A THEORY OF
PREDICATES

CSLI LECTURE NOTES
NUMBER 76

A THEORY OF PREDICATES

FARRELL ACKERMAN
GERT WEBELHUTH

CENTER FOR THE STUDY OF
LANGUAGE AND INFORMATION
STANFORD, CALIFORNIA

Copyright © 1998
CSLI Publications
Center for the Study of Language and Information
Leland Stanford Junior University

02 01 00 99 98   5 4 3 2 1

Library of Congress Cataloging-in-Publication Data

Ackerman, Farrell.
A theory of predicates / Farrell Ackerman, Gert Webelhuth.
p.   cm. — (CSLI lecture notes ; no. 76)
Includes bibliographical references and index.

ISBN 1-57586-087-2 (hardback : alk. paper).
ISBN 1-57586-086-4 (pbk. : alk. paper)

1. Grammar, Comparative and general–Verb phrase.   I. Webelhuth, Gert.
II. Title.   III. Series.

P281.A27   1997
415—dc21   97-28186
CIP

CSLI Publications reports new developments in the study of language,
information, and computation. In addition to lecture notes, our publications
include monographs, working papers, revised dissertations, and conference
proceedings. Our aim is to make new results, ideas, and approaches available as
quickly as possible. Please visit our website at
HTTP://CSLI-WWW.STANFORD.EDU/PUBLICATIONS/
for comments on this and other titles, as well as for changes and corrections by
the author and publisher.

This book is dedicated to

Barbara, Jan, Jordan, and Molly.

May they stay forever young!

Contents

Acknowledgments

The collaboration that produced this book was less motivated by large overlaps in the theoretical convictions of the authors than by our shared conviction that the cross-linguistic profile of (complex) predicates provides central insights for the form of linguistic theory. When we met, Farrell Ackerman was working in Lexical-Functional Grammar and Gert Webelhuth in Government and Binding Theory, two research communities whose members often have little to say to each other. In reflection, we tacitly adopted some heuristics for useful collaboration: (i) to ignore short-lived theory-internal trends in favor of building a theory based on empirical generalizations from a disparate set of languages; (ii) to heed insights and results from different linguistic traditions; and (iii) to adapt and devise whatever assumptions and representational tools seemed necessary for the development of a universal theory of predicates. For practical purposes, we have focused in this book primarily on a subset of widespread predicate phenomena exemplified by German and have formulated our theory generally in a formal idiom which was native to neither of us, namely, a variant of Head-Driven Phrase Structure Grammar.

Against the background of our respective earlier theoretical convictions, many of the moves we found it necessary to make came as a surprise to one or both of us: as in Lexical-Functional Grammar and Head-Driven Phrase Structure Grammar, the lexicon is viewed as a central component of grammar; only the lexicon, i.e., not the syntactic component, forms new predicates and new morphological words; the lexicon consists of two parallel submodules, one for predicates and one for morphological words; much of the information associated with functional structures and contributed by independent elements in constituent structure in Lexical-Functional Grammar is associated with lexical representations in our proposal; lexical entries can consist of more than one morphological word; the morphological module of the lexicon is a word and paradigm model; the construct predicate is construed functionally or relationally, rather than categorially, as in Relational Grammar and Lexical-Functional Grammar; the explanatory role of principles and parameters in structure-based theories is replaced by a theory of grammatical archetypes; complex predicates form constructions in the sense of Construction Grammar that are part of construction families whose interrelationships can be captured with the typed feature structures and multiple inheritance hierarchies of Head-Driven Phrase Structure Grammar.

We want to thank many colleagues and students who over the past six years have expressed encouragement and constructive criticism or have contributed ideas, insights, example sentences, and comments on various drafts of this book.

Ivan Sag and Carl Pollard are role models of precision, explicitness, and data coverage in linguistic theorizing. We were keenly aware that by largely formulating our theory in terms of HPSG our work would be measured against the superior quality standards they have set for their own work and HPSG in general. We believe that the field of linguistics would be well-served if these quality standards were accepted at large and have made an attempt to meet them in this book. In immediate terms, we are deeply indebted to Ivan Sag for carefully reading a previous draft of this work and for providing us with characteristically incisive and insightful comments, many of which we incorporated into these chapters. Ivan was extremely generous with his ideas, his time and his resources and this book is a better work because of his influence. Joan Bresnan has been another abiding source of theoretical inspiration and a model of cogent argumentation: many of her views of grammar and various aspects of LFG find expression in much of what follows. Bob Kasper and Andreas Kathol helped us out with advice and insights whenever we needed it in writing this book. We have appreciated their help very much! Phil LeSourd's clarity and precision of thought as well as mastery of complex empirical phenomena provided an indispensable resource in identifying many conceptual issues underlying the present proposal and in pointing to likely theoretical solutions, particularly in morphology. Mark Gawron has been encouraging of this enterprise from the outset and has provided hours of thoughtful and probing conversation. As students of Emmon Bach and Chuck Fillmore, we hope that they will see their deep influence in this work. Our warmest thanks and appreciation also go to Alex Alsina, Chris Barker, Hans Boas, Jim Blevins, Bob Carpenter, Mary Dalrymple, Franco Diener, Stan Dubinsky, Mirjam Fried, Adele Goldberg, Alice Harris, Paul Kay, Tracy Holloway King, Manfred Krifka, Yuki Kuroda, Chris Manning, John Moore, Rachel Nordlinger, Orhan Orgun, David Perlmutter, Maria Polinsky, Marga Reis, Peter Sells, Henriëtte de Swart, Elisabeth Traugott, Tom Wasow, and Leyla Zidani-Eroglu.

We gratefully acknowledge the badly needed help Gert Webelhuth received from the HPSG group at the Center for the Study of Language and Information at Stanford University in implementing a version of our theory of predicates for the purpose of a "reality check." We realize that it must have been an ordeal to teach a complete novice a sophisticated piece of grammar development software. Ivan Sag and Dan Flickinger generously made their resources available to us and Ann Copestake, Dan Flickinger, Rob Malouf, and Peter Skadhauge patiently taught Gert how to use the system. During a brief visit, Stephan Oepen lent his expertise as well. Many thanks to all of them!

We had the opportunity to present the material that went into this book before several audiences and are extremely grateful for the helpful feedback we received on those occasions. We would like to thank the participants of courses that Gert Webelhuth taught in the Department of Linguistics at Stanford University, the Institut für Maschinelle Sprachverarbeitung and Germanistik-Linguistik at the University of Stuttgart, and the Holland Institute of Linguistics. Gert Webelhuth would like to thank Ivan Sag, Rob Malouf, Susanne Riehemann, Judith Berman, Martin Everaert, and Hans Broekhuis for making these teaching opportunities possible and for making them so enjoyable. Gert's only complaint is that these events each had to end and that this made it harder for him to interact with these wonderful linguists (some of them graduate students with stellar careers ahead of them) on a day to day basis. We also want to express appreciation to the audiences at various conferences and departmental colloquia and contributors to Linguist List.

We feel extremely lucky to publish this book with CSLI Publications. Dikran Karagueuzian, Tony Gee, and Maureen Burke have been the greatest pleasure to work with and have been helpful with every detail in the preparation of the book's physical manuscript. We would like to thank them for their advice, their courtesy, and their patience with us throughout the whole process!

Patrick Murphy took time out from writing his dissertation in linguistics at the University of North Carolina at Chapel Hill and prepared the book's index. We gratefully acknowledge the wonderful job he has done. Special thanks go to Chip Gerfen for allowing us to print the final manuscript on his equipment at a time when he was under pressure to finish a book manuscript of his own.

Gert's wife Barbara Levergood, who has combined qualifications in linguistics and library science, insisted that the book's bibliography meet the standards of a professional university librarian. She tried to track down every last reference and formatted the bibliography to make it the professional state of the art. However, this contribution pales in comparison to the love and support she has unfailingly shown Gert in all of his endeavors, professional and otherwise. Without her, he fails to be a complete person and life loses all color!

We want to publicly thank each other for the mutual support shown over the years, despite obvious differences in background, sensibilities, and talents. This collaboration was challenging, but rewarding, forcing us to reexamine and abandon many previously held commitments and to reinvent ourselves in the process. It is our hope that the synthesis of ideas informing our theory of predicates goes some way toward promoting further productive convergence among theories and theorists.

The deep friendship that has grown between us extends to our whole families. We apologize to them that working on this book has made us spend many hours that were rightfully theirs away from them on the phone, at the office, or out of town. Our companions Jan and Barbara are owed a debt of gratitude for their support that will be hard to pay back, but we'll xiv / A THEORY OF PREDICATES

try. We also want to take the opportunity to thank our parents and siblings for continuing to show their love and giving moral sustenance, despite perpetual bafflement about what we are doing and why we are doing it. We suspect that some of them even feel that they have no choice, given that we persistently refuse to grow up! But we are grateful anyway.

1

Complex Predicates and Lexicalism

1 Overview of the Problems

It is a commonplace of linguistic investigation that the information packaged into a single word in one language is sometimes expressed by several independent words in another language. This observation raises a classic challenge for linguistic theory: how can we represent what is the same among languages, while also accounting for the patent differences between them? In the present work we address this issue by examining a class of constructions, mainly exemplified by German, where the information ordinarily associated with a single clausal head is distributed among several (not necessarily contiguous) elements in constituent structure. This informational head, irrespective of surface expression, will be referred to here as the *predicate*. We argue that there is a recurring class of *predicate* constructions across languages which should receive a uniform theoretical treatment: we develop a lexicalist proposal that synthesizes certain results and architectural assumptions from Lexical-Functional Grammar, Head-Driven Phrase Structure Grammar, Construction Grammar, and the word-based tradition of morphology. The theory of *predicates* we propose is one which is responsive to many issues raised cross-theoretically in the recent literature on complex predicates, but which additionally, is designed to address certain clear patterns of grammaticalization or morphologization evident in the domain of predicate formation cross-linguistically.

Ever since Chomsky (1965, 1970) it has been standard within generative frameworks to postulate a component called the lexicon. This component contains lexical entries minimally possessing information about their categorial status, morphological class, and semantic properties. In addition, if the element is an argument-taking entity, the lexical entry also provides information concerning its valence, i.e., the number of its arguments, the semantic roles of its arguments, as well as some representation concerning the syntactic status (i.e., grammatical relations) of these arguments. Lexical information such as valence, semantic role, and grammatical relational values is presumed to help determine central properties of the clause. Moreover, it has seemed natural to assume that the projector of such information, leaving aside the special case of idioms, is associated with a single morphological object such as a verb, a noun, an adjective, etc.

In accordance with the *Weak Lexicalist Hypothesis* the morphological objects that express lexical representations are fully derived word forms, while on the *Strong Lexicalist Hypothesis* they are both fully derived and inflected word forms. Additionally, these morphological word forms are further constrained to be phonologically integrated and syntactically atomic: this follows from the Lexical Integrity Hypothesis which, roughly speaking, states that pieces of complex morphological objects are opaque to syntactic operations that would treat these pieces as independent elements in phrase structure.

Finally, the lexical operations claimed to alter the information associated with lexical entries are likewise standardly constrained to relate objects with a morphological status. That is, they manipulate the information associated with such categories as V(erb), N(oun), or A(djective). For example, lexical rules have been proposed to account for causative formation, applicative formation (dative shift), inversion (psych predicates), resultative formation, and passivization.

The conception of lexicalism as constrained by some variant of the Lexicalist Hypothesis and Lexical Integrity has over the years been the main focus of proponents and detractors.[1] For detractors, demonstrated violations of Lexical Integrity have often sufficed to argue against lexicalism per se and, as a consequence, for the need to develop an alternative keyed to phrase structure representations. Lieber (1992), for instance, appears to assume this standard view of lexicalism as a backdrop for developing her view of the need for syntactic word formation. For example, she demonstrates that some phrasal entities are clearly within the purview of morphology and concludes that, consequently, lexicalist theories are empirically problematic. In particular, following Subramanian (1988), she cites nominalization processes with the suffix *tal* in Tamil which seem to operate on the phrasal constituent VP.

(1)

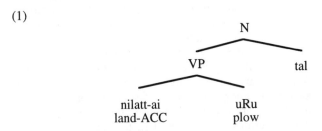

As can be seen in (1), the derived nominal *nilatt-ai uRu tal* 'plowing the land' can be accurately described by a phrase structure representation in

---

[1] There is a recent review of the role of lexical integrity in generative theory found in Bresnan and Mchombo (1995) and Ackerman and LeSourd (1997). There are two interpretations of lexical integrity which often get conflated and which will play a role in subsequent discussion. Broadly characterized the two interpretations are as follows: lexical integrity can refer to the claim that words are indivisible elements fully formed in the lexicon and that syntax cannot effect the morphological composition of word forms (this contrasts with claims in the Principles and Parameters framework according to which "head" movement can create word forms), or lexical integrity can refer to the notion that lexical representations must be associated with morphophonologically integrated and syntactically atomic morphological objects. See discussion below for elaboration.

which the case marked nominal *nilatt* 'land' is interpreted as the OBJECT of the verb *uRu* 'plow', within a VP constituent: the suffix *tal* can, accordingly, be interpreted as concatenating with a VP, rather than with a lexical category.

The challenge raised by such phenomena is obvious: how, given the fundamental assumptions of lexicalism, could the relevant entities be lexical, if the morphology must apply to them as phrasal objects and if morphological operations, by hypothesis, must apply prior to the appearance of words within phrases? There is, of course, nothing wrong with the observation that such a phenomenon presents a problem for one (albeit prevailing) interpretation of lexicalism, but it is arguable whether such data should be construed as an argument against lexicalism per se or as demonstrating the necessity for a syntactic account of such facts.

The type of challenge represented by nominalization phenomena such as those cited above is particularly prevalent in the domain which represents the major focus of inquiry in this book, namely, predicate formation of several types. Consider the following representative phenomena in this light.

It is well-known that Russian contains morphological predicates consisting of a prefix and a verbal stem. These predicates are standardly analyzed as morphophonologically integrated units representing atomic entities with respect to the syntax. We will refer to them as synthetic forms of predicates. An example is provided in (2), containing the prefix *ob* 'around': this prefix correlates with an increase in transitivity for the verbal stem yielding the direct object argument 'lake'.

(2)   guljajuščie pary *ob*xodjat   ozero
        strolling   pairs around-go-3/pl lake-ACC

        'The strolling couples walk around the lake'

As is to be expected, given the morphological status of this word form, predicates such as these have clear derivatives, both nominal (3) and adjectival (4), related to them:

(3)   *ob*xod   N   'round' (as in 'make the rounds')
(4)   *ob*xodnyj A   'roundabout'

As in Russian, Hungarian has predicates where a preverbal (PV) element modifies certain lexical properties associated with the verbal stem.

(5)   András *bele*szolt   a vitába
        András into spoke the dispute-ILL

        'András intervened in the dispute'

For example, in (5) we see an instance where the preverb *bele* 'into' correlates with an alteration of both the case government pattern and the meaning
associated with the verbal stem *szol* 'speak, say, talk': whereas *szol* is a one-
place predicate, *beleszol* is a two-place predicate which governs the illative
case for its oblique complement.

Once again, as in Russian, the predicate appears to have a morphological status, serving as a base for derivational processes such as nominalization. In the present instance, the verb *beleszol* 'intervene' corresponds to
the derived nominal *beleszolás* 'intervention.'

These obvious parallelisms between the predicates in Russian and
Hungarian clearly suggest a uniform analysis and such an analysis would be
compatible with a lexical treatment. On the other hand, there is a property
characteristic of Hungarian complex predicates that distinguishes them from
their Russian analogs: in Hungarian the preverb and the verb can function as
independent elements in phrase structure. This independence is exemplified
in (6) where the presence of the sentential negation element *nem* 'no' immediately to the left of the verbal stem correlates with the postposing of the
preverb:

(6) András *nem* szolt *bele* a vitába
     András not   spoke into the dispute-ILL

     'András didn't intervene in the dispute'

Formations whose pieces exhibit this sort of syntactic independence
are often referred to as phrasal predicates given their analytic or periphrastic
expression.

Estonian, like Hungarian, possesses phrasal predicates. In (7) the
preverb *ära* 'away' is associated with the predicate *ära ostma* 'corrupt, suborn'. This predicate is based on the simple verb stem *ostma* 'buy, purchase'.
The preverb appears discontinuous from the verbal stem at the end of the
clause.

(7) mees ostab   ta sõbra   *ära*
     man   buy-3sg his friend-GEN away

     'The man is bribing his friend'

Predicates consisting of a separable preverb and a verbal stem can
serve as bases for derivational operations. The following deverbal adjectival
and nominal forms related to *ära ostma* 'corrupt, suborn' typify this possibility:

(8) äraostmatu   A   'incorruptible'
     äraostmatus   N   'incorruptibility'
     äraostetav   A   'venal, corrupt'
     äraostetavus   N   'venality'

Finally, the phrasal predicates of Hungarian and Estonian resemble in relevant ways one of the types of German predicates which will be closely examined in chapter 10, namely, predicates containing so-called separable particles.[2] An example is provided below containing the predicate *abrufen* 'call up'.

(9) weil   wir die Informationen jetzt *ab-rufen* können
     because we the information   now up-call   can

     'because we can call up the information now'

(10) Wir *rufen* die Informationen jetzt *ab*
     we call   the information   now up

     'We call up the information now'

As can be seen, the separable preverb *ab* appears at the end of the finite matrix clause in (10): the verbal stem and the preverb are discontinuous in the syntax. As in Hungarian and Estonian, German phrasal predicates may serve as bases for derivational operations. This is exemplified by the possibility for a phrasal predicate to participate in adjective formation with the suffix *-bar* 'able' as in (11):

(11) weil   die Informationen jetzt *ab-ruf-bar*   sind
     because the information   now up-call-able are

     'because the information is obtainable now'

The predicates in Russian, Hungarian, Estonian, and German all: (i) exhibit lexical effects, i.e., the preverb-V may differ from the verb stem with respect to argument adicity, semantics, case government, (and grammatical functions) and (ii) exhibit morphological effects, i.e., the preverb and V together constitute a morphological base for derivational and inflectional operations. On the other hand, Hungarian, Estonian, and German differ from Russian in allowing the preverb and verb to exhibit syntactic independence.[3]

The existence of phrasal predicates with the profile exhibited by Hungarian, Estonian, and German is widespread cross-linguistically and has elicited the following characterization by Watkins (1964: 1037):

---

[2] Though not addressed in the present work, English particle verb constructions also exemplify this problem. For example, whereas it is acceptable to say 'the teacher dressed the boy down' the related nominalization is preferably 'the teacher's dressing down of the boy', rather than 'the teacher's dressing of the boy down.'

[3] For additional evidence concerning the lexical status of German verb-particle combinations, see Stiebels and Wunderlich (1992) and Stiebels (1996).

PV V compositions constitute "single semantic words", comparable to simple lexical items; yet they permit *tmesis*, or syntactic separation, suggesting that internal parts are independent syntactic entities.

As with the compounds presented by Lieber, phrasal predicates represent an "analytic paradox" with respect to standard assumptions of lexicalism [cf. Nash (1982)]. In particular, their semantic and morphological unithood conflicts with their syntactic separability if the lexicon is interpreted as the source for words employed as syntactic atoms and the syntax as a system for combining and ordering them.

In line with the basic representational apparatus assumed in the present work we believe that it is illuminating to illustrate these similarities and differences in terms of a type hierarchy: the transition from root node to leaves in such a representation calibrates the relation between (possibly) universal to language-particular instantiations of types and subtypes of (complex) predicates. A schematic example of such a type hierarchy can be seen below (a formal representation with different technical vocabulary will be developed in chapter 10 for the analysis of German verb-particle constructions):

predicate
α properties

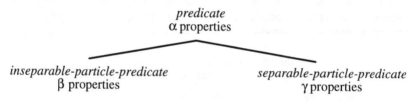

inseparable-particle-predicate   *separable-particle-predicate*
β properties   γ properties

Broadly speaking, there is a supertype possessing certain properties (indicated by α), referred to above as *predicate*, which comprises several subtypes: that is to say that the subtypes *inseparable-particle-predicate* and *separable-particle-predicate* possess the same properties as their supertype, as well as their own distinctive properties.

In this book we develop a lexicalist proposal for the construct predicate construed as the determiner of central properties of clauses. The lexical representation for the predicate encodes both the content and the form associated with the Sausurrean sign. From a content-theoretic point of view it contains functional-semantic information concerning the meaning of the predicate, its semantic arguments and their grammatical function status, as well as morphosyntactic content providing values for such properties as tense, aspect, polarity, agreement etc.[4] It is in other words the content-theo-

---

[4] We use the term "morphosyntactic content" in order to convey the sense that this information is often associated with both classically morphological and syntactic properties or features. Note that "morphosyntactic content" is a kind of *content* and not a kind of form. It expresses the kind of *information* on predicates that in formal semantic theories is often modeled by operators (excluding quantifiers and WH-words), i.e., tense, aspect, or negation functions. This kind of content is typically expressed morphologically or by auxiliaries and particles and this is what motivates our reference to it as 'morphosyntactic content' as opposed to the functional-

retic head of a clause. The distinction between two types of information correlates with a distinction between two basic sorts of predicates examined in this book. First, each language possesses an inventory of basic predicates: these are lexical representations containing only functional-semantic information, with respect to content. For example, the functional-semantic information of the Hungarian predicate *beleszol* 'intervene' in (5) above differs from that for the related predicate *szol* 'speak with' respect to meaning, the semantics of their arguments, and the grammatical functions of those arguments. On the other hand, the two basic predicates with their different basic contents can participate in the same paradigms concerning tense and agreement: from the present perspective, this morphosyntactic content complements the functional-semantic information of the basic predicate and yields what we will refer to as an expanded predicate. The content side of the predicate can be schematized as follows:

Functional-semantic content: basic meaning, semantic roles, and
                                 grammatical functions;
Morphosyntactic content: tense, aspect, negation,
                                 agreement, etc.;
Expanded predicate content: functional-semantic content +
                                 morphosyntactic content.

We contrast the content-theoretic aspect of a predicate with its form-theoretic aspect, i.e., those aspects of the sign which most closely relate to the structure of the physical signal representing the sign's content as defined above:

Predicate form: categorial properties (e.g., part of
                                 speech and morphophonological
                                 properties)

The sign as a whole (with predicates being one special case) is a combination of the various aspects of form and content:

The Sausurrean Aspects of a Sign

A.   The Content-theoretic Aspect of the Sign
      • Functional-semantic content
      • Morphosyntactic content

---

semantic content of a predicate (its core meaning, the semantic roles it assigns, and their grammatical functions) which typically is expressed by stems or words belonging to an open class part of speech rather than a morphological process or an auxiliary/particle. In drawing a difference between these two kinds of content and their prototypical linguistic expressions, we follow the lead of Sapir (1924).

B. The Form-theoretic Aspect of the Sign
   • Categorial form
   • Morphophonological form

   With respect to the form-theoretic aspect of signs, predicates as interpreted here are not uniformly expressed by a single lexical category such as V(erb), as on standard lexicalist assumptions, nor can they be freely formed from syntactically created phrases as is possible in logically informed linguistic theories such as Montague Grammar and Categorial Grammar. So, we will accordingly focus on both the morphological and syntactic expression of predicates in this book as well. Thus, all of our predicates will receive full representation in terms of both their content and form.
   Though we will address both aspects of the predicate sign, we argue that the predicate represents a natural content-theoretic unit (in the sense of "content-theoretic aspect of the sign" just discussed). The notion of naturalness appealed to here is simply this: there are several linguistically significant notions (e.g., tense-aspect, causative, or passive) which recur cross-linguistically and differ primarily in the surface forms employed to express them. If what commonly recurs in quite different languages is entitled to be called natural, then the content-theoretic units (referred to subsequently also as "contentive units") examined here are prime candidates for theoretical constructs in a theory of grammar that attempts to capture essential properties of language.
   We provide evidence for the hypothesis of a content-theoretic predicate, often inclusive of morphosyntactic content, on the basis of those cross-linguistic operations which affect lexical semantics, valence, case government, and/or grammatical function assignments independent of the way in which these predicates are formally expressed, i.e., their form-theoretic expression type. The cross-linguistic frequency of these informational configurations and the tendency toward similar behaviors, both synchronic and diachronic, associated with elements employed to express them, suggests a privileged status for these phenomena.
   A central concern of this book is the development of a representational system for a lexical submodule containing contentive aspects of the sign and another containing morphological aspects of the sign: elements of these submodules are placed in correspondence to yield predicates (at various levels of generality). Since discernible patterns of regularity or markedness in such correspondences are facilitated by several of our representational assumptions, we regard them as a crucial prerequisite for any explanatorily adequate theory. Throughout we therefore speculate on the nature of the explanatory assumptions that could account for the widespread recurrence of certain predicates as well as their contentive and formal profiles. Specifically, in chapter 4 we outline a theory of archetypal and language-specific templates which can provide explanations within the unifica-

tion-based type-driven assumptions that we believe are conceptually as well as empirically superior to explanations in terms of principles and parameters within approaches such as Government and Binding Theory and the Minimalist Program.

It bears noting that the predicates examined here are also distinguishable from the enormous class of predicates made possible by such formal operations as lambda abstraction: as is well known, such a device makes it feasible to confer predicate status on any expression with a free variable. That is, it permits the creation of predicates which constitute a superset of the small class of natural predicates which have been demonstrated to recur cross-linguistically (see chapter 2 for a more detailed discussion).

The remainder of this chapter provides an informal introduction to the basic phenomena examined here, the problems they raise for linguistic theories and the nature of the answers proposed in the present work. After presenting four types of predicates which will be closely examined in later chapters we provide an overview of standard lexicalist assumptions in order to place the present analysis of these phenomena among competing theoretical accounts. Following this we identify and discuss three central problems concerning theory construction in the domain of predicate formation.

The first problem is referred to as *the expression problem*. Roughly this concerns the fact that the same construction can receive different surface expressions across languages and sometimes within a single language. The theoretical challenge, of course, is to provide an appropriate vocabulary and representations to reveal how languages can be similar in certain respects, while differing—sometimes radically—in others. The second problem often arises in an effort to address the first.

What we will call *the proliferation problem* is a familiar one within linguistics ever since Kiparsky (1973). In this classic article Kiparsky raises the issue as to how abstract linguistic representations should be permitted to be, using phonology as the domain of inquiry. One way in which abstractness becomes an issue is that representational assumptions found to be useful for explaining certain phenomena are exploited in increasingly abstract fashion to account for new phenomena or different expressions of familiar phenomena. The basic issue here is one of achieving tolerable abstractness. In this regard we will see that lexicalist frameworks make possible in principle the proliferation of lexical entries, potentially yielding unconstrained homophony. Structure-oriented frameworks, in contrast, have proliferated phrasal categories yielding structural configurations whose only effective constraint is often a uniform two bar level expansion of binary branching trees.

Since our framework is lexicalist, the issue of proliferation of lexical entries arises as much as in other versions of lexicalism. We will discuss various ways of addressing proliferation and lay out the reasons for our particular choice of dealing with this problem over other techniques that have been proposed.

The last problem, the *grammaticalization or diachrony problem,* takes as its foundation the widely held claim that the expression side of predicate formation exhibits a similar profile cross-linguistically. That is, the constructions examined here frequently trace a diachronic unidirectional path from syntactically independent elements to synthetic morphological objects. Moreover, cross-linguistic research reveals that a recurrent class of predicate constructions tend to exhibit morphologization.

2 Representative Phenomena

Throughout this book we focus on the examination of several content-theoretic constructions. Recall that the term content-theoretic unit as used here covers both morphosyntactic content such as tense etc., as well as the functional-semantic information concerning lexical semantics, number of arguments, argument structure, and/or grammatical function assignment to arguments: both of these types of information, as mentioned previously, are interpreted as information within lexical representations. In particular, we examine expanded predicates containing morphosyntactic content as well as basic predicates containing functional-semantic information which participate in derivational relations. In all instances we juxtapose synthetic and analytic expressions of these construction types. That is, we investigate constructions which share certain central content-theoretic properties, although they may be realized as a single morphological word or as several co-occurring words. In this section, we present examples of the four construction types we examine in detail in later chapters of this book.

It should be noted that our presentation in this chapter is strictly introductory and we forego explicit discussion of important properties of these constructions.

2.1 Expanded Predicates and Morphosyntactic Content

In Chapter 7 we will examine how our theory of predicates provides analyses for predicate constructions containing morphosyntactic content such as tense, aspect, and agreement. Typically, these notions can either be expressed synthetically or analytically. For instance, both French and German have a way of expressing future tense. However, as (12) and (13) show, French expresses the future tense synthetically whereas German uses a combination of the infinitive of a main verb and an inflected form of the auxiliary *werden* 'to become:'

Synthetic Expression: French

(12)   Je le   **verrai**
        I   him   will see

        'I will see him'

Analytic Expression: German

(13)   weil   ich ihn **sehen werde**
         because I   him see-inf will

       'because I will see him'

Our treatment of the analytic expressions of these constructions will associate all of the contentive and expression properties of these entities with a
single lexical representation. This contrasts with syntactic proposals that
compose the information of independent morphosyntactic content-bearing
elements with the information of a dependent lexical category: this is accomplished by positing an extended functional projection domain, as in GB,
or a single functional structure set in correspondence with multiple syntactic
co-heads, as in LFG (see below for a discussion of this type of analysis in
LFG.)

2.2   Synthetic and Analytic Passives

The passive is one of the most commonly analyzed constructions
within linguistics. There are two frequently attested patterns for the encoding of passive predicates. These are exemplified by the morphological (i.e.,
synthetic) passive in Vogul [from Kulonen (1989: 75)] and the periphrastic
(i.e., analytic) passive of German:

Synthetic Expression: Vogul (Ugric)

(14)   por-nēn   ań ńāwram   **tot-wes**
         Por-woman-LAT now child-NOM take-PASS-3sg/past

       'The child was taken away now by the Por-woman'

Analytic Expression: German

(15)   weil   die Blumen dem Mann **geschenkt wurden**
         because the flowers the man given   were

       'because the flowers were given to the man'

As can be seen, the passive morpheme appears as a suffix to the
Vogul verb in (14), whereas passive is conveyed by the co-occurrence of a
non-finite participle and an inflected auxiliary in German in (15).

Chapter 8 provides an account of the relation between universals of
passive formation and the language-particular encoding of passives. We pay
particular attention to several German passives encoded analytically when

used in a predicative function but encoded synthetically when used in an attributive manner.

2.3 Synthetic and Analytic Causatives

There are causative constructions in many languages. In typical instances the causativized predicate exhibits one more semantic argument than the base predicate, i.e., it has a causer argument. Since this new argument bears the subject function, the grammatical functions borne by the arguments of the base predicate must be readjusted in some manner. The semantics, argument valence, case government, and function assignment of the base predicate are often affected by the operation of causativization. That these effects can occur independent of the surface form of the causative predicate becomes evident from the following pair of predicates in (16) and (17) from Hungarian:

Synthetic Expression: Hungarian

(16) a   fiú   **elvonszoltatta**   Jánost
      the boy away-drag-CAUS-3sg/DEF John-ACC

      a hölggyel/a hölgy   által
      the lady-INSTR/the lady by

      'The boy had Janos dragged away (by the lady)'

Analytic Expression: Hungarian

(17) a fiú   **hagyta**   Jánost   **elvonszolni** (a hölgy által)
      the boy let-PAST-3sg/DEF John-ACC away drag   (the lady by)

      'The boy let Janos be dragged away (by the lady)'

(16) contains the morphological (synthetic) expression of the causative of a transitive base predicate: the causee is expressed as an oblique, while the theme of the base predicate retains its object status. In contrast, (17) contains the analytic or periphrastic causative of a transitive base predicate: the causee again appears as an oblique, while the theme of the base predicate retains its object status. Since the base predicate in this latter construction is an active infinitival form, it is obvious that the composition of the causative predicate *hagy* and the active infinitive yields grammatical function assignments different from those associated with the active infinitive alone. In fact, the function assignments associated with (17) are identical to those associated with (16).

In Chapter 9 we will provide an analysis of the frequently attested cross-linguistic patterns of causative formation, paying particular attention to the interactions of grammatical function assignment, bi- vs. mono-clausality effects, and the synthetic vs. analytic expression types associated with these constructions.

2.4 Predicates with Separable Particles

We have already seen in (2)–(11) that several languages possess predicates consisting of a verbal stem and some element which precedes it. The preceding element can be either bound like a standard prefix (or the first member of a compound) or is separable from the verbal stem under some syntactic conditions. Despite formal differences concerning separability of the pieces of these compositions, many of the same lexical semantic, argument valence, case government, and grammatical function effects are evident irrespective of the prefixal (compound) or preverbal status of the element accompanying the verb. That is, in an intuitive sense we are confronted by the same phenomenon independent of whether we encounter a synthetic or an analytic expression type.

Chapter 10 will be devoted to various aspects of constructions exemplifying this type of (complex) predicate. Given the variety and variable degrees of regularity exhibited by this class of constructions both within and across languages, we focus on the analysis of German. We observe that this analysis provides an appropriate representational schema for the whole class of phenomena when adjusted to the properties of the constructions in other languages.

2.5 Summary

The preceding subsections have presented four widespread grammatical phenomena involving predicates. In each case we have seen that predicates of a single type, i.e., phrasal predicates, passive predicates, and causative predicates, can receive either synthetic or analytic expression.

The relative informational invariance of each of these construction classes and their reported recurring cross-linguistic diachronic profiles raise the issue of how to account for the systematic existence of both synthetic and analytic encodings for their surface forms. We will argue that these observations provide exactly the kind of empirical justification for the postulation of the predicate as a theoretical construct and that predicates are best understood as units of lexical representations. This leads us to a discussion in the next section of what lexicalism is taken to claim and how this concept will be employed in the present book.

3 Lexicalism as a Cluster Concept

In our view lexicalism is usefully interpreted as consisting of three central proto-concepts, while lexicalist frameworks can be distinguished according to the role these concepts play in them. In this section we identify these three proto-properties and use them to characterize the nature of lexicalism propounded by several different recent approaches depending on which of the principles are recognized in the particular theory. In addition, we can compare the views developed in the present work to these competing conceptions of lexicalism.

(18) Overview of Lexicalism

Theory	Lexical Adicity	Morphological Integrity	Morphological Expression
Classical LFG and HPSG[5]	yes	yes	Principle
Some recent views in LFG and HPSG	**no**	yes	Principle
This book	yes	yes	**Preference**

The table in (18) provides an overview of our comparison. A characterization of the principles and the values that we have assigned to each theory are discussed below.[6]

---

[5] The identification of Classical LFG and HPSG with respect to the three principles discussed here underdetermines an important difference between these theories with respect to an insight that guides the proposal in the present book. In particular, LFG has a tradition of distinguishing between functional (what we refer to as information theoretic) and structural lexicalism. This distinction is appealed to for the explanation of various grammatical phenomena in early work by Simpson (1991) on Walpiri, Ackerman (1984, 1987) on Hungarian, Vogul and Ostyak and more recently for the analysis of Japanese complex predicates in Matsumoto (1996), to name the work of only a few researchers. The architectural assumptions of LFG permit one to distinguish between the functional and structural or categorial heads of phrasal domains: most importantly it permits there to be discrepancies between the functional and structural heads of syntactic constructions. As mentioned, this view of distinctive headedness in different informational domains underlies much of the conceptual motivation for the theory of predicates proposed, as well as some of the implementational assumptions discussed in chapter 3. Moreover, it informs an important development concerning the interaction between phrasal structure and functional structure in much recent work within LFG. (See footnote 4 in chapter 3 for further discussion.)

[6] We refer the reader to Jackendoff (1995, 1997) for cogent criticisms of standard lexicalist assumptions as well as a reconceptualization of lexical representations which shares much in spirit with the proposal developed here. This is not accidental, since the present work is formulated within the architectural assumptions referred to and adopted by Jackendoff as "representational modularity": this general approach is characteristic of constraint-based lexicalist theories such as LFG and HPSG which provide many of the representational assumptions of the present theory. Within this theoretical tradition there have been empirical motivations adduced to challenge certain standard lexicalist assumptions. See for example Abaitua (1988), Ackerman (1987), Dahlstrom (1987), Matsumoto (1996) and Simpson (1991). Constraint-based theoretical assumptions and considerations of certain empirical phenomena have converged in the present work to yield many conceptual parallelisms between Jackendoff's work and our own. In addition, we have relied explicitly in several aspects of our theory on certain of

We will call the first lexicalist proto-principle *Lexical Adicity* since it relates to constraints on establishing a set of adicity structures for lexical items:

(19)   Lexical Adicity

The adicity of a lexical item is lexically fully determined and cannot be altered by items of the syntactic context in which it appears.

Lexical adicity is intended to cover three different types of information associated with a lexical item: the number and type of its semantic arguments, the number and type of its functional arguments, and the number and grammatical categories of its phrase-structural dependents. For a verb such as *hit,* lexical adicity would require that its semantic arguments "hitter" and "hittee", its functional arguments "subject" and "object", and its categorial arguments "NP[nom]" and "NP[acc]" already be specified in its lexical entry. The passive lexical entry (or predicate) based on *hit* likewise would be lexically completely specified for semantic, functional, and categorial selection, because (19) reserves the power of specifying these selectional properties for the lexicon and expressly withholds this privilege from the mechanisms applying in the syntactic component.

As the table indicates, classical LFG and HPSG both incorporated lexical adicity. In the context of the theories presented in Bresnan (1982b) or Pollard and Sag (1987) the selectional properties of lexical items were completely determined in the lexicon and all changes in the meaning of a predicate or its selectional properties were achieved in the lexicon (via lexical rules) and were independent of the syntactic context into which the lexical entry was inserted.[7]

Jackendoff's proposals: most notably, we adopt a variant of his metric for calculating the information cost of lexical representations in our discussion of archetypes and markedness in chapter 4. Finally, it should be observed that from an empirical perspective Jackendoff (1995, 1997) develops his proposals with keen attention to fixed phrases and idioms (including idiomatic phrasal verbs): due to considerations of length we do not discuss idioms here, although in other work [Webelhuth and Ackerman (1998)] we provide evidence for accommodating German idioms to the class of complex predicates treated here.

[7] The view of Lexical Adicity represents in some sense a variant of Direct Syntactic Encoding in LFG as formulated in Kaplan and Bresnan (1982: 32):

Direct Syntactic Encoding: No rule of syntax may replace one function name with another.

They characterize the consequent difference between lexical versus syntactic operations as follows: (1982: 32)

"The principle of direct syntactic encoding sharpens the distinction between two classes of rules: rules that change relations are lexical and range over finite sets, while syntactic rules that project onto an infinite set of sentences preserve grammatical relations."

Lexical Adacity obviously adheres to this distinction, as well as making explicit that what obtains for grammatical functions also obtains for valence and lexical semantics (as well as case government).

Some recent work in LFG and HPSG approaches to complex predicate phenomena, however, extend the privilege of creating new argument
structures from the lexicon to the syntax, in direct violation of *Lexical
Adicity*.[8] In the case of LFG, Alsina (1993: iv, v, 280) admits "partially
specified predicates" whose adicity is only fixed in the syntactic component,
as can be inferred from the two quotes below:[9]

> The operations that affect the way that arguments are overtly expressed are assumed
> to be operations on the argument structure of a predicate and are treated as partially
> specified predicates that must compose with other predicates to yield fully specified
> predicates. Thus, predicate composition is responsible for operations such as pas-
> sivization, causativization, applicativization, etc.

> Most work within LFG, and other lexicalist theories, has assumed that predicate
> composition, or the equivalent notion in each particular theory, can only take place
> in the lexicon. However, the evidence indicates that causative (and other) complex
> predicates in Romance are not derived in the lexicon because the two verbs that
> compose the complex predicates do not constitute a word. If the lexicon is the word
> formation module of the grammar and words are the terminal nodes of the c-struc-
> ture, we have to conclude that causative constructions in Romance contain two
> words that jointly determine the predicate of the clause. This forces us to design a
> theory that allows predicate composition to result not only from combining mor-
> phemes in the lexicon, but also from combining words and phrases in the syntax. In
> what follows, *I will first present evidence that the causative complex predicate in
> Romance does not correspond to one word (a morphological unit) or even one sin-
> gle X^0 or terminal node in the syntax, and that it is, therefore not formed in the lexi-
> con; and I will then indicate the necessary assumptions for an LFG theory to allow
> predicate composition in the syntax.* [Italics added by Ackerman and Webelhuth]

The italicized portion of the latter passage is worth focusing on for a moment, since it helps both to distinguish our assumptions from the trend represented by Alsina as well as to identify certain crucial assumptions that we
share with LFG. From the perspective of certain basic assumptions within
LFG (see footnote 6) it is evident that Alsina conflates two independent aspects of "lexical integrity" in order to argue against the lexical composition
of Romance causative predicates: he identifies the structural conception of
"lexical" or "morphological" integrity (i.e., being a zero level category oc-
cupying a leaf node in phrasal structure) with the functional conception (i.e.,
being associated with information corresponding to a single predicator).[10] In
principle, however, LFG permits the possibility that the information associated with a single predicator could be associated with multiple indepen-

---

[8]Frank (1996) challenges syntactic composition accounts within LFG on the basis of Romance
auxiliary selection and reflexivization. We share the intuitions guiding this proposal although
we capture relevant effects for the data examined here in a different fashion.

[9]For a similar view, see Butt (1995: chapter 5 and elsewhere in her book).

[10]We thank Joan Bresnan for discussion on this point. See the discussions of Morphological
Integrity and Morphological Expression further below in the text for an elaboration of these issues.

dent elements each functioning as a syntactic atom. It is precisely this option that is suggested in Ackerman (1984, 1987), Ackerman and LeSourd (1997) and developed in greater detail in this book. In consequence of this conflation of two independent aspects of lexicality,[11] it does not follow that if one adduces evidence *"that the causative complex predicate in Romance does not correspond to one word (a morphological unit) or even one single X^0 or terminal node in the syntax"*, that this licenses the conclusion *"that it is, therefore not formed in the lexicon."*

Within HPSG, the highly influential proposal of Hinrichs and Nakazawa (1989, 1994) allows lexical entries to subcategorize for another lexical entry as a complement. As a consequence, the selecting lexical entry may inherit some or all of the selectional properties of that complement. This yields a configuration where a selector with an initially underspecified argument structure comes to have a fully specified argument structure. Thus, an auxiliary that selects for a main verb complement and inherits all of that complement's arguments will have a different number of arguments depending on whether the embedded complement has zero, one, two, or three arguments. Since the identity of the verb that serves as the complement to the auxiliary will only be known once the two verbs appear together in phrase structure, the argument structure of the auxiliary will be finally specified only in the syntactic component as a function of the syntactic context in which the auxiliary appears. This is in clear violation of the principle of *Lexical Adicity*.

Thus, some recent work in LFG and HPSG exhibits a conceptual innovation in that the trends it displays effectively reset the boundaries between the applicability of lexical and syntactic mechanisms in favor of the syntax: what we have referred to as the classic versions of both approaches (inclusive of present variants that reflect classic assumptions in various ways) gave certain analytical privileges to the lexicon and withheld them from the syntax, whereas certain recent proposals within these frameworks allow the syntax to move further into the territory once held exclusively by the lexicon.

In this connection it is important to appreciate that the empirical motivation for this relative loss of distinction on the part of the lexicon is precisely the set of phenomena dealing with analytically expressed clausal heads (i.e., predicates). Alsina (1993), Butt (1995), and Hinrichs & Nakazawa (1989, 1994) all motivate the need for the creation of new argument structures in the syntax on the basis of constructions involving a combination of two verbs which jointly define the semantic, functional, and categorial properties of a clause, e.g., a combination of a causative verb and a main verb or a combination of an auxiliary and a main verb.

As the entry in the final row of table (18) indicates, the theory of predicates developed in this book retains the strongly lexicalist position of classical LFG and HPSG: the lexicon and *only the lexicon* has the privilege

---

[11] See Mohanan (1995) for an informative discussion of the theoretical notion "lexicality".

of specifying the properties that make up the adicity of a phrase-projecting head. We believe that it is the wrong theoretical choice to weaken the influence of the lexicon relative to the syntax in the face of analytically expressed predicates and—as will be stated shortly—instead take the position that this problem is most effectively solved by realigning the relative influences of the lexicon and the syntax in the other direction. In other words, the theory of this book will force the syntax to cede some further analytical ground to the lexicon and hence in this respect is an even more strongly lexicalist theory than that explicitly formulated in classical LFG and HPSG.

Our second proto-principle of lexicalism deals with the relationship between the lexical component and morphology:

(20)   Morphological Integrity

       Syntactic mechanisms neither make reference to the daughters
       of morphological words nor can they create new morphologi-
       cal words in constituent structure.

In the words of Di Sciullo and Williams (1987), *Morphological Integrity* creates a "bottle neck" represented by morphological words: the sole morphological information that syntax can access is the morphology of the topmost node of a morphological constituent structure tree. Syntax cannot "look" lower in the tree at the word's daughter constituents. Bresnan and Mchombo (1995) present this point as follows (note that these authors prefer the term *Lexical Integrity* to the somewhat more specific *Morphological Integrity):*

A fundamental generalization that morphologists have traditionally maintained is the *lexical integrity principle,* that words are built out of different structural elements and by different principles of composition than syntactic phrases. Specifically, the morphological constituents of words are lexical and sublexical categories—stems and affixes—while the syntactic constituents of phrases have words as the minimal, unanalyzable units; and syntactic ordering principles do not apply to morphemic structures ... it has been hypothesized that *the lexical integrity principle holds of the morphemic structure of words, independently of their prosodic or functional structure.*

We take *Morphological Integrity* to mean that syntax and morphology are separate but interacting domains of grammar. Syntax, interpreted as phrasal structure, can neither "look into" morphological words to see internal structure nor can it create new morphological words.[12] The lexicon is

---

[12]This has led to what is referred to as 'Relativized Lexical Integrity' in Bresnan and Mchombo (1995), and Bresnan (forthcoming) [see also Ackerman and LeSourd (1997)] and is adopted here:

COMPLEX PREDICATES AND LEXICALISM / 19

not subject to either of these two constraints and hence has a more privileged relation to morphology than the syntax.

Each of the theories compared in our overview table (18) claims this morphological privilege of the lexicon over the syntax and in so doing they all differ from other theories that do allow morphological and syntactic operations to be intermixed, e.g., many versions of Government and Binding Theory and classical Montague Grammar.

The third and final diagnostic entering into an explication of lexicalism will be referred to as *Morphological Expression:*

(21) Morphological Expression

Lexical entries are uniformly expressed as single synthetic (syntactically atomic) word forms.

The concept of morphological expression, we believe, has been mistakenly conflated with morphological integrity as characterized above. Specifically, whereas morphological integrity constrains syntactic operations from creating morphological word forms, morphological expression concerns assumptions about the surface means by which lexical representations are expressed. LFG and HPSG have traditionally held the lexicon to the strict requirement that each lexical representation be expressed by at most one single morphophonologically integrated word form. This requirement privileges the syntax to create all collocations that consist of more than one morphologically free piece, even if the ensemble of words behaves as one content-theoretic unit with one argument structure, e.g., the analytical causatives discussed in Alsina (1993) and the auxiliary-verb combinations discussed in Hinrichs and Nakazawa (1989, 1994). It is precisely this required connection between clausal heads inserted from the lexicon and single morphological surface forms that leads these three authors to abandon the restriction against the formation of new argument structures in the syntax as was discussed in connection with the principle of *Lexical Adicity.*

There is thus conceptual tension between *Lexical Adicity* and *Morphological Expression,* and this tension becomes most obvious in the treatment of analytically expressed clausal heads. Classical LFG and HPSG maintained both principles but were unable to provide optimal analyses of these types of heads. Two obvious types of responses to this state of affairs are imaginable and both involve a realignment of the relative privileges of the lexicon and the syntactic component, albeit in opposite directions. If one considers it of paramount importance to retain the morphological restrictions of the lexicon vis-à-vis the syntax, then one is led to create analytically expressed clausal heads in the syntax by allowing phrase-structural opera-

---

"Morphologically complete words are leaves of the constituent structure tree and each leaf corresponds to one and only one c-structure node." [Bresnan (forthcoming: 84)]

tions to invade into the previously exclusively lexical domain of the formation of new argument structures. This leads to the departure from classical lexicalism that is represented by works such as Alsina (1993) and Hinrichs and Nakazawa (1989, 1994). Accordingly, lexicalism is in a weaker position relative to the syntax in recent LFG and HPSG compared to the classical versions of these theories (see the first and second rows in (18)).

Alternatively, if one considers *Lexical Adicity,* i.e., the exclusive privilege of the lexicon to create the functional-semantic information associated with clausal heads, to be the conceptual heart of lexicalism, then one is more inclined to lessen the strong constraint posed by *Morphological Expression* concerning the surface expression of lexical representations. Toning down the effects of this latter principle by downgrading it to a markedness preference strengthens the relative analytical role of the lexicon vis-à-vis the syntax: whereas classical lexicalism allowed the syntax to deal with collocations without joint morphological status and withheld this option from the lexicon, *Morphological Expression* as a preference principle makes the syntax only the preferred locus of composition for analytically expressed elements but extends this option to the lexicon as a marked choice.

It is important to mention that there is another and deft response compatible with classical LFG and licensed by LFG architectural assumptions which has been developed in several recent analyses (see Kroeger (1993), King (1995), Nordlinger and Bresnan (1996), Niño (1995, 1997), and Bresnan (forthcoming) for detailed exposition.)[13] In particular, certain independent constituent structure elements can be analyzed as constituent structure or phrasal co-heads that contribute their combined information to a functional structure associated with a single clause nucleus. In this way, two or more independent categorial elements can be construed as constituting a unit at some level of representation, specifically at the functional level. This type of proposal has provided elegant analyses of analytically expressed tense and other constructions involving auxiliary-like elements. On such an approach morphological integrity is maintained, since the leaf nodes of constituent structure trees are fully formed syntactic atoms, while the information associated with these syntactic atoms is pooled into a single functional structure. Crucially, the resulting f-structure is not interpreted as part of a lexical representation expressed by multiple syntactic atoms, as it is in the present work: rather it is a composite of information created by the co-occurrence of the co-heads in phrase structure. It is not interpreted as a projection from the lexicon in the same manner that it would be if the skeletal f-structure derived from a single morphological entity in the lexicon: the skeletal f-structures ordinarily associated with lexical representations can also be associated with concatenations of syntactic co-heads. In this respect

---

[13]This was a way of attacking the relevant problem which was basically inchoate at the time we developed our theory. Its outlines are evident in the early distinction between functional and structural heads and the work that employed this distinction cited previously in this chapter.

the mappings of form and function associated with e.g., analytically expressed tense and a verb is not stored as a part of a pattern for a predicate paradigm in the lexicon, but is presumably only extant as a syntactic pattern. Co-head analyses of the sort under discussion have been proposed primarily for syntactic constructions containing auxiliaries bearing modal and inflectional (i.e., morphosyntactic) information.[14] A question arises as to how a co-head analysis would work when applied to the derivation of complex predicates, e.g., causatives, expressed by independent c-structure elements. If these latter should be lexically represented and derived, as argued in Frank (1996), the question naturally arises as to why a similar analysis should not be assumed for the types of constructions ordinarily addressed by co-heads expressing combinations of lexical and morphosyntactic information? In fact, the uniform lexical treatment of the derivation of complex predicates as well as the participation of all types of predicates in morphosyntactic content paradigms, irrespective of synthetic or analytic surface expression, is the position developed throughout this book. As previously stated, our operative characterization of (complex) predicate includes both those sorts standardly assumed in this connection, e.g., causatives, analytically expressed passives involving auxiliaries, as well as analytic expressions of tense, modality, etc. It will be seen in chapter 6 that this broad view of the class of complex predicates is one of the factors that motivates the adoption of word and paradigm models of morphology in our implementation: it will be seen that certain word-based morphological assumptions facilitate locating both the derivational types and the inflectional types of analytically expressed predicates within the view of the lexicon espoused here.

To sum up our discussion of lexicalism as a cluster concept: this book takes the view that the data from predicates expressed by syntactically independent elements do not warrant abandoning what we take to be foundational principles of lexicalism, in particular the principle we called *Lexical Adicity* which prevents the syntactic component from creating new argument structures. The proposals developed in this book are guided by the conviction that this content-theoretic view of lexicalism should only be abandoned if the puzzles created by (complex) predicates prove to be thoroughly incommensurable with all defensible implementations of this view. From a more positive perspective, we will demonstrate that adherence to these content-theoretic principles raises important questions and yields important results. Accordingly, our overall view can perhaps best be characterized as follows:

---

[14]Co-head analyses have also been proposed for mixed category constructions such as gerundial constructions in Bresnan (to appear b) and Mugane (1996).

(22)   The Primacy of Function over Form

> Lexicalism is first and foremost a hypothesis about content-theoretic
> objects (containing functional-semantic and/or morphosyntactic con-
> tent) and secondarily a hypothesis about form.[15]

It is important to recall that in the present theory lexical adicity refers
to the functional-semantic information associated with lexical predicates.
Another type of information, as previously mentioned, comprises the morphosyntactic content often expressed synthetically by inflectional morphology, but frequently expressed analytically by clitics, particles, or auxiliaries
of several sorts. The specific manner in which each of these information
types is encoded is the subject of chapters 3–5 in which we introduce our
representations for lexical predicates.

Given this general perspective on lexicalism, we are led to postulate
the profile of principles in the last line of the overview table of lexicalism.
This proposal can be summed up for easy reference as follows:

(23)   Assumptions of the Present Book

- Only lexical and not syntactic rules can create new argument structures
  (Lexical Adicity).
- Only lexical but not syntactic rules can create or analyze morphological
  words *(Morphological Integrity)*.
- Lexical representations are preferably expressed by single synthetic word
  forms but can also be expressed by combinations of words without joint
  morphological status *(Morphological Expression)*.

Familiar accounts of "lexical insertion" deal only with synthetically
expressed predicates. On our alternative view the question arises how the
parts of an analytic predicate are associated with positions in syntactic
structure. [Cf. Jackendoff (1997) for similar considerations concerning
lexical entities and lexical insertion]. This is one of several issues which
will be addressed in due course. As can be seen, it is an immediate
consequence of an interpretation of lexicalism that separates content-
theoretic notions from morphological status that the types of problems for
lexicalism adduced by Lieber and alluded to earlier are limited to the
standard view of lexicalism. In fact, it is precisely this type of challenging
data that, we will argue, supports the strengthened view of lexicalism
propounded here and argues against alternatives that would seek solutions

---

[15]Of course a theory of signs such as is proposed here must necessarily address both content-
theoretic and form-theoretic aspects of lexical representations. It is important to observe that we
do not propose here a substantive theory of the principled relation of content to form, but note
that there seem important markedness considerations that an adequate theory must address
here. (See Bresnan (to appear b) for an intriguing proposal concerning the relation between
content, form, and markedness.)

to the problems posed by analytically expressed clausal heads in terms of a syntacticization of argument structure specification.[16]

By positing the notion predicate as an independent construct we expect to find empirical evidence suggesting that grammatical operations appeal to this entity just as it has been shown that they appeal to syntactic categories and grammatical relations [cf. Perlmutter (1979) for similar considerations]. In chapter 2 we will address this issue in detail from the perspective of two basic types of evidence: we adduce (1) several operations of morphology that refer to the predicate irrespective of the nature of its formal expression and (2) several syntactic operations that refer to the notion predicate.

We turn now to a discussion of three problems which any adequate theory of predicates must satisfactorily address.

4   The Expression Problem

This problem has already been amply demonstrated in sections 1 and 2 with data from preverbs, causatives, and passives. All of these constructions and others to be discussed later in this book uniformly display the property that what is content-theoretically essentially the same construction can find very different surface expressions in the world's languages. In particular, they can be expressed either synthetically or analytically. An acceptable linguistic theory should have a design from which this observation follows readily.

5   The Proliferation Problem

Modern linguistics concerns itself with developing a theory of *linguistic representations*. The history of the field in the last few decades provides ample illustration that the explanatory force of a particular linguistic theory depends in large measure on the types of linguistic constructs it posits and the manner in which it manipulates them in order to yield well formed linguistic representations. The task of identifying the right representations and the appropriate relations between them is quite challenging. In practice it has proven easy to postulate representations that account well for

---

[16]Our operative notion of predicate obviously resembles certain analyses in Montague Grammar and Categorial Grammar [Dowty (1979), Bach (1983), Hoeksema (1991)]. This becomes particularly clear in Dowty (1979) where syntactic and morphological *operations* are distinguished from syntactic and lexical *rules*. Lexical rules on Dowty's account relate entities that are not necessarily expressed by synthetic morphological objects: for example, English resultative constructions (called factitives in his account) are associated with lexical rules and syntactic operations. A somewhat similar view, of particular relevance to our analysis of German analytic predicate expressions as associated with lexical representations, is the proposal found in Bierwisch (1990). Some recent lexicalist analyses of phrasal verb constructions, sometimes addressing other "related" constructions, are found in Booij (1990), Neeleman & Weerman (1993), and Neeleman (1994).

certain syntactic phenomena. Moreover, in many instances, a notion of global theoretical parsimony has suggested that the representations and assumptions found serviceable for certain phenomena be pressed into service elsewhere. On the other hand, it has often been observed that such representational assumptions (1) predict the existence of phenomena which are unattested or counter-exemplified in the languages of the world and (2) have dubious applicability beyond the phenomena which they were formulated to address since they entail increasingly abstract interpretations with respect to these new domains of application.

This reliance on apparently effective sources of explanation for more and more seemingly disparate distributions of data has a consequence that we will refer to as *the proliferation problem.* It has different manifestations in different approaches. In lexicalist approaches it can lead to the proliferation of homophonous lexical entries. In certain versions of structure based approaches, in contrast, it has led to a proliferation of structure in terms of functional categories. This raises the issue of how to extend the empirical coverage of a theory without suffering unacceptable proliferation of postulated entities. At the end of this section we will discuss this problem in connection with our own theory.

5.1 Proliferation in Lexical-Functional Grammar

As mentioned in a previous section, German frequently expresses passive analytically: a non-finite form of the verb co-occurs with an auxiliary. One type of passive construction consists of a participle and a finite form of the auxiliary *werden* 'become'. This is shown in (24) which contains the participial form of the verb *zeigen* 'to show' and the 3rd person singular present tense form of the auxiliary.

(24)　weil　das Buch dem Jungen *von Maria* **gezeigt** wird
　　　because the book the boy　by Mary　shown becomes
　　　'because the book is shown to the boy by Maria'

On the early LFG account of passive, the active form of the verb would be related to its passive form via lexical rule. Ignoring for the moment recent developments in this framework, a lexical operation will assure that the argument bearing the SUBJECT function in the active lexical entry will correspond to an OBLIQUE function or an unrealized argument in the passive lexical entry, while the OBJECT of the active will correspond to the SUBJECT of the passive lexical entry. Bresnan's (1982a) formulation distinguishes between functional and morphological properties of this operation:

(25) Functional Change: SUBJ --> OBL/Ø
                                  OBJ   --> SUBJ

      Morphological Change: V   --> V [part]

The functional aspect of this rule can be regarded as universal: the formal expression is expected to vary from language to language. Indeed, the only (implicit) assumption with respect to function and form in this formulation appears to be that the function changes will be associated with a morphological object. In the present case, the passive function assignments are associated with a participial form of the verb.

The preceding rule of passive is applicable to German without alteration. In particular we could posit lexical entries related by the passive lexical rule. The active lexical entry

(26) *zeigen* , V, 'show < SUBJ, OBJ, OBL >'

is relatable in this manner to the passive lexical entry:

(27) *gezeigt* , V, 'shown < OBL/Ø, SUBJ, OBL >'

Like its English counterpart, the observed participial form of German has a use where it is associated with an active set of function assignments:

(28)   weil   Maria das Buch dem Jungen **gezeigt** hat
       because Maria the book the boy   shown   has
       'because Maria has shown the book to the boy'

The active and passive participial forms can be treated as homophonous entities: each lexical item is associated with its own function assignments. The relevant entry for the active participle would be

(29) *gezeigt* , V, 'shown < SUBJ, OBJ, OBL >'

There are consequently at least three different but related lexical items at issue in the present case. In an obvious sense this represents a proliferation of lexical items.

Now consider the following additional German passive construction:

(30)   weil   der Junge das Buch *von Maria* **gezeigt** bekommt
       because the boy the book by Maria shown   gets
       'because the boy gets the book shown by Maria'

In this construction we can see that the same participial form with passive force appears as in (24) above. However, in the present case the OBJ of the active does not appear as the SUBJ of the passive, rather the IN-DIRECT OBJ does. Given this state of affairs one could posit a homophonous participial form with different function assignments than that hypothesized for (27), increasing the number of homophonous participial forms to three:

(31)   *gezeigt*, V, 'shown < OBL/Ø, OBJ, SUBJ >'

The forms *gezeigt* that appear in both (27) and (31) must represent two different (though related) lexical items, because the sentences they are contained in have properties which according to standard lexicalism must be due to lexical differences: they display distinct function sets.

Given the fact that the same participle appears with different functional-semantic (specifically, adicity) properties in conjunction with different auxiliaries, it might be argued that passive should be formulated over the participle and a particular auxiliary. Recent proposals within LFG [e.g., Alsina (1993)] and HPSG [e.g., Hinrichs and Nakazawa (1989, 1994), Kathol (1994)] have made possible such an account of analytically expressed predicates. An analysis formulated within these assumptions might avoid the need to proliferate homophonous participial forms with different function assignments in favor of permitting passive to apply to a participle in conjunction with an auxiliary when they actually co-occur, i.e., by necessity in phrase structure. The proliferation problem would then be eliminated. In particular, one could extend the syntactic predicate composition operations proposed by Alsina for periphrastically expressed causatives to periphrastically expressed passives. The auxiliary participating in passive could be analyzed as an incomplete predicate on analogy with independent causative verbs. The auxiliary would accordingly need to compose with another verbal entity bearing an appropriate argument structure. A passive mapping algorithm would apply to the composite argument structure resulting from the composition of the two syntactically independent predicates.[17]

An analysis along these lines would lead to a loss of linguistically significant generalizations, however, as can be shown by the interaction of German passives and resultatives [following a parallel argument from English in Goldberg (1995)]:

---

[17]It should be noted that Alsina (1996) does not develop such a proposal, but rather one in which a passive argument structure is associated with a passive participle that combines in the syntax with an auxiliary. That is, passive is not interpreted as associated with the construction consisting of a participle and an auxiliary, but is associated with the participle alone. See chapter 8 for our analysis of passive.

COMPLEX PREDICATES AND LEXICALISM / 27

(32)   Sie hat die Schuhe krumm gelaufen
       she has the shoes   crooked walked

       'She walked the shoes crooked'

(33)   Die Schuhe sind von ihr krumm gelaufen worden
       the shoes   are by her crooked walked become

       'The shoes were walked crooked by her'

(34)   Die krumm gelaufenen Schuhe zieht sie nicht mehr an
       the crooked walked   shoes wears she not   more particle

       'She doesn't wear the shoes any more that she walked crooked'

As can be seen in (32), a verb which is ordinarily intransitive, i.e.,
'gelaufen', appears with a direct object in the active variant of the resultative. (33) is a personal passive analog of (32). If there are no lexical passive
participles (in order to avoid proliferation), then 'gelaufen' is the active perfect participle taken from the lexicon which combines with the resultative
secondary predicate in the syntax to form an argument structure to which
passive might apply. Assuming that passive does apply, the application of
passive either alters the categorial status of the participle so that it becomes
a passive participle or it does not and the participle remains perfect.

If the first option obtains, then some instances of syntactic predicate
composition would seem to alter the lexical status of elements within the
syntax, thereby raising the issue of whether there can be morphological
word formation in the syntax in LFG in violation of *Morphological Integrity*
after all: previously, it was assumed that although certain types of *information* (i.e., argument structures) could combine in the syntax, the *morphological* status of the elements participating in such compositions was determined in the lexicon.

If, in contrast, the second option is taken and the participle in (33)
remains a perfect participle, then the question arises as to how to relate the
syntactically composed '*krumm gelaufen* worden' to the attributive form
'*krumm gelaufenen*' in (34), given that in the latter context the participle has
undergone the morphological processes that allow it to signal such categories as number, case, etc. in which it agrees with the nominal that the passivized resultative predicate modifies in (34).

The theoretical and analytical issues which arise with respect to the
German examples presented above are paralleled by passive and related adjectival forms from Marathi.[18] Consider the following passive sentence containing two inflected verbal forms: the verb 'hit' is followed by the verb
'go' which functions as a "passivizer" in such constructions.

---

[18]This presentation follows the discussion in Dalrymple (1993: 12).

(35)   mulaa-naa   tyaa gurujiin-kaḍuun maarle   jaate
        children-ACC   that teacher-by   hit-AGR PASS-AGR

'Children are (usually) beaten by that teacher'

Marathi possesses an adjective-forming suffix *-raa* which affixes to a verbal form to create a new category. When *-raa* is affixed to active verbs it can appear in nominals such as in (36):

(36)   maarṇaare mule
        beat-RAA   children

'Children who beat/*Children who are beaten'

Similarly, the presence of this suffix on a passive construction yields the following:

(37)   maarlii jaaṇaarii   mule
        hit   PASS-RAA   children

'Children who are beaten/*Children who beat'

As can be seen, *-raa* suffixes to the "passivizing" verb 'go' to yield an adjectival form with a passive sense: passives consist formally of two independent verbs. In both the clausal use of the passive and the adjectival use the verbal forms exhibit agreement morphology.

The German and Marathi data create the following paradox: if analytically expressed predicates must be composed syntactically either because of the syntactic independence of their component parts or because we want to avoid proliferation of homophonous lexical entries, then how can they be related in a principled way to forms which clearly bear a derivational relation to them but must have been created in the lexicon because they have undergone further morphological operations?

One way to achieve descriptive adequacy would be to form the predicative structures through predicate composition in the syntax while deriving the attributive form through some morphological operation in the lexicon. But clearly this solution undoes the anticipated advantages of allowing passives to be formed in phrase structure. Not only do we have to list homophonous entries (including at least one passive entry) for 'gelaufen' after all—avoiding this was the goal of allowing predicate formation in the syntax to begin with—but in addition even though we now do have a passive entry of the participle 'gelaufen' in the lexicon, we compose its predicative analog in the syntax from the active participle 'gelaufen' and an auxiliary rather than exploiting the existence of the lexical passive participle. The linguistically relevant generalizations that the attributive and predicative passives share thus fail to be captured.

The issue of how to capture the relevant generalizations while avoiding the detrimental effects of proliferation arise in our theory as well, as in fact they do in every approach to the kinds of problems we are concerned with in this book. For the reasons just discussed in connection with the German and Marathi passives, we believe that syntacticizing predicate formation yields no effective solution to the problem of the proliferation of homophonous lexical entries in heavily lexicalist theories of grammar. In fact, in our view splitting predicate formation between two components of the grammar not only does not present a solution but even stands in the way of a principled solution to the proliferation problem! In contrast, a theory that locates all predicate formation in one component can reduce proliferation to a minimum without losing generalizations.

Recall that in the approach advocated in this book all predicates are formed in the lexicon, no matter how many words make up their surface exponence.[19] As a result, all predicates are accessible to the inheritance hierarchy of lexical types which allows generalizations across lexical entries to be extracted from them and expressed in a common lexical supertype. Besides a specification of its supertypes, a lexical entry then only needs to explicitly spell out those properties that it does not share with other lexical entries. With this general approach it is possible for several different lexical entries to all inherit the same morphological information (e.g., "participle") while being assigned different content-theoretic information depending on which predicate is being formed, e.g., predicative vs. attributive, active vs. passive, etc. Each such lexical predicate formation process can determine which auxiliary becomes part of the exponence of the newly formed predicate if any. In this manner, the theory simultaneously defines a set of predicates including their surface exponences such that all those predicates which comprise a participial exponent will be related because they all inherit from the same *morphological* type and all the passive predicates will be related because they inherit from the same *functional-semantic* type. Only one sort of entity is being proliferated in such a system, namely predicate constructions which specify which combinations of exponents express which content-theoretic units of information. This strikes us as the minimal core that every adequate theory of predicates will have to state and as an acceptable solution to the proliferation problem.[20]

---

[19]As mentioned previously Frank (1996) provides an alternative to syntactic composition within LFG that is in the same spirit as the proposal developed here. She writes (1996: 187):

"Our lexical rule of complex predicate formation ... then constitutes just another class of lexical rule, which applies to *two* verb stems, to yield two discontinuous verb stems ..."

Our lexical operations are likewise designed to address the possibility of multiple exponence by several syntactically independent elements. It should be noted that a variant of this position is presented and defended in Jackendoff (1997).

[20]It bears mentioning that Bresnan (1994) proposes, in effect, an alternative way to avoid the proliferation of lexical entries within LFG. In particular, she posits a supralexical construction which can superimpose its own argument structure and function assignments on lexical entries that would otherwise not meet the lexical requirements to participate in locative inversion.

5.2   Proliferation in Government and Binding Theory

Government and Binding Theory also exhibits a *proliferation* problem. What proliferates in GB are not lexical items (whose phonological matrices provide evidence for their existence, if not for a multiplication of homophonous elements) but abstract binary branching structures projected by
so-called *functional heads.*

Government and Binding Theory, especially its classical version as
described in Chomsky (1981), hypothesizes that phrase structure configurations play a central role in the explication of syntactic phenomena. The theory further postulates that phrase structure in general is "projected" from
units of lexical size as are other important properties, e.g., argument structure and Case features which enter into well-formedness conditions such as
the θ–criterion and Case theory. These well-formedness conditions in turn
refer to phrase structure configurations such as sisterhood, command, and
government which are assumed to hold uniformly across categorial heads
and their uniformly postulated syntactic projections (this is the X-bar theory
of phrase structure).

Given this singular emphasis on phrase structural explanations over
other kinds of explanations and the desire to achieve uniformity of phrase
structure configurations, it is not surprising that GB theory frequently postulates categorial heads to do work which is done through different means in
other theories. For instance, while tense and agreement marking are completely handled in the lexicon in unification type theories, most versions of
GB theory postulate the existence of categorial heads which express this information in phrase structure: in Chomsky (1981) this information was
stored under the Infl(ection) node, but in more recent theories this node has
been "exploded" into a set of separate nodes whose precise number differs
from author to author. Following the "exploded Infl" theory pioneered by
Pollock (1989) there have been many proposals to solve problems by appealing to functional heads. The following table presents a list of such heads
that have been proposed in the literature over the years:[21]

---

[21]We ignore here and in what follows more recent proposals, since the list of proposed heads
continues to grow in unconstrained and unexplanatory fashion. In addition, we do not discuss
recent work within the Minimalist Program, since, to the degree that it is "lexicalist", it seems
to adopt certain basic insights of standard lexicalist frameworks, while retaining some of the
phrase-structure theoretic commitments rendered superfluous by the formalisms ordinarily
employed in standard lexicalist theories.

(38)   Proposed Category   Source

       AGR_A Chomsky (1995)
       Agr_{IO} Mahajan(1990)
       AGR_N Johns (1992)
       AGR_V Johns (1992)
       AGR_1, AGR_2 Collins and Thráinsson (1996)
       Aspect   Hendrick (1991)
       Aux   Mahajan(1990)
       Clitic voices   Sportiche (1992)
       Deg   Corver (1997)
       F   Uriagereka (1995)
       Gender   Shlonsky (1989)[22]
       Honorific   Kim (1992)
       K   Bittner and Hale (1996)
       μ   Pesetsky (1989), Johnson (1991)
       Neg   Pollock (1989), Benmamoun (1992)
       Number   Shlonsky (1989), Ritter (1991)
       Person   Shlonsky (1989)
       Predicate   Bowers (1993)
       Tense   Pollock (1989)
       Z   Stowell (1992)

The theory of this book is conservative in the postulation of phrase structure. Following the spirit of much of the work within LFG, we posit categorial structure only when there is categorial evidence for it [cf. Bresnan (1995)]. There will be no need to proliferate categorially unmotivated phrase structure representations in the present account, since the interaction of other independently motivated sorts of information will be shown to cover the same ground.

6 The Grammaticalization Problem

It is a frequent observation in different grammatical traditions that a single lexical unit can consist of several syntactically separate elements. The basic issues can be conveyed by looking briefly at representatives from two traditions which explicitly address complex predicates in this fashion. These linguists are associated with the descriptive linguistic traditions in Russia and Australia.

Though the problems presented to X-bar theory and the principles of lexical insertion by analytically expressed predicates may be novel, the notion of analytic predicates viewed as members of paradigms is not. Soviet linguists have traditionally acknowledged the existence of synthetic and an-

---

[22]Reported in Benmamoun (1992: 167, fn. 5).

alytic forms: whereas lexical and grammatical (i.e., morphosyntactic) information appear together within morphophonologically integrated units for synthetic expression, these types of information appear separately in analytic forms. The typical profile for an analytic expression is characterized as follows by Jartseva (1963: 53):

The specific property of analytic forms is that lexical and grammatical meanings are transmitted disjointly and that the degree of coalescence between the elements of analytic word forms varies according to the historical development manifest in a given language.

She contends that these forms are not only distinguished by discrete syntactic expression of different types of information , but that (op. cit.):

The constitutive components of analytic forms, although representing a single lexical unit, are capable of altering their linear relations to one another and of permitting the interposition of elements between them.

Both disjoint expression of information and syntactic separability of the exponents of this information are aspects of complex predicates we have already encountered.

Meshchaninov (1982) is representative of scholars describing the nature of the so-called auxiliary verb in these analytic predicates (1982: 158):

Having become a linking verb, the verb loses one of its obligatory meanings—lexical meaning—and preserves another meaning—syntactic meaning. A verb [i.e., a predicate; the authors] exists only in the union of both [meanings].

Meshchaninov points here toward the common observation that verbs which function as auxiliaries typically derive from (or are sometimes synchronous with) verbs which function as independent predicators. In addition, he suggests that the analytic form resembles the synthetic form in that for both the predicate, i.e., his verb, is only complete as the integration of functional-semantic and morphosyntactic, i.e., his syntactic, meaning.

The characterization of analytic predicates provided by Russian linguists is remarkably similar to the descriptions offered by several linguists examining verbal constructions found in Australian aboriginal languages. These are presented in Dixon (1976).[23] A typical profile of compound predicates is proposed by Vászolyi (1976: 640) for Wunambal:

The non-finite head-verb, reminiscent of a gerund or infinitive, functions as the semantic nucleus of a compound and carries its lexical meaning. It appears that the fol-

---

[23]Topic E: Simple and compound verbs: conjugation by auxiliaries in Australian verbal systems.

lowing auxiliary (at least on a descriptive plane) has but grammatical functions, indicating mood, tense, subject, object etc.

Once again, on the origins of the auxiliary we find the following (1976: 640):

The auxiliary is one of the simple verbs [i.e., an independent, synthetic verb form; the authors] ... which follows the head-verb and carries most of the syntactic load of the compound... Semantically, the lexical meaning of a simple verb appears more often than not obscured or neutralized when functioning as an auxiliary.

The observations of these Russian and Australian descriptivists converge in two important ways: they both posit a distinction between lexical vs. grammatical (morphosyntactic) meanings and they both hypothesize that the manner in which these meanings are expressed viz. synthetic vs. analytic, is not criterial for determining the lexicality status of the relevant predicates.

It should be noted that the diachronic development of complex predicates consisting of a preverb (or particle) and a verbal stem parallels, in striking fashion, the development of V + V compositions presented above. For example, Nichols (1986) presents the following data from Chechen:

(39)   čaj-na ^{M}ču šieker ^{H}tasa
         tea-DAT in   sugar-NOM sprinkle-IMP

         'Sprinkle some sugar in the tea'

(40)   čaj-na šieker ^{M}ču-^{H}tasa
         tea-DAT sugar-NOM in-sprinkle-IMP

         'Sprinkle some sugar in the tea'

She describes this as follows (1986: 84):

Here the postposition ^{M}ču governs the dative case (as postpositions regularly do in Chechen). In [40], it is a preverb, and its former object has now become a second object (in the dative, as are most second objects). Both constructions are possible in all possible orders... This example is a particularly strong demonstration of the universality of headward migration, since Chechen and Ingush are among the world's most consistently dependent-marking languages.

Noting, as can be seen, that the development of such preverbal systems arises independent of whether a language tends to mark its head or dependent elements, Nichols additionally observes that it cannot be explained either in terms of the original linear orders of the participating pieces. She concludes (1986: 85):

What is now needed is a positive understanding of the mechanics and motivation of the processes which turn words into affixes. One principle has been given here: dependents (or parts of them) become affixes on heads. A complete account of the causation must also establish hierarchies of syntactic relations, pronominal categories, semantic functions, lexical classes, etc. which favor migration.

It is our belief that it is desirable for this pre-theoretical and descriptive consensus on the diachrony of complex predicates to be reflected in the formal account of these constructions: an optimal proposal would be responsive to the recurrent cross-linguistic developmental profile of these constructions.[24] We believe that the representational apparatus we develop for predicates in this book does precisely that.

Beyond the Russian and Australian sources cited above, analysis along similar lines has been the standard assumption within Algonquian linguistics since the pioneering work of Jones (1904, 1911) suggested that preverb-V sequences represent some type of complex stem. Michaelson (1917: 50–52) argued that such sequences reflect a process of "loose composition", that is to say a process that derives compound stems whose members retain considerable syntactic independence. Similarly within Ugric linguistics Rombandeeva (1973: 180) observes of some Vogul separable preverbs that "they evince a transitional function between word-formative affixes and components of compound words." This parallels the remarks of Soltész (1959: 8) concerning Hungarian preverb-V constructions:

If certain prefixed verbs occupy a place between a compound word and a derived word, then from another perspective we must locate prefixed verbs along the border between syntagmata and compounds.

In effect, the proposal in this book represents a formal reconstruction of a pretheoretical consensus that predicates in many languages evince mismatches between their status as lexical items and their syntactic behaviors. We treat synchronic instances of such discrepancies as the reflexes of a pervasive and well-documented tendency for certain types of syntactically independent elements to exhibit a historical development into lexical representations. This process is generally interpreted as grammaticalization [see Steever (1993), Heine (1993), Hopper and Traugott (1993), and many others]. In addition, it is often observed, with requisite caveats [see Nevis (1988) on an analytic tendency in Estonian and Harris and Campbell (1995)], that this historical change tends to display a unidirectional character toward creating synthetic units from analytic expressions.

---

[24]This view is also expressed in an excellent article by Börjárs, Vincent, and Chapman (1996) with respect to the synthetic versus analytic expression of the morphosyntactic information traditionally represented in paradigms. Our proposal bears a natural affinity with theirs in terms of both some basic assumptions and certain representational commitments. This will be particularly evident in chapter 3 where we present our representations for the information-theoretic aspects of predicates.

The account of Harris and Campbell (1995) argues against assuming an independent theoretical status for grammaticalization, and argues for capturing "grammaticalization effects" associated with diachronic change as being facilitated by two mechanisms, namely reanalysis and extension. These mechanisms are described as follows (p. 50f; all footnotes and indication of emphasis omitted for convenience):

Reanalysis is a mechanism which changes the underlying structure of a syntactic pattern and which does not involve any modification of its surface manifestation. We understand underlying structure in this sense to include at least (i) constituency, (ii) hierarchical structure, (iii) category labels, and (iv) grammatical relations. Surface manifestation includes (i) morphological marking, such as morphological case, agreement, and gender class, and (ii) word order.

Extension results in changes in the surface manifestation of a pattern and which does not involve immediate or intrinsic modification of underlying structure.

As can be seen, reanalysis involves an alteration of content information, while extension concerns the manner in which content information is formally realized or expressed.

Harris and Campbell argue that these mechanisms are broadly operative in historical changes and specifically evident in the development of particle-verb combinations of the sort presented previously. For example, they demonstrate that within the Kartvelian family of Caucasian languages, exemplified by Svan and Georgian, there are numerous prefixed verb constructions that trace their origins to the combination of independent adverbial elements with verbs. In several ways these constructions synchronically still display different stages of development from independent elements to clitics, to affixes. Similarly, Harris and Campbell argue that these mechanisms are at play in the development of monoclausal from biclausal predicate constructions (see chapter 9 in the present book for an analysis of causative constructions in which clausality plays a prominent role).

Whether one adopts some variant of the standard grammaticalization hypotheses or the type of alternative proposed in Harris and Campbell, we believe that the representations and assumptions of linguistic theory should be adaptable enough to reflect convergent patterns of diachronic development where they are attested.

Guided by the insights and observations of these historical and typological studies, we will occasionally speculate that the surface form of particular predicates in particular languages is due to factors involving diachronic change and grammaticalization. From a synchronic theoretical perspective we have chosen to connect the cross-linguistic prevalence and consistency evident in such historical development to the hypothesis that many instances of reanalysis, in the sense provided, are best interpreted in terms of the lexicalization in the form of analytically expressed predicates of formerly syntactically related distinct predicates.

7 Conclusions

In this chapter we have discussed the synthetic and analytic expression of four predicate constructions involving alteration of various types of non-categorial information associated with a lexical representation. We have argued that the existence of a cross-linguistically recurring set of predicate constructions which evince a unidirectional diachronic development toward synthetic morphological expression represents an instructive challenge for theory construction with respect to three important problems. The *expression problem* challenges the theoretician to look past obvious surface differences between languages in order to see what is common between them. In the service of this goal it raises the issue concerning the most apposite and well-motivated representation. This yields the *proliferation problem* since there is an understandable desire on the part of theoreticians to be parsimonious regarding representational assumptions. Such parsimony often yields proliferation without obvious limit and somewhat more importantly sometimes without true explanatory force. Finally, what we have referred to as the *grammaticalization problem* suggests that the expression of predicates falls into a small number of well-defined types and that representational assumptions should accordingly be developed to reflect this. That is, it is desirable for our notions of lexical entries, phrase structures and constructions to be represented in such a manner as to be able to be set in principled correspondence with what we know about the morphological and phrasal expressions of predicates. This is the position we develop and argue for in the remainder of this book.

2

The Construct 'Predicate'[1]

In the preceding chapter we suggested that grammatical theory should represent the notion predicate independent of its surface expression within particular languages. Discussing the *grammaticalization problem,* we observed that the predicate types of interest here exhibit a recurrent cross-linguistic and diachronic profile: they tend to exhibit a unidirectional tendency to develop into morphophonologically integrated units from syntactically independent elements. Pervasive parallelisms in this domain suggest the possibility that we may be dealing with a natural class of entities.[2] More generally, if the construct predicate is to be attributed a theoretical status, it is to be expected that operations of grammar will appeal to it in much the same way that other theoretical constructs have been motivated empirically. Accordingly, much of this chapter is devoted to an examination of numerous phenomena which seem to require appealing to the construct predicate in grammatical theory, independent of categoriality and expressible by a single syntactic atom or by multiple syntactically independent elements.

Before examining the empirical evidence for a content-theoretic notion of predicate, it is important to say a few things about traditional logical and generative linguistic interpretations of the term predicate in order to better see how our use of the term relates to them. We then turn to an investigation of both morphological and syntactic phenomena from numerous languages which motivate the theoretical need for a linguistic construct predicate.

1   Some Previous Views of Predicates

The functional division of clauses into subject and predicate has a venerable history. The standard interpretation traces back to Aristotle where it corresponds to the bipartite division of propositions into subject and predicate. Following the discussion in Kneale and Kneale (1962: 64):

The subject-term may be taken to indicate or refer to a number of individuals distributively by expressing a property or group of properties which these individuals have in common. The copula then expresses the not further analyzable notion of

---

[1] We would like to express appreciation to Phil LeSourd for collaboration on some of the central conceptual issues explored in this chapter. See Ackerman and LeSourd (1997) for discussion relating to some issues considered here.

[2] Of course, we are not claiming that morphologization implies that participating elements are predicates: there are numerous instances of morphologization of non-predicates. Rather, we are observing that the class of elements interpretable as predicates for independent reasons exhibits a tendency to morphologize.

predication and the predicate simply expresses the property which it is the function of the whole sentence to ascribe to the individuals indicated by the subject-term.

Obviously, this description characterizes predicative constructions such as 'All men are animals.' On the other hand it is commonplace to extend this notion of 'predication' to many sorts of sentence, including transitive ones such as 'Jones owns Ulysses', as typified by the discussion in Kamp and Reyle (1993). Adapting their account, such sentences are roughly representable as in Figure 1:

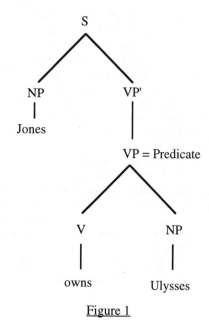

Figure 1

The VP, consisting of the verb 'own' and its object, constitutes the predicate. This constituent is predicated of the subject, represented here as the daughter of S.

There are many elements that function as predicates within the logical tradition of formal semantics. If, for example, we decided to do so we could create a predicate out of 'X owns four copies of Ulysses in Abkhaz' in order to create a sentence where this predicate combines with the NP 'Jones' to form a sentence 'Jones owns four copies of Ulysses in Abkhaz'. Alternatively, we could make a predicate out of 'Jones owns four copies of X in Abkhaz' which would combine with 'Ulysses' to form the sentence 'Jones owns four copies of Ulysses in Abkhaz.' An important linguistic question raised by the ability to specify predicates in such enormous variety is what sorts of natural language entities they correspond to? In the same vein, is there a class of natural language entities that constitute a (proper) subset of the entities characterizable by these means and how might we identify and most perspicuously represent such a class?

The enormous range of predicates permitted by logical notations and the consequent conception of the notion predicate within the logical tradition differs from the one presently proposed in that we limit the notion predicate to the entity that, among other things, determines all of the complement requirements for the domain which it heads. For the sentence 'John owns Ulysses', the relevant domain is the entire clause and the projector of complement requirements for the clausal domain is 'own'. 'Own' is interpretable as a predicate since it projects argument requirements for both a subject and an object. Once again following Kamp and Reyle (1993) we can characterize the predicate X OWNS Y as *irreducible*. On the other hand, 'own Ulysses' is not regarded as the predicate of the clause in the desired sense, since one of the arguments of the clausal projector is already saturated, i.e., the object: on Kamp and Reyle's account this is a *reducible* predicate. Having saturated one of its argument requirements this unit no longer represents the basic informational core of the clause.

It is important to observe that by distinguishing between the standard interpretation of 'predication' (i.e., either a reducible or an irreducible predicate) and our own (i.e., roughly speaking, an irreducible predicate), we neither reject the standard notion nor many of the uses for which the traditional construct has been profitably employed. Rather, we believe that another, and somewhat neglected, notion of predicate is also relevant for linguistic theory. It is this restricted notion of predicate as argument-taker, clausal complement determiner and locus for clausal operator notions such as tense, modality, etc. that we develop in the present work.[3]

There is another point worth making in connection with our emphasis on the argument-taking and clausal property determining aspect of predicates. This emphasis is intended both to (i) distinguish this aspect of predicates from their categorial expression, i.e., as to whether they are verbs or nouns or adjectives etc., as well as to (ii) suggest their independence from *morphological expression,* i.e., that they need not correspond to a single synthetic morphological object.

Several relevant issues concerning logical vs. linguistic notions of the predicate as well as speculations concerning the nature of the representations appropriate for encoding a linguistic notion of predicate can be made plain by reviewing some previous generative literature. For example, our notion of predicate parallels, on some construal, the notion of V(erb) advanced in Chomsky (1957). Among the rewrite rules presented in Chomsky (1957) we find the following:

---

[3]See Bybee et al. (1994), Traugott and Heine (1991), Heine (1993), Steever (1993), among others for proposals concerning the morphologization/grammaticalization of clausal operator information.

Verb --> Aux + V
V   --> hit, take, walk, etc.
Aux --> C(M) (have+en) (be+ing) (be+en)

<u>Figure 2</u>

There is, we would suggest, a useful intuition encoded in these early rewrite rules: they suggest that Aux(s) and a V warrant recognition as a unit, distinct from the VP. We will assume, informally for the present, that the construct *predicate* can be characterized as follows: it is the determiner or projector of certain core properties of clauses, i.e., valence, semantic roles for arguments, grammatical functions associated with arguments, as well as morphosyntactic content such as tense, mood, aspect etc.

The postulation of an accessible information unit consisting of grammatical information such as agreement, tense, mood, etc. as well as the projection of argument structure (and associated functions) clearly parallels the intuitions underlying Grimshaw's (to appear) Extended Projections as well as earlier [Mohanan (1982), Ackerman (1984, 1987)] and recent work within LFG on the organization of phrase structure [see King (1995), Austin and Bresnan (1996), Butt et al. (1996)]. It is information of the sort characteristic of skeletal functional structures within LFG. Our quarrel, such as it is, is with the assumption that the relevant information is most explanatorily encoded in terms of syntactic configurations, as in Chomsky-based proposals, or in terms of the composition of information among multiple constituent-structure heads, as in recent X-bar proposals within LFG.

We see that there was an early recognition of the need for a linguistic construct predicate which could include the 'main verb' and bearers of clausal operator information such as auxiliaries. This was complemented by the recognition that there were certain entities interpretable as constituting single semantic entities but expressed by multiple syntactically independent elements.

The role of the predicate in linguistic theory suggests a parallel with another construct that has figured prominently in pretheoretical and some theoretical speculation, namely, the syllable. Despite efforts to dispense with it in early generative phonology, the arguments of numerous phonologists over the past few years [Hooper (1972), Vennemann (1972), Kahn (1976), Clements and Keyser (1983), Levin (1985), among others] have demonstrated the need for such a construct in order to explain a wide array of phenomena and this has ensured it a prominent place in phonological theory. Kenstowicz (1994: 250) provides motivation for generative efforts to circumvent positing the syllable:

One reason the syllable has proved so elusive is that it lacks any uniform direct phonetic correlates: it is not a sound, but an abstract unit of prosodic organization through which language expresses much of its phonology. Furthermore, the exact shape of the syllable varies from one language to another. Finally, the organization of sounds into syllables can take place at a certain level of abstraction: more superficial features often obscure the underlying organization.

Similarly, it is the contention of the present work that the predicate is an abstract unit of clausal organization which does not exhibit a unique mapping into a single formal expression cross-linguistically, although it does exhibit a diachronic tendency to be encoded by a single morphological object. As with the syllable, its existence is more evident in its explanatory force for treating disparate language phenomena than in any reductive superficial properties used to define it.

Kenstowicz concludes the previous passage as follows:

Phonologists have only begun to grasp the factors determining syllabification. Much work still remains to be done. But there can be no doubt that the syllable is an essential unit of phonological organization and hence a principal research objective.

It is our belief that the time has come for a similar recognition of the need for the construct predicate. The weight of empirical arguments pointing to the existence of the syllable has elicited much effort to provide a theoretical formulation of this entity. In the present book we develop a particular formal interpretation of the primarily descriptive and pretheoretical content-theoretic construct predicate, and do so from a lexicalist perspective.

There are, of course, alternative ways to argue for the sharp differentiation between form-theoretic and content-theoretic considerations, and these lead to different conceptualizations of grammar than those that find their source in Chomsky's early reflections. Linguists working within both Relational Grammar and Lexical-Functional Grammar have provided evidence for the value of distinguishing the categorial from the functional (or relational) status for complements of predicators: they have argued for the value of notions such as subject, object, oblique, etc. In an innovative departure Perlmutter (1979) argues for distinguishing between the categorial and the functional (relational) status of the predicate [see Davies and Rosen (1988) and related work for recent developments]. He provides several types of evidence for positing a predicate relation independent of its categorial expression (see below for further discussion), including data from yes/no question formation in Russian. He hypothesizes that the neutral order of clausal constituents for yes/no questions is predicate initial and that the question particle -*li* follows the predicate: (1a) contains a verbal predicate, (1b) an adjectival predicate, (1c) a nominal predicate, and (1d) contains a predicate of problematic categoriality.

(1a)　Rabotaet li　　　　Boris　na tom　　　zavode
work-3sg　Q-PART　Boris　in this-LOC　factory-LOC

'Does Boris work in this factory?'

(1b)　Molod　li　　　　Boris
young　Q-PART　Boris

'Is Boris young?'

(1c)　Učitel' li　　　　Boris
teacher　Q-PART　Boris

'Is Boris a teacher?'

(1d)　Žal' li　　　　Boris tvoju　　　sestru
pity　Q-PART　Boris　your-ACC　sister-ACC

'Does Boris pity your sister?'

The distribution typified by Russian yes/no question formation straightforwardly indicates that the categorial status of an element is in some measure independent of its clausal function.[4] The clausal function or relation that permits the appropriate cross-categorial generalization is the *predicate.*

Kaplan (1989) observes that the predicate function is part of the fundamental architectural assumptions of LFG. On the other hand, there has been little explicit exploration of the broad theoretical and empirical uses to which this function might be put [see Mohanan (1994) for a notable exception].

The distinction between categorial versus functional headedness has been a central element with respect to the LFG analyses of some types of phenomena examined here. For example, Mohanan (1982) has argued that Malayalam compound predicates, consisting of syntactically independent elements, are categorially headed by an auxiliary verbal element, while they are functionally headed by a non-finite verbal element: the auxiliary serves as the structural head of a constituent structure domain, the non-finite verbal element serving as a functional head, i.e., the predicate in a functional level of representation. Within the LFG literature apparent discrepancies exhibited by surface expression versus functional representations in the domain of predicate formation have been noted from two directions. Several researchers examining morphological causatives have posited "functionally complex" words, i.e., single morphological objects that provide evidence for the need to assume more than one clause associated with a single word form [see Ishikawa (1985), O'Connor (1992), Dahlstrom (1991), Abaitua (1988),

---

[4]See Sadock (1991) and Jackendoff (1987), among others, for similar views from different theoretical perspectives.

Matsumoto (1992), among others]. Others have explored the converse of this situation, namely, the existence of syntactically independent elements that correspond to only a single clause, previously referred to as an extended projection domain. For example, Ackerman (1987) analyzes several different types of analytically expressed predicates in Hungarian which exhibit this property. He observes in connection with these two types of mismatch that (1987:13):

> The lesson here is simple: morphophonological integrity does not entail functional simplicity... The present enterprise might be interpreted as the converse of this lesson: the absence of morphophonological integrity does not entail functional complexity.

The analysis of complex predicates expressed by syntactically independent elements as constituting a single predicate in functional structure has been subject to intensive research in the past few years. For causative constructions there is the influential work of Alsina (1993) as well as the adaptation of Jackendoff's lexical conceptual structures to the LFG framework found in Butt (1995). Finally, there have been several recent efforts to provide analyses of auxiliary plus verb constructions [see Niño (1995, 1997), Nordlinger (1995)] and serial verb constructions [see Bodomo (1996, 1997)]. These proposals all share the property, mentioned in chapter 1, that operations in the syntax are assumed to be responsible for composing the information associated with syntactically independent constituents.

In sum, both Relational Grammar and LFG have attempted to adduce evidence for the need to appeal to functions independent of categoriality and phrase structure. In addition, both frameworks propose essentially syntactic accounts of the information associated with syntactically separate elements. Finally, while the majority of effort has gone into examining evidence for standard grammatical functions, there has been some explicit recognition of the relevance of a predicate construct.

In the remainder of this chapter we present arguments for the construct predicate, providing some of Perlmutter's original arguments as well as several of our own. The basic argument form employed below exemplifies the strategy for demonstrating the need for a predicate relation presented in Perlmutter (1979). To show that a

> given notion is relational [= functional; the authors] rather than categorial is simply to show its independence of category membership... the arguments used here show that elements that differ in category membership behave alike in cases where they bear the same grammatical relation—the predicate relation. (p. 130)

For purposes of the present inquiry it is important to observe the type of phenomenon which Perlmutter explicitly excludes from consideration in his investigation: he proposes to ignore instances of predicates which would receive expression by independent entities in the clause. These are precisely the phenomena that are of central interest in the present work. In this regard it is significant to note that many of the arguments presented as evidence for the existence of a predicate expressed by a synthetic morphological expression on his account can equally be shown to apply to predicates consisting of separate pieces on the present account.

As a further point of differentiation between the RG approach and our own it is important to note that throughout this discussion we will suggest that, unlike in RG where the predicate is interpreted as a syntactic notion, we are concerned with these entities as lexical representations exhibiting variable morphological and phrasal expression.[5]

Finally, it will become clear that some of the phenomena examined here admit of different analyses via standard mechanisms and assumptions in several syntactic theories. As a consequence it is important to make explicit the reason for citing the diverse data types we examine below. It is our contention that all of these disparate phenomena in the aggregate implicate the existence of a construct predicate. In the absence of such a unifying construct a theory would be forced to address various of these phenomena in ways that would obscure their essential relatedness.

2   Arguments for the Construct 'Predicate'

2.1   Morphological Evidence

There are several ways in which the distribution of morphology provides evidence for the construct predicate. First, we examine the distribution of the subject agreement inflectional paradigm in the Samoyedic language Nenets and the Mayan language Tzotzil. In these languages the distribution of agreement morphology cannot be given a satisfactory categorial explanation, but can be elegantly explained by appealing to the construct predicate. In a second type of agreement distribution we examine instances where syntactically independent elements associated with complex predicates serve as co-hosts for morphology ordinarily hosted by a single entity functioning as a simple predicate. The data here come from negative verb constructions in the Uralic language Finnish, modal constructions in Hungarian, and separable preverb and verb constructions in the Algonquian language Fox. Finally, we examine the agreement paradigm for subject and object complements of predicates in the Ugric language Hungarian as well as the subject, object, and indirect object agreement paradigm in Basque. In all three instances, in different ways, the distribution of agreement morphology is shown to be explicable by appealing to a predicate which heads a single clausal domain within which the local phenomenon of agreement is observed to operate.

---

[5]Those works of Government and Binding Theory which make reference to a predicate syntacticize the notion as well, along with all other grammatical properties that find expression in that framework. For some examples, see Williams (1980), Napoli (1989), and Bowers (1993).

2.1.1 Distribution of Subject Agreement Paradigms

In this section we show that in several languages the distribution of agreement morphology cannot be unified by referencing the categoriality of the morphological base. Within generative frameworks it has been standard to provide feature analyses of categories such that combinations of features yield natural classes. For example, one well-known set of binary features is $\pm$ N and $\pm$ V to define the four categories V (= +V, -N), N (= -V, +N), P (= -V, -N) and A (= +V, +N). As in phonology, entities contained in the same class are supposed to share behaviors, while entities in different classes are not.

On all such feature decompositions of categories there is a sharp disjunction between Noun and Verb: there is accordingly a prediction that entities expressed by these categories will not share any grammatically significant behaviors. However, as the examples from Samoyedic below indicate, the distribution of agreement morphology in some languages references an "unnatural class" covering Noun and Verb from a categorial perspective.[6]

Indeterminate Agreement Paradigms
(Present tense)

Substantival: (Hajdú 1968:47)   Verb: (Hajdú 1968:59)

		Allo 1	Allo 2	
Sg.	1	-dm,	-tm	-dm?, -m?
	2	-n,	-t	-n
	3	-Ø		-Ø
Du.	1	-ńi?		-ńi?
	2	-di?,	-ti?	-di?
	3	-xV?,	-k(a)?	-xV?
Pl.	1	-wa?,	-ma?	-wa?
	2	-da?,	-ta?	-da?
	3	-?		-?

Figure 3

The Samoyedic language Nenets contains three agreement paradigms: the so-called *indeterminate paradigm* reflects agreement with a subject, the *determinate paradigm* reflects agreement with both subject and object, and constructions in which there is referential identity between the subject and the object call for a *reflexive paradigm*. Agreement encodes the

---

[6]The data here is taken from Hajdú (1968).

person and number features of a subject argument for three persons (1st, 2nd, and 3rd) and three numbers (i.e., singular, dual, and plural), as well as the number feature (i.e., singular, dual, or plural) of the object. Only the indeterminate paradigm is of relevance here: the present paradigms for N and A (referred to together as Substantival in Figure 3), and V are presented.

As can be seen, the paradigm for substantives generally contains two allomorphs, i.e., Allo 1 and Allo 2, while the paradigm for verbs, with the exception of the first person singular, contains a single suffixal form identical to Allo 1 of the Substantival agreement paradigm.

Representative constructions are illustrated by the partial paradigm in Figure 4 where we find the present tense dual forms of the predicate nominal *xāsawa* 'person' and the verbal form *nūs* 'stand'.

Representative Agreement Forms
(Dual)

Noun: xāsawa 'person' (Hajdú 1982: 47)			Verb: nūs 'stand' (Hajdú 1982: 60)	
1 mańi?	xāsawańi?	'we (2) are people'	nūńi?	'we (2) stand'
2 pidańi?	xāsawadi?	'you (2) are people'	nūdi?	'you (2) stand'
3 pidi?	xasāwaxa?	'they (2) are people'	nūxu?	'they (2) stand'

Figure 4

Whereas a generalization for agreement marker distribution in purely categorial terms, stated as the Category Condition in (A) below, is clearly unilluminating, i.e., N and V do not represent a natural class, an explanation in terms of function is easily motivated. That is, the relevant agreement markers are not solely sensitive to the categoriality of their host, but are sensitive to whether elements function as predicates in a clause. This is stated as the Predicate Condition in B.

(A) Category Condition: agreement markers appear on a disjunction of categories, i.e., there is no need for reference to a predicate.

(B) Predicate Condition: agreement markers appear on the predicate of a clause irrespective of categoriality.

It might be argued that subject agreement is actually categorial in nature and, as per standard assumptions, sensitive to the verb(al) status of the base: predicate nominals and adjectives would be construed as undergoing zero conversion into verbs. This is formulated as Hypothesis 1 below. The alternative hypothesis is that they remain substantival. This is formulated as Hypothesis 2.

Hypothesis 1: Zero category conversion of substantival into verb.

Hypothesis 2: No category conversion—substantival remains substantival

Below, we provide one type of morphological evidence which speaks in favor of Hypothesis 2, and against Hypothesis 1, namely paradigm allomorphy in substantivals.

There are two basic substantival declension classes. In particular and simplifying for expediency, substantivals are divisible into two basic declensional classes, namely, Class 1 and Class 2. Whereas Allo 1 of the indeterminate agreement paradigm in Figure 3 co-occurs with nominals from Class 1, Allo 2 co-occurs with nominals from Class 2. Tereshchenko (1973: 164) comments:

In the Nenets (and Enets) languages personal predicate suffixes joined to nominal bases of the second class undergo several phonetic changes in comparison with those suffixes when added to nominal stems of the first class.

This distribution is illustrated in Figure 5 with partial paradigms for the Class 1 noun *xańena* 'hunter' and the Class 2 noun *jane?* 'neighbor': [adapted from Décsy (1966: 29)]

Class 1 Noun: *xańena* 'hunter'   Class 2 Noun: *jane?* 'neighbor'

xańenani?	'we (2) are hunters'	jane?ni?	'we (2) are neighbors'
xańenadi?	'you (2) are hunters'	janeti?	'you(2) are neighbors'
xańenaxa?	'they (2) are hunters'	janek?	'they(2)are neighbors'

Class 1: Stem + AGR$_{ALLO1}$ Class 2: Stem + AGR$_{ALLO2}$

Figure 5: Indeterminate Agreement Paradigms for Noun Types

In other words, the different allomorphs in the indeterminate agreement paradigm are keyed to the declension class of the nominal which serves as its host. Crucially, the nominals here exhibit declension class based allomorphy reflecting contrasts seen elsewhere in nominal paradigms, such as possessive marking and case. This can be seen by comparing the allomorphy patterns in Figure 3 to the allomorphy patterns for the possessive and determinate or objective agreement paradigm in Figure 6. Possessive morphology reflects the person/number of the possessor and the number of the possessed, while determinate agreement reflects the person/number of the subject and the number of the object. The possessive paradigm in Figure 6 displays two allomorphs, while the determinate paradigm displays a single variant identical to Allo1 of the possessive paradigm. As was evident in the indeterminate paradigm, the determinate verbal paradigm shows little suffix allomorphy, while the possessive paradigm shows systematic allomorphy: [adapted from Hajdú (1968: 42 & 59)]

		Possessive Paradigm: Sg.		Possessed Determinate Conjugation: Sg. Object
		Class 1 Noun:	Class 2 Noun:	Verb:
		Allo 1	Allo 2	
Sg.	1	-w , -mí	-mí	-w
	2	-r	-l	-r
	3	-da	-ta	-da
Du.	1	-mí?	-mí?	-mí?
	2	-rí?	-lí?	-rí?
	3	-di?	-ti?	-di?
Pl.	1	-wa?	-ma?	-wa?
	2	-ra?	-la?	-ra?
	3	-do?	-to?	-do?

Figure 6: Possessive Paradigm and Determinate Conjugation

The Nenets possessive paradigm is sensitive to nominal stem type, while the clearly related determinate conjugation for verbs does not display suffixal allomorphy.

In summary, noun stem types consistently correlate with suffixal allomorphy in Nenets: this is evident both when the nominal hosts indeterminate agreement markers, functioning predicatively, and when it hosts nonverbal markers such as those from the possessive paradigm. If predicate nominals maintain their categoriality when inflected, as on Hypothesis 2, then their behavioral differences from verbs are easily explained: if, on the other hand, zero conversion applies, as on Hypothesis 1, it becomes unclear why the nominals functioning as predicates do not exhibit the same inflectional repertoire as indisputable verbs and, additionally, why they do exhibit the suffixal allomorphy patterns characteristic of nominals. In other words, suffixal allomorphy patterns suggest that the subject agreement markers are differentially sensitive to the category of the host. In addition, as will be shown below in the discussion of negative verbs in Uralic, there are certain morphological and syntactic differences between categorial verbs and other categories used predicatively.[7]

The distribution of agreement morphology demonstrated for Nenets parallels the distribution of agreement morphology for the language Tzotzil as described in Aissen (1987). She writes: "All and only members of these three major lexical classes [V, N, and A] can be inflected. All and only these can function as (heads of) predicates." Aissen provides the following paradigm for the SET B agreement markers in Tzotzil:

Set B affixes:

SUFFIX		PREFIX	
B1sg	-on	B1	-i-
B2sg	-ot	B2	a-
B1plinc	-otik		
B1plexc	-otikotik		
B2pl	-oxuk		

Figure 7

The distribution of these affixes over the three major categories (V, N, and A) is illustrated below:

(2) Tal   -em   -on   (3) Krem -on
     come perfect B1sg   boy B1sg

     'I have come'   'I am a boy'

(4) Tzotz -on
     strong B1sg

     'I am strong'

As can be seen, the 1st singular marker -*on* from Set B appears three separate times in (2)–(4). In particular, it appears with a categorial verb functioning as the predicate of a simple clause in (2). In addition, it appears with both a nominal, in (3), and an adjective, in (4), when these function predicatively.

In sum, Tzotzil resembles Nenets in displaying a distribution of agreement morphology which is sensitive to the function of the morphological host rather than the categoriality of word forms per se. As a consequence, explanation for the distribution of agreement in both of these languages appears to require reference to the notion predicate.

---

[7] The distribution of agreement morphology observable in Nenets is also found in the Finnic language Mordvin (see Keresztés (1990) for details).

2.1.2 Distribution of Agreement Paradigms

It is assumed cross-theoretically that agreement is a local phenomenon, reflecting a relation between the head of some phrasal domain and some other constituent within that domain.

In Finnish, the simple present and simple past tense for affirmative polarity verb forms are expressed synthetically. Finnish verb forms exhibit person and number agreement with their subject complement. The conjugations associated with the features simple present tense and affirmative polarity are exemplified by the paradigm for the verb *lukea* 'read':

lue-**n**	I read	lue-**mme**	We read
lue-**t**	You (sg.) read	lue-**tte**	You (pl.) read
lukee	S/he reads	lue-**vat**	They read

Figure 8

In contrast, negative polarity is expressed by a *negative verb* which bears person and number agreement information concerning the subject: this inflected negative verb co-occurs with a non-finite form of the basic verb stem which itself bears number information with respect to the subject. This distribution of agreement morphology is presented in Figure 9. Markers from the person/number agreement paradigm are suffixed to the negative verb *e* and this form co-occurs with the bare stem of the 'main' verb, signaling singular agreement or with an inflected form of the stem, signaling plural agreement.

e-**n** lue	I don't read	e-**mme** lueneet	We don't read
e-**t** lue	You (sg.) don't read	e-**tte** lueneet	You don't read
e-i lue	S/he doesn't read	ei-**vät** lueneet	They don't read

Figure 9

The distribution of agreement marking appears to be located with respect to the predicate. In particular, the subject exhibits agreement with the predicate, but the precise locus of the person/number marking depends on the manner in which the predicate is expressed. Whereas certain constellations of properties—including affirmative polarity in the present examples—are realized synthetically, other constellations—including negative polarity in the present examples—are realized periphrastically. The agreement markers appear on the synthetic verbal expression in the former case, but on the categorial verb bearing the negative polarity feature in the latter.

There are, of course, several ways to describe this agreement pattern and many of these have been proposed for similar phenomena in other languages: clitic climbing and clause union, inheritance of arguments of a dependent VP, restructuring. These proposals all share the following property: an essentially syntactic dependency is implicated in the relation between the auxiliary and the dependent verb. By this we mean that the auxiliary and the non-finite verb are not only assumed to have an independent phrase structural status (an assumption with which we concur), but that the operation responsible for the location of the agreement markers is itself syntactic in some fashion.

An alternative analysis of the relation between such auxiliary elements and a "dependent" verbal form is to assume that the composition is associated with a lexical representation: in particular, it is possible to interpret the "auxiliary" element and the "dependent" verb as constituting a single predicate.

On this interpretation the distribution of agreement morphemes is explicable in the following manner: the markers conveying the relevant morphosyntactic content appear in the lexical representation for the predicate. The surface difference in their appearance concerns the way in which predicates with certain sorts of information are expressed: sometimes the predicate is expressed by a single categorial verb and in this instance agreement appears on this form, while in other instances the predicate is expressed by multiple syntactically independent forms and in this case agreement appears on the pieces that make up the analytic predicate.

Notice two immediate consequences of a proposal such as this. First of all, agreement is not explained in terms of syntactic relations between an auxiliary and a dependent argument taking verb. These elements can be treated as independent entities in phrase structure without the need to assume that they exhibit special syntactic relations requiring or permitting the composition of certain sorts of information in the syntax. Second, the relation between the "auxiliary" and the "dependent" verb is interpretable as simply representing one particular way that morphosyntactic content is expressed for the event denoted by the "dependent" verb: agreement and polarity display the type of paradigmatic patterning typical of inflectional morphology. Differences in formal expression concerning synthetic vs. analytic encoding are superficial: they reflect various means to encode particular combinations of features internal to a paradigm. The existence of analytic encoding need not be regarded as implicating the need to posit significant syntactic relations between the participating pieces of this predicate. The representational apparatus developed in chapters 3–6 formalizes these intuitions concerning the role of the paradigm in these and similar constructions presented below. In chapters 7–10 we readdress from a more theoretical perspective some of the phenomena presented descriptively here.

Tereshchenko (1973) and Hajdú (1968) describe the basic word order in Nenets as Subject Object Predicate. For convenience we refer to simple expressions of the predicate when we are concerned with a single categorial expression, but to complex expressions when we are concerned with multiple categorial expressions. The basic order for affirmative clauses containing simple expressions is presented schematically below which spells out in categorial terms the order SOP:

$$S ----> X(P)^* \, V/N$$

Figure 10: Word order for simplex predicates

Previously we saw that Nenets indeterminate subject agreement morphology appears on the category functioning as the predicate of the clause. Though non-verbal categories such as nouns and adjectives can host such agreement morphology, they participate in 'defective' paradigms: they cannot occur with the full set of morphosyntactic content distinctions permitted to occur with verbs. In particular, non-verbal predicates can host simple past tense markers, yielding a tense contrast between past, as in (5) below, and non-past, as in example (6). However, these categories cannot host the full set of tense, mood, and aspect markers which can occur with verbs.

(5) pidar   ńiśan-aś   (6) pidar   ńiśan
     PRO-2SG father-2SG-PAST   PRO-2SG father-2SG

     'You were a father'   'You are a father'

Hajdú (1982: 122) identifies these restrictions on morphological marking as one of the ways in which nominal and adjectival predicates are not "genuine" verbs. In addition, he cites differences in the behavior of verbal vs. non-verbal predicates with respect to negative clauses.

Nenets, like Finnish, possesses a negative verb. In Nenets this form is *ni* and it can host derivational suffixes and agreement markers from various paradigms; the indeterminate paradigm reflects person/number properties of the subject, the determinate paradigm reflects person/number properties of the subject and the object, and the reflexive paradigm. The negative verb, derived and inflected, appears immediately to the left of a non-finite form of the main verb in clause structure. Relevant distributions are illustrated in (7) where the negative verb hosts an agreement marker from the indeterminate paradigm, (8) where it hosts a member of the determinate paradigm, reflecting properties of the object complement ostensibly selected by the non-finite form and (9) where the negative verb bears reflexive marking semantically associated with the non-finite form of the verb [from Hajdú (1982: 115 & 116)]:

(7)   ńidm?   tat?
      NEGV-1SG-INDETERMINATE give
      'I don't give'

(8)   ńiw   namt?
      NEGV-1SG-DETERMINATE hear
      'I didn't hear it'

(9)   pido? ńid?   jamdaŋku?
      PRO-3 NEGV-3PL-REFLEXIVE set out
      'They are not setting out with a caravan'

Non-verbal predicates display differences from verbal predicates concerning the expression of clausal negation. As we have seen, in clauses with verbal predicates the negative verb is inflected with markers from the appropriate agreement paradigm and appears to the left of the 'main' verb. In contrast, in non-verbal predicate negation constructions the predicate nominal or adjective and the negative verb both exhibit agreement markers, while the negative verb appears to the right of the predicate nominal/adjective. This latter pattern is exemplified in (10) where the 2sg marker appears on the predicate nominal and the negative verb:

(10)   pidar   ńiśan   ńin
       PRO-2SG father-2SG NEGV-2SG
       'You are not a father'

In summary, affirmative clauses contain simple expressions of categorially diverse predicates, while negative clauses contain complex expressions of categorially diverse predicates. Positing that Nenets is predicate final, we see that there are, additionally, more refined generalizations concerning the categoriality of the predicate. For example, if the predicate is simple, then it is final irrespective of categoriality, while if the predicate is complex, then the clause is verb final irrespective of whether we are dealing with a verbal or nominal predicate. In general, there appears to be a preference for categorial verbs to be final, but when the simplex predicate does not contain a categorial verb, the element expressing this predicate is final. In complex predicates there is an apparent mismatch between the categorial head of the clause, i.e., the negative verb, and the element that appears to determine the lexically specified arguments and function assignments for the clause, i.e., the non-finite verbal form. In such constructions the categorial head appears to bear information associated with the semantic and functional arguments of the non-finite verbal form. If these two elements were regarded as a single unit, i.e., a predicate, then this distribution of information would be motivated: the negative verb is simply reflecting argument and function information associated with the predicate interpreted as a composite entity.

Finally, one must know whether the predicate is verbal or nominal in order to know how the negative is formed, i.e., the categoriality of the predicate is relevant to syntactic sequencing as well as to morphological expression (i.e., double marking with nominals). Positing the construct predicate permits us to address what is similar while allowing differences to be attributed to such properties as categoriality.

Hungarian possesses an intriguing distribution of agreement markers. When a verbal predicate is expressed synthetically in this language both person/number marking of the subject as well as tense and certain modality marking appear on the verb. This is exemplified in (11) where the verbal predicate *csokol* 'kiss' hosts both the 1SG subject agreement morphology and the past tense morphology:

(11)   csokol-t-am   a nyuszit
       kiss-PAST-1SG the bunny-ACC

       'I kissed the bunny'

In contrast, there are certain constructions in which modality is expressed by the co-occurrence of a syntactically independent modal element and a non-finite verbal form. In these instances the inflectional markers reflecting both agreement and tense are distributed among the pieces representing the analytic predicate. This is illustrated in (12) where the modal verb *kell* 'must' hosts the past tense marking, while the non-finite form of *csokol* 'kiss' bears markers from the possessive paradigm, reflecting person/number properties of a (optionally present dative marked) subject:[8]

(12)   (Nekem) kell-ett   csokoln-om   a nyuszit
       I-DAT   *must-PAST* kiss-1SG/POSS the bunny-ACC

       'I had to kiss the bunny'

The markers which appear on a predicate when it is expressed synthetically are distributed among the pieces of a predicate when it is expressed analytically.

Moving away from Uralic, consider the following representative example of agreement marking for simple versus phrasal predicates in the Algonquian language Fox.[9] Transitive verbs in Fox may take a primary object, a secondary object, or both. In forms of the so-called *Independent Order*, occurring in various types of main clauses, both the subject and the object are indicated in the form of a verb by the combined use of a person-

---

[8]For discussion of the dative complement as a subject, see Kiss (1987: chapter 5).

[9]The presentation of Fox here reproduces the discussion of joint research by Ackerman and LeSourd (1994a). We thank Phil LeSourd for the careful exposition of this difficult data.

marking prefix [first person *ne(t)-,* second person *ke(t)-*] and one or more suffixes. This distribution of person-marking can be seen in examples (13a) and (13b). (13a) shows that inflectional markers (underlined) appear as a prefix and suffix on the simplex verbal stem: the prefix indicates person, while the suffix indicates person and number. (13b) on the other hand illustrates that these inflectional markers mark the pieces of a discontinuous complex predicate consisting of a (separable) preverb and a verbal stem (both boldfaced): in this case, the person marking appears on the preverb, while the person and number marker appears as a suffix to the verb stem. As can be seen in (13b), these markers bracket the preverb-verb complex. Descriptively, the person-marking prefix occurs on the first preverb of the clause, if there is one, otherwise on the verbal stem; the suffixes always appear on the verb stem [Dahlstrom (1987: 65)]. That the preverb is syntactically independent from the verbal stem can be seen in (13b) from the fact that an object argument, 'your daughter', has been interposed between the preverb and the verb. Given arguments against the incorporation of this complement presented in Dahlstrom (1987), the preverb and verb are interpretable as discontinuous in constituent structure.

(13a)   <u>ne</u>wa:pam<u>a:pena</u>
       1PERSON-look at-1PL/3SG.INDIC

       'We look at her'

(13b)   **<u>ne</u>pye:či**   keta:nesa   **wa:pam<u>a:pena</u>**
       1PERSON-come your daughter look at 1PL/-3SG.INDIC

       'We have come to see your daughter'
       [Michaelson (1917: 51)]

The following descriptive generalization accounts for the distribution of agreement marking in Fox: agreement marking is borne by the pieces that make up the predicate. When the predicate is expressed by a single morphological object as in (13a), then the relevant markers are borne by that form. In contrast, when the predicate is realized by syntactically independent elements, as is done with phrasal predicates typified by (13b), the agreement markers are distributed among the pieces used to express the predicate.

    Number prefixes are not the only elements whose distribution requires referencing the simple verbal stem or the preverb and verbal stem combination. The tense markers *e:h=* for indicating 'aorist' and *wi:h=* for indicating 'future' have been analyzed by Goddard (1988: 63) as proclitic preverbs. Both the phonological and syntactic properties of these tense markers are consistent with the hypothesis that they are proclitics. Either proclitic preverb may precede a non-clitic preverb if there is one, as shown in (14): (14a) exhibits the aorist marker cliticized to the preverb *pwa:wi* 'not', while (14b) shows the future marker cliticized to the preverb *mawi* 'go'.

(14a) e:h=**pwa:wi** owi:ye:ha ke:ko:hi **inowe:-**či.
AOR-not someone something say.so-3.SG.CONJ
'No one said anything'
[Dahlstrom (1987: 69)]

(14b) wi:[h]=**mawi** wi:hpe:m-a:tehe
FUT-go sleep.with-3/3OBV (unreal)
'When he was going (somewhere) to lie with her'
[Bloomfield (1925–1927: 212)]

As expected, since the proclitics are preverbs, the person markers precede them in these combinations. This is exemplified in (15) where the 2person marker precedes the future marker: second person *ke* plus the future marker *wi:h=* yields *ki:h=*, where the allomorphic variant of the clitic is underlined and the *k* indicates second person.

(15) k-i:h=**wi:šiki**=ča:h=meko **nenehke:net-**a.
2-FUT-strongly-EMPH-EMPH think.of-2SG/3IN.INDIC
'You (sg.) must keep it firmly in mind'
[Dahlstrom (1987: 72)]

On the other hand, when there is no preverb, then the tense markers cliticize to the verbal stem. This is illustrated in (16a) where the aorist marker cliticizes to the verb 'think so' and in (16b) where the future marker cliticizes to the verb 'be thus'.

(16a) e:h=iš-ite:he:-yani
AOR-thus-think-2sg CONJ
'because you (sg.) thought (so)'
[Bloomfield (1925–1927: 205)]

(16b) i:niki:='ni wi:h=iš-ike-nikiki
those-that FUT-thus-be-3iN.OBV PART
'those (animate) for whom it (medicine) will be efficacious' (literally: it will be that way)
[Goddard (1987: 112)]

Thus the aorist and the future proclitics, like the relevant person-marking prefixes, are involved in a system of discontinuous dependencies.

A process of ablaut, known as *Initial Change*, similarly targets the beginning of the preverb-verb complex. In forms in several subordinate clause paradigms, the first vowel of the first preverb is subject to ablaut, or the first vowel of the verb itself if no preverb is used. [Goddard (1987: 106)]. Only short vowels are affected in the regular cases: /a/ and /e/ are replaced by /e:/; /o/ is replaced by /we:/. This phenomenon is exemplified below. In (17) the first /e/ of the stem *keteminaw*- 'take pity on, bless' is lengthened, since no preverb precedes the stem in this case. In (18), the /o/ of the preverb *oči* undergoes ablaut instead. That contiguity of the preverb and verb is irrelevant for the application of this operation is evident in (19) where the preverb *iiši* 'thus' appears in its changed form *e:ši* : the preverb in this sentence is followed by an enclitic particle and is consequently an independent syntactic element. It should also be noted that since *Initial Change* occurs on the preverb in (19), the first /e/ on the verb stem *kehke:net*- 'know' remains short.

(17) ke:teminaw-ita
    take pity on-3/1SG PART
    'the one that blessed me'
    [Goddard (1987: 109)]

(18) mani we:či keteminaw-aki
    this why take pity on-1SG/3SG PART
    'this is why I blessed him'
    [Goddard (1987: 111)]

(19) meše=meko e:ši=meko kehke:net-amokwe:ni,
    maybe-EMPH thus=EMPH know-3/3IN INTER,

    i:ni=meko a:mi 'š-awi-či
    that-EMPH could do thus-3 (CONJ)
    'Any knowledge he may have (lit. whatever he may know),
    he can simply practice it.'
    [Michaelson (1925: 66.1–2)]

In summary, we see that the inflectional morphology of the Fox verbal system treats the preverb-verb sequence as a unit. The person-marking prefixes, the proclitics *e:h=* and *wi:h=*, and *Initial Change* are all involved in discontinuous dependencies with material which is affixed to the verb word.

Finally with respect to Fox preverb-verb combinations, Goddard (1990a, b) has referred to the need to preserve evident *paradigmatic relations* between certain uses of these word forms. We consider below two phenomena from Fox presented in Goddard (1990a) and (1990b): stem allomorphy and PV bumping.[10]

---

[10]This discussion reproduces the presentation found in Ackerman and LeSourd (1994b).

First we present the phenomenon of *stem allomorphy*. In example
(20b) the aspectual marker functions as a prefix, while in (21b) the same aspectual marker functions as a syntactically separate preverb.

(20a) wi:seni -wa
      eat   3SG.INDIC

      'S/he eats'

(20b) kiš-**is**enye: -wa
      finish-eat- 3SG.INDIC

      'S/he has finished eating'

(21a) meno -wa
      drink 3SG.INDIC

      'S/he drinks'

(21b) ki:ši meno -wa
      finish drink 3SG.INDIC

      'S/he has finished drinking'

Whether the exponent of the aspectual notion of completiveness surfaces as
a bound morpheme as in (20b) or as a syntactically independent preverb as
in (21b) appears to be a function of idiosyncratic morphological information. In particular, if a verb stem has a corresponding so-called *derived final*
form [such as the boldfaced element in (20b)], then the aspectual marker is
prefixed to the *derived final*. If, however, a verb stem does not have a corresponding *derived final* [as indicated by the formal identity of 'drink' in
(21a) and (21b)], then the aspectual marker surfaces as a preverb. There is
obviously a paradigmatic relation between aspectually unmarked verbs and
their perfective counterparts [cf. the contrast between the (a) and (b) sentences in (20) and (21)]: (20b) and (21b) differ solely with respect to the
boundness or separability of the aspectual marker and this appears to be
morphologically conditioned. Goddard writes: (1990a: 41)

The resulting forms in [20b] and [21b] are both single syntactic words: word-initial
processes, such as prefixation, operate on the first preverb... A paradigmatic relationship links these two morphologically disparate but functionally parallel types of
stem ([20b] and [21b]). This paradigmatic relationship should lead us to consider the
theoretically interesting possibility that the derived expressions in [20b] and [21b]
have the same lexical status.

This 'theoretically interesting possibility' is precisely the insight we develop
in this book, namely that syntactically discontinuous expressions may function as one predicate. It is worth noting that there is an additional notion of
paradigmaticity at play here as well: there are paradigmatic relations between the class of all aspectually marked predicates versus predicates that
are not marked for aspect. The former class consists of both synthetic and
analytic or phrasal expressions of predicates.

    Goddard mentions a second phenomenon where idiosyncratic mor-
phological constraints yield paradigmatically related entities with either synthetic or analytic expression. He refers to this as *PV bumping*:

(22a)   pem-   ose:wa
        along- walk-3sg.INDIC

        'S/he walks along'

(22b)   pemi we:p- ose:wa
        along start- walk-3SG.INDIC

        'S/he starts walking along'

In (22a), the so-called initial *pem-* 'along' is prefixed to the verb, losing the characteristic final *-i* associated with preverbs, while in (22b) it is displaced or bumped by the aspectual *we:p-* 'start' and functions as a preverb. Goddard suggests plausibly that there is a paradigmatic relation between 'walk along' and 'start to walk along': he observes that even though *we:pi* 'start' exists as a preverb, in all attested cases where 'along' and 'start' co-occur it seems that *pemi* 'along' surfaces as a preverb and *we:p-* 'start' as a prefix. There thus appears to be a sequencing constraint such that *pemi* 'along' must precede *wepi* 'start'. This, of course, creates a mismatch between formal expression and the paradigmatic relation which obtains between the two forms: given that 'walk along' should be related to 'start to walk along', i.e., that *wep(i)* 'start' has scope over the complex verb 'walk along', it might be expected that we could get the form listed as (23):

(23) * we:pi pem-   ose:wa
         start along- walk-3SG.INDIC

         'S/he starts walking along'

However, according to Goddard this does not correspond to any attested form. The phenomenon of preverb bumping, then, represents an instance where certain morpheme sequencing constraints determine (in)separability.

In conclusion, Fox provides data of several sorts which make it sensible to treat both preverb-verb combinations and simple verbs as expressing a single unit such as a predicate.

In the Ugric languages Hungarian and Vogul a verb functioning as the predicate and head of the clause shares certain morphosyntactic features with its subject and object. In Hungarian the verb registers the person and number features of its subject and the definiteness of its object, while in Vogul it registers the person and number features of its subject and the number feature of its object. These agreement properties are illustrated below for Hungarian. In (24a) the DEFINITE agreement marker co-occurs with an object NP modified by a definite determiner, but is incompatible with the presence of an indefinite determiner, as indicated by the ungrammaticality of (24b). These judgments are reversed in (25a) and (25b) when the INDEFINITE conjugation is employed.

(24a)   csokol-om   a   nyuszit
         kiss-1SG/DEF the bunny-ACC

         'I am kissing the bunny'

(24b) * csokol-om   egy nyuszit
         kiss-1SG/DEF a   bunny-ACC

         'I am kissing a bunny'

(25a)   csokol-ok   egy nyuszit
         kiss-1SG/INDEF a   bunny-ACC

         'I am kissing a bunny'

(25b) * csokol-ok   a   nyuszit
         kiss-1SG/INDEF the bunny-ACC

         'I am kissing the bunny'

The Hungarian sentences are grammatical when the properties associated with the verb and its subject and object complements concur, while conflicts with respect to the relevant properties yield ungrammaticality. The present cases exhibit clauses which contain a synthetic verbal form: this form clearly serves as the host for elements from the agreement paradigm.

In contrast to this situation, there are constructions in Hungarian and Vogul in which the determinant of the semantic information and the grammatical function assignment for the arguments of a clause does not host these agreement markers. This happens in those instances where the 'main' verb co-occurs with certain 'auxiliary' elements. This phenomenon is exemplified for Hungarian with the future auxiliary *fog* 'will' in (26) and (27). The grammaticality judgments parallel those in (24–25) containing a synthetic form of the predicate. (26a) is acceptable because DEFINITE agreement co-occurs with a definite determined object NP, while (26b) is unacceptable because of the incompatibility of the DEFINITE agreement marker with an indefinite object. The converse compatibility requirements explain the judgments in (27).

(26a)   fog-om   csokolni a   nyuszit
         will-1SG/DEF kiss-INF the bunny-ACC

         'I will kiss the bunny'

(26b) * fog-om   csokolni egy nyuszit
         will-1SG/DEF kiss-INF a   bunny-ACC

         'I will kiss a bunny'

(27a)   fog-ok   csokolni egy nyuszit
         will-1SG/INDEF kiss-INF a   bunny-ACC

         'I will kiss a bunny'

(27b) * fog-ok   csokolni a   nyuszit
         will-1SG/INDEF kiss-INF the bunny-ACC

         'I will kiss the bunny'

In these examples the auxiliary hosts the agreement features properly associated with the arguments of its ostensible complement, i.e., the dependent
or 'main' verb. If we assume that the subject and object are properly interpreted as belonging to the predicate, then the agreement markers reflecting
properties of these complements appear on only the pieces comprising the
predicate. When it is expressed periphrastically, the distribution of agreement morphology is restricted to one piece of the analytically expressed
predicate: that piece, of course, bears the relevant marker only by virtue of
being a part of the predicate, since the auxiliary alone does not select for the
relevant complements.

    The Ugric languages are not alone in permitting auxiliary elements to
host agreement markers which reflect grammatical function requirements of
'dependent' non-finite verbal elements. It is well-known that Basque exhibits agreement behavior that resembles the agreement patterns found in
Hungarian and Vogul. There are two noteworthy properties that make the
Basque agreement facts somewhat more dramatic. First of all, agreement
with an auxiliary in Basque is extremely pervasive: it is generally claimed
that Basque has few synthetic verb forms and that as a consequence the unmarked form of agreement in Basque involves some form of an argument
taking predicate and an inflecting auxiliary. In addition, whereas agreement
in Hungarian and Vogul is limited to the subject and object functions, it includes the indirect object (IO) in Basque. In (28) we see some conjugated
forms of one of the few synthetic verb forms in Basque: this form reflects
agreement with both subject and object complements: [examples from
Manandise (1988: 23)]

(28a)   n-   a-   rama- zu
         ABS/1SG NON-PAST carry ERG/2SG

         'You carry me'

(28b)   d-   a-   rama- t
         ABS/3SG NON-PAST carry ERG/1SG

         'I carry him'

In contrast, the periphrastic forms in (29) and (30) display an interesting
distribution of marking. Manandise writes:

Periphrastic verbs are those whose verbal root can only be inflected with aspectual markers (perfective, imperfective, future)... periphrastic verbs do not allow their root to serve as a base for person, number, tense, and/or modality markers to attach upon. The person, number, tense, and/or modality markers are attached to the base of two verbal roots which are traditionally analyzed as the auxiliary verbs *izan* 'to be' and *ukan* 'to have'... (1988: 24)

This distribution of markers is illustrated below: [examples from Manandise (1988: 25)][11]

(29a)　Jan　　　n-　　　a-　　　　u-　　zu
　　　　eat-PERF ABS/1SG NON-PAST have ERG/2SG

　　　　'You have eaten me'

(29b)　Jango　 n-　　　a-　　　　u-　　zu
　　　　eat-FUT ABS/1SG NON-PAST have ERG/2SG

　　　　'You will eat me'

(30)　　Irakurri　d-　　　i-　　　z-　　　ut
　　　　read-PERF ABS/3SG DAT DAT/2SG ERG/1SG

　　　　'I have read to you'

In (29) the auxiliary reflects agreement with both the subject and object complements and the 'main' verb hosts aspect morphology yielding a perfect interpretation for (29a) and a future interpretation for (29b). (30) contains an auxiliary which exhibits agreement for all three of the complements of the 'main' verb, specifically, the subject, object, and indirect object.

　　　Abaitua (1988) develops a lexical treatment within LFG of the Basque auxiliary verb system. He follows Falk's (1984) treatment of English 'do', in analyzing these auxiliaries as minor categories which do not themselves project a clause nucleus. He proposes a lexical restructuring operation which operates on the auxiliary and verbal noun prior to lexical insertion and which creates a mono-clausal complex predicate (1984: 70). Obviously on such an analysis the type of agreement exhibited above is local, since the lexical restructuring operation creates a mono-clausal complex lexical predicate.

　　　Whereas in Basque periphrastic predicates person/number agreement for subjects appears on the auxiliary verb and aspect on the 'main' verb,

---

[11]Manandise observes that whereas the perfective marker is null, the imperfective is *-te/tzen*, and the future marker is *-ko/go*. She suggests that "the morphological category of aspect holds, so to speak, independently for the category AUX..." (1988: 55). By this she seems to intend that though the formal markers of aspect can appear on the auxiliary, the notional distinctions associated with such markers are relegated solely to marking on the verbal root. This claim is relevant to the comparison of Basque with Tzotzil below.

Aissen (1994) illustrates that the opposite distribution of verbal elements and marking exists in the Mayan language Tzotzil. We demonstrate this pattern by contrasting the synthetic verbal expression in (31a) with the analytic expression in (31b). The verb in (31a) contains the incompletive aspect marker (= ICP) as well as the agreement marker from set B agreement affixes (see section 2.1.1 above). The two verb forms in (31b) show that the aspectual prefix occurs on the auxiliary verb while the agreement marker appears on the 'main' verb: [examples from Aissen (1994: 659)]

(31a)   chi- i- chonolaj   (31b)   ch- ba chonolaj-ik-on
        ICP B1 trade   ICP go trade-SUBJ-B1SG

        'I'll trade'   'I'll go trade'

    In summary, we have seen several sorts of morphological distributions which indicate the need for the construct predicate. First of all, in some languages there are morphological markers which typically occur with verbal predicates but also appear with members of other categories when these function predicatively. The morphological paradigm in these instances appears sensitive to the function rather than the category of forms. Second, we have seen several examples where the morphological distribution of various markers singles out an entity functioning as the predicate irrespective of whether this is formally expressed synthetically or analytically. This suggests that these markers too are sensitive to the function rather than the formal expression of certain co-occurring elements in the clause.
    In our view, the data presented in this section cannot be analyzed without loss of explanation, unless reference is made to the theoretical construct predicate. While many of the descriptive generalizations can be captured without predicates, approaches that proceed in this manner seem to get the facts right by stipulation rather than by invoking natural linguistic notions. For instance, the Russian word order facts in (1) could be captured by making the word order of this language sensitive to some feature on the signs of the language (i.e., a feature +Predicate). Unless such a proposal associates this feature with conceptual content, however, (and explains why the elements bearing this feature are categorially so heterogeneous), it is little more than a restatement of the factual situation in Russian.
    Descriptive adequacy can also be achieved regarding the agreement paradigms we have presented, but, again, theories without predicates don't capture the facts on principled enough grounds and lose generalizations. Consider how the Hungarian data described in (11) and (12) might be handled in the theory of argument attraction proposed in Hinrichs and Nakazawa (1989, 1994), or similar approaches. Synthetically expressed finite verbs bear both subject agreement and tense inflection. Analytic predicates expressed by a verb-auxiliary combination depart from this and express tense on the auxiliary and the subject agreement features on the nonfinite main verb. The closest one can come to analyzing the auxiliary and

the verb in (12) as one content-theoretic unit in the argument attraction paradigm is to assume that the auxiliary selects the non-finite main verb and attracts its argument structure. The result is the presence in the structural analysis of the clause of two categorial heads with an overlap in argument structure. One could now capture the agreement facts by enforcing the following two conditions on verbs in Hungarian: (i) finite verbs that are *not* argument attractors express both tense and subject agreement; (ii) finite verbs that *are* argument attractors express only tense and require the X^0 they select to express subject agreement.

While these assumptions are sufficient to generate all and only the correct agreement patterns, they clearly miss a global generalization about Hungarian morphosyntax: *in finite sentences, the predicate bears tense and agrees with its subject.* Many languages of the world follow this same agreement pattern (whereas they may differ on how they distribute the various markers among the exponents of an analytically expressed predicate). From this point of view, Hungarian instantiates a typologically natural condition.

Note, now, that under the argument attraction analysis of (11) and (12), there is no unit in the structural description of these sentences that could be said to encode the simple condition we just stated: in (11) there would be one finite synthetic verb form and it indeed bears both tense and subject agreement information. But in (12), the finite verb form only bears tense and lacks agreement. It selects for another verb and forces that verb to express subject agreement, but this is simply an accident of its selectional properties and finds no explanation in a constraint that all the heads of finite clauses in Hungarian have to obey. If instead of forcing the embedded verb to show subject agreement, the governing auxiliary forced it to express aspect or polarity, no larger pattern would get disrupted.

On the other hand, in a theory based on predicates viewed as content-theoretic entities independent of their surface realization, the systematic existence of agreement patterns in the world's languages that require the same type of information to be expressed by predicates no matter whether the predicate is synthetic or analytic is a matter of natural expectation, given the underlying choice of predicates as primitives and the function they perform in the grammatical systems of natural languages.

2.2   Syntactic Evidence

2.2.1   The Expression of Passive

In lexicalist accounts of passive it has been traditionally assumed that passive is an operation on lexical items which alters the function assignments of a predicate: the lexicon contains a lexical representation for active and passive forms of a predicate and these are generally related by lexical rule. Each form has an invariant set of semantic arguments associated with different grammatical functions. One of the early motivations for passive as a lexical operation was that it has local effects, as would be expected if it were limited to manipulating the sort of information typically found within the lexical entry for a verb [cf. Bresnan (1982a)]. In accordance with *Morphological Integrity* and *Uniform Morphological Expression* the data structure associated with function assignments was assumed to be expressed by a synthetic morphological object. Over the years it has become clear that many languages possess passive constructions that seem to require appealing to information which goes beyond the bounds of a single synthetically encoded lexical item. In the present section we discuss several languages where the passive predicate can be expressed analytically and where the morphological marker of passive exhibits an intriguing distribution in such constructions.

There has been considerable research into passive constructions that appear to violate locality constraints, e.g., constructions in which an auxiliary verb (bearing tense, modality, etc.) co-occurs with a 'dependent' element and where the auxiliary exhibits passive morphology: the latter exhibits passive morphology despite the fact that (i) it does not contain a passivizable argument and (ii) the surface subject in these constructions appears to be an argument of the 'dependent' argument taking predicate. In addition, the "dependent" verb appears in an active non-finite form. Passive in such instances, like certain of the agreement phenomena mentioned previously, appears to be non-local: it looks like the argument of a dependent predicate functions as the subject of the passive predicate. In particular, consider the examples in (32a) and (32b) from Spanish. In (32a) we see the active form of the clause that has a passive analog in (32b). (32b) also demonstrates that the 'matrix' predicate exhibits the shape ordinarily shown by a passivized predicate, i.e., a copular element and a participial form, while the 'main' verb appears in an active infinitival form.

(32a) Los obreros acaberon   de pintar   las casas   ayer
       the workers finish-PAST/3PL   paint-INF the houses yesterday

       'The workers finished painting the houses yesterday'

(32b) Las casas fueron   acabadas de pintar
       the houses COP-3PL finish-part   paint-INF

       [por los obreros] ayer
       by   the painters yesterday

       'The houses were finished being painted (by the workers) yesterday'

[Aissen and Perlmutter (1983: 391)]

Western Armenian is a language where two complex predicate formation operations interact in an interesting way with respect to passive.[12] This language possesses both a morphological causative marker, e.g., *-ts-*, and a morphological passive marker, e.g., *-v-*. The paradigm for a basic transitive and its passive variant is exemplified below, where (33b) contains the passive affix and the agentive argument in the ablative case:

(33a) Hagopə godrets   seʁanə
       hagop   break-PAST-3SG table

       'Hagop broke the table'

(33b) seʁanə godr-v-etsav   Hagopen
       table   break-PASS-PAST-3SG   Hagop-ABL

       'The table was destroyed by Hagop'

As mentioned above, Western Armenian also possesses an affix for creating a morphological causative. The relevant form is illustrated by the causativized intransitive base predicate *tsadgel* 'jump' in (34):

(34)   Sarkisə tsadge-ts-uts   Hagopin
       Sarkis   jump-CAUS-PAST-3SG   Hagop-DAT

       'Sarkis made Hagop jump'

Given the transitivity of the causative in (34), one might expect it to be possible to place a passive marker after the causative to get a sentence such as 'Hagop was made to jump by Sarkis.' However, as indicated by the questionable status of (35), it is somewhat problematic to create a morphological passive in this instance:

(35) */? Hagopə tsadge-ts-v-etsav   Sarkisen
           Hagop   jump-CAUS-PASS-PAST-3SG   Sarkis-ABL

           'Hagop was made to jump by Sarkis'

In order to create a passive from this causative and many others, Western Armenian appeals to an analytic strategy whereby the causativized intransitive co-occurs with a passivized form of the verb *dal* 'give'.[13] This is illustrated in (36):

---

[12]The data discussed here represent a subset of a far more complex pattern presently being investigated by one of the authors. We thank Araxy Tatoulian for providing the relevant examples.

[13]There appears to be some degree of variability concerning which causativized intransitives permit the co-occurrence of the causative and passive markers within the same stem. This is an issue under investigation.

(36)   Hagopə tsadge-ts-nel   dr-v-etsav   Sarkisen
       Hagop   jump-CAUS-INF   give-PASS-PAST-3SG   Sarkis-ABL

       'Hagop was made to jump by Sarkis'

Restricting ourselves to the patterns illustrated above, the following generalization seems to obtain: the passive morpheme appears internal to the stem
of the verb whose arguments are affected by passivization when this predicate is a basic transitive predicate, but appears internal to the verb 'give'
when the arguments affected by the passive are associated with a
causativized form of a base intransitive predicate.

    Two anomalies associated with the constructions in Spanish and
Western Armenian are addressed if we assume that we are confronted with
the analytic expression of a single passive predicate. First, the argument
functioning as the subject in (33b) and (36) bears a local relation to the
'matrix' verb. For example, there is just as much reason to assume that passive is clause bounded when it applies to basic transitives in Western
Armenian as when it applies to increase the valence of intransitives under
causativization. If we assume that the difference in surface expression for
Western Armenian passives in (33b) and (36) is simply a matter of knowing
the lexical representations for the passivized predicates, i.e., whether they
are basic transitive or causativized intransitives, then an analysis based on
access to such information would be able to directly account for the attested
patterns. Passivization would be uniformly lexical in both instances, with
surface differences attributable to the lexical nature of the input predicate.
Second, the 'matrix' verb would be construed as appropriately reflecting
this relation by virtue of being a portion of the passive predicate consisting
of the 'auxiliary' verb and the participle in Spanish or infinitival form in
Western Armenian.

    A schematic proposal such as this, of course, covers the same empiri-
cal ground as the standard interpretation of these passives in terms of clause
reduction.[14] On the other hand, a lexical representation analysis in terms of
the functional notion predicate has the theoretical advantage of assimilating
phenomena such as these to other phenomena for which clause reduction is
an unsuitable explanation. It also is consistent with the principle of *Lexical
Adicity* discussed in chapter 1: passive as a function altering operation is
limited to the lexicon. The surface spell-outs for the passive predicates exhibit the synthetic versus analytic expression options characteristic of discontinuous lexical items such as phrasal predicates.

    A second well-attested pattern of passive morpheme distribution is
exemplified in those languages where there seems to be multiple exponence
of the passive morpheme despite there being only a single instance of passive from a functional-semantic perspective. Consider the following exam-

---

[14]We include here the recent work in LFG X-bar theory according to which multiple constituent structure heads combine their information into a single functional clause nucleus: this,
in effect, yields clause reduction.

ples from Turkish where active forms in the (a) examples are contrasted with passive forms in the (b) examples. As can be seen, the passive marker is suffixed to the synthetic exponent of the predicate in (37b), while it is suffixed to the auxiliary verbs 'want' and 'begin' and a co-occurring non-finite verb in (38b) and (39b):[15] [examples from Orhan Orgun, personal communication]

(37a)   onlar bina-yɨ   yɨk-tɨ-lar
         they building-ACC destroy-3PL

         'They destroyed the building'

(37b)   bina   onlar tarafɨndan yɨk-ɨl-dɨ
         the building they by   destroy-PASS-PAST

         'The building was destroyed (by them)'

(38a)   onlar bina-yɨ   yɨk-ma-ya   başla-dɨ-lar
         they building-ACC destroy-NOMLZ-DAT start-PAST-3PL

         'They began to destroy the building'

(38b)   bina   onlar tarafɨndan yɨk-ɨl-ma-ya
         the building they by   destroy-PASS-NOMLZ-DAT

         başla-n-dɨ
         start-PASS-PAST

         'The building was begun to be destroyed (by them)'

(39a)   onlar bina-yɨ   yɨk-mak   iste-di-ler
         they building-ACC destroy-INF   want-PAST-3PL

         'They wanted to destroy the building '

(39b)   bina   onlar tarafɨndan yɨk-ɨl-mak
         the building they by   destroy-PASS-INF

         iste-n-di
         want-PASS-PAST

         'The building was wanted by them to be destroyed'

---

[15]Multiple exponence of the passive marker among the pieces of an analytically expressed predicate is also attested in Lithuanian: the passive marker appears on both the copula element and the co-occurring non-finite verbal form. For discussion and examples see Keenan and Timberlake (1985).

George and Kornfilt (1977) have argued that constructions of this sort are best analyzed as *a single application of passive* where the two verbal elements participate in clause reduction, yielding a monoclausal structure. Monoclausal effects are evident with respect to such behaviors as the scrambling (i.e., variable clausal position) of sentential adverbs such as *dün* 'yesterday'. Consider the active Equi sentence in (40) where the time adverbial can appear, among other places, clause initially or between the matrix Equi predicate and the non-finite form of the verb contained in the complement clause:

(40)　(dün)　yazarlar　viskiyi　içmeye (dün)　razɨ ol-du-lar
　　　yesterday the authors whiskey drink　yesterday consent-PAST-3PL

　　'Yesterday the authors consented to drink the whiskey'

In contrast, similar scrambling distributions yield ungrammatical sentences in both the active clause containing the matrix auxiliary verb *iste* 'want' in (41a) and its passive analog in (41b):

(41a)　(dün)　　yazarlar　viskiyi　içmek
　　　(yesterday) the authors whiskey drink

　　　(*dün)　　iste-di-ler
　　　(*yesterday) want-PAST-3PL

　　'Yesterday the authors wanted to drink the whiskey'

(41b)　(dün)　bu viski　yazarlar tarafɨndan iç-il-mek
　　　(yesterday) this whiskey authors　by　　　drink-PASS-INF

　　　(*dün)　　iste-n-di
　　　(*yesterday) want-PASS-PAST

　　'Yesterday the authors wanted to drink the whiskey'

　　　George and Kornfilt argue that scrambling as well as adverbial scope suggest the monoclausal status of these constructions. They propose that a syntactic process of clause reduction creates a monoclausal structure and that the double passive marking results from a rule that copies the passive marker from the matrix verb onto the dependent verb. They acknowledge that "this copying rule is entirely ad hoc (1977: 74)." On the other hand, they mention that doubling occurs not only with analytic expressions of the sort illustrated above, but in synthetic expressions containing the abilitative suffix *-Ebil,* as in (42) where the passive morpheme appears both before and after the abilitative marker:

(42) bu mesele halled-il-ebil-in-ir
      this problem solve-PASS-ABLE-PASS-AOR

      'This problem can be solved'

The adhocness of George and Kornfilt's 'copying rule' is apparent in the fact that, among other things, it is not clear why the passive markers appear where they do. In other words, why do they appear on the pieces of a presumable predicate? Moreover, the copying rule does not stand in any principled relation to their demonstration that there is clause reduction and that the surface result of clause reduction in these cases is the formation of a single unit which prohibits the interposing of elements between its identifiable pieces. What one would like, of course, is an insight into why these apparently disparate properties might correlate with one another. In the context of the present inquiry, multiple marking is to be expected irrespective of the synthetic versus analytic expression of predicates, since the marked elements represent pieces of a single predicate.

Recent innovations within lexicalist frameworks which posit the syntactic composition of predicates (see chapter 1 for discussion) are able to address phenomena such as these. In particular, if passive is interpreted as an operation on argument structures—on analogy with causative formation—[cf. Alsina (1993), Manning (1996), among others], then it is possible to apply passive over the composite argument structure which results from the composition of the argument structures associated with the relevant independent syntactic entities. That is, passive would no longer be an operation relegated to the lexicon in the languages of the world: rather it would apply in the syntax in certain languages or under certain conditions in some languages. Syntactic predicate composition, thus, would seem to provide an analysis of the passive constructions examined here.

On the other hand, the present proposal also explains the cases at hand: in fact, the basic nature of the proposal predicts that such expressions of passive should be attested in the languages of world, since the basic constructs of our theory, namely, predicates are explicitly designed to separate information concerning function assignments from the formal expression of the entities that convey this information. Moreover, as mentioned previously, when the predicate consists of several pieces, it is reasonable that their status as a single unit might be indicated by marking several of its constitutive pieces with identical morphemes.

In addition, our proposal accounts for another aspect of these analytically expressed passive predicates that seems problematic for a syntactic composition account. Specifically, we expect that analytically expressed passive predicates might be able to participate in the types of derivational processes accessible to passive predicates expressed by synthetic morphological objects. This follows from our account since derivation is keyed to lexical representations, rather than to a particular morphological expression type. Relevant data from German and Marathi has been presented in examples (32)–(37) in chapter 1.

Once again, on the present account this is precisely the sort of phenomenon we expect to find in the languages of the world. Specifically, since syntactic independence (or, expression type) is orthogonal to the lexical status of predicates, our proposal straightforwardly addresses instances where syntactically independent pieces of predicates can serve as bases for derivational operations standardly limited to the lexicon. We will develop this proposal in greater detail in later chapters.

2.2.2   Basic Word Order

Perlmutter (1979) argues that word order or linear order generalizations in many languages are best interpreted in terms of the functional/relational construct predicate, rather than in terms of categoriality. In other words, the standard hybrid of functional and categorial notions, i.e., SVO etc., is better analyzed as SPO (P = predicate), etc. In the present section we will examine the evidence for this position adduced by Perlmutter and augment it with similar data from other languages which illustrate that the word order generalizations formulated to account for the distribution of predicates expressed by synthetic word forms often also account for distributions of predicates expressed by multiple syntactically independent elements.

Perlmutter observes that the Philippine language Cebuano, as analyzed in Bell (1983), possesses a neutral word order which is verb-initial. (43) provides evidence for this order: [examples from Perlmutter (1979: 132)]

(43)   **Magluto'** si Rosa   ug bugas
        ACT-cook NOM Rosa   OBL rice

        'Rosa will cook some rice'

As Perlmutter suggests, if the conditions on neutral linear sequence are formulated in terms of the relative order of functions associated with constituents, then it is to be expected that nominals functioning predicatively will exhibit the same order as verbs. That this is so is illustrated in (44), where the predicate nominal *maestra* 'teacher' is clause initial.

(44)   **Maestra** si Rosa
        teacher   NOM Rosa

        'Rosa is a teacher'

Clearly if linear sequence were sensitive to categoriality, the relevant generalization would have to be formulated disjunctively, i.e., either V or N is clause initial. On the other hand, this disjunctive statement would be insufficient to yield the correct sequences since it turns out that not all nominals appear clause-initially (after all, sometimes verbs do), but only those nominals which function predicatively. In other words, the appropriate generalization concerning linear sequence can be simply stated in terms of predicates: Cebuano is a PSO language.

Given that the functional/relational status of clausal elements proves superior in explaining linear sequence generalizations in languages such as Cebuano (and other languages as well, e.g., Tzotzil), it is to be expected that it is likewise relevant for the explanation of orders in languages displaying other basic orders of elements. In fact, it is to be expected that languages ordinarily analyzed as SOV, for example, are actually SOP. Perlmutter presents data from the Muskogean language Choctaw, presented in (45), to demonstrate that this language is SOP: (45a) contains a verbal predicate in final position, while (45b) contains a predicate nominal in final position.

(45a)   Hattak-at   oho:yo-y-ã   chokka **i-kãchi-tok**
        man-NOM   woman-OBJ   house   3DAT-sell-PAST

        'The man sold the house to the woman'

(45b)   Mary-at   **alikchi**
        Mary-NOM   doctor

        'Mary is a doctor'

In this section we have so far seen that the construct predicate is essential for insightful generalizations concerning the linear sequence of clausal constituents in numerous languages. In the cases we have examined, the element interpreted as the predicate has been expressed by a synthetic morphological entity. Indeed, Perlmutter's arguments for the recognition of a predicate relation within Relational Grammar were all directed at instances where the predicate was identified with a synthetic morphological object. On the other hand, if predicates can receive variable types of formal expression, as argued here, then there should be word order generalizations that extend to non-synthetic expressions of predicates: that is, the standard word order generalizations formulated in terms of SPO should find application in the languages of the world irrespective of the formal expression of the entity functioning as P. We conclude this section by presenting data which demonstrate that, as expected on the present account, it is sometimes necessary to interpret P in terms of syntactically independent elements in order to address basic word order distributions. This point becomes clear when examining two prevalent word order sequences, namely, POS and SOP.

Aissen (1987) observes that the unmarked order of constituents in a Tzotzil clause is POS. As can be seen from the examples in (46), what counts as a P can be either a single morphological element, as in (46a), or several syntactically independent elements, as in (46b). [examples from Aissen (1987: 1, 17)]

(46a) **7i-**   **s-** **pet**   lok'el   7antz   ti   t'ul-e
       COMP/ASP- A3- carry away   woman the rabbit-CL
       'The rabbit carried away the woman'

(46b) **ba** **j-** **ta-** **tikotikl** j7ilol
       went A1- find- 1PL-EXC shaman
       'We went to find a shaman'

In both instances the neutral order of elements places the P in initial position.

In contrast to languages with basic POS order, there are numerous languages which display a basic SOP order. Hindi, for example, is often described as SOV, which on the present account would be more appropriately interpreted as SOP. The value of P in this language can be either a synthetic word form or an analytically expressed predicate consisting of an auxiliary verb and a 'main' verb Irrespective of the surface exponent of the predicate, the neutral or canonical order finds the predicate in clause final position. This is exemplified by the clauses in (47) taken from Mohanan (1994). (47a) contains a simple predicate realized by a single morphological object, while (47b) contains a complex predicate consisting of the nominal *madad* 'help' and the verbal element *kar* 'do' yielding a two place predicate meaning 'help'.

(47a) ilaa-ne anuu-ko haar   **b^{h}ejaa**
       Ila-ERG Anu-DAT necklace-NOM send-PERF
       'Ila sent Anu a/the necklace'

(47b) raam-ne niinaa-kii **madad** **kii**
       Ram-ERG Nina-GEN help-NOM do-PERF
       'Ram helped Nina'

Finally, there are several languages which have been described as possessing a basic SPO order. Among them Hungarian will be used to illustrate how the elements associated with P in this description must be construed as either single morphological objects or entities whose pieces exhibit syntactic independence. Following the presentation found in Kálmán et al. (1989), the clauses containing various types of formal expressions of predicates in (48) exemplify the neutral order of constituents: (48a) contains a predicate expressed by a simplex morphological object, (48b) a predicate expressed by a complex morphological object with a modal suffix, (48c) an analytic predicate consisting of an independent infinitival form and a future auxiliary inflected for subject agreement, and (48d) contains an analytic predicate consisting of an infinitival form inflected for person features of the subject and a present tense form of a modal auxiliary.

(48a)   a   holló **énekel**   egy dalt a   rokának
        the raven sing-3SG/INDEF a   song the fox-DAT

'The raven sings a song to the fox'

(48b)   a   holló **énekel-het**   egy dalt a   rokának
        the raven sing-ABLE-3SG/INDEF a   song the fox-DAT

'The raven is able to sing a song to the fox'

(48c)   a   holló **énekelni fog**   egy dalt a   rokának
        the raven sing-INF will-3SG/INDEF a   song the fox-DAT

'The raven will sing a song to the fox'

(48d)   a   hollónak **énekelnie**   **kell** egy dalt a   rokának
        the raven-DAT sing-INF-3SG must a   song the fox-DAT

'The raven must sing a song to the fox'

On the defensible assumption that it is important to distinguish neutral orders from other orders in Hungarian, the sentences in (48) suggest that both synthetic and analytic expressions of predicates conform to the same word order generalization concerning an SPO neutral order.

From the perspective of arguing for the shared properties of several different types of predicates with syntactically independent parts, it is important to observe how 'auxiliary' elements like those found in (48c) and (48d) interact with separable preverb and verb combinations of the sort presented in chapter 1. The neutral order of these elements can be schematized as follows: preverb > aux > verb. Examples are presented in (49) with the preverb-verb combination *meg-mond* 'say':

(49a)   a holló   **meg** fog   **mondani** valamit
        the raven PV   will-3SG/INDEF say-INF   something-ACC

        a rokának
        the fox-DAT

'The raven will say something to the fox'

(49b)   a hollónak   **meg** kell **mondania** valamit
        the raven-DAT PV   must say-INF-3SG something-ACC

        a rokának
        the fox-DAT

        'The raven must say something to the fox'

As can be seen from (48) and (49) a satisfying account of word order should address the obvious parallelisms between predicates of different types with respect to neutral linear sequences.

In this section we have seen that word order generalizations concerning the neutral sequence of clausal constituents require reference to the notion predicate. In addition, in order to achieve maximal coverage such generalizations must be able to separate the function of clausal elements from both their categorial status and their encoding with respect to synthetic versus periphrastic expression.

2.2.3   Sentential Negation in Hindi

Mohanan (1994) demonstrates that in Hindi certain complex predicate constructions are categorially indistinguishable from one another. On the other hand, they are functionally distinct. In particular, she contrasts complex predicates such as *prasamsaa kar* 'praise' with *yaad kar* 'remember'. She distinguishes these predicates on the basis of such behaviors as whether the verb *kar* 'do' can exhibit agreement with the co-occurring nominal *prasamsaa* 'praise' vs. *yaad* 'memory': agreement occurs with the former, but not with the latter. She argues that such behaviors argue for the factorization of complex predicates into distinct levels of information in correspondence with one another. The two levels utilized in her analysis are *argument structure* and *grammatical category structure*. From a categorial perspective, both complex predicates are argued to be phrasal expansions. The two complex predicates can be represented as follows (adapted from Mohanan (1994):

prašamsaa kar 'praise':

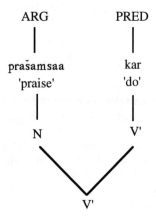

Figure 11

yaad kar 'remember':

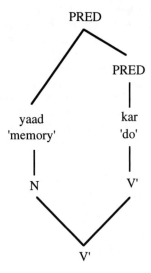

Figure 12

It is important to observe that these constructions are minimally distinct. They differ with respect to what is considered to be the predicate: whereas the predicate is limited to the inner V' in 'praise', it comprises the whole outer V' in 'remember'.

Mohanan observes a particular restriction on sentential negation with the negative word *nahĩĩ* 'no/not'. She proposes the following condition on the distribution of this element in order to account for its different interaction with these predicates:

In sentential negation:

(A) NEG is attached to the left of the verb in grammatical category structure; or

(B) NEG must be adjacent to the predicate in argument structure/f-structure.

These conditions account for the distributions in (50) and (51):

(50a)   anil-ne   ilaa-ko   [yaad]   nahĩĩ [kiyaa]
        Anil-E(M) Ila-ACC(F) memory-N(F) not   do-PERF.M
        'Anil didn't remember Ila'

(50b)   anil-ne   ilaa-ko nahĩĩ [yaad   kiyaa]
        Anil-E(M) Ila-A(F) not   memory-N(F) do-PERF.M
        'Anil didn't remember Ila'

(51a)   anil-ne   ilaa-kii [prašamsaa] nahĩĩ [kiyaa]
        Anil-E(MA) Ila-G(F) praise-N(F) not   do-PERF.M
        'Anil didn't praise Ila'

(51b) * anil-ne   ilaa-kii nahĩĩ [prašamsaa kiyaa]
        Anil-E(M) Ila-G(F) not   praise-N(F) do-PERF.M
        'Anil didn't praise Ila'

As can be seen, the negative element *nahĩĩ* appears immediately before the V in (50a) and (51a), in accordance with condition (A). In contrast, condition (B) permits this element to additionally appear before *yaad* in the complex predicate *yaad kar* in (50b), since the N and V together constitute the predicate (see Figure 12). *nahĩĩ* cannot appear before *prašamsaa* in *prašamsaa kar* 'praise' in (51b), since the N in this construction is interpreted as an argument which is not part of the predicate (see Figure 11).

It is important to note that, on Mohanan's account, conditions on the distribution of the negative word in Hindi appear to require an accessible notion of predicate: in effect, the negative word can appear before the predicate of the clause. The crucial aspect of this analysis for the proposal we develop here is that two syntactically independent elements can jointly represent the predicate or one word can represent the predicate. Mohanan's analysis consequently provides support from Hindi for a content-theoretic construct predicate independent of its categorial expression or surface exponence. Like the evidence we have cited earlier from word order, this sort of phenomenon suggests that the linear distribution of certain elements is instructively analyzed by postulating the construct predicate.[16]

3 Conclusions

We began this chapter by reviewing several approaches to the notion predicate. We have adopted a more restricted interpretation of this notion than the one traditionally found in logic and categorially oriented generative linguistic traditions. In addition, we have demonstrated several problems with efforts to reduce the construct predicate to categorial notions.

The major part of this chapter has provided a small selection of evidence from the distribution of morphology and certain syntactic behaviors which suggest that grammars refer to content-theoretic entities that may be discontinuous in constituent structure. The cross-linguistically widespread existence of such behaviors evident in connection with quite disparate grammatical phenomena suggests that linguistic theory requires a construct suitable to accommodate them. We have informally proposed that the appropriate construct is the predicate.

We believe that the status of the predicate in syntactic theory is not unlike that of the syllable in phonology: theoretical parsimony always dictates that the linguist keep the inventory of concepts as small as possible. However, when the price of excluding some concept from the theory is the systematic loss of linguistically significant generalizations, then considerations of theoretical parsimony must be put aside in favor of the most explanatory inventory of notions. In our view, in analogy to the syllable, the generalizations made possible by postulating predicates as part of linguistic representations overwhelmingly justify their inclusion.

Even though predicates have no invariant surface expression (neither do subjects and objects!), there are strong indications that like in the case of the syllable, we can state preference principles for their surface exponence:

---

[16]Another type of evidence for the postulation of lexical predicates with multiple syntactic exponence comes from so-called morphological blocking phenomena. In Ackerman and Webelhuth (in press) we present arguments from Hungarian on inflecting separable preverbs. We propose that morphological blocking is better interpreted as "lexical blocking" and that viewed this way there is evidence that synthetic lexical items block analytic lexical items: this limits the domain of relevant blocking to the lexicon. (See King (1995) for an examination of analytic versus synthetic expression of future tense in Russian with a different theoretical interpretation, i.e., a lexical entity is argued to block a syntactic phrase.) There are additionally some compelling recent proposals, developed independently of our proposal, which address some of the same basic types of data we examine and offer solutions broadly compatible with our solution [see Blevins (1995), Bresnan (to appear a), Sadler (1997), and Sells (to appear a, b)].

predicates are preferably expressed by single categorial words but can also be expressed by combinations of such words. If this principle holds true for the elements which we identify as predicates on other grounds (and evidence is in principle available from typological studies as well as from studies of the diachronic development of predicates), then this is a substantive prediction about the surface form of clausal heads that does not follow from a theory that fails to postulate predicates.

However, since predicates—like syllables—are abstract units of grammatical organization, we would expect to find evidence for their existence in the role they play as content-theoretic units. This chapter has made a case for that view, based on the convergence of syntactic and morphological phenomena which remain mysterious unless they are viewed as symptoms of the presence of predicates. Recall from our discussion of the morphological distribution of tense and agreement that many languages have agreement markers that go onto all and only categories which we would analyze as predicates. If predicates are the content-theoretic heads of clauses irrespective of the category that expresses them, then such clausal operator information as tense, aspect, or modality should be expressible on them independently of their own categorial status. This chapter has demonstrated that this prediction is borne out. Moreover, given the role of predicates as argument-taking items and the analysis of agreement (in unification-based approaches) in terms of structure-sharing of information, we would also expect predicates to express agreement information about their arguments. More particularly, given that all the exponents of a predicate collectively express the content-theoretic information inherent in that predicate (both clausal information and agreement), it is functionally irrelevant which exponent of an analytically expressed predicate bears which morphological marker. We thus expect to systematically find languages where such information is spread out over the exponents of the predicate. This prediction is borne out as well, sometimes dramatically as in the case of the separable preverb of Fox in (13b) which carries a subject person agreement affix. If instead of analyzing that preverb as part of the predicate of this sentence we postulate it as some complement of the verb, we end up with the completely uninsightful description that in finite sentences there are always two inflectional markers one of which is always suffixed to the verb and the other is either prefixed to the verb as well or is prefixed to a particle complement of that verb. Under a complement analysis of the preverb in (13b), its choice as the carrier of the prefixal inflectional marker is no more motivated than the choice of some adverb or the indirect object, etc. Other examples from other languages cited in this chapter replicate this argument on the basis of morphology distributed over the pieces of analytically expressed predicates.

Given that the pieces of a predicate collectively express one content-theoretic unit, there is nothing to prevent the same content to be expressed morphologically on more than one exponent of the predicate. Niño (1995, 1997) and Nordlinger (1995) present relevant evidence of this (providing a different theoretical interpretation than the one offered here) and the Turkish examples (38b) and (39b) with two passive markers reinforce this point.

Finally, it is hard to see how the evidence from word order can be understood without positing predicates as content-theoretic units with variable surface expression. Why would many languages systematically position certain elements together in the same clausal location if they didn't have some crucial property in common? Given the distinct categoriality of the initial elements in (1), what could that common property be other than the category-independent property of predicatehood?

And why should there be languages like Tzotzil as discussed in (46) or Hindi [see (47)] that keep the different pieces of their analytically expressed predicates linearly adjacent? A plausible answer is that predicates are content-theoretic units and languages follow the tendency stated in Behagel (1932) that "What belongs together semantically, stands together in the sentence."[17] Under any reasonable conception of "belonging together semantically", the pieces that express the information in one predicate fall under this notion and hence should frequently be found adjacent.

The additional functional tendency to avoid synonymous lexical entries or to use the entry with the most specific content also provides a plausible explanation for the blocking effects we have addressed elsewhere [Ackerman and Webelhuth (in press)], provided we recognize the existence of both synthetically and analytically expressed predicates: analytic expressions will legitimately participate in so-called morphological blocking, if they are interpreted as analytic expressions of lexical representations and morphological blocking is interpreted more broadly as *lexical blocking*.

In sum, like in the case of the syllable, there is no one datum that can be used as an all-decisive argument for the existence of the predicate. Yet, the evidence from a large number of disparate phenomena that find plausible and intuitively satisfying accounts converges on the reality of the construct predicate as a part of linguistic representations. In its entirety, we believe that the case for postulating a predicate with the profile suggested here is compelling.

In the following four chapters we provide the formal means we have developed for implementing the hypothesis that the predicate is best interpreted in terms of lexical representations. As will be seen, we will argue that the lexical representation associated with the predicate is formally an object referred to as a *lexical combinatorial item (lci)* which may receive surface expression as one or more *morphological items (mi)*.

---

[17]See Behagel (1932: Vol. IV, 4) writing on word order: "Das oberste Gesetz ist dieses, daß das geistig eng Zusammengehörige auch eng zusammengestellt wird."

3

Lexical and Phrasal Signs

1 Introduction

Recent work within Head-Driven Phrase Structure Grammar [see Pollard and Sag (1987, 1994), among others] and Construction Grammar [see Fillmore and Kay (1996), among others] has demonstrated the usefulness of modeling language phenomena in terms of type theoretic data structures: both lexical and phrasal elements are interpreted as attribute/value matrices providing information sufficient to classify and cross-classify them in terms of types and subtypes. Hierarchically organized systems of such data structures have been proposed, providing a detailed and formally precise exposition of Saussure's notion of the linguistic sign as a mapping between notional content and its formal expression at various levels of representation, i.e., at the level of the word and at the level of the phrase. For example, morphological items, can be simplex or compound and serve as the surface representations of signs or what Saussure (1986) calls the signifiant of the sign.

Signs, i.e., the signifiant together with the sign's notional information which Saussure referred to as the signifiee, can combine with each other to form new signs which have their own signifiant and signifiee. Every language imposes constraints on how signs can be formed from other signs. In the more formal passages of this book, we often refer to signs as "combinatorial items" to highlight the central role that the recursive combinatory potential of signs plays in the unbounded linguistic creativity of native speakers of natural languages. We will, however, continue to use "sign" and "combinatorial item" interchangeably in informal passages.

Like traditional grammar and most other current linguistic theories we draw a distinction between lexical and phrasal items: we formalize this distinction in terms of a contrast between *lexical combinatorial items* versus *phrasal combinatorial items*. There are two aspects of these items that are central for the ensuing analysis and which are adopted from the research in Head Driven Phrase Structure Grammar. First, all signs (i.e., both lexical and phrasal) are represented as *attribute-value matrices* (AVMs). This permits one to refer to distinct properties of both lexical and phrasal entities, rather than treating them as atomic units. Second, all signs are *typed* and arranged within a multiple inheritance type hierarchy. The different properties associated with signs can be used to relate different signs with one another and to organize signs into networks of relations in terms of shared and implied properties.

In this chapter we will introduce the grammatical formalism that will be used in the remainder of this book. The upcoming subsection presents the representations of synthetically and analytically expressed predicate nominals from the Nenets paradigm that was already discussed informally in chapter 2 in connection with examples (5)–(10). It is shown how these predicates are instances of the wider class of sign structures that our formalism makes possible. Following this we discuss the syntactic schemata that create the complex phrase structures in which predicates can be realized.

2 A Short Overview of Sign Structures with an Illustration from Nenets

Jackendoff (1997: 4) observes the following with respect to the presentation of theoretical ideas:

... a theory's choice of formalism can set up sociological barriers to communication with researchers in other frameworks.

The presentation of our representational apparatus is guided by an expository strategy that seeks to make it possible for our proposals to be comprehensible across theoretical boundaries: we introduce and focus only on those analytic ingredients and constructs that we are strongly committed to theoretically, while remaining silent on many routine specificities and details concerning implementation. We do this both for the sake of brevity and clarity, since there are many routine and repetitive aspects to full specification which may impede the reader's understanding of what we consider to be linguistically significant assumptions. The full grammatical formalism we have developed is able to represent synthetically and analytically expressed lexical entries and to combine these lexical entries with their arguments and modifiers to form phrasal expressions. A more detailed version of the analyses presented in this book has been implemented in the *Platform for Advanced Grammar Engineering*, a grammar development environment created by the Deutsche Forschungsgesellschaft für Künstliche Intelligenz.[1]

2.1 Nenets Revisited

In chapter 2 we encountered data from the Samoyedic language Nenets. Recall that in this language predicate nominals and adjectives (= substantivals) host agreement morphology similar to that found with verbs and the language contains an independent negative verb which itself hosts agreement morphology and co-occurs with some form of a substantival or

---

[1]German Research Association for Artificial Intelligence in Saarbrücken, Germany. We would like to express our gratitude to this organization and to the Center for the Study of Language and Information for allowing us to use their software and hardware and for instructing us in using it.

verb. Additional examples of affirmative and negative variants of substanti-val predicates appear below: [Hajdú (1968: 72)]

(1)   mań   xańenadm?
       I-NOM hunter-1SG

       'I am a hunter'

(2)   mań   xańenadm? ńidm?
       I-NOM hunter-1SG NEGV-1SG

       'I am not a hunter'

As can be seen, the predicate nominal 'hunter' in the affirmative variant (1) bears the agreement marker for a 1st person singular subject. In contrast, the negative variant in (2) shows that both the predicate nominal and the nega-tive verb bear this inflectional marker.

As indicated in chapter 2, we wish to analyze *xańenadm?* in (1) as a synthetically expressed predicate and *xańenadm? ńidm?* in (2) as an analyt-ically expressed predicate related to the predicate of (1). The representations of these predicates should express the information that they have in com-mon and also the properties where they differ, in particular that the negative meaning in (2) correlates with the presence of a negative auxiliary in the surface expression of the predicate.

The lexical representations for the predicates in (1) and (2) appear in (3) and (4) in the formalism to be explicated in this chapter.

(3) The predicate *xańenadm?* 'am a hunter' in sentence (1)

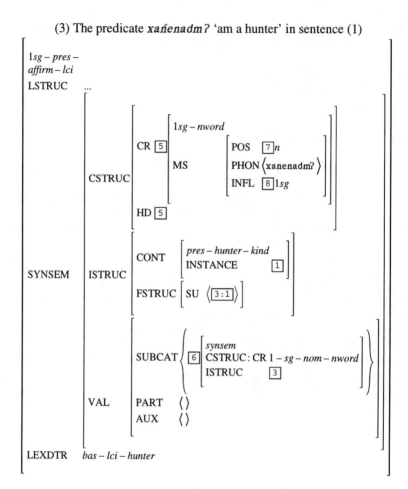

The following subsections will introduce our formal theory of signs in schematic fashion and will use (3)–(4) to illustrate how the schemas can be employed in the formation of concrete signs such as the two Nenets predicates.

(4) The predicate *xaṅenadm? ṅidm?* 'am not a hunter' in sentence (2)

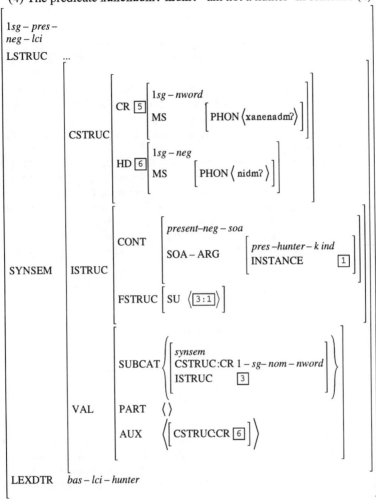

$$
\begin{bmatrix}
\textit{1sg} - \textit{pres} - \\
\textit{neg} - \textit{lci} \\
\text{LSTRUC} \quad ... \\[2pt]
\text{SYNSEM} \begin{bmatrix}
\text{CSTRUC} \begin{bmatrix}
\text{CR } \boxed{5} \begin{bmatrix} \textit{1sg} - \textit{nword} \\ \text{MS} \quad \left[\text{PHON} \langle \text{xanenadm?} \rangle \right] \end{bmatrix} \\[8pt]
\text{HD } \boxed{6} \begin{bmatrix} \textit{1sg} - \textit{neg} \\ \text{MS} \quad \left[\text{PHON} \langle \text{nidm?} \rangle \right] \end{bmatrix}
\end{bmatrix} \\[20pt]
\text{ISTRUC} \begin{bmatrix}
\text{CONT} \begin{bmatrix} \textit{present-neg} - \textit{soa} \\ \text{SOA} - \text{ARG} \begin{bmatrix} \textit{pres} - \textit{hunter} - \textit{k ind} \\ \text{INSTANCE} \quad \boxed{1} \end{bmatrix} \end{bmatrix} \\[12pt]
\text{FSTRUC} \left[\text{SU} \; \langle \boxed{3:1} \rangle \right]
\end{bmatrix} \\[24pt]
\text{VAL} \begin{bmatrix}
\text{SUBCAT} \left\{ \begin{bmatrix} \textit{synsem} \\ \text{CSTRUC:CR } 1 - \textit{sg-} \textit{nom} - \textit{nword} \\ \text{ISTRUC} \quad \boxed{3} \end{bmatrix} \right\} \\[12pt]
\text{PART} \quad \langle \rangle \\[4pt]
\text{AUX} \quad \langle \left[\text{CSTRUC:CR } \boxed{6} \right] \rangle
\end{bmatrix}
\end{bmatrix} \\[20pt]
\text{LEXDTR} \quad \textit{bas} - \textit{lci} - \textit{hunter}
\end{bmatrix}
$$

(5) The structure of combinatorial items *(= ci)* aka signs

$$
\begin{bmatrix}
\textit{ci} \\
\textbf{LSTRUC} \; \textit{word order properties} \\[4pt]
\textbf{SYNSEM} \begin{bmatrix}
\text{CSTRUC} \; \textit{categorial properties} \\
\text{ISTRUC} \; \textit{meaning and grammatical functions} \\
\text{VAL} \quad \textit{categorial selection}
\end{bmatrix}
\end{bmatrix}
$$

2.2 Combinatorial Items (= Signs)

(5) is a schematic representation of the information contained in the signs that we will employ. As can be seen in the graph, we draw a "Saussurean" distinction between the observable linear structure properties of the sign (encoded in the value of the attribute LSTRUC = linear structure) and its more abstract syntactic/semantic properties (SYNSEM).

Thus, the single word *xañenadm?* 'am a hunter' of (1) represents the information contained in the value of the SYNSEM attribute of (3), while the two word linear sequence *xañenadm? ñidm?* 'am not a hunter' is the surface realization of the syntactic and semantic properties of the lexical combinatorial sign in (4).

One crucial distinction between combinatorial items of the lexical sort illustrated in (3) and (4) and those of the phrasal sort is that the two can have different internal structures. In particular, a phrase (i.e., a *pci* = phrasal combinatorial item) can have several lexical or phrasal phrase-structural daughters that make up its internal phrase structure. Beyond the information in (5) that characterizes all combinatorial items, phrases will thus have a DTRS attribute whose value is its phrase structure, i.e., a phrase structure tree:[2]

(6) Phrasal combinatorial items *(= pci)* aka syntactic phrases

$$
\begin{bmatrix}
pci \\
\text{LSTRUC } word\,order\,properties \\
\text{SYNSEM} \begin{bmatrix} \text{CSTRUC } categorial\,properties \\ \text{ISTRUC } meaning\,and\,grammatical\,functions \\ \text{VAL } \quad categorial\,selection \end{bmatrix} \\
\text{DTRS} \quad tree\,structure\,of\,the\,phrase
\end{bmatrix}
$$

Lexical combinatorial items, in contrast, may or may not have daughter constituents and in case they do, their daughter always has to be lexical as well. These considerations allow for two kinds of structures in lexical items. First, those which are lexically underived and have no attribute for daughter information of any kind:

---

[2]This tree will not, however, necessarily reflect the linear order of the terminal nodes, since that is represented in the LSTRUC of the sign, following similar proposals in GPSG and more recently in HPSG by Reape (1992) and Kathol (1995), among others.

(7) Underived lexical combinatorial items *(= underived-lci)* aka predicates
(Example: the underived lci *hunter*

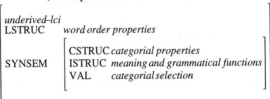

$$\begin{bmatrix} \textit{underived--lci} \\ \text{LSTRUC} \quad \textit{word order properties} \\ \\ \text{SYNSEM} \quad \begin{bmatrix} \text{CSTRUC} \, \textit{categorial properties} \\ \text{ISTRUC} \, \textit{meaning and grammatical functions} \\ \text{VAL} \quad \textit{categorial selection} \end{bmatrix} \end{bmatrix}$$

and, secondly, those lexical predicates which are themselves derived from other predicates:

(8) Derived lexical combinatorial items *(= derived-lci)* aka predicates
(Example: the derived lci *be a hunter,* derived from (7))

$$\begin{bmatrix} \textit{derived--lci} \\ \text{LSTRUC} \quad \textit{word order properties} \\ \\ \text{SYNSEM} \quad \begin{bmatrix} \text{CSTRUC} \, \textit{categorial properties} \\ \text{ISTRUC} \, \textit{meaning and grammatical functions} \\ \text{VAL} \quad \textit{categorial selection} \end{bmatrix} \\ \\ \textbf{LEXDTR} \; \textit{the lexical source of the whole lci} \end{bmatrix}$$

As (8) illustrates, derived lexical entries do have a daughter attribute but as its name suggests, the daughter has to be another lexical entry.

Both of the predicates in (3) and (4) are derived predicates as is indicated by the presence of the attribute LEXDTR: they each are formed from the non-finite basic Nenets nominal predicate meaning 'hunter.'

The lexical sign type represented by (7) and (8) will have specific subtypes that can be defined for it universally or in a language-particular fashion. For instance, we will want to recognize that lci's can be either finite or non-finite, that they can be active, passive, or causative, etc. Each subtype will then impose certain SYNSEM properties on the sign: finite lci's might be required to have a finite categorial head, they should be semantically tensed, and they might select a nominative NP to express their subject function. Passive and causative lexical item types bring their own SYNSEM properties, many of which we will argue are made available by universal grammar.

Fillmore and Kay (1996), Sag (1997), and Ginzburg and Sag (forthcoming) propose that phrases should also be cross-classified by construction types such as interrogative phrase, relative clause phrase, etc. Based on the general phrasal type in (6), these proposals can be incorporated into our approach and combined with the powerful theory of lexical entries that it offers. All that is needed is to define the types of phrases proposed by the authors mentioned above as subtypes of our type (6).

2.3 Combinatorial Items in More Detail

The two SYNSEM attributes CSTRUC and VAL (= valence) determine how many words make up the surface representation of a predicate and what grammatical relationship has to hold between those words: these are form-theoretic properties of the sign. We first take a look at the information we expect to find in morphological words.[3] (9) presents a typical underived word:

(9) The structure of an underived word

$$
\begin{bmatrix}
word \\
\text{MS} \begin{bmatrix}
\text{LME} & \textit{the lexeme the word is a form of} \\
\text{PHON} & \textit{the word's pronunciation} \\
\text{POS} & \textit{the word's part of speech} \\
\text{INFL} & \textit{the word's inflection}
\end{bmatrix}
\end{bmatrix}
$$

Words in essence are bundles of morphosyntactic form information (= MS): each word instantiates a particular lexeme, it has a phonological representation, the word belongs to a part of speech, and finally, it has some inflectional behavior (including the value *none* for particles and other uninflected items). Items of the morphological module of the lexicon, like the combinatorial items in the sign module of the lexicon, can also be derived, of course. Under those circumstances, they have the same morphosyntactic form information as the underived items described by (9), but they carry the additional attribute MDTR which specifies the morphological base from which the overall word has to be derived:

(10) The structure of a derived word

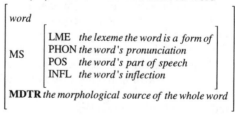

As the name MDTR suggests, our approach to morphology requires that each derived word is based on one other word, rather than a combination of

---

[3]Chapter 5 presents the details of our approach to morphology.

underlying words or a combination of words and affixes. In this, we follow the tradition of *word-based morphology* or as it is also known *word and paradigm morphology*. Our reasons for this decision and a discussion of the word based tradition appear in chapter 5.

A concrete example of a derived morphological word appears in (11):

(11) The first person singular word *xańenadm?* 'am a hunter' (Nenets)

$$
\begin{bmatrix}
1sg - nword \\[4pt]
\text{MS} \quad
\begin{bmatrix}
\text{LME} \ \langle \text{hunter} \rangle \\
\text{PHON} \langle \text{xanenadm?} \rangle \\
\text{POS} \quad n \\
\text{INFL} \ \begin{bmatrix} \text{NINFL} \begin{bmatrix} \text{PER} & first \\ \text{NUM} & sg \end{bmatrix} \end{bmatrix}
\end{bmatrix} \\[4pt]
\text{MDTR} \quad
\begin{bmatrix}
stem \\
\text{MS} \ \begin{bmatrix} \text{LME} \langle \text{hunter} \rangle \end{bmatrix}
\end{bmatrix}
\end{bmatrix}
$$

We are dealing with a data structure of type *first person singular noun word*. The morphosyntactic form information specifies that this word is a realization of the lexeme *hunter* with a certain pronunciation (here represented by the orthography). The part of speech of the word is of course noun and the inflection is a nominal inflection (NINFL) in this case and is first person singular, as expected. Finally, the MDTR information states that this word is morphologically derivative and, in particular, that it is derived from a stem that is also a realization of the LME *hunter*. The word in (11) is the complete surface expression of the synthetically expressed predicate (3) but forms only one part of the two word surface expression of the analytically expressed predicate (4), as we will see shortly.

With this preliminary look at the structure of words, we are now ready to examine the informational contribution of the SYNSEM attribute CSTRUC:

(12) The structure of CSTRUC

$$
\begin{bmatrix}
\text{CR } \textit{the word serving as the categorial core of the predicate} \\
\text{HD } \textit{the word serving as categorial head of the predicate}
\end{bmatrix}
$$

Note that within the categorial structure of a predicate we draw a distinction between its CR = categorial core and its HD = categorial head.[4] The core of

---

[4]This distinction derives from the fundamental contrast between functional and structural heads within LFG mentioned in chapter 1. (See footnote 6 in chapter 1 for references.) This distinc-

a predicate models what might be called its "semantic head," i.e., the element felt to contribute its core meaning. The head, on the other hand, may be "meaningless" as in the case of certain dummy auxiliaries or may express certain operator type meanings, e.g., tense, aspect, negation, including meaning operations on the core that lead to grammatical function changes such as causativization, middle formation, etc.

In synthetically expressed predicates, the categorial core and head of course have to be identical, given that the predicate is expressed by only a single word. Likewise, we assume that in analytically expressed predicates the core and the head can only be distinct when an auxiliary is part of the categorial surface expression of the predicate. When there is no auxiliary, the core and the head have to be identical:

(13) The CSTRUC[5] of synthetically expressed predicates and analytically expressed predicates without auxiliaries

$$\begin{bmatrix} \text{CR } \boxed{1}\ \textit{word} \\ \text{HD } \boxed{1}\ \textit{word} \end{bmatrix}$$

Note that the CSTRUC of (3) has the structure of (13), i.e., the categorial core and the categorial head of this predicate are identical, given that the predicate is synthetically expressed.[6]

In analytically expressed predicates with auxiliaries we typically find that the semantic core is represented by a "main verb" (or noun, adjective, etc.) whereas canonical categorial head properties like tense inflection and agreement are associated with an auxiliary. The CSTRUC of such a predicate would look as follows:

---

tion plays a prominent role within recent versions of LFG phrase structure where phrase structure co-heads can contribute information to a single clause nucleus represented in functional structure. (see Bresnan (forthcoming) for details and references.). In general, the entities treated as co-heads in syntactic representations which contribute information to a single functional structure within recent work in LFG are represented as CR and HD in the present work and analyzed as the pieces required to express a single lexical representation. In LFG the co-occurrence requirements on multiple c-structure elements associated with a single f-structure may be achieved by appealing to constraint equations. Frank (1996), following a proposal in Butt et. al. (1996) for introducing a level of m(-orphological) structure into LFG, develops an analysis along these lines. Both the LFG proposal and our own represent alternative implementations of the claim found in Falk (1984) on English 'do' and Ackerman (1984, 1987) on Hungarian modals and analytic tense constructions, that certain syntactically independent elements correspond to single clausal domains, rather than to multiple domains as in standard raising analyses of e.g., auxiliaries.

[5]Instead of using the technically correct but verbose "the value of attribute X has property P" we will from now on often take the liberty to shorten this to the technically sloppy "Attribute X has property P." The coindexation of CR and HD in (4) represents token-identity between the two values. Thus, (13) is satisfied only if CR and HD describe one and the same thing, a word in the present case.

[6]For reasons of space the morphological word that is both the head and the core of that predicate had to be abbreviated in (3). To make up for that, its fully specified representation was used as an illustration of morphological words in (11) above.

(14) The CSTRUC of an analytically expressed predicate with an auxiliary

$$\begin{bmatrix} \text{CR } \boxed{1}\, word\,("main\ predicator") \\ \text{HD } \boxed{2}\, word\ ("supporting\ auxiliary") \end{bmatrix}$$

In (14), $\boxed{1}$ and $\boxed{2}$ must be distinct. Looking back at the analytically expressed predicate in (4), we see that here the categorial core contains the predicate nominal which expresses the semantic core of the predicate whereas the auxiliary serving as the categorial head in this case contributes the operator information of negation to the meaning of the predicate as a whole.

The fact that a predicate has an auxiliary in its surface expression is also expressed in its valence which has the following general topology:

(15) The Structure of VAL

$$\begin{bmatrix} \text{SUBCAT} & subcategorized complements \\ \text{AUX} & auxiliaries\ required\ to\ express\ the\ predicate \\ \text{PART} & particles\ required\ to\ express\ the\ predicate \end{bmatrix}$$

Postponing discussion of SUBCAT for now, note that the valence of a predicate can specify which (if any) auxiliaries and particles are required for the surface realization of the predicate to be complete. Both AUX and PART are (possibly empty) lists of SYNSEM objects, where each such SYNSEM object describes the syntactic/semantic properties of an auxiliary or particle sign that is part of the analytically expressed predicate.

While we want both particles and auxiliaries to be part of the surface spell-out of predicates, we want only auxiliaries but not particles to take on the function of categorially heading the predicate. It is thus natural to impose the following constraint on all lexical combinatorial items:

(16)   The Categorial Head Principle[7]

Each lexical combinatorial item satisfies either (a) or (b):

(a) its VAL:AUX list is empty and its CSTRUC:CR is token-identical to its CSTRUC:HD;

(b) its VAL:AUX list is non-empty and the word that expresses the first auxiliary in VAL:AUX is token-identical to the item's

---

[7]This principle applies only to lexical and not to phrasal combinatorial items, since the core vs. head distinction is only made for predicates but not for phrases.

CSTRUC:HD and consequently the item's CSTRUC:HD and CSTRUC:CR are distinct.

Principle (16) has the desired effect of allowing predicates to select both particles and auxiliaries as part of their surface expression while excluding particles from serving as the head of the predicate. Auxiliaries, however, and in particular the first auxiliary on the predicate's AUX list, can and in fact must act as the predicate's categorial head. In the absence of an auxiliary, this function is performed by the predicate's categorial core.

Returning to our Nenets examples, let us examine the valences of the two predicates in (3) and (4) and how the relationship between the valences and the CSTRUCs of these respective signs satisfies the Categorial Head Principle in (16).

First, both valences specify that neither predicate has a particle in its surface expression. This is done by giving the attribute PART the empty list as its value. Secondly, both predicates select for one subcategorized complement, but we will postpone discussion of subcategorization until later. Finally, the predicate in (3) has an empty auxiliary valence whereas the analytically expressed predicate (4) must combine with one auxiliary, given that its auxiliary valence is a one member list.

The predicate in (3), being synthetic, is an instance of the case (16a) in that the predicate's auxiliary list is empty and consequently the predicate's core must also act as its categorial head. On the other hand, (4) instantiates the case of analytically expressed predicates covered in (16b): since this predicate is forced to combine with an auxiliary sign by its non-empty auxiliary valence, the word that morphologically spells out this auxiliary (being the leftmost selected auxiliary) must act as the categorial head of the whole predicate. In this case, therefore, the categorial core and head of the predicate are realized by different morphological words.

We turn to providing a schematic description of the information that can be expected to appear in VAL:SUBCAT and in ISTRUC.

Following the lead of HPSG, heads select their subcategorized complements (subjects and objects) by governing properties in the SYNSEM of these complements.[8] A look back at the schematic representation for phrasal combinatorial items in (6) shows that this allows heads to restrict the syntactic/semantic properties of their complements but makes the linear (LSTRUC) and phrase-structural properties (DTRS) of a complement non-selectable. A typical subcategorization frame would then look as follows:

---

[8]Evidence of the need for categorial selection is presented, among others, in Webelhuth (1992: chapter 1) and in Pollard and Sag (1994: chapter 3). Note that LFG handles selection for particular prepositions through the functional attribute PCASE which has strong categorial overtones in that its value always correlates with the *form* of a member of the syntactic *category* preposition.

(17) A typical subcategorization frame

$$
\left[\text{SUBCAT} \left\{ \left[\begin{array}{l} synsem \\ \text{CSTRUC } categorial selection \\ \text{ISTRUC } functional selection \end{array} \right], \left[\begin{array}{l} synsem \\ \text{CSTRUC } categorial selection \\ \text{ISTRUC } functional selection \end{array} \right], ... \right\} \right]
$$

On the basis of (17) we would expect heads to select their complements on categorial and semantic grounds and that is of course the normal case. On the other hand, heads that require their complements to have some particular complement-internal linear order or phrase structure should not exist, at least if these internal properties can be shown not to correlate in any systematic way with the categorial and/or semantic properties of the complement as a whole.

Both (3) and (4) have subcategorization frames with a single selected *synsem* constituent. In each case, the predicate selects for a sign whose categorial core is represented by a first person singular nominative noun word. Since the categorial heads of both of these predicates are also first person singular, we thus are witnessing a case here where a predicate enforces agreement of person and number between its categorial complement and its categorial head and the predicate likewise governs the nominative case on its complement.

Finally, we present the schematic structure of an information structure:

(18) The information contained in a typical *istruc*

$$
\left[\begin{array}{ll} \text{CONT} & \textit{the meaning of the sign} \\ \\ \text{FSTRUC} & \left[\begin{array}{ll} \text{SU} & \textit{properties of the subject} \\ \text{DO} & \textit{properties of the direct object} \\ \text{IO} & \textit{properties of the indirect object} \\ \text{OBL} & \textit{properties of oblique complements} \\ \text{CCL} & \textit{properties of complement clauses} \end{array} \right] \end{array} \right]
$$

The information structure of a sign of course specifies the sign's meaning which is typically an attribute-value structure naming an event and specifying which individuals (= semantic indexes) play which semantic roles in the event. The functional structure reflects the functional-semantic properties of the grammatical functions governed by a predicate. Each grammatical function can enter into two relationships: (i) the semantic index of the grammatical function may be token-identical to an index bearing a semantic role in the meaning of the predicate; and (ii) the whole information structure corresponding to a grammatical function may be part of the *synsem* of a subcategorized complement. In (19) we illustrate these two dependencies:

(19) Grammatical functions mediate between subcategorization and semantic roles

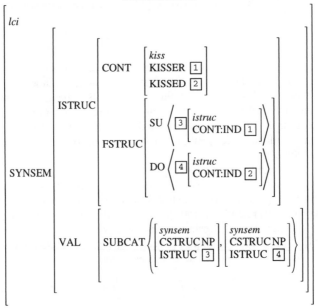

The predicate captured with the representation in (19) is subcategorized for two NP complements. The valence of the predicate determines via the tag [3] that the information contained in the initial complement specifies the predicate's grammatical function subject and the predicate's functional structure in turn requires that the semantic index [1] of the subject is assigned the kisser role in the event denoted by the predicate. The lci's second subcategorized complement is the categorial surface realization of the predicate's direct object which is interpreted as the kissed participant of the kissing event, as the tags [4] and [2] show.[9]

In the representations of the two Nenets predicates which we have been explicating, we can also follow the tags from subcategorized complements through the f-structure to the content representation to see the

---

[9]Though we establish the relation between semantic roles and their function assignments by stipulating identical indices, our formalism is compatible with a more principled alignment of arguments and their grammatical function status. However, we forego consideration of (current) mapping proposals in the present book. See Davis (1997) for a recent formulation of mapping designed to be compatible with much of the formal apparatus employed here and Levin and Rappaport-Hovav (1997) for an excellent review of competing mapping proposals.

"linkings" between surface arguments, grammatical functions, and semantic roles which predicates impose on the expressions they project. However, in (3) and (4) we have introduced an abbreviatory convention which we will use frequently in this book: in ⌐3:1⌐ , the first integer denotes an ISTRUC that serves as the value of a grammatical function and the second integer refers to a semantic index contained in that information structure. Given that notational convention, we can see from inspection of the SUBCAT valence in (3) and (4) that the single subcategorized first person singular nominative pronoun must be paired with an information structure ⌐3⌐ . The functional structure of both signs tells us that this information structure of the pronoun acts as the grammatical function SUBJECT of the predicate and that the index of that subject is assigned the semantic role INSTANCE of the *hunter* kind in the semantic representation of the predicate.

Keeping semantic government (CONT), functional government (FSTRUC), and categorial government (SUBCAT) independent of each other allows us to capture cases of systematic and idiosyncratic mismatches between these three classes of information contained in a sign. For instance, while in languages like English and German the subjects of finite predicates must be spelled out in surface categorial structure, this is not the case in pro-drop languages like Italian. Here we typically find certain categories to be omissible in surface structure, even though the grammatical functions that would be specified by these categories are still present, as evidenced by agreement, binding, or interpretive phenomena. Our theory would in this case make available a version of the sign that links each grammatical function to a semantic role but would not have categorial complements that spell out the grammatical function. This is the intuitively most satisfactory analysis of "pro drop," since it directly captures our intuition that the "missing" category's information is already contributed by the governing predicate itself and the spell-out of the category would therefore be redundant.

Another kind of mismatch that is possible is a grammatical function that is categorially selected in the valence of the lci but is not linked to a semantic role in the sign's content. This is the case of expletives and grammatical functions in semantically non-compositional idioms.

Finally, our theory makes it possible for a sign to subcategorize for a categorial complement which neither bears a grammatical function nor a semantic role. Arguably, one instantiation of this is the German pronoun *es* 'it' which appears in the initial position of German main clause existential sentences like (20):

(20)   **Es** sitzen drei Leute im   Wartezimmer
        It   sit-pl three people in the waiting room

        'Three people are sitting in the waiting room'

This *es* only appears in main clauses of existential sentences and must fill their first position. There is no reason to believe that this element is anything more than a filler of the first position in these clauses whose function it is to maintain the verb-second property of German main clauses. If this *es* bore a grammatical function to the predicate, in particular the grammatical function subject, then it would be mysterious why it cannot follow the finite verb in (10) as other subjects can and why it has to disappear completely in subordinate clauses. Moreover, this *es* certainly does not bear an index that is assigned a semantic role in the predicate's semantics. It thus seems to be a category that is subcategorized by certain predicates that don't assign it either a grammatical function or a semantic role. The architecture of our signs allows for this case.

The discussion above ought to give the reader a good idea of the internal structure of signs (both lexical and phrasal) that we postulate and how that structure has been deliberately modeled to formally capture the key proposal we are putting forth in this book: the information in predicates can sometimes be expressed by single words in categorial surface structure but sometimes also by a collocation of words. In other words, the various structural components that make up the representation of a predicate (e.g., semantic content, grammatical functions, surface spell-out) are all conceptually independent of each other and it is only in the formation of a whole sign that all this information cooccurrs in one logical place and that the question of possible correspondences (in the sense of 'linking') between the pieces of the various levels of representation within the sign arises. We believe that there is a one-to-one mapping between units within the sign only under unmarked conditions and that an optimal theory of grammar will be flexible enough to allow the mismatches in semantic, functional, and categorial selection discussed in the last few paragraphs as well as the synthetic vs. analytic expression of the predicate as a whole that was empirically demonstrated in chapter 2. Our theory of signs was designed to achieve that very goal.

3   Syntactic Schemas for Creating Phrasal Structures

Let us take stock of what we have accomplished so far: we have sketched the internal structure of lexical combinatorial items which function as predicates and also the internal structure of the morphological words that (alone or in combination) serve as the spell-out of the information in predicates.

From a predicate's CSTRUC and VAL we can determine which categorial words have to be present for a sentence to contain the surface realization of a predicate and hence also the predicate's semantic content and the grammatical functional structure it imposes on the sentence.

In this section, we introduce three syntactic schemas that build syntactic structures on the basis of the valence requirements of predicates. Each phrase-building operation combines a predicate with another sign that satisfies one of the predicate's valence requirements, e.g., a complement, a particle, or an auxiliary valence requirement.[10]

Technically, the syntactic "schemas" are just different types of phrases. Remember from our earlier preliminary discussion of phrasal combinatorial items in (6) that phrases are combinatorial items which happen to be equipped with a DTRS attribute allowing for the description of syntactic phrase structure:

(21) Phrasal combinatorial items *(= pci)* aka syntactic phrases

$$
\begin{bmatrix}
pci \\
\text{LSTRUC } \textit{word order properties} \\
\text{SYNSEM } \begin{bmatrix} \text{CSTRUC } \textit{categorial properties} \\ \text{ISTRUC } \textit{meaning and grammatical functions} \\ \text{VAL } \textit{categorial selection} \end{bmatrix} \\
\textbf{DTRS} \quad \textbf{DTR–1, DTR –2, ..., DTR–n}
\end{bmatrix}
$$

Note that (21) in fact has the structure of a local categorial phrase structure tree where the branches connecting the mother node to its various daughter nodes have been omitted: the mother's grammatical properties are described by the information in the attributes LSTRUC and SYNSEM. The same kind of information is available about its daughters in the form of the value of the DTRS attribute. If one wanted to convert (21) into the familiar tree representation for phrases one would simply take the part of speech from the mother's CSTRUC, write it at the top of the page, and then downwards-connect it with branches to the parts of speech of the various daughters.

But the representation in (21) is in fact much more useful than a standard categorial tree because the nodes of the 'tree' in (21) aren't mere category symbols but whole signs! This makes the representations big (sometimes too big to fit on one of our pages!) but it allows the linguist to state in one and the same representation what contribution the information in the daughter signs makes to the representation of the mother sign. For instance, following Kathol (1995) we can impose constraints on how the linear orders of the various daughters must be combined to form the linear structure of the newly created phrasal sign. We can simultaneously correlate linear orders with specific semantic properties (e.g., quantifier scope, topic-focus) without having to invoke theoretically suspect structure-deforming transformations like quantifier raising or numerous empirically insupportable 'functional' heads required by beliefs about the relation of language to putative conceptual minimalism as in the Minimalist Program.

A formal representation of phrasal signs that has many of the desirable properties just mentioned appears in (22):

---

[10]We are postponing discussion of modification constructions until later.

(22) The "Phrase Schema"

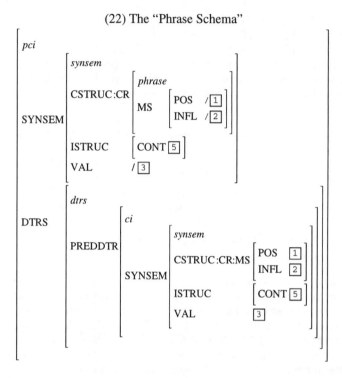

With one exception, the information in (22) should by now look familiar to the reader: the phrase (aka *pci* = phrasal combinatorial item) has a SYNSEM containing attributes describing the categorial structure (CSTRUC) and the information content (ISTRUC) of the phrase. Observe that the value of the mother's path SYNSEM:CSTRUC:CR is *phrase*, i.e., the schema requires that a sign that has syntactic daughters must be labeled with a phrasal part of speech.

The schema (22) also requires that in every phrase a predicate daughter is present and that this PREDDTR be a combinatorial item (either a lexical or a phrasal sign).

The predicate daughter completely determines the meaning of the phrase it heads: if there are other daughters in the phrase, they can contribute to the mother's meaning only indirectly. In the case of particle and auxiliary daughters, they are considered part of the surface spell-out of the predicate and hence their semantic contribution is already reflected in the meaning of the PREDDTR. In the remaining case of subcategorized complements, their semantic contribution is also channeled through the predicate: recall from our discussion in connection with (19) that, as in LFG, grammatical functions mediate between categorial structures and semantic interpretation (in order to capture the intuition that the predicate itself can contribute the information of pro-dropped "constituents" via its f-structure). Consequently, by saturating a subcategorization valence of a predicate, an argument may informationally specify one of the predicate's grammatical functions and indirectly one of the semantic indexes in the predicate's semantic content [cf. the example in (19)].

In sum, PREDDTRs fully determine the functional structure of a functional clause and they completely determine the semantic contribution of AUXDTRs and PARTDTRs they combine with. In addition, they "route" the information contributed by subcategorized complements through the PREDDTRs f-structure. Given this, the predicate as the determiner of this information acts as the content-theoretic head of a clause. Auxiliaries and particles may have to be present to saturate valence requirements of a predicate that must be satisfied in syntactic phrase structure. But their presence and their functional/semantic/valence contribution is guaranteed in the lexical entry of the predicate and at the level of syntactic phrase formation, these elements play a purely categorial role. In this sense, in our theory the lexicon is the grammatical component in which predicates are created or listed and the syntax is the domain in which predicates are expressed and their valence requirements are saturated.

With these observations in mind we return to the details of the phrase schema in (22). The schema also requires that the PREDDTR 'percolate' its POS and INFL information to the phrase (via the tags $\boxed{1}$ and $\boxed{2}$) and that the valence of the phrase ($\boxed{3}$) be inherited from its predicate daughter as well, rather than some other daughter. In this sense, the predicate daughter is both the categorial head and the valence head of the phrase projected from it.

Observe, however, a notational convention in (22) [borrowed from Sag (1997)] which we have not seen so far and are introducing here for the first time: three of the tags correlating information in the predicate daughter with information in the corresponding slots in the phrase are preceded by a slash in the mother's representation. This notation indicates information that is *present by default, i.e., unless contradicted by an overriding statement elsewhere in the representation.* For phrases, (22) thus says that in the general case the categorial and valence properties of a phrase are determined by its predicate daughter. Turning now to the three phrasal schemas that deal with the specific situations where a subcategorized complement, a particle, or an auxiliary daughter is co-present with a predicate daughter in a sign, we see that the default assignments spelled out for the general case in (22) sometimes have to be overridden.

We first examine the case where a phrase like that in (22) not only has a predicate daughter but also an argument daughter. This situation is handled by a subtype of the type *pci* of (22), namely the subtype *argdtr-pci* which is defined as follows:[11]

(23) The "Argument Schema" [formally of type *argdtr-pci,* a subtype of the type *pci* illustrated in (22)]

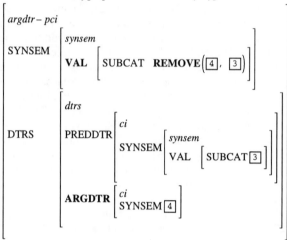

The reason (23) is a subtype of (22) is that a phrase where a PREDDTR combines with one of its subcategorized complements is one of the general ways of forming a new phrase. (22) describes the general case and (23) the more specific case. Not surprisingly, therefore, (23) introduces a second daughter into the DTRS description of the phrase, namely an ARGDTR (= argument daughter). This ARGDTR has to be a combinatorial item which can either be phrasal or lexical.

   Let us track what has happened to the default information specified for the general case of phrase formation in (22). The general case required that the part of speech and inflection information of a phrase be identical to that of its predicate daughter. (23) contains no statement that is inconsistent with that requirement and therefore, taken together, (22) and (23) imply that when a predicate combines with one of its subcategorized arguments, then the predicate daughter determines the part of speech and inflectional properties of the newly formed phrase. In other words, (23) does not override the categorial percolation default of (22). With respect to valence, things are different, however. Recall that generally the valence of a phrase should be

---

[11]In a fuller treatment, the "Argument Schema" will allow the SUBCAT valence of the argument selected by a predicate to be either empty or to be a singleton set containing the valence element corresponding to the subject of the argument expression. Since both lexical items and phrases must of course have a VALENCE and the value of this attribute is part of SYNSEM (the level at which subcategorization takes place), an expression's information concerning its unrealized subject is available for selection by other predicates. This is sufficient for the modeling of raising and control.

identical to the valence of its predicate daughter. (23) explicitly overrides that information partially in that it sets the valence of the mother node to the result of removing the argument daughter's SYNSEM from the PREDDTR's subcategorization frame.[12] The default remains in effect for all other valence features of the mother, i.e., the mother still has the same particle and auxiliary valences as its PREDDTR. It should be clear why the general valence default has to be overridden in the fashion indicated in (23): each time a predicate combines with one of its arguments, the predicate's mother node has one less argument to combine with; in other words, each argument cancels a predicate's subcategorization requirement.

The schema that forms phrases by combining a predicate with a particle is almost identical to the schema for arguments:

(24) The "Particle Schema" [formally of type *partdtr-pci,* a subtype of the type *pci* illustrated in (22)]

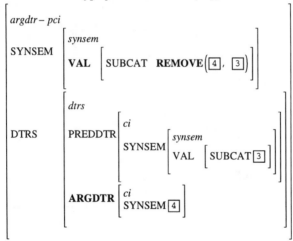

This schema achieves for particles what (23) does for arguments: it adds a particle daughter to the PREDDTR that is introduced into the phrase by the definition of the general case in (22). (24) makes no provisions to override the general regularity for categorial percolation that gives the PREDDTR of a phrase the privilege to determine the categorial properties of the newly formed phrase. And like (23), the particle schema overrides the default va-

---

[12]Subcategorization frames in our theory are sets. Therefore, the REMOVE function used in (23) is defined as follows:

REMOVE(α, β) = γ (where β is a set) iff β - $\{\alpha\}$ = γ, i.e., the result of removing α from a set β is γ if and only if the set difference of β and the singleton set containing α is equal to γ.

lence assignment to register in the mother phrase that a particle valence of the PREDDTR has been saturated by the particle daughter.[13]

The auxiliary schema completes the review of phrase-forming operations. This schema explicitly overrides both the categorial and the valence defaults of the general case expressed in (22):

(25) The "Auxiliary Schema" [formally of type *auxdtr-pci,* a subtype of the type *pci* illustrated in (22)]

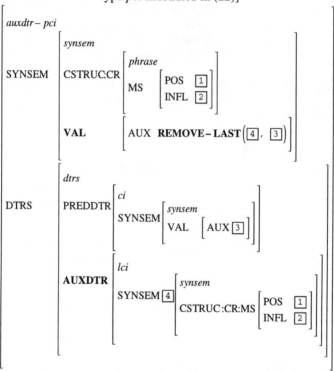

In phrases with an auxiliary daughter, the auxiliary's rather than the predicate's categorial features percolate to the mother's category slots and the mother's valence is identical to that of the predicate daughter except that the

---

[13]There is one qualitative difference between the two schemas, however. For technical reasons, we are modeling SUBCAT frames as sets of SYNSEMs but particle valences as ordered lists of SYNSEMs. Therefore, the function REMOVE-FIRST is used to remove the first saturated SYNSEM from a particle valence list. The additional definition we need is presented below:

REMOVE-FIRST(α, β) = γ (where β is a list) iff the concatenation of the singleton list containing α with the list γ is equal to β.

mother is looking for one auxiliary less than its PREDDTR does (the auxiliaries are removed from the PREDDTR'S auxiliary valence from right to left so that the predicate's categorial head is saturated last).[14]

4   An Illustration of the Interplay between Predicate Representations and Syntactic Schemas

In combination with the lexical representations of our theory, the three syntactic schemas allow us to accomplish formally what the arguments in chapters 1 and 2 of this book have demanded that an empirically and conceptually satisfactory theory of grammar should be able to do: they make it possible for an indeterminate number of categorial constituents of a categorial phrase (i.e., the pieces of the surface expression of a predicate) to collectively determine the inventory of grammatical functions, the semantic content, and the number of categorial arguments in a sentence or clause. Using the two predicates (3)–(4) from the Nenets sentences (1)–(2), we will now illustrate how sentences can be created from synthetically and analytically expressed predicates without resorting to any predicate formation in the syntax.

The predicates in (3) and (4) are obviously related. As inspection of their representations shows, we express this relatedness by deriving both predicates from the same basic lexical entry, the nominal predicate 'hunter.' Nenets has two different predicate formation patterns, one that takes a nominal sign as input and creates a new sign like that in (3) that is usable as the predicate of an affirmative sentence. This predicate is expressed by a single noun and must combine with one nominal argument to saturate its subcategorization valence. This argument bears the grammatical function subject and is interpreted as an instance of the kind of thing the predicate denotes, in this case the *hunter* kind. The second predicate pattern derives a lexical predicate which denotes the semantic negation of the first. This clearly related predicate has the same subcategorization requirements as its affirmative counterpart but differs in the surface expression of the predicate: the negative predicate is expressed by an auxiliary-noun combination. Additionally, these two pieces of the predicate must both signal agreement with their common subject argument.

Which syntactic schemas can the predicates in (3) and (4) occur in respectively? Since all the valences except the SUBCAT valence of (3) are empty, (3) can only appear as the PREDDTR in the Argument Schema (23). After one application of this schema, the PREDDTR's valences have all been saturated and no further phrases can be projected from it. In contrast, (4) has two non-empty valences: like (3) it must combine with an argument, but in addition it must also combine with an auxiliary sign whose CSTRUC

---

[14]Like particle valences, auxiliary valences are treated as lists. The auxiliary schema thus uses a list method of REMOVE-LAST whose definition differs from the definition of REMOVE-FIRST of the previous footnote only in reversing the arguments of the concatenation operation.

is part of the expression of the predicate expressed by the PREDDTR. The lexical entry in (4) thus must undergo two phrase-forming operations to become saturated.

In (26), we see the result of feeding the synthetically expressed predicate in (3) the categorial complement it seeks to combine with:

(26) The representation of the sentential sign in sentence (1)

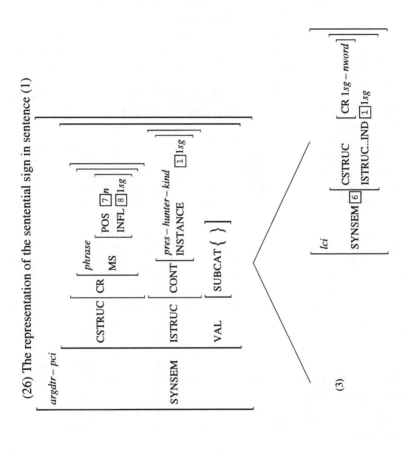

(3)

The pci's PREDDTR appears on the left and its ARGDTR on the right. These two daughters hence form an *argdtr-pci,* a phrasal combinatorial item like (23) where a predicate combines with an argument that satisfies one of the predicate's SUBCAT valences. The information flow in the new phrase is as follows: via tag ⑥ the predicate in (3) seeks to combine with a noun phrase whose information structure it identifies with its own subject via tag ③. The semantic index of its subject (①) is passed to the predicate's semantic content as the instance of the *pres-hunter-kind* that the predicate denotes. Since the SYNSEM of the nominal argument sign on the right in (26) must unify with the SYNSEM selected in the predicate's SUBCAT valence, the semantic index of the argument daughter has to be ① as well. Consequently, the ARGDTR's description of index ① as first person singular finds its way into the semantic representation of the predicate and also the semantic representation of the mother phrase. The new phrase inherits the empty PART and AUX valences of its PREDDTR (not shown in (26) due to lack of space) and now also has an empty SUBCAT valence, since its right-hand daughter has saturated the SUBCAT valence of its left-hand daughter. Language-particular linearization constraints will concatenate the spell-out of the subject complement with the predicate's spell-out to yield the correct word order of (1) in the *argdtr-pci.*

The end result of (26) is therefore the nominal sentence (1) which pairs the observable surface form *mań xańenadm?* with the semantic content *I am a hunter.*

Sentence (2) is the semantic negation of sentence (1) and this semantic difference is reflected in that the predicate of sentence (2) contains an extra auxiliary signaling negation. This predicate, whose lexical representation was presented in (4), thus has to undergo an extra step of phrase formation to saturate its valences completely. We present the structure of sentence (2) in two parts. In (27a), we form a phrase by combining the two pieces that realize the predicate in (4), i.e., the predicate's categorial core and the auxiliary that serves as its categorial head. In (27b), this newly formed phrase is combined with the categorial complement the predicate is subcategorized for.[15]

---

[15](27a, b) uses another abbreviatory convention.

$$NP_{③}$$

abbreviates a *synsem* object whose part of speech is a NP and whose ISTRUC (= information structure) is ③.

(27a) The phrase-structural realization of the predicate of sentence (2)

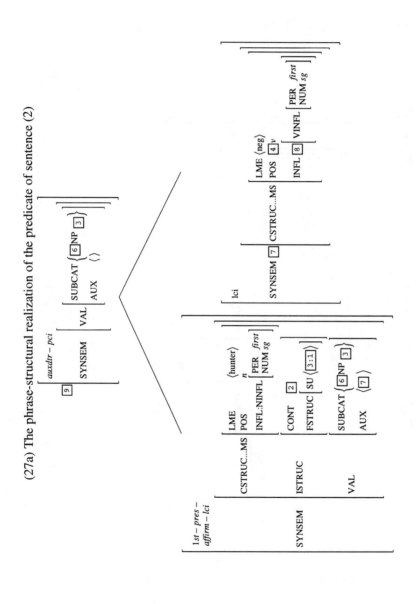

(27b) The top node of the phrase structure tree of sentence (2)

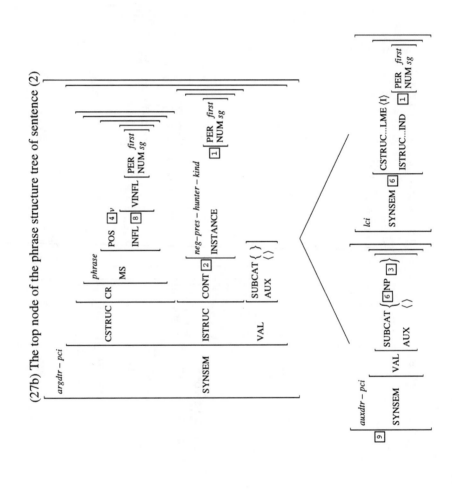

The phrase that results from these two applications of syntactic schemas is a verb phrase, since in accordance with (25) the auxiliary is the categorial head of the phrase and makes the phrase categorially verbal. The presence of the negativizing auxiliary indicates that this verbal sentence is the negative variant of the nominal sentence in (24). The categorial difference is irrelevant for the semantic interpretation of these clauses, as the interpretation of the clause is a matter of the semantic content of the predicate and the semantic interpretations of the grammatical functions governed by the predicate. Except for the feature of negation, the predicates of (26) and (27) are identical in both cases and in a function-based theory of predicates semantic interpretation is tied to the information content of the predicate rather than to such incidental factors as the part of speech of the predicate or whether it is spelled out by one or more than one word.

We conclude this illustration with a final remark: since our theory is function-based rather than form-based, it does not matter in which order the PREDDTR of (27) saturates its two unsaturated valences. In our illustration we arbitrarily chose to combine the PREDDTR with the auxiliary it selects before taking care of the SUBCAT valence requirement. A little thought will convince the reader that reversing the order of these operations will yield exactly the same result. Each phrase-forming operation has three effects: (i) it saturates a valence requirement of the PREDDTR but the order in which the valences are saturated is irrelevant, since the schemas will 'percolate' the valences that remain unsaturated to the PREDDTR's mother for later saturation; (ii) it integrates the meaning of the predicate's arguments (the meaning of auxiliaries and particles is already contained in the PREDDTR's meaning) into the phrase's meaning, but since the semantic contribution of each argument is fully determined by its grammatical function, it is irrelevant in what order the PREDDTR combines with its arguments; (iii) it builds the linear LSTRUC representation of the phrase but in theories of linearization like that of Reape (1992) and Kathol (1995) which we assume to be in operation here, the linear order of a phrase is in principle independent of its tree structure. Instead, the serialization of the surface spell-out of a phrase may depend on a whole set of grammatical factors other than its tree configuration, e.g., grammatical functions, part of speech, prosodic factors, topic-focus effects, etc. Consequently, the order of operations that create the 'tectogrammatical structure' in the sense of Curry (1961) and Dowty (1996) is not essentially relevant and no general ordering principles need to be imposed.[16]

---

[16]This does not mean, however, that there are no ordering constraints in particular cases. These can be encoded in the structure of the predicate, however. In fact, that is the reason why we chose to model auxiliary and particle valences as lists which have to be saturated from left to right. By building up the LSTRUC representation of phrases in a manner that is sensitive to the order of saturation we can make sure that the various auxiliaries that appear with a PREDDTR appear in a certain order (e.g., that the Dutch auxiliary order is the mirror image of German in many grammatical environments, etc.). But it has to be realized that this is a language-specific and often even construction-specific matter and that no universal ordering principles are called for.

This concludes our discussion of the three schemas that produce phrasal signs from other signs.

5 Conclusions

In this chapter we have sketched the general structure of lexical and phrasal signs as it is determined by our theory of predicates. We have applied these structural assumptions to two concrete predicates from Nenets which are lexically related and differ only in the presence of the semantic feature of negation in their semantic representations. Otherwise, there is virtually a complete overlap in the functions performed by these predicates: their non-operator meanings are identical, they govern the same grammatical functions, and they have identical subcategorization valences. Yet, despite this functional equivalence, one predicate is expressed by one word and the other one by a two word combination of a noun and an auxiliary.

We have demonstrated that it is possible to capture the functional equivalence of the two Nenets predicates by postulating lexical entries for them which are structurally homomorphic in those properties which define a predicate functionally: semantic content, grammatical functions, and subcategorization valence. At the same time, the lexical entries differ minimally in one purely surfacy way: whereas (3) has empty PART and AUX valences, its negative equivalent requires that the functional properties of the predicate be signaled simultaneously by the categorial core of the predicate and an auxiliary the predicate selects via its AUX valence.

The three syntactic schemas in (23)–(25), which are all subtypes and hence different specific instantiations of the general definition of phrasal combinatorial items in (22), interface with the lexical representations of predicates in such a way that their utilization of the *information* contained in a predicate is completely independent of the requirements that the lexical

---

Similarly, it might be advantageous to fix a language-particular order of combination in what are often called 'configurational' languages (see Hale (1983), Simpson (1991), Webelhuth (1992), among others). For English, for instance, it will probably be efficient to set up the phrasal system in such a way that all the predicate's non-subject complements are combined with the verb first, followed by all auxiliaries, followed by the predicate's subject. For languages with comparatively free phrase order (e.g., German, Hindi, Japanese, and Hungarian) such a combinatorial straightjacket arguably leads to very inefficient grammars. Besides, it has proved to be both difficult and often desirable only from a narrow theory-internal perspective to motivate the phrase structural asymmetries predicted to exist by highly configurational theories of combination (see the endless and arguably ultimately unresolved discussion in the 1980s of whether or not the languages mentioned above have VP constituents creating subject-object asymmetries). All of these problems disappear largely once one recognizes that in natural language function takes primacy over form. The 'deeper' properties of language are found in the semantic, functional, and selectional properties of predicates and the surface categorial form of predicates, their arguments, and the phrases formed from their combinations is just that: incidental surface realization.

In other words, we are convinced that the correct theory of predicates and arguments and their respective *information* contribution to a clause reveals as fruitless pseudo-issues such questions about pure surface form as whether every language must have a VP constituent or how many empty 'functional' heads to postulate in a clause architecture based on 'exploded INFL.'

entry of the predicate's core imposes on the *surface categorial expression* of the functional predicate. In turn, the creation of the surface form of the predicate by the syntactic schemas is completely independent of the predicate's functional features.

The desirability of this principled dissociation of the semantic, grammatical-functional, and valence functions of the predicate on the one hand and its categorial surface spell-out on the other was the outcome of the conceptual and empirical argumentation of chapters 1 and 2. In particular, in conformity with the Principle of Primacy of Function over Form, the desideratum was stated that the grammatical formalism should uniformly capture the defining *functional* properties of *predicates* in their *lexical representations* independently of how many words happen to be necessary to express the predicate. With the concepts developed in the present chapter the ideas discussed informally in chapters 1 and 2 have been given a formal enough expression to allow our theory to make predictions about what kinds of predicates we expect to find instantiated in the languages of the world. It is to this issue that we turn in the next chapter.

4

Grammatical Archetypes

1 Introduction

One of the main hypotheses we pursue and formalize in this book is that the reason we find many of the same functional-semantic constructions and morphosyntactic spell-outs of predicates in different natural languages is that Universal Grammar defines predicate types in a type hierarchy which the grammars of individual languages can import as whole chunks. We assume that such universally configured types are particularly "cheap" in a system of markedness and that individual grammars benefit from importing types from Universal Grammar because that keeps their overall degree of markedness lower than if they created their own fully language-particular types to perform the same functions that can be performed by the universally available types. We will refer to the elementary types that are available for incorporation into individual grammars as *archetypes*.

Two sorts of archetypes are of particular importance to us in that they parallel the two basic functions of a linguistic sign: to express a semantic content and to do so via a surface arrangement of morphological words. We find archetypes along both of these dimensions:

> Content-theoretic archetypes: these contain functional-semantic and morphosyntactic content information about a predicate.

> Form-theoretic archetypes: these contain information about the number and arrangement of the morphological words in the surface expression of a predicate. We will also often refer to these as "arrangement archetypes."

We will proceed by introducing the major arrangement types that can be found in the languages of the world and then illustrate how these arrangement types interact with a central content-theoretic archetype, specifically, the expanded predicate containing tense-aspect information.

2 The Form-Theoretic Archetypes *simplex-lci* and *compd-lci*

In our overview of the sign system presented in the previous chapter, we saw that lexical combinatorial items (= predicate signs) have a feature structure that allows their c(ategorial) structure to describe a categorial core and a categorial head which may or may not be identical. As (1) shows, both the core and the head of the predicate must be realized by morphological words:

(1) The structure of lexical combinatorial items *(lci)*

$$
\begin{bmatrix}
lci \\
\text{SYNSEM} \begin{bmatrix} \text{CSTRUC} \begin{bmatrix} \text{CR } word \\ \text{HD } word \end{bmatrix} \end{bmatrix}
\end{bmatrix}
$$

For the moment, we will concentrate on the structure of the categorial core. Given that its value has to be of type *word,* the core can be realized either by a morphologically simplex word or by a morphological compound. Depending on this choice, we can define two subtypes of the general type *lci* in (1) which is neutral between this distinction. Since these two subtypes frequently recur in the world's languages, we assume that they are predefined in Universal Grammar and can be drawn on cheaply by individual grammars. They are thus examples of what we call *archetypes* and in particular they are *arrangement archetypes,* since they influence the surface expression of a predicate:

(2) The arrangement archetype *simplex-lci:*
its core is morphologically simplex

$$
\begin{bmatrix}
simplex\text{--}lci \\
\text{SYNSEM} \begin{bmatrix} \text{CSTRUC} \begin{bmatrix} \text{CR } simplex \end{bmatrix} \end{bmatrix}
\end{bmatrix}
$$

(3) The arrangement archetype *compd-lci:*
its core is a morphological compound

$$
\begin{bmatrix}
compd\text{--}lci \\
\text{SYNSEM} \begin{bmatrix} \text{CSTRUC} \begin{bmatrix} \text{CR } compd \end{bmatrix} \end{bmatrix}
\end{bmatrix}
$$

3 The Form-Theoretic Archetypes *auxd-lci* and *nauxd-lci*

Orthogonal to the simplex vs. compound distinction is the distinction between auxiliated and non-auxiliated predicates. An auxiliated predicate (i.e., *auxd-lci)* is specified as having a non-empty list as the value of its AUX valence attribute whereas a non-auxiliated predicate (i.e., *nauxd-lci)* takes the empty list as the value of that attribute and hence is not required (and, in fact, not even allowed) to combine with any auxiliaries. The fact that both of these predicate types recur systematically in the world's languages leads us to postulate them as archetypes as well:

(4) The arrangement archetype *auxd-lci:* (preliminary definition)[1]
    has a non-empty list *(= nelt)* as its AUX valence

$$\begin{bmatrix} auxd-lci \\ \text{SYNSEM} \begin{bmatrix} \text{VAL} \begin{bmatrix} \text{AUX } nelt \end{bmatrix} \end{bmatrix} \end{bmatrix}$$

(5) The arrangement archetype *nauxd-lci:* (preliminary definition)
    its AUX valence is the empty list

$$\begin{bmatrix} nauxd-lci \\ \text{SYNSEM} \begin{bmatrix} \text{VAL} \begin{bmatrix} \text{AUX} \langle \rangle \end{bmatrix} \end{bmatrix} \end{bmatrix}$$

Recall that auxiliaries are pieces of the spell-out of lci's that may be required to appear in the valence list of a predicate, depending on the predicate's morpho-syntactic properties. That makes the two types in (4)–(5) examples of arrangement archetypes.

4 The Form-Theoretic Archetypes *partld-lci* and *npartld-lci*

This brings us to the third and final pair of arrangement archetypes we find frequently instantiated in the world's languages. Predicates either require a particle as part of their surface spell-out or they do not. The two arrangement archetypes *partld-lci* and *npartld-lci* differ in whether the particle valence of the lci is empty or non-empty:[2]

(6) The arrangement archetype *partld-lci:*
    its PART valence is a singleton list

$$\begin{bmatrix} partld-lci \\ \text{SYNSEM} \begin{bmatrix} \text{VAL} \begin{bmatrix} \text{PART } sglt-synsem \end{bmatrix} \end{bmatrix} \end{bmatrix}$$

---

[1] The final definitions of the auxiliary archetypes appear in (20) and (21).
[2] All the applications of particled lci's in this work require at most one particle for any predicate. If phenomena in other languages require the postulation of more than one particle per predicate, then the type that *partld-lci* imposes on the path SYNSEM:VAL:PART should be changed from *singleton-list* to *non-empty-list*.

(7) The arrangement archetype *npartld-lci:*
its PART valence is the empty list

$$
\begin{bmatrix}
\textit{npartld} - \textit{lci} \\
\text{SYNSEM} \quad \begin{bmatrix} \text{VAL} \begin{bmatrix} \text{PART} \langle \rangle \end{bmatrix} \end{bmatrix}
\end{bmatrix}
$$

5 Assumptions about Markedness

Empirical evidence from typological studies suggest that within each pair of arrangement archetypes one member is less marked than the other:

Less marked	More marked
simplex-lci	*compound-lci*
nauxd-lci	*auxd-lci*
npartld-lci	*partld-lci*

Based on these assumptions, we would expect that predicates instantiating the less marked value of each pair would be found more frequently in the world's languages and that predicates which instantiate all the three values on the left display the cross-linguistic properties typical of unmarked categories, e.g., they are acquired relatively early, are perceived relatively easily, are found more frequently than more marked categories, develop historically from more marked categories (cf. the discussion concerning unidirectional diachronic change in the first two chapters), etc.[3] We will occasionally point to corroborating evidence of this point later in the book.

6 Sketch of a Content-Theoretic Archetype

We will use tense-aspect to illustrate the possible pairings of content-theoretic archetypes and form-theoretic arrangements, since this is the topic that will concern us in the upcoming chapters on morphology (chapter 5) and sign formation (chapters 6–7).

All languages of the world express tense-aspect in some fashion. One notion that is typically instantiated is future tense/prospective aspect. For our present illustrative purposes relating to the possible combinations of content-theoretic and form-theoretic archetypes it will be appropriate to avoid the semantic details and simply postulate one type of semantic content called *future-content*. On this basis we can define a subtype of *lci* which is defined via the requirement specified in (8):

---

[3]For a full-fledged discussion of the properties that are typically associated with unmarked vs. marked categories, see Mayerthaler (1981) or its English translation.

(8) The content-theoretic archetype *future-lci:*
     its CONT is of type *future-content*

$$
\begin{bmatrix}
\textit{future} - \textit{lci} \\[2ex]
\text{SYNSEM} \begin{bmatrix} \text{ISTRUC} \begin{bmatrix} \text{CONTENT} \textit{ future} - \textit{content} \end{bmatrix} \end{bmatrix}
\end{bmatrix}
$$

The type definition of the future archetype restricts the value of the i(nformation)-structural attribute CONTENT to a data structure of type *future-content*. Note, crucially, that it does *not* impose any conditions on the arrangement of the morphological material that will realize the morphosyntactic content on the visible surface. That makes this archetype a *content-theoretic* as opposed to a form-theoretic archetype.

As we will argue throughout, this content-theoretic archetype pattern is typical for Universal Grammar: UG makes available many patterns of this sort and also makes available a set of arrangement archetypes which individual languages can combine into patterns for the surface realization of predicates, including the predicates whose content-theoretic properties are identical to or derived from one of the functional-semantic archetypes.

The necessity for individual grammars to find ways of creating language-particular surface realizations for the content-theoretic archetypes they import from Universal Grammar follows from the setup of UG: on the one hand UG makes available content-theoretic archetypes which are unmarked and thus "cheap" to incorporate into individual grammars; on the other hand, UG does not universally associate the content-theoretic archetypes with form-theoretic archetypes but crucially *does require that every well formed lexical combinatorial item be expressed on the surface in one way or the other.* In particular, every predicate must be either auxiliated or non-auxiliated, particled or non-particled, and its core must be either morphologically simplex or a compound. While in accordance with Saussure's doctrine of the arbitrariness of the sign, UG thus does not force *particular* arrangements or *particular* phonological realizations of the morphological parts of the arrangements on the functional-semantic archetypes inherited by individual grammars, it does force the requirement on them to create *one* of the universally possible and phonologically interpreted arrangements as the surface realization of every content-theoretic archetype employed by the individual language.

The tendency for unidirectional grammaticalization cited in chapter 1 provides evidence to support a preferred relation between predicates and the form-theoretic types employed to express them: following section 5 above, we assume that there is a universal markedness pressure for lci's to be expressed by synthetic morphological items. The manner in which such expression occurs in particular languages is, of course, the result of the effects of the universal markedness principle above and systemic pressures that operate in particular languages. Given the hypothesis just expounded concerning the discrete availability of content-theoretic and arrangement archetypes we would expect to find that a content-theoretic archetype like *future-lci* occurs with different surface expressions in the languages of the world. The next section provides empirical evidence for this claim.

6.1 The Future Archetype Expressed by a Single Non-compound Word

Recall the arrangement we postulated as being the most unmarked surface realization of predicates: the categorial core is realized by a morphologically simplex item and there is neither an auxiliary nor a particle. If a language combines this arrangement with the future archetype in (8) we get the following data structure:

(9) The unmarked surface expression of the future archetype[4]

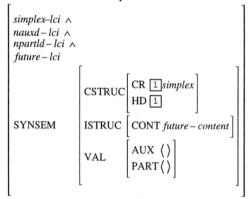

As expected, there are languages whose future predicates are realized by simple morphological words. The following example is from French:

(10)   Je le **verrai** quant il arrivera
       I him will see when he arrives

       'I will see him when he arrives'

In this language, verbs are made to express future by the addition of an affix, yielding a morphologically simple future predicate.

---

[4]Recall that the *Categorial Head Principle* in (16) from the previous chapter requires a predicate's core and head to be identical in the absence of an auxiliary; when the predicate selects auxiliaries, then the categorial expression of the leftmost auxiliary on the AUX valence list serves as the categorial head of the whole predicate. Later in this chapter, we will show that the *Categorial Head Principle* can be derived as a theorem from the final definitions of the two archetypes *auxd-lci* and *nauxd-lci*.

6.2 The Future Archetype Expressed by a Single Non-compound Word Supported by an Auxiliary

In German we find that the future tense is expressed by a main verb supported by an auxiliary:

(11)   Barbara **wird** den Vortrag **halten**
       Barbara will   the talk   give

'Barbara will give the talk'

(12) The future archetype expressed with the help of an auxiliary

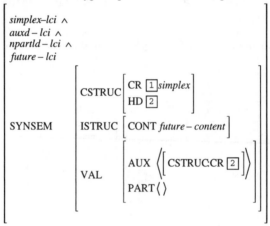

The categorial core in the above example is the infinitival main verb form *halten* and the auxiliary that supports the main verb is the third person singular present tense of *werden* 'to become'. Note that the auxiliary serves as the categorial head of the predicate.

6.3 The Future Archetype Expressed by a Single Non-compound Word Supported by a Particle

Finally, Modern Greek shows that the future tense can also be expressed by a combination of a verb and a particle. In (13) the present tense form of the verb *catch* and the particle θà combine to express futurity: [Adams (1987: 52)]

(13)   **θà piáuw**
       fut catch-1sg-pres

'I will be catching'

The predicate of (13) would be the following straightforward combination of the content-theoretic archetype of *future-lci* with several of the arrangement archetypes we postulated earlier in this chapter:

(14) The future archetype expressed with the help of a particle

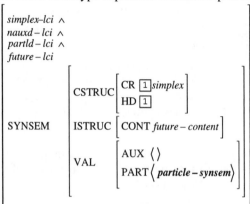

The lci has a particle valence containing the description of the particle that the predicate's categorial core must combine with to create the complete surface realization of this future predicate. Applied to the Greek case illustrated in (13), the core of (14) would describe the present tense verb *piáuw* and the particle valence would describe the SYNSEM of the *partld-lci* expressed by the particle *θà.*

7 Derivational Archetypes

There is a third kind of archetype that we recognize. Its instantiations were already presented in chapter 3 but are repeated here to make the presentation of the archetypes self-contained.

(15) The derivational archetype *underived-lci:*
it lacks the attribute LEXDTR

$$
\begin{bmatrix}
\textbf{\textit{underived–lci}} \\
\text{LSTRUC} \quad \textit{word order properties} \\
\text{SYNSEM} \begin{bmatrix}
\text{CSTRUC} \; \textit{categorial properties} \\
\text{ISTRUC} \; \textit{meaning and grammatical functions} \\
\text{VAL} \quad \textit{categorial selection}
\end{bmatrix}
\end{bmatrix}
$$

Recall that we have drawn a distinction between underived predicates and those predicates which are derived from other predicates.[5] Since these predicate types recur systematically in the world's languages, we treat them as archetypes as well. Their representations appear in (15) and (16).

(16) The derivational archetype *derived-lci:*
it bears the attribute LEXDTR

$$
\begin{bmatrix}
\textbf{\textit{derived–lci}} \\
\text{LSTRUC} \quad \textit{word order properties} \\[4pt]
\text{SYNSEM} \begin{bmatrix} \text{CSTRUC} \, \textit{categorial properties} \\ \text{ISTRUC} \; \textit{meaning and grammatical functions} \\ \text{VAL} \quad \textit{categorial selection} \end{bmatrix} \\[4pt]
\textbf{LEXDTR} \quad \textbf{\textit{the lexical source of the whole lci}}
\end{bmatrix}
$$

The derived-underived dichotomy not only exists in the predicate inventory of lexical signs but also in the morphological module of morphological items employed to express predicates:

(17) The derivational archetype *underived-mi*
(= underived morphological item):
it lacks the attribute MDTR

$$
\begin{bmatrix}
\textbf{\textit{underived – mi}} \\[4pt]
\text{MS} \begin{bmatrix} \text{LME} \quad \textit{the lexeme the word is a form of} \\ \text{PHON} \, \textit{the word's pronunciation} \\ \text{POS} \quad \textit{the word's part of speech} \\ \text{INFL} \quad \textit{the word's inflection} \end{bmatrix}
\end{bmatrix}
$$

(18) The derivational archetype *derived-mi (= derived morphological item):*
it bears the attribute MDTR

$$
\begin{bmatrix}
\textbf{\textit{derived – mi}} \\[4pt]
\text{MS} \begin{bmatrix} \text{LME} \quad \textit{the lexeme the word is a form of} \\ \text{PHON} \, \textit{the word's pronunciation} \\ \text{POS} \quad \textit{the word's part of speech} \\ \text{INFL} \quad \textit{the word's inflection} \end{bmatrix} \\[4pt]
\textbf{MDTR} \quad \textbf{\textit{the morphological source of the whole morphological item}}
\end{bmatrix}
$$

(17) and (18) complete the set of derivational archetypes.

---

[5] It should be emphasized that the use of the term "derivation" should not be understood in a procedural manner. Rather, the system we propose is completely declarative.

8 Type Partitions

Based on the archetypes defined in this chapter, we are in a position to employ a very simple method to impose powerful restrictions on the signs that can be formed in natural language grammars. We are referring to the *partitioning* of types, i.e., the grouping together of a number of subtypes of a given type T with the requirement that every data structure that belongs to the original type T must also belong to one of the subtypes and in particular to *exactly* one subtype. The types we want to partition are of course the two types *lexical combinatorial item* and *morphological item,* and the grouping we wish to establish was already anticipated in our pairwise definitions of the archetypes. For instance, we defined the types *simplex-lci* and *compd-lci* together because we eventually wanted to be able to require that every *lci* has to fall into one of these two classes of lexical combinatorial items. And the same applies to all the remaining archetypes of lci's that we have presented in this chapter. (19) contains the crucial information about the type *lci:*

(19) a. The type *lci* has the following subtypes (among others):

> *simplex-lci, compd-lci, auxd-lci, nauxd-lci, partld-lci, npartld-lci, underived-lci, derived-lci, future-lci, ...*

b. Partitions of the type *lci:*

- The types *simplex-lci* and *compd-lci* partition the type *lci,* i.e., every data structure of type *lci* must belong to either the subtype *simplex-lci* or *compd-lci,* but not both.
- The types *auxd-lci* and *nauxd-lci* partition the type *lci,* i.e., every data structure of type *lci* is either auxiliated or non-auxiliated, but not both.
- The types *partld-lci* and *npartld-lci* partition the type *lci,* i.e., every data structure of type *lci* is either particled or non-particled, but not both.
- The types *underived-lci* and *derived-lci* partition the type *lci,* i.e., every data structure of type *lci* either is a derived lci or an underived *lci,* but not both.

Note that while some partitioning statements are trivial (for instance, it is logically necessary that every predicate be particled or non-particled, there is no intermediate option), partitioning can do some substantive work for us in capturing linguistic generalizations. As an example, consider the preliminary definitions of the two auxiliary archetypes in (4) and (5). As presently defined, the two types are incompatible and if every sign must have information about AUX valence, every sign must logically belong to one of the two subtypes *auxd-lci* or *nauxd-lci*. Given the present definitions, the second partitioning statement under (19b) thus does no work for us. Imagine, however, that we give the revised definitions in (20) and (21) to these two types:

(20) The form-theoretic archetype *auxd-lci:* (final definition)

$$
\begin{bmatrix}
auxd-lci \\
SYNSEM \begin{bmatrix} CSTRUC \begin{bmatrix} HD\ \boxed{1} \end{bmatrix} \\ VAL \quad \begin{bmatrix} AUX:FIRST:CSTRUC:CR\ \boxed{1} \end{bmatrix} \end{bmatrix}
\end{bmatrix}
$$

(21) The form-theoretic archetype *nauxd-lci:* (final definition)

$$
\begin{bmatrix}
nauxd-lci \\
SYNSEM \begin{bmatrix} CSTRUC \begin{bmatrix} CR\ \boxed{1} \\ HD\ \boxed{1} \end{bmatrix} \\ VAL \quad \begin{bmatrix} AUX\langle\rangle \end{bmatrix} \end{bmatrix}
\end{bmatrix}
$$

In addition to specifying whether or not the lci has to combine with an auxiliary to produce the surface realization of the predicate as the preliminary definitions in (4) and (5) did, the final definitions in (20) and (21) correlate the status of the auxiliary valence with the identity of the predicate's categorial head. In (21) where no auxiliary is selected, the predicate's core element simultaneously serves as its categorial head (typically bearing tense-aspect inflections and showing agreement). In contrast, where there is at least one auxiliary as in (20), the word realizing the first auxiliary on the auxiliary valence will act as the categorial head of the whole predicate.

With the revised definitions in (20) and (21), the second partitioning statement in (19b) now makes a substantive claim about natural language predicates: every predicate, whether universally defined or defined in a language-particular fashion, belongs to one and only one of the two subtypes in (20)–(21): this rules out imaginable predicate definitions that would deny the role of categorial head to the first auxiliary on the auxiliary list and also denies the possible existence of predicates where a particle or a subcategorized complement acts as the predicate's categorial head. These are substantive claims about the nature of natural language grammars that can be put to empirical tests and potentially be falsified.

The type *morphological item* also has groups of subtypes that partition it. For instance, the types *derived morphological item* and *underived morphological item* form one such partition. The next chapter will deal with morphological items in detail.

9 Archetypes and Universal Grammar

We conclude this chapter by exploring how the information in archetypes can be transferred from Universal Grammar to individual grammars in the process of language acquisition. This process of *archetype activation* is designed to replace the parameters of the principles and parameters approach. In our view this paradigm has not delivered on its provocative conceptual and empirical promises, despite much rhetoric to the contrary. We begin with a brief discussion of the drawbacks of parameter setting and then illustrate that archetype activation operates in ways which avoid these problems.

9.1 The Overestimation of the Principles and Parameters Approach

Beginning in the late 1970s and early 1980s, Chomsky and others developed the concept of principles and parameters in an attempt to systematically account for similarities and differences between natural languages. Government and Binding Theory became closely associated with this analytical approach, see Chomsky (1981).

A principles and parameters approach to syntax attempts to compile a small list of parametric options in an otherwise completely fixed set of universal principles such that by making different choices from among the options one obtains a possible natural language grammar and each possible natural language grammar can be composed in this manner.

The principles and parameters conception of natural language is very appealing conceptually because in principle it is able to deliver solutions to problems that linguists in general and generative linguists in particular have been concerned with. Three such problems come to mind.

First, there is the problem of what counts as a linguistically significant generalization. Linguistic expressions have properties in many different dimensions, from the physical properties of speech sounds studied by phonetics to their ability to express such vexing semantic concepts as intensionality. By delimiting a fixed set of universal principles of grammar that have to hold in all grammars and a fixed set of universally determined choices where individual grammars can differ from each other, the overall system explicitly constrains which correlations are linguistically significant and which ones are either accidental or significant in some other, non-linguistic, domain (e.g., general memory limitations affecting language processing).

Second, a principles and parameters approach is appealing from the point of view of language acquisition. Assuming the principles and parameters to be innate and available to the learner during language acquisition, the learners are led to process the primary linguistic data they encounter for cues concerning which parametric choices they have to make to generate this data. In other words, among the many possible hypotheses learners could form about the language they are acquiring, they would automatically filter out all those which do not correspond to linguistically significant generalizations.

The third problem is typological: what language types can in principle exist? It should be obvious that a principles and parameters model makes typological predictions via the particular clusters of parametric choices it makes available to individual grammars.

Despite efforts to provide answers to these important questions, the principles and parameters model has not lived up to its promises in practice: presently there does not exist nor is there reason to believe that there will exist a specific proposal for parametric choices that can solve the three problems described above.

One of the reasons leading to this negative assessment is the immense heterogeneity of the individual proposals within the principles and parameters model. While there are many interesting and even inspired analyses of different natural language phenomena offered by *different* versions of the principles and parameters model, there is *no one single version* of the model that can offer the combined insights of all these analyses and still be constrained enough to maintain the vaunted advantages of a principles and parameters model. The difficulties underlying this problem are one of specificity: for any given specific set of data one can set up a constrained system of specific parametric options that provides an elegant account of that specific data. But unfortunately all attempts to generalize from any one specific set of parameters designed for one *specific* set of language-particular facts to a set of parameters that can handle a *general* data sample from the languages of the world have led to unconstrained and unprincipled proliferations of parametric options, mostly motivated by theory internal considerations.[6]

A second reason for questioning the empirical value of the parameters proposed in the principles and parameters model are their inability to make available *comprehensive and concrete* grammatical analyses. In part, this problem is related to the specificity problem referred to in the previous paragraph. As was already indicated there, the parameters proposed in the analyses of the principles and parameters framework haven't really matured from tools for the analysis of restricted sets of grammatical phenomena in particular languages to general purpose tools for general descriptions of natural languages. This is shown most clearly by two developments in the practice of the principles and parameters work in the last decade. (i) The proliferation of so-called 'functional' heads which are found useful in the

---

[6]This issue is discussed in more detail and with concrete examples in Webelhuth (1992) and Webelhuth (1995b).

analysis of some languages but then must either be postulated for all languages or must be viewed as parametric options.[7] If the first choice is made, as is usually the case, then frequently analyses result where invisible and empirically insupportable empty categories are proliferated whose exact properties are not spelled out because they cannot be determined on empirical grounds. This results in incomplete and sketchy analyses that rely on the reader's ability and willingness to connect the analysis to the observable empirical evidence. This is unfortunate, since generative grammars were invented, among other reasons, to overcome certain perceived limitations concerning the impressionism of traditional grammars. (ii) Another serious problem is the increasing diacriticization of parameters in the principles and parameters framework which is due to the combined effects of the proliferation of 'functional' categories and the systematic empirical underdetermination of their properties. Since 'functional' heads are postulated as empty categories in many if not most languages, it is impossible to verify their existence in theory-neutral fashion and equally impossible to verify by observation whether the theory has assigned them the correct properties. As a result, while there were still parameters in the 1980s that were meant to express such substantive and observable linguistic properties as 'head-initial' vs. 'head-final,' in the Minimalist Program of the 1990s parameters almost exclusively express such abstract and non-observable 'morphological' properties as 'strong' or 'weak.'[8]

Concluding this discussion, we briefly mention three additional problems with the principles and parameters theory. First, given that parameters are supposed to capture category-wide or system-wide generalizations of a

---

[7]Spencer (1997), among many others who have thoroughly studied the matter, comes to the following conclusion about the usefulness of 'functional' heads:

"I have examined several aspects of the functional-heads approach to inflectional morphology, and then shown that the patterns of historical change one might expect given this theory are simply not observed. Thus, the theory saddles inflectional morphology with baroque syntactic structures for which no good use can be found. On the other hand, certain patterns are observed which are incompatible with any kind of rigorous interpretation of the model. In particular, those aspects of inflectional morphology which are traditionally problematic for morpheme-based accounts, and especially extended exponence, pose particularly severe problems for the functional-heads variant of the morpheme theory. In addition, the wholesale loss of inflectional paradigms due to shifts in the morphosemantic system cannot be handled on any theory that takes inflection to be conveyed by lexical morphemes. Echoing the words of Henning Andersen (1980), I would argue that the best way to understand historical change and inflectional morphology is to make sure you start out with a decent theory of inflectional morphology in the first place. This entails abandoning the functional-heads approach to inflection."

[8]The source of this development can be located in the theory of pro-drop of Chomsky (1981, 1982). In order to protect the Extended Projection Principle of GB theory which requires that every sentence have a subject from direct empirical falsification by pro-drop languages, Chomsky (1982) postulates phonologically null categories in the subject positions of these languages. The availability of this option was dependent on whether the INFL of this language was 'strong' or 'weak.' While this choice of wording suggests a correlation between pro-drop and the observable properties of inflectional morphology, this is misleading, since what is 'weak' or 'strong' is an abstract AGR feature in INFL. Chomsky never tried to establish a concrete theoretical connection between this abstract diacritical status and any observable properties of inflectional morphology and later attempts to do so [e.g., Jaeggli and Safir (1989)] failed on empirical grounds.

language, it is difficult to account for lexical idiosyncrasies in a principles and parameters type approach, especially in the absence of a commonly accepted theory of lexical entries in that framework. Such lexical studies as Gross (1979) and detailed examinations of lexical items in quality dictionaries [e.g., the German verb lexicon Helbig and Schenkel (1980)] or idiom dictionaries [e.g., the German idiom dictionary Friederich (1976)] point to the empirical requirement that promising theories of grammar must be able to assign rich and often idiosyncratic representations to lexical entries. The principles and parameters approach is almost completely unresponsive to these empirical needs.[9] Secondly, Abney (1996: 2) rightly points out that with respect to language acquisition under standard assumptions of the principles and parameters approach:

we would expect the course of language development to be characterized by abrupt changes, each time the child learns or alters a rule or parameter of the grammar.

This is, of course, empirically false. The same empirically wrong predictions of abrupt changes are made for language change:

We might expect some poor bloke to go down to the local pub one evening, order "Ale!", and be served an eel instead, because the Great Vowel Shift happened to him a day too early. [Footnote omitted.] [Abney (1996: 3)]

To conclude this section: a systematic comparison of the hypothetical insights of the principles and parameters framework with its actual achievements shows a wide gulf between the two. A similar sentiment is expressed in the following quote from a review of the Minimalist Program, the currently fashionable version of the principles and parameters theory [Freidin (1997: 580)]:

The overall character of the minimalist program is highly speculative, as Chomsky notes throughout *MP*. In a recent paper (Chomsky 1996) he is virtually categorical on this point 'There are minimalist questions, but no specific minimalist answers' ... Whatever answers can be discovered will result from following the research agenda of the program. Unfortunately, how this is to be done is rather unclear ...

---

[9] Abney (1996) makes the same point::

"The largest piece of what must be learned is the lexicon. If parameter-setting views of syntax acquisition are correct, then learning the syntax ... is actually almost trivial. The really hard job is the lexicon."

Of course there is a venerable and substantive tradition of lexical semantic analysis within this general approach to language analysis, but the question remains as to how much of a role a generally accepted theory of lexical semantics plays in large numbers of its analyses. (See Levin and Rappaport-Hovav (1997) for an illuminating overview of various approaches to lexical semantics and mapping.)

Contrast the sentiments in the quote above ("highly speculative," "no specific minimalist answers," "how this is to be done is rather unclear") with the following remarks about the Minimalist Program made just two years earlier [Marantz (1995: 380f)]:

... this detailed and highly successful work on a wide range of languages [in GB theory in the early 1980s and since; the authors] has inspired Chomsky to envisage the end of syntax per se... A vision of the end of syntax—the end of the sub-field of linguistics that takes the computational system, between the interfaces, as its primary object of study—this vision encompasses the completion rather than the disappearance of syntax.

In sum, we believe that much of the literature systematically overestimates the value of the principles and parameters framework in several ways:

(22) (i) by pointing to individual successes it has achieved but failing to mention that this success does not generalize to one single inherently consistent theory of grammar of the kind that has been successfully implemented in HPSG or LFG;

(ii) by failing to recognize that many proposals within the principles and parameters framework, despite being articulated in some respects, are ultimately schematic and unlikely to carry over into extended analyses that meet the higher descriptive standards of competing theories like HPSG or LFG;

(iii) by failing to mention that the principles and parameters theory lacks a generally accepted and empirically adequate theory of lexical representations that can deal with lexical idiosyncrasies, idiomaticity, etc.;

(iv) by failing to point to the inability of the principles and parameters approach to account for gradual rather than abrupt changes typical in the processes of language acquisition and linguistic change. In contrast, theories that represent grammatical information in attribute-value form allow the association between attributes and their values to be modeled by the kind of statistical relations that allow gradual transitions between states.

A realistic appraisal of results within the principles and parameters framework encourages one to question foundational assumptions within that approach and to look for alternatives. We believe that a unification-based lexicalist theory offers a better general framework within which to develop an explanatory theory of grammar, and more specifically, a more explanatory theory of predicates.

9.2   Archetype Activation

The previous section argued that the principles and parameters framework has been unable to achieve its central goals and that presently there are no hopeful signs to point to that this evaluation is about to change. This realistic evaluation of the *practice* of this framework does not compel us to dismiss all of its goals, however, because it may be possible to meet some of its attractive and realizable goals in a *different* theory of grammar.

In our view, it seems hasty to claim that because structure theoretic reductions of universal grammatical constraints on linguistic options have failed empirically, there are no universal aspects of linguistic competence. This latter position sometimes seems to be taken in certain parallel distributed processing approaches to language where the goal is to get networks of nodes to induce certain aspects of language without prespecifying the weights of connections between nodes: all weightings between connections and behaviors associated with networks of connections are determined by the data to which the nets are exposed and in the absence of any predisposing biases. (See Rumelhart and McClelland (1986) or Plunkett and Marchman (1991, 1993), but Clark (1993) for a consideration of models with initial weightings of connections). This type of radical empiricist approach is evident as well in some recent conjectures within HPSG by Green (1997) on "emergentist" learning.

Even a superficial consideration of these issues reveals that there is a sufficiently large logical space between the pure nativist and the pure empiricist ends of the theoretical spectrum that we see no reason to choose one of these extreme views, given the incomplete knowledge base that is presently available. In fact we believe that recent research on the perception and segmentation of speech in infants which advocates an approach referred to as "innately guided learning" [see Jusczyk (1997), Mehler and Dupoux (1994)] provides a promising, substantive alternative to these competing extremes. In connection with the type of problem represented by speech segmentation for the child Jusczyk (1997: 76) summarizes as follows:

> The point is that any innate or early capacities that infants possess should allow them to begin to make sense of sound patterns in the input and help them to detect any inherent regularities that are present. In this sense, the initial categorization skills of infants provide a foundation for what might be described as *innately guided learning* (Gould and Marler 1987; Jusczyk 1993; Jusczyk and Bertoncini 1988; Marler 1990).
> The basic notion behind innately guided learning is that many organisms are preprogrammed to learn particular things and to learn them in particular ways.

In domains of language other than speech perception, one might speculate that there are similarly small classes of distinctions that children are predisposed to attend to and that the learning of specific grammars represents the interaction between these predispositions and the distinctions actually made in particular languages. Karmiloff-Smith (1992) provides intriguing speculation about how such interactions may proceed in several domains of grammar (see Mandler (1992) for evidence concerning early abstract conceptual categories).

In our estimation, two facts about language need to be accounted for by an explanatory theory of grammar. On the one hand there *are* linguistic structures that seem to reappear systematically in the world's languages with greater than chance frequency [see Greenberg (1978), Comrie (1981), Hawkins (1983), and others on statistical universals in various grammatical domains]. From the grammatical area that this book is concerned with, we might mention the systematic use in the world's languages of predicates expressing such notions as tense-aspect, passive, causation, etc., as well as the systematic recurrence of synthetic and analytic spell-outs of these notions in different and unrelated languages. On the other hand, an explanatory theory of grammar should also be capable of allowing for purely language-particular structures that seem to be the result of unusual diachronic developments and hence don't recur systematically in other languages.[10] In our view, while the extreme nativist account grossly overstates the similarity between languages, the extreme empiricist view grossly overstates their differences. We are not convinced that the first approach has sufficiently sophisticated tools to account for the myriad micro-differences between languages that lay hidden behind their superficial similarities. On the other hand, we are aware of only a handful of unsystematic attempts to derive significant cross-linguistic generalizations from general cognitive principles. Additionally, within the latter research paradigm there is an absence of convincing and detailed analyses which would make it initially plausible that linguistic universals such as the general form of grammars, i.e., the number and nature of dimensions of linguistic information, the internal structuring of linguistic expressions, the nature of the lexicon as opposed to the syntax, the recurrent clusters of semantic notions with grammatical functions, etc. can be derived without recourse to specifically linguistic principles, either applying universally or in the manner of preference principles.

We cite one of a very long list of examples that could be given here. Proto-Roles and Proto-Properties:

Proto-Agent properties	*Proto-Patient properties*
• volitional involvement in event or state	• undergoes change of state
• sentience	• incremental theme
• causing an event or change of state	• causally affected
• movement (relative to position of other participant)	• stationary (relative to an-another participant)
• exists independently of the event	• does not exist independently of the event or not at all.

---

[10]In chapter 10 we will argue that the intriguing properties of German verb-particle predicates are the result of a diachronic merger of two earlier constructions.

As noted previously in chapter 1, numerous researchers from different theoretical perspectives have identified a small set of "grammatically relevant features or notions" that tend to recur in the languages of the world. For example, Dowty (1991) has argued that SUBJ and OBJ selection in natural languages appeals to the semantic entailments above.

Essentially, the argument of a transitive predicate with the most proto-agentive properties tends to be associated with the SUBJ function, while a co-occurring argument with the most proto-patientive properties is associated with the OBJ function. In this domain there are many imaginable properties of the referent that could, in principle, be appealed to: size, color, danger, usefulness, attractiveness, age, distance etc. All of these represent general cognitive categories accessible to human beings and many of them would seem to have considerable salience and/or topicality. And yet, unlike Dowty's categories, the alternative properties we have listed seem to be routinely ignored in grammatical function selection. A credible theory of language should explain why Dowty's properties (or some augmented set) seem relevant to argument selection cross-linguistically. We believe that regularities such as those evident in argument selection indicate the existence of guiding principles specific to language in linguistic phenomena other than speech segmentation and perception.

In our view, the idea of grammatical archetypes developed in this chapter for classes of predicates, when combined with the concept of a multiple inheritance hierarchy borrowed from HPSG, provides a sensible middle ground between the extreme nativist and empiricist views. It can account for the fact that there is a well defined core of notions and structures that we find in most languages, but that each language significantly extends that core in unpredictable ways.[11] Thus, our quarrel with the principles and parameters theory is not so much with some of its general goals but rather with the practical grammatical tools with which it hopes to realize these goals, as well as with the empirical foundation which motivates many of its claims.

Let us consider how some of the effects of parameters can be achieved with archetypes and inheritance. Our theory draws a distinction between universally available types (archetypes) and language-particular types. The different types can be associated with different markedness values as follows:

---

[11]Our inventory of contentive archetypes is likely to be grounded in the sorts of event structures or conceptual schemata that underlie much recent speculation in the domain of lexical semantics (see Levin and Rappaport-Hovav (1997) for an intriguing exploration and Slobin (1997) for a consideration of prototypical scenes as guiding grammar growth in children).

(23)   General Markedness Values of Types

Less marked archetypes < more marked archetypes <
language-particular types.

Thus, language-particular types are more marked than universally available types and among the universal types we specify on a one by one basis their relative markedness values.

It is natural to assume that the notional predicates which are found to exist in many genetically, areally, and diachronically unrelated languages express content-theoretic information contained in a maximally unmarked universal archetype. Predicates which are still found frequently but which occur more rarely represent more marked universal archetypes, and predicates which are found very unsystematically are language-particular. Note that any particular predicate is probably a mixture of universal and language-particular information but the degree to which a predicate is composed of information belonging to one of the three markedness types will determine its overall degree of relative markedness and, by hypothesis, the frequency with which it is instantiated in the world's languages.

To illustrate these distinctions we anticipate some of the discussion of passive to be found in greater detail in chapter 8. Passives which promote the direct object to subject appear to be the most widely used passives in the world's languages. Our theory will therefore make available an archetype for this kind of passive. Impersonal passives also are found in many languages but they occur more rarely and usually if a language has a construction of this kind, then it will also have the direct object passive. This leads us to propose archetypes for impersonal passives as well and to designate them as more marked variants of the passive predicate construction relative to direct object passives. On the other hand, Baker (1988: 33) mentions that Turkish and Lithuanian have double-passive constructions in the sense that passivized predicates can undergo further passivization. If these are truly multiple applications of passive, rather than merely multiple passive morphology exponence as suggested in chapter 2, this type is so extremely rare in the languages of the world that in our view there would be significant loss in linguistic explanation if a theory of grammar would give this passive the same theoretical status as the systematically attested variations of the passive construction. Our theory draws the relevant distinctions by making available universal archetypes for direct object passives and impersonal passives (where the first are less marked than the second) but failing to make available analogous archetypes for double passivization. All double passives therefore must be language-particular innovations and according to (23) they will incur a higher markedness cost than direct object passives and impersonal passives.

In what follows, we will develop a theory that is designed to explain why certain structures systematically reappear in natural languages and others don't. Theories which are successful in that regard are said to achieve explanatory adequacy. We believe that our approach is explanatorily more adequate than either a principles and parameters approach or a connectionist approach.

Recall that we make a distinction between Universal Grammar and individual grammars. UG, in our conception is not a set of principles and parameters but rather a system of logical and substantive constraints on the types of linguistic representations and inheritance hierarchies. Among others, UG specifies a number of archetypes (content-theoretic, form-theoretic, derivational) which contain information available for use in individual grammars. This informational transfer is accomplished as follows.

Our theory allows for a process of *archetype activation* which consists of two parts:

(24) *Archetype activation =*
    archetype declaration + archetype configuration.

Remember that an archetype is simply a type defined in Universal Grammar. To allow individual grammars to make use of the information in such archetypes,[12] we make available the process of *archetype declaration*. This is a statement in an individual grammar that one of the types in its language-particular type hierarchy is a subtype of a universal archetype. A grammar that declares such an archetype imports all the archetype's information.

As the division into content-theoretic, form-theoretic, and derivational archetypes shows, archetypes usually aren't fully specified signs but contain information about one aspect of a sign, e.g., its content-theoretic information, or whether or not the sign's surface exponence contains an auxiliary, etc. In that sense, archetypes are informationally incomplete: content-theoretic archetypes need to be combined with surface spell-out information to become complete signs and the form-theoretic archetypes need to be complemented with content-theoretic information for a whole sign to result. A second step beyond archetype declaration is thus necessary for an individual grammar to put to use archetypal information: this second step of enriching an archetype informationally we refer to as *archetype configuration*.

Technically, archetype declaration proceeds as follows. Universal Grammar specifies a set of types that are available to all individual languages. In the particular case of lexical combinatorial items, it specifies the

---

[12]Note that individual grammars are *allowed* to make use of archetypes to decrease their degree of markedness but are *not* forced to use all of them. This avoids the significant empirical and conceptual disadvantages of the typical claim of principles and parameters theories that all languages must fit into the same sentence-structural straitjacket.

type *type-of-lci* as the type of all universally available predicate archetypes. On the other hand, individual grammars have to specify the types that they actually use. These types will typically define *patterns* for the productive generation of expression types, e.g., a passive pattern, a third person singular present morphological pattern, etc. To express this pattern quality, we assume that every individual language defines a number of sign pattern types and morphological pattern types. For lexical combinatorial items, we thus assume that each language has a type called *lc-pat (= lexical combinatorial pattern)*.

The following graphs illustrate the archetype activation process that leads to the explanatory transfer of information from Universal Grammar to individual grammars.

(25) The relationship between UG and an individual grammar before archetype activation has taken place:

Universal Grammar: Individual Grammar G:

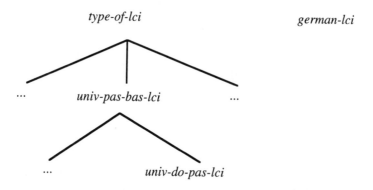

(25) shows the state of the system before the individual grammar has activated any archetypes. The archetypes made available by Universal Grammar are all present but the individual grammar has not made any connections to them yet. In particular, the portion of the universal archetype tree contains an unused universal passive basic lci *(= univ-pas-bas-lci)* and a universal direct object passive lci *(= univ-do-pas-lci)*. These are two functional-semantic predicate types that we will define in detail in chapter 8. For our present purposes, their exact definitions do not matter.

In the next state, we see the result of a language having declared the universal direct object passive archetype.[13] This is done by defining a language-particular lexical pattern type that is constrained as inheriting all the information of *univ-do-pas-lci:*

(26) The relationship between UG and an individual grammar that has declared the archetype *univ-do-pas-lci* via its language-particular type *german-do-pas-lci:*

Universal Grammar:　　　　**Individual Grammar G:**

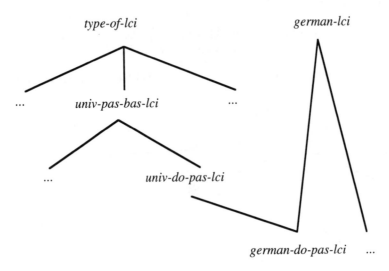

The transition from (25) to (26) represents the first half of the archetype activation process in (24): by declaring a language-particular type which inherits from a universal archetype, a grammar is ensured to contain the information captured by the archetype. Recall, however, that archetypes typically are not complete expressions. In the case at hand, chapter 8 will illustrate that the direct object passive archetype requires that predicates belonging to this type must be derived from active predicates whose subject has been demoted and whose direct object bears the grammatical function of subject in the passive predicate. In the languages where this type is declared, the type functions as a pattern that (productively) relates active predicates to direct object passive predicates. However, given that the archetype is of the content-theoretic kind, specifically of the functional-semantic kind,

---

[13]This illustration of archetype declaration and configuration using the German direct object passive does not accurately or completely reflect our analysis of this construction. The analysis of this passive that we *are* theoretically committed to appears in chapter 8.

it specifies the semantic and functional effects of direct object passivization but does *not* in any way constrain the surface spell-out of the predicate. This has to be done via the second step involved in archetype activation, the step we have referred to as *configuration.*

The representation in (26) thus is only an intermediate step in the full development of a direct object passive pattern in German or any other language. The final representation might look like (27):

(27) The relationship between UG and an individual grammar that has declared and configured the archetype *univ-do-pas-lci:*

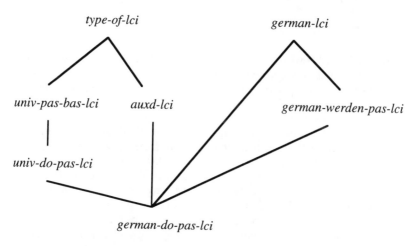

Universal Grammar: **Individual Grammar G:**

At this final stage the German direct object passive predicate type inherits the universal properties of the functional-semantic universal direct object passive archetype and those of the form-theoretic archetype *auxiliated lci.* The form-theoretic arrangement archetype requires that the surface expression of these German predicates consist of a main verb supported by at least one auxiliary acting as the categorial head of the predicate. What the arrangement archetype leaves open is *which* form of the main verb appears in this predicate construction and *which* auxiliary/ies must be present. These two pieces of information are contributed by a third type which *german-do-pas-lci* inherits from, namely *german-werden-pas-lci.* The definition of this type (to be presented in chapter 8) will guarantee that the main verb in the construction under discussion will appear in the participle of the perfect and the auxiliary will be a form of the verb *werden.* An example involving such a predicate is shown in (28):

(28)   weil   die Katze **geküßt wurde**
        because the cat   kissed   was

        'because the cat was kissed'

The two pieces expressing the predicate appear in bold-face: as required, the main verb *küssen 'kiss'* is represented by its participle of the perfect and is supported by a form of the auxiliary *werden*. Note that it is an accident of the German subordinate clause word order in (28) that the two pieces of the predicate are adjacent. (29) shows that they can be separated in main clauses and therefore that they don't form an inseparable morphologically created lexical unit:

(29)   Die Katze **wurde** oft   **geküßt**
        the cat   was   often kissed

        'The cat was kissed often'

A final look at (27) will show that the analysis of the German direct object passive predicates is composed mostly of chunks of information predefined in the form of archetypes by Universal Grammar: the German predicate inherits both its functional-semantic content and the form-theoretic arrangement of the words in its surface spell-out by declaring universal archetypes. Besides these archetype declarations, the grammar of German need only specify the precise lexemes and their morphological categories to complete the definition of the predicate pattern. Given the design of the system, we would expect many other languages to make use of the same functional-semantic and arrangement archetypes but we have no expectation that any language uninfluenced by German will spell out its predicates with a combination of the participle of the perfect and a form of the auxiliary *werden*. This last information is completely language-particular and there is no markedness advantage to any language to reuse these precise forms.

Under the right assumptions about markedness, however, a language does benefit from archetype activation instead of defining its own language-particular types that contain the same information as some archetype. One approach that goes in the right direction is the following constraint on evaluation metrics:

(30)   Let A be some aspect of a language-particular predicate P. Then A contributes less to the markedness cost of P if P inherits A from a universal archetype than if P specifies A as part of its language-particular definition.

What (30) requires of any evaluation metric is that it rewards languages for using the information in archetypes. With respect to a construction like passive, we thus make the following predictions: (i) passive is an archetype and thus potentially accessible to all natural languages; (ii) not all natural languages need to have a passive construction;[14] (iii) the most frequently attested passives are those resulting from the activation of the most unmarked passive archetypes in UG (the direct object passive); we expect to find more marked instantiations of passive archetypes (e.g., impersonal passive) systematically but infrequently in the world's languages; language-particular passive constructions like the double passives of Lithuanian that don't correspond to any universal passive archetype result in the highest markedness cost by (30) and therefore should be found most rarely in the languages of the world.

10   Conclusion

In this chapter we have argued that whereas some of the main goals for positing parameters in principles and parameters approaches are laudable, the actual record of results is weaker than advertised. We have presented as an alternative a single, comprehensive framework which makes it possible to represent systematically recurring components of grammatical information in the form of archetypes. These archetypes are viewed as universal templates that individual grammars can but do not have to use. We have also provided a principled means by which particular languages can partake of the universal inventory of archetypes, while also exhibiting their own idiosyncratic properties: archetype activation is responsive to markedness factors in language. Our theory makes available powerful and precise representational devices for lexical entries and therefore is able to achieve adequacy for all regular formations as well as for domains of lexical idiosyncrasy and idiomaticity that make up much of a native speakers' knowledge of their language.

This flexible theory of archetypes thus seems a promising and plausible answer to the questions as to why languages can be so much alike, while also differing quite broadly from one another. It also provides a way of accounting for why a single language can exhibit degrees of regularity with respect to specific constructions.

---

[14]Keenan (1985, 247) mentions languages in New Guinea, Chadic languages, and Tamang (Sino-Tibetan), Isthmus Zapotec (Oto-Manguean), and Yidin (Australian) as languages that lack a passive construction. See the passage cited for references to sources.

5

Morphology and Lexical Representations

1 Introduction

The present chapter develops the morphological assumptions underlying our analysis of predicates. As in Jackendoff (1975, 1995, 1997), we assume that lexical representations of predicates are not solely expressible by synthetic morphological objects. Instead, our formalism endows predicates with several "categorial slots" for morphological words that in combination function as the surface expression of the content of that predicate (what we have also called the predicate's *form-theoretic aspect*). The reader will recall that the following slots are available for that purpose:

(1) Morphological spell-out slots in the structures of predicate signs[1]

$$
\begin{bmatrix}
lci \\
\\
\text{SYNSEM}
\begin{bmatrix}
\text{CSTRUC}\begin{bmatrix} \text{CR } word \end{bmatrix} \\
\\
\text{VAL}
\begin{bmatrix}
\text{AUX } list-of-word\,(possibly\,empty) \\
\text{PART } list-of-word\,(possibly\,empty)
\end{bmatrix}
\end{bmatrix}
\end{bmatrix}
$$

From a morphological point of view, a predicate minimally must be associated with a morphological word that spells out the predicate's categorial core. A predicate with this minimal morphological specification (i.e., whose auxiliary and particle lists are empty), is a *synthetically expressed predicate*. If either of a predicate's auxiliary/particle lists is non-empty, then we are dealing with an *analytically expressed predicate*. The present chapter deals with the grammar of the morphological words that can serve as categorial cores and as members of the auxiliary and particle valences of lexical predicates.

Our theory of predicates employs a word and paradigm (WP) model of morphology that incorporates many of the insights from Anderson (1992), Aronoff (1976,1994), Bochner (1993), Carstairs (1987), Matthews (1972, 1991), Stump (1991), Orgun (1995, 1996), Riehemann (1993, to appear), Börjárs et. al. (1996), Zwicky (1990), and others. This type of

---

[1]In addition, there is the path SYNSEM:CSTRUC:HD. However, the value of this path is identical to one of the other paths and hence does not contribute any independent morphological information.

morphological system fits naturally into our assumptions about parallel levels of linguistic representation whose constituent elements do not necessarily stand in a one-to-one relationship with each other. Just like our theory allows one predicate content to be expressed by more than one categorial word in a syntactic representation, a word and paradigm morphology allows one morphosyntactic feature to be expressed by any number of morphological pieces ("affixes"). The parallelism between the two cases is brought out in (2)–(3) below.

Example (2) shows that the single morphosyntactic content (= meaning) of future tense is expressed by a combination of two word-sized morphosyntactic forms in German: to find the syntactic expression of the future tense of any predicate P, one first finds the infinitive of the morphological lexeme that corresponds to the predicate P and makes it the categorial core of the predicate; then one finds a present tense form of the lexeme *werden* 'to become' (depending on the person-number of the predicate's subject) and adds it to the predicate's AUX valence.

(2) Violations of one-to-one mapping in the syntax

Future tense in German—one meaning is expressed by a combination of two forms which are potentially discontinuous in phrase structure:

Schematic:

Future = (infinitive of main verb) + (present form of auxiliary *werden)*

Example:

fragen + wird
(ask-inf) + (will-3-sg-pres)

Example (3) illustrates the same kind of absence of a one-to-one relationship between morphosyntactic features and the morphological forms that express them. For one class of morphological lexemes in German, to create the word form that expresses the single morphological feature of the participle of the perfect, a stem has to undergo two morphological processes, one which prefixes the phonological material *ge* to the stem and another one which suffixes *t* to it.[2]

---

[2]We reemphasize: future tense is a semantic concept and German does not have a morphological category that corresponds to it, since this semantic concept is expressed by a combination of words in German. Participle of the perfect is not a semantic concept, however, but a morphological category in this language. The word forms belonging to this paradigmatic category enter into the expression of predicates with various meanings and functions, e.g., the active predicative participle of the perfect, passives, etc. Our use of the name "participle of the perfect" for this morphological category follows traditional usage but is potentially misleading insofar as it suggests that the morphological category itself is associated with the meaning of the participle of the perfect. Much confusion has arisen

(3) Violations of one-to-one mapping in the morphology

Participle of the perfect in German—one morphosyntactic feature is expressed by two forms (phonological operations of prefixation and suffixation):

Schematic:

Part. perfect = (prefix: *ge)* + (participle stem of lexeme) + (suffix : *t)*

Example:

ge + **frag** + **t**
(prefix: *ge)* + (participle stem of lexeme *ask)* + (suffix : *t)*

Mismatches as in (3) present obvious and long-standing problems for a system of morphology that seeks to store morphological information in morphemes and views the morphological information of complex words as the sum of the morphological information in their pieces or a function thereof. Which piece of a German participle of a perfect bears the information "participle of the perfect", the prefix or the suffix? Worse yet, other languages signal certain information by truncating parts of words. Again, which piece of the word could be said to carry the additional information—the truncated piece?[3]

---

because other theories do not make a clean distinction between the meaning of a predicate and the morphological forms that spell out the predicate. The crucial relationships are as follow. *Signs* have content-theoretic and form-theoretic aspects. *Morphological words,* in contrast, have no meaning per se but become indirectly associated with meanings because they form the spell-out of predicate signs *which do have meaning.* Reference to a form such as *gefragt* in (3) of the main text as the "participle of the perfect" is thus justified in the sense that this word form is used as the core of the categorial expression of a predicate whose meaning is a perfect (in combination with a supporting auxiliary). However, the "participle of the perfect" might instead be referred to as the "participle of the passive," since the same word form is involved in the expression of passive predicates. Throughout, the reader should resist the impulse to attribute contentive or grammatical-functional information to words and see words as pure pieces of morphological form (e.g., *gefragt)* that are characterized by morphosyntactic features (e.g., 'participle of the perfect' of the lexeme 'fragen') through which predicates bearing meanings and functional inventories find their categorial surface expression.

[3]The same phenomenon exists not only in morphology but at the level of signs as well. Den Besten (1989: 60ff) discusses the case of "Haben/sein Deletion" illustrated by examples like the following:

(i)   daβ er noch nicht gekommen (ist)
         that he yet   not   come   has

         'He has not come yet'

(ii)   -- warum er geweint (hat)
         -- why   he wept   has

         '-- why he has wept'

By adopting a word and paradigm organization of the morphological module, our theory of predicate formation achieves an attractive conceptual unification of the grammatical domains that govern the structure of predicates (as the grammatical units that bear meanings and function inventories) and the structure of morphological words (as the grammatical units that express predicates). The conceptual unification consists of the uniform design decision to strictly separate the *functions* that a grammatical unit performs from the *form* through which this unit is expressed. By not arbitrarily tying functions to certain forms, form does not take primacy over function in either the predicate or the word domain and we can capture generalizations across grammatical units performing the same functions even if the units are expressed very differently either in their phrasal or their morpho-

---

Den Besten comments: "An archaic rule of German syntax deletes the finite forms of the temporal auxiliaries *haben* and *sein* (in this case *hat* and *ist* respectively) only if these are in sentence (or at least VP) final position... Both rules are optional."

Crucially, the two sentences mean the same and have the same function inventories *whether the auxiliary is present or not!* This causes no problem for our theory of predicates. For each of (i) and (ii) we can postulate a lexical entry for a predicate with the meaning and function inventory necessary to capture the semantic and grammatical-functional properties of the sentence. In addition, we will specify that the perfective auxiliary is optional in the form-theoretic aspect of these predicates. Consequently, the predicate's meaning and functions are expressed no matter whether the auxiliary appears in the sentence, since this information is part of the *content-theoretic aspect* of the predicate and this information is conveyed no matter how many words make up the predicate's *form-theoretic aspect*. This simple and intuitive treatment is possible because our theory gives primacy of function over form.

Contrast this with the difficulties that the phenomenon illustrated with (i) and (ii) causes for form-based approaches to predicates, in particular theories of syntactic predicate formation like Hinrichs and Nakazawa's HPSG approach or the various LFG approaches mentioned in chapter 1 which allow independent constituent structure co-heads to contribute their combined information to a functional structure associated with a single clause nucleus. According to these approaches, in the version of the sentences (i) and (ii) where the auxiliary is present, the tense-aspect meaning of their predicates would result from the presence of the auxiliary in the syntax, with the main verb contributing a tenseless description of a coming event in (i) and a weeping event in (ii) and the auxiliary contributing the tense-aspect. By tying the tense-aspect meaning in (i) and (ii) to the auxiliary *form* rather than to the lexical representation of the *functional* predicate as a whole, these theories have no natural account of why the meaning of the sentence does not become non-tensed when the auxiliary is left out of the sentence. The only recourse would seem to be the postulation of another lexical entry for participles of the perfect which assigns them the same meaning that would be created by syntactically combining them with a perfective auxiliary. Why there should be two predicates, one created in the lexicon and the other one in the syntax, that have identical meanings and identical main verb forms but differ in whether or not they contain an auxiliary remains mysterious, however. The linguistically significant pattern that in some constructions the perfective auxiliary (be it *haben* or *sein*) is optional is the result of the postulation of three distinct predicate constructions, two of which are formed in the syntax by combining a perfect-participial main verb with either the auxiliary *haben* or *sein* and another unrelated lexical construction which happens to apply to perfect-participial main verbs as well. By insisting that predicate form takes analytical precedence over predicate content, it is impossible to locate all three predicate constructions in one component and thereby to capture the contentive and formal identities that hold across them.

Den Besten (op. cit.: 18f), following Andersson and Dahl (1974), cites another construction where these theories would fail in the same way and for the same reason: "There is an optional rule in Swedish that deletes the auxiliary *ha* (have) in subordinate clauses only."

phonological makeup. According to our grammar design, the primary question is always "What grammatical information does a predicate or a word carry?" and only then do we ask "How many words express the form of this predicate," or "How many 'affixes' express a given morphosyntactic feature in this word?" In this sense, our theory gives primacy of function over form generally.[4]

---

[4]The general conception of morphology that guides the present proposal has been called *separationist* by Aronoff (1994: 8), following the work of Beard (1981, 1995). Aronoff (1994: 8) stresses that a word based morphology treats sound and meaning as separate systems, while the concept of the morpheme is based on an isomorphism of sound and meaning beyond the morpheme.

While the morphological conception we use follows Beard and Aronoff in being word based rather than affix based, it nevertheless differs in one crucial respect from their overall stance. In order to solve the problem that the morphosyntax/meaning of a word does not stand in a one-to-one compositional relationship to the word's internal arrangement of morphemes, these authors "lift" the attachment of these *functional* properties from the lower *form* level of the morpheme to the higher *form* level of the word (hence, the name *word based morphology* or *lexeme based morphology*). We go one radical step further and end up with a theory which we believe to be qualitatively different. We accept that there are no affixes as bearers of morphosyntactic information, meanings, or function inventories and consequently that it is wrong to view the morphosyntactic properties of words to be the result of combining the morphosyntactic features of the roots, stems, and affixes contained in the word. Where we do not agree, however, is that morphosyntactic information has the same grammatical status as meaning and function inventories in that they are all attached to form at the morphological word level. Instead, we assume that morphosyntactic information is information about *form* and hence *is* tied to morphology (at the word level); meanings and function inventories, in contrast, are *contentive,* however, and are attached to grammatical *functional* units such as predicates and clauses. As we have been arguing throughout, none of these *functional* units are tied to any specific level of *form.* In particular, the contentive information associated with a predicate is *not* to be associated with only a single *form* level of expression, i.e., the word [the same is, of course, true for functional clauses, i.e., there are languages where the clausal information which requires a whole sentence to express in English (e.g., "I like you") is expressible by a single morphological word].

We are set apart in the same way from Matthews (1991: 219) which gives a pertinent discussion of Latin active and passive predicates in several tenses:

"In Latin, schoolboys learned *amo* 'I love' as Present Active, *amor* 'I am loved' as Present Passive, *amavi* 'I loved' as Perfect Active, but then *amatus sum* (a form consisting of a Masculine Nominative Singular Participle, *amatus,* and the form for 'I am', *sum*) as the Perfect Participle. The last is clearly two words, which obey separate syntactic rules (for example, of agreement). Nevertheless, they are taken together as a *term* [emphasis added by FA and GW] in what are otherwise morphological oppositions."

This Latin data, like the dozens of other cases we discuss elsewhere in this book, shows that it doesn't help to merely lift the level of form from morpheme to word at which meanings and function inventories are attached. The opposed terms that Matthews refers to in the last sentence are not terms of *form,* be it morphemic, word-sized, or phrasal, but rather terms of *function,* i.e., predicates bearing meanings, active or passive voice, etc. Even though Matthews seems to realize this, he comes to the following confusing conclusion about the Latin data (1991: 221):

"... the essential point is that in such cases the paradigm of a lexeme, which is basically a morphological concept, is extended beyond the word."

By referring to the lexeme as a "morphological" concept, Matthews seems to accept the traditional distinction between syntax and morphology based on something like our principle of the Morphological Integrity of words presented in chapter 1. Yet, simultaneously he makes the claim that the paradigm of a lexeme is "extended beyond the word." Clearly, the

The following table attempts to illustrate how we see the division between form and function in both the predicate and the morphological systems:

(4) Form and function of predicates and words

Domain	Function	Form
Predicates	the contentive aspect of the predicate, i.e., its meaning and its function inventory	its categorial core, the auxiliaries and particles needed to express the predicate in the syntax
Words	the morphosyntactic features the word expresses, e.g., 'participle of the perfect'	the word's morpho-phonological structure, e.g., that it was created by simultaneous prefixation and suffixation to a stem

2 Predicates and the Words that Express Them

A lexicon in our theory consists of two separate but interacting modules: a sign module containing all the lexical combinatorial items and a morphological module containing all the morphological roots, stems, and words. Both modules should be understood as "intelligent" in the sense that they are not merely long static lists of items with all their irregularities but instead are the repositories of the underived predicates/words of a language plus the set of patterns of forming new predicates/words from old ones. It is precisely by building and putting to use a powerful lexical engine using state of the art knowledge representation techniques that we can maintain the strong kind of lexicalist theory of grammar described in chapter 1 and yet derive powerful linguistic generalizations that are often thought to be derivable only with highly syntacticized grammars.

'paradigm' under discussion cannot be a morphological paradigm, because each member of such a paradigm by Morphological Integrity is no larger than a word.

As before, the problem is that Matthews does not cleanly enough separate morphosyntactic information such as being a participle of the perfect from predicate information such as having a passive functional structure. He locates both of these kinds of information in "basically a morphological concept," i.e., a unit of form. (See Behrens (1995/1996) for similar considerations.)

The confusion dissipates immediately once we recognize the following important distinction: morphosyntax is a way of categorizing *word-sized* units of *form*, but meanings, voice, and function inventories are ways of specifying *predicates* whose *content* is realized by one or more word-sized units identified via their morphosyntactic profiles.

In this section we will lay out how the two modules of the grammar, the sign module and the morphological module interact with each other. It is clear that information has to be able to flow between the two modules somehow, because otherwise we couldn't guarantee that a predicate sign in the sign module that has a present tense meaning and a third person singular subject will be realized morphologically by a word form characterized as third person singular present as opposed to some other person-number-tense combination.

The interaction between the sign module and the morphological module should be constrained as follows: a predicate or predicate pattern has to be able to signal to the morphological module that it requires a form of a specific lexeme that satisfies a description articulated with features such as part of speech, person, number, gender, etc. Following Pullum and Zwicky's (1988) principle of phonology-free syntax, the sign should *not,* however, be able to specify the particular morphophonological operations (e.g., "Add the suffix *s"* to spell out the plural of English *dog* as opposed to "Add the suffix *ren"* to spell out the plural of *child)* that are used to compose the shape of the word that satisfies this featural description. This goal can be achieved by giving morphological words the schematic structure in (5) which we already saw in chapter 3 in connection with our discussion of the spell-out of signs:

(5) The structure of a derived word

$$
\begin{bmatrix}
word & \\
& MS \begin{bmatrix} \text{LME} & \textit{the lexeme the word is a form of} \\ \text{POS} & \textit{the word's part of speech} \\ \text{PHON} & \textit{the word's pronunciation} \\ \text{INFL} & \textit{the word's inflection} \end{bmatrix} \\
& \textbf{MDTR} \quad \textit{the morphological source of the whole word}
\end{bmatrix}
$$

(6) contains a concrete exemplar of such a morphological word, the word that realizes the categorial core of a first person singular present tense usage of the German predicate meaning 'kiss.' The representation encodes that this finite form of the lexeme *küssen* is morphologically derived from the present tense stem of the same lexeme. By comparing the phonology values of the input and output we see that the phonology of the finite form is created by the morpho-phonological operation of suffixing 'e' to the phonology of the input stem.

(6) The 1-sg-pres form of the German lexeme *küssen* 'kiss'

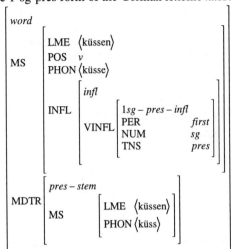

To achieve a phonology-free syntax, we have to make sure that (i) the sign module of the lexicon does not have access to the value of the phonology attribute of words and (ii) does not have access to the derivational history of words from which the phonological operations that have applied to a word would be recoverable. To this effect, we formulate the constraint in (7):

(7) The Morphological Accessibility Constraint

A sign or sign pattern can only constrain the attributes LME, POS, and INFL in a morphological word.

Given the constraint in (7), no predicate formation operation and no syntactic operation should in any way depend on the phonological makeup or the phonological history of an expression. For instance, the syntactically determined word order of English plural nouns should be independent of whether the noun forms its plural regularly or irregularly. This of course does not rule out that the phonology of an expression influences sentence structure or even word order, as long as that word order is not syntactically determined. For instance, one can imagine a case where a clitic needs to cliticize onto a prosodic host with particular phonological properties. In a given sentence, the word order of the clitic might be restricted, but crucially by factors which are phonological and not syntactic.

With the general structure of words in (5) and the Morphological Accessibility Constraint in (7), we can now illustrate how the sign module and the morphological module work together to create predicates with their correct surface spell-outs, be these surface spell-outs synthetic or analytic.

In chapter 7 we begin to discuss predicate formation patterns in detail. Among the first patterns that we will study will be the different tense-aspect realizations of basic predicates, including the past tense and the perfect. As (8) and (9) illustrate, the past and perfect tense realizations of the basic predicate meaning 'ask' are synthetic and analytic expressions involving word forms of the lexeme *fragen:*

(8)   weil   Maria Hans **fragte**
      because Maria Hans ask-3-sg-past

      'because Maria asked Hans'

(9)   weil   Maria Hans **gefragt**   **hat**
      because Maria Hans ask-part-perf has-3-sg-pres

      'because Maria has asked Hans'

In anticipation of the morphological needs of these predicate formation operations whose other details will be postponed until chapter 7, we will here illustrate how the morphological system creates the various word forms of the lexeme *fragen* which appear in (10):

(10) The morphological paradigm of the lexeme *fragen*

	Predicative use	Attributive use
Finite forms:		
present	frage, fragst, fragt, fragen, fragt, fragen,	
past	fragte, fragtest, **fragte**, fragten, fragtet, fragten	
bare infinitive	fragen	
zu infinitive	zu fragen	zu fragende, zu fragender, ...
part. perfect	**gefragt**	gefragte, gefragten, ...
part. present	fragend	fragende, fragenden, ...

Note that the two forms of *fragen* which appear in (8) and (9) are bold-faced in the paradigm (10).

Without going into unnecessary detail at this point, let us consider why it is illuminating to compare the predicates in (8) and (9): they have one interesting property in common but differ in two interesting ways. What they have in common is that from a contentive point of view, the two predicates are very similar. They share the same basic meaning and assign the same semantic roles. In addition, they govern the same grammatical functions (one subject and one direct object), assign the same cases and semantic roles to these grammatical functions, and they both agree with the subject in person and number. Regarding morphosyntactic content, they both add a tense-aspect component to the basic atemporal meaning of the predicate. The morphosyntactic contents expressed by the past tense and the perfect in German are very similar, in fact in Webelhuth's dialect (9) substitutes for (8) in colloquial speech (but not vice versa).[5] From a content-theoretic point of view, these two predicates thus have identical or nearly identical structures. Form-theoretically, they differ in two interesting respects, however. One is that the past tense predicate is expressed by a single word that is specialized to express past tense meanings *(fragte)*, whereas the perfect predicate is expressed by a combination of the participle of the perfect of the lexeme *fragen* and the third person singular present of the lexeme *haben* which here represents an auxiliary sign. The second interesting difference is purely morphological. The word form *fragte* has a relatively unremarkable derivational history:

(11a) The morphological derivation of the word form *fragte*

    a. The root of the lexeme *fragen* is *frag*.

    b. The past stem of the lexeme *fragen* is formed by suffixing *t* to the lexeme's root: *frag + t = fragt*.

    c. The 3-sg past tense word of the lexeme *fragen* is formed by suffixing *e* to the past stem of the lexeme *fragen*: *fragt + e = fragte*.

(11b) The morphological derivation of the word form *gefragt*

    a. The root of the lexeme *fragen* is *frag*.

    b. The perfect stem of the lexeme *fragen* is identical to the lexeme's root: *frag*.

    c. The 'predicative participle of the perfect' word of the lexeme *fragen* is formed by simultaneously prefixing *ge* and suffixing *t* to the perfect stem of the lexeme *fragen*: *ge+ frag + t = gefragt*.

Recall from our earlier discussion in (3), however, that the morphological form of the participle of the perfect *gefragt* is more interesting in that it in-

---

[5] Some dialects of German mostly avoid the past tense form in favor of the perfect form throughout.

volves a case of overlapping exponence: the single morphosyntactic feature of 'participle of the perfect' is expressed simultaneously by the prefix *ge* and the suffix *t*. The derivational history of that word is shown in (11b).

We now proceed to show (i) how the content-theoretic similarities of the predicates in (8) and (9) can be captured by assigning them representations in the sign module that are nearly identical; and (ii) how the surface spell-out differences between these two predicates fall out from the form-theoretic aspects of their sign representations and the inventory of morphological patterns in the morphological module of the German lexicon.

(12) provides a simplified representation of the third person singular past tense predicate meaning "ask." This is a predicate (= lexical combinatorial item, lci) in the sign module of the German lexicon. Rather than being listed as an underived lexical sign, it will be shown to be the product of a general predicate formation pattern that takes untensed predicates as input and returns tensed predicates like (12) as output:

(12) The third person singular past tense predicate meaning "ask"

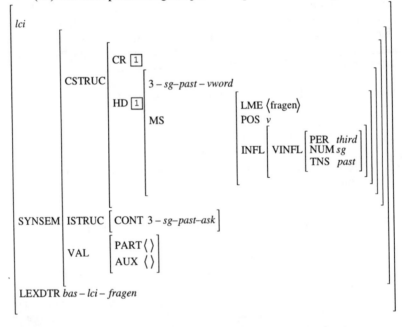

A few things are noteworthy about this predicate representation: the LEXDTR specification indicates that this predicate is derived from the basic combinatorial item *fragen*, i.e., the basic meaningful predicate *fragen* (not to be confused with the morphological lexeme *fragen!*). The value of the path SYNSEM:ISTRUC:CONT identifies the meaning of the predicate as a past event of asking whose subject is a third person singular asker. When we will present the representation for the perfect version of this predicate below, we will see that the value of its CONT attribute will be very similar: *3-sg-perf-ask,* the only difference being the value of the tense-aspect feature. In addition, if we were to represent the functional structure and the valence of the two predicates, we would find them to be identical. From a contentive point of view, the past and perfect versions of the predicates will thus structurally be nearly identical.

This leaves us with the form-theoretic aspects of (12). Note that the particle and auxiliary valence lists are both empty, making (12) a synthetically expressed predicate. The particle list is empty because the basic predicate *fragen* does not draw on a particle lexeme in its spell-out and hence none of its derived forms do either. The auxiliary list is also empty and this is due to the interaction of the basic properties of the predicate *fragen* and the predicate formation operation that forms past tense predicates: this particular predicate pattern does not add any auxiliaries to the spell-out of the newly formed predicate but instead requires that the categorial head of the new predicate bear the verbal inflection in (13):

$$(13) \quad \begin{bmatrix} \text{PER } \textit{third} \\ \text{NUM } \textit{sg} \\ \text{TNS } \textit{past} \end{bmatrix}$$

Since the basic predicate *fragen* does not have an auxiliary and the past tense predicate pattern does not add one, the auxiliary list of the newly formed predicate must be empty.

However, as we see, the predicate does specify the morphological word form that acts as its categorial head (and because there is no auxiliary, also the categorial core). Any morphological word that can act as the categorial core/head of this synthetically expressed predicate must be compatible with the following structure:

$$(14) \quad \begin{bmatrix} 3-sg\text{--}past-vword \\ \\ \text{MS} \quad \begin{bmatrix} \text{LME } \langle \text{fragen} \rangle \\ \text{POS } v \\ \\ \text{INFL} \begin{bmatrix} \text{VINFL} \begin{bmatrix} \text{PER } \textit{third} \\ \text{NUM } \textit{sg} \\ \text{TNS } \textit{past} \end{bmatrix} \end{bmatrix} \end{bmatrix} \end{bmatrix}$$

The predicate imposes restrictions on the three attributes that it is allowed to constrain in accordance with the Morphological Accessibility Constraint in (7): (i) it requires the word form to be taken from the morphological paradigm of the lexeme *fragen;* (ii) it specifies that the word form belong to the part of speech verb; and (iii) the word form must bear verbal inflectional features identifying it as a third person singular past tense form.[6]

It is at this point that the task of the morphological module of the lexicon begins. (14) is not a fully specified data structure of a morphological word. Because of the Morphological Accessibility Constraint, predicates aren't allowed to make reference to the phonological or daughter information of morphological words, as a consequence of which they systematically underspecify the morphological representations that act as their morphological spell-out slots [see (1)]. The privilege of taking basic morpho-phonological forms and applying morpho-phonological operations to them and pairing the resulting forms with morphosyntactic information like that contained in (14) is reserved for the morphological module of the grammar.

Our lexicon thus consists of two modules: one module contains a set of underived predicates and patterns to form new predicates. Another module contains a stock of underived morphological items and patterns for forming new morphological items. Items in the sign module have various morphological spell-out slots through which they constrain the words that can act as their categorial spell-outs. The morphological module contains (either as underived items or as the output of a morphological pattern) complete word representations that can fill the spell-out slots of predicates in the sign module. The Morphological Spell-out Constraint in (15) assures that each morphological spell-out slot of any predicate is eventually filled by a fully specified morphological word from the morphological module of the lexicon:

(15) The Morphological Spell-out Constraint

If a predicate P is the head daughter of a syntactic phrase, then each morphological spell-out slot of P is filled with an entry of the morphological module of the lexicon.

According to (15), once a predicate is to used in the syntax, each of its morphological spell-out slots must contain a fully formed morphological word that satisfies the constraints the predicate lexically imposes on that spell-out slot. In our specific case, this means that the morphological representation in (14) which represents the constraint the predicate in (12) imposes on the morphological spell-out of its categorial core/head will be enriched to the morphological representation in (16) which now contains the phonological string that actually represents the word:

---

[6]In case the reader is wondering why we specifically identify the inflectional features as "verbal" via the attribute VINFL, a look at the paradigm in (10) will show that verbs in German can carry both verbal and nominal inflection, depending on their use. Thus, the predicative participle of the perfect *gefragt* bears only verbal inflection, but its attributive counterpart (in the second column) in addition bears the nominal inflectional marker *e* to signal agreement with the noun its predicate modifies when it is used attributively. In the case we are presently discussing, we only need to mention verbal inflection, since finite verbs are unable to carry any other inflection.

$$
(16) \quad
\begin{bmatrix}
3 - sg\text{--}past - vword \\[2ex]
MS \quad
\begin{bmatrix}
\text{LME} \quad \langle \text{fragen} \rangle \\
\text{POS} \quad v \\
\text{PHON} \langle \text{fragte} \rangle \\[2ex]
\text{INFL} \quad
\begin{bmatrix}
\text{VINFL} \begin{bmatrix} \text{PER} \; third \\ \text{NUM} \; sg \\ \text{TNS} \; past \end{bmatrix}
\end{bmatrix}
\end{bmatrix} \\[4ex]
MDTR \qquad \ldots
\end{bmatrix}
$$

(16) is the representation of the word form *fragte* that represents the synthetically expressed predicate (12) in sentence (8).

Let us then turn to sentence (9) and ask what the representation of its predicate would look like. Recall that we wish to capture the similarity in content between the predicates in (8) and (9) but at the same time account for the spell-out differences (synthetic vs. analytic) and the morphological differences (repeated suffixation vs. circumfixation) that exist between them.

In chapter 7 we will formulate a perfect tense-aspect predicate formation pattern that creates the entry (17) [here simplified] in the predicate module of the German lexicon. As mentioned earlier, from a contentive point of view, this perfect predicate is almost identical to the past tense predicate in (12): the content attribute specifies a different tense-aspect for the predicate but both predicates refer to the same basic event, they have identical f-structures and valences (neither shown here).

Despite this near-isomorphy of the contentive aspects of these two predicates, they differ in how they are expressed. As will be shown in chapter 7, the predicate formation pattern that creates perfect predicates like (17) from basic predicates like *fragen* affects two morphological spell-out slots of the new predicate: first, it requires that the categorial core of the new predicate be realized by the participle of the perfect of the lexeme specified in the categorial core; second, it prefixes an auxiliary to the new predicate's auxiliary list and requires this auxiliary to be spelled out by a present tense form of the lexeme *haben*. Both of these restrictions can be observed in (17). Together they model the traditional insight that German predicates form their perfect tense-aspect through a combination of the "main verb" appearing in the participle of the perfect and a present tense form of the auxiliary *haben*.[7]

---

[7]Some predicates form their perfect with the auxiliary *sein*. We will ignore this distinction for the purposes of the following illustration.

(17) The third person singular perfect tense-aspect predicate meaning "ask"

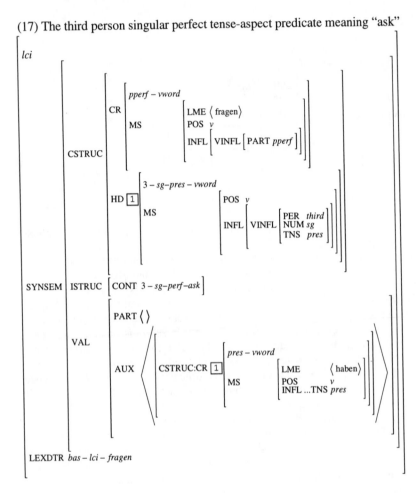

(18) $\begin{bmatrix} \text{MS} & \begin{bmatrix} pperf - vword \\ \begin{bmatrix} \text{LME} \langle \text{fragen} \rangle \\ \text{POS} \quad v \\ \text{PHON} \langle \text{gefragt} \rangle \\ \text{INFL} \begin{bmatrix} \text{VINFL} \begin{bmatrix} \text{PART } pperf \end{bmatrix} \end{bmatrix} \end{bmatrix} \end{bmatrix} \\ \text{MDTR} \quad \dots \end{bmatrix}$

Once the predicate in (17) is used in a syntactic context, only one word created by the German morphological module is compatible with the restrictions that (17) imposes on the morphological spell-out of its categorial core. This is the word in (18).

Since there is an auxiliary on the auxiliary valence list in (17), the word in (18) must be accompanied by an auxiliary word for the predicate in (17) to be syntactically expressed. Which form of the auxiliary *haben* must be chosen? Note that the auxiliary valence restricts the word to any present tense morphological form of the auxiliary *haben*. However, recall that in auxiliated predicates, the first auxiliary on the auxiliary list serves as the predicate's categorial head. Since (17) is a third person predicate, the categorial head slot requires that the categorial head carry these morphological features. In other words, the word spelling out the categorial head of (17) must meet the unification of the constraints that this predicate imposes on its categorial head and the first auxiliary on its auxiliary list [this is signaled by the tag ⊡ of (17)]. The resultant constraints appear in (19):

$$
(19) \quad \begin{bmatrix} 3-sg-pres-vword \\[2ex] \text{MS} \quad \begin{bmatrix} \text{LME } \langle \text{haben} \rangle \\ \text{POS } v \\ \text{INFL} \begin{bmatrix} \text{VINFL} \begin{bmatrix} \text{PER } third \\ \text{NUM } sg \\ \text{TNS } pres \end{bmatrix} \end{bmatrix} \end{bmatrix} \\[2ex] \text{MDTR} \qquad \ldots \end{bmatrix}
$$

The only word in the morphological module of the German lexicon that fulfills all these constraints is (20):

$$
(20) \quad \begin{bmatrix} 3-sg-pres-vword \\[2ex] \text{MS} \quad \begin{bmatrix} \text{LME } \langle \text{haben} \rangle \\ \text{POS } v \\ \text{PHON } \langle \text{hat} \rangle \\ \text{INFL} \begin{bmatrix} \text{VINFL} \begin{bmatrix} \text{PER } third \\ \text{NUM } sg \\ \text{TNS } pres \end{bmatrix} \end{bmatrix} \end{bmatrix} \\[2ex] \text{MDTR} \qquad \ldots \end{bmatrix}
$$

The combination of the participial word in (18) and the auxiliary (20) forms the surface spell-out of the perfect predicate (17) as it is used in sentence (9).

3 Morphological Patterns

We have described what role the morphological module of the lexicon plays in the overall grammatical system: it contains morpho-phonological forms that are labeled with such morphosyntactic information as (i) the lexeme whose paradigm the form belongs to, (ii) the part of speech of the form, and (iii) the inflectional properties of the form. The predicates in the sign module of the grammar specify these three kinds of information for their morphological spell-out slots and the Morphological Spell-out Constraint in (15) ensures that each slot is spelled out in the syntax by the morphological word that the morphological module associates with this morphosyntactic information.

An important aspect of both the morphological submodule and the sign submodule of the lexicon is that they are "intelligent" in the sense that they are not mere lists of items but rather have tools for the generation of new items from old ones which in principle are as productive as the tools of syntactic phrase formation. We have already referred to these tools as *patterns* on several occasions. In this section, we will illustrate how these patterns work in the morphological module. It should become clear what we mean when we say that our theory of grammar incorporates a powerful "lexical engine" (however, the other half of that power, the predicate formation patterns, will only be discussed in chapter 7).

Let us take as a starting point the third person singular word form *fragte* in (16). Clearly, any theory that merely lists this lexical entry without relating it to other items misses several important generalizations that a good linguistic theory should capture. First, as the morphological paradigm of the lexeme in (10) shows, *fragte* is part of a morphological system of forms based on the same lexeme. There are many other such morphological systems whose structure is isomorphic to the system in (10), e.g., the morphological paradigm of the lexeme *glauben* 'believe.' By listing (16) in isolation, we fail to capture the systematic recurrence of isomorphic morphological systems throughout the morphological module of German. Secondly, by failing to tie (16) and all similar forms to a larger pattern, we have no account of native speaker intuitions about new forms entering into their vocabulary. Without effort, speakers who have internalized the German morphological system are able to create all the morphological forms of a new lexeme they have just learned.[8] Third, if all words were listed independently of patterns, it would be hard to explain why frequently all of them undergo certain (diachronic) changes together, e.g., the assimilation in voic-

---

[8]This is an oversimplification that only applies in cases where there is exactly one regular and productive pattern. In other circumstances, several patterns may compete with each other and then native speakers' intuitions may be less clear. Thus, even in that circumstance we have evidence that speakers try to associate words with larger patterns.

ing of the English noun plural marker, the optionality or loss of inflectional affixes, etc.[9]

The morphological patterns that we will postulate will address all three of these issues. They serve to reduce the isolation of words in the morphological module by integrating them into larger linguistic structures that can be formally described with the same modern knowledge representation techniques that we are using throughout the grammar: typed feature structures organized into hierarchical multiple inheritance hierarchies.

The existence of patterns (whether they are morphological patterns or sign patterns) has the same rationale as the existence of archetypes in universal grammar. In fact, patterns are best thought of as language-particular archetypes and the universal archetypes are best thought of as patterns that have universal validity. The difference is not so much one of kind but of scope of application. What makes patterns and archetypes functionally equivalent is that both devices serve to reduce the amount of independence ("arbitrariness", "entropy") in natural languages in the sense discussed above in connection with the desirability of relating morphological words to larger patterns in the morphological module. Both archetypes and patterns weave linguistic units into larger groups and allow for the formulation of generalizations across all members of the group. The groups can be thought of as natural classes of elements which are likely to behave alike in certain synchronic and diachronic respects. This creates a higher conformity among the items in a module than would be the case in the absence of archetypes or language-particular patterns and therefore reduces the average amount of information that needs to be stated independently for each unit. From a functional point of view, it is easy to see the advantages of why a knowledge representation system should be organized in this way. Since it is known that generally human beings can memorize things more easily that have affinities to other things they already have memorized, an organization that systematically weaves individual units into larger patterns that hold across them facilitates the acquisition of similar units. The postulation of archetypes (which have universal scope and get the assimilation and generalization process started in the beginning when no language-particular patterns are available yet to assimilate to) and the language-particular patterns therefore not only have strong typological and language-internal motivation but can in addition be functionally motivated as well.

Let us examine, then, what we need to postulate to see (16) not as an isolated entry in a "dumb" lexicon that statically lists all entries in isolation from each other but in an "intelligent" system that is able to dynamically

---

[9]To cite a concrete case, in Webelhuth's German the final schwa of the first person singular present tense ending is optional across verbs (*ich lache* ~ *ich lach* 'I am laughing'). This alternation is not phonologically conditioned, since the final schwa of the first person singular past tense ending is obligatory, e.g., *ich lachte* ~ **ich lacht* 'I was laughing.' Verbs ending in *t* allow optional schwas in the present tense, showing that the obligatoriness of the schwa in the past tense cannot be blamed on the preceding alveolar stop: *ich schalte* ~ *ich schalt* 'I am switching.'

account for the native speaker's recognition and productive use of larger patterns.

We begin by taking another look at the paradigm of the lexeme *fragen* in (10). It is easy to see that all the members of that paradigm are formally similar to each other and the same similarities can be shown to hold if we look at the paradigms of other regular German verbs. In particular, it is possible to define a set of patterns over the members of the paradigm that allow all members to be generated from one single listed form that underlies all the other forms. And the same patterns that are postulated for (10) will extend to organize the paradigms of the other hundreds or thousands of regular German verbs, making it possible to list no more than one single form for each paradigm. In light of such an organizing effect, the utility of having patterns available to a grammar should be obvious.

There are several ways that one can organize a paradigm of the kind in (10) and it is not obvious to us that there is one unique best organization or that all speakers necessarily use the same organization. We will sketch one paradigmatic organization that is simple and that has been shown to be consistent through a computer implementation. According to this organization, every verbal morphological paradigm contains one root form from which three stem forms are derived which in turn underlie all the remaining forms of the paradigm. The roots and stems for *fragen* are presented in (21):

(21) The roots and stems of the lexeme *fragen*[10]

Root: *frag*

Present Stem:	*frag*
Past Stem:	*fragt*
Perfect Stem:	*frag*

(22) The verb root "fragen"

$$\begin{bmatrix} vroot \\ MS \begin{bmatrix} LME & \langle fragen \rangle \\ POS & v \\ PHON & \langle frag \rangle \\ INFL & no-infl \end{bmatrix} \end{bmatrix}$$

---

[10]Note that we postulate the root, the present stem, and the perfect stem to be identical. Instead, we could have postulated only one of these three types, e.g., the root and derive all the forms from it which in the present system we derive from the two stems which are identical with it. For many irregular verbs, we would need to postulate additional stems, however, since the identities there don't hold. There are no empirical differences that follow from the various design decisions, as far as we can tell. In any event, each system can easily be changed into the other one if that is thought to be desirable.

Let us assume that only the root *frag* is listed as an underived morphological item in the morphological module of the German lexicon. Following the general format for morphological items that we have postulated, its entry would have the structure in (22).

The type *vroot (= verb root)* is a subtype of the type *morphological item* which has other subtypes such as *vstem, vword,* similar types for non-verbal parts of speech, and more specialized subtypes such as *3-sg-pres-vword.* Lacking the attribute MDTR, the verb root is an underived morphological item which is what we want since the verb root is supposed to be listed as the keystone of a morphological paradigm from which all other members of the paradigm are derived via morphological patterns. Like all morphological items, (22) has the attribute MS which specifies the morphosyntactic attributes of the morphological item. From top to bottom, (22) specifies that this verb root is a form of the lexeme *fragen,* that its phonological spell-out is the list of characters <frag>, that the root's part of speech is verb and that it carries no inflectional features.

Assuming similar listed entries for the roots of all regular German verbs, we now need morphological patterns that can take these root representations as input and for each root derive the three stems mentioned in (21). We will present the patterns for the present and past stems, since the treatment of the perfect stem will be trivial once we have handled the phonologically identical present tense stem.

What is a morphological pattern, then? Not surprisingly, no more than just another morphological subtype of the type *morphological item.* In contrast to the *vroot* subtype which we see in (22), the pattern types must be *derived morphological items* rather than the *underived morphological items* which list the underived items in the morphological module of the lexicon. (23) shows a small and highly simplified part of the type hierarchy that illustrates these differences in status for the German system under discussion:

(23)

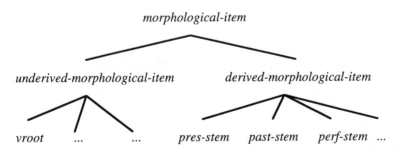

The crucial difference between underived and derived morphological items is that the latter have an additional MDTR attribute missing in the former which allows derived items to specify the properties of an underlying morphological item from which the whole item is derived. In (24) we see the type *past-stem* as an example of such a derived morphological item:

(24) The German past stem pattern

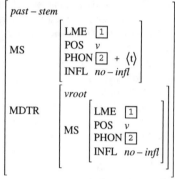

Note that the type in (24) not only specifies that the past stem has a morphological daughter (MDTR) but in addition constrains the properties of this morphological daughter and how the daughter's information contributes to the information in its own MS (= morphosyntax). Note that (24) can be viewed as a lexical rule written from bottom to top rather than from left to right. This can be seen by comparing its structure with the following lexical rule:

(25) A lexical rule that has the same effect as the pattern in (24)

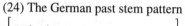

The left-hand side of the lexical rule in (25) imposes conditions on the item that serves as input to the derivation. The value of the MDTR attribute in (24) serves that same purpose. The role of the output of the derivation is played by the right-hand side of the lexical rule in (25) and the whole structure in (24) excluding the bottom attribute-value pair. Using pattern types like the one illustrated in (24) allows us to apply the tools we have available in our grammar anyway and to dispense with lexical rules altogether.

It is now easy to see how we can generate the content of the past tense stem slot of the paradigm whose verbal root is the listed entry in (22)

or any other similar listed root. Applying the morphological pattern (24) to
the morphological item (22) means to unify (22) as a whole with the value
of the MDTR slot of (24). The result of doing this looks like (26):

(26) The result of applying the past stem pattern (24) to the verb root (22)

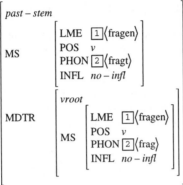

Note that the pattern in (24) leaves the identity of the lexeme and the
phonology of both the MDTR and the whole structure unspecified but constrains the relative values of LME and PHON in the mother and the daughter
of the structure. The lack of specification of a value identifying a particular
lexeme is what gives (24) the status of a morphological pattern rather than a
specific morphological item. By applying this pattern to the verb root in
(22), the pattern's MDTR comes to be identified as the verb root of the lexeme *fragen,* as can be seen in the lower half of the representation in (26).
The LME and PHON attributes of the morphological daughter in (26) are
now instantiated to the LME and PHON values of the verb root of *fragen.*
As a consequence, the values of the corresponding attributes of the mother
structure now are instantiated as well: since the pattern type requires that the
mother inherit the daughter's LME value, the mother is now identified as a
morphological form of the lexeme *fragen* as well. Secondly, since the past
tense pattern specifies that the mother's phonology is the result of suffixing
the list of characters <t> to the list of characters making up the phonology
of the verb root, the mother's phonology comes to be fully specified as
<fragt>. The result is a data structure of a specific morphological item,
namely the past tense stem of the lexeme *fragen,* with a specific
phonological representation.

Had we applied the pattern in (24) to a verb root other than that of
fragen, we would have received the past tense stem of that lexeme instead.
We can guarantee that this system is completely general by stating the following principles:

(27)   The Fundamental Morphological Inventory

        The morphological module of the lexicon contains a finite fundamental morphological inventory of underived morphological items.

(28)   The Morphological Inventory of Language L

        A. If M is a member of the fundamental morphological inventory of a language L, then M is a member of the morphological inventory of L.

        B. If M is a member of the morphological inventory of L and MP is a morphological pattern type of L, then the result of applying MP to M, if well-formed, is also a member of the morphological inventory of L.

        C. Nothing else is a member of the morphological inventory of L.

(27) and (28) guarantee that besides the fundamental underived morphological items (cf. [28A]), all and only the derived morphological items which can be derived from other morphological items by the morphological patterns of a language are contained in the morphological inventory of this language (cf. [28B–C]).

In the concrete case of the pattern (24), this means that for any (regular) verb root that is listed in the fundamental morphological inventory of the German lexicon, the morphological inventory not only contains that verb root but also a past tense stem for the same lexeme which is phonologically identical to the verb root. Having available the past stem of *fragen* in (26), it is now easy to see that by formulating additional morphological patterns that take the past stem as input and forms specified for the various person-number combinations as output we can derive all the past tense forms of *fragen* in the paradigm (10), in particular the third person singular past tense word *fragte* in (16) which we had set out to generate with the help of patterns. The same is true for any other regular verbal lexeme of German.

With this result in hand, let us turn to the other word form we wanted to account for, the participle of the perfect in (18). This is somewhat more interesting from a morpho-phonological point of view, since the derivation of this word specifies simultaneous prefixation and suffixation of phonological material. Assume that we have already derived the perfect stem of *fragen* and that it is phonologically identical to the verb root in (22). We can feed this stem into the following word formation pattern deriving participles of the perfect from perfect stems (for regular verbs):

(29) The German 'Participle of the Perfect' pattern

$$
\begin{bmatrix}
pperf - vword \\[2ex]
\text{MS} \quad
\begin{bmatrix}
\text{LME} \quad \boxed{1} \\
\text{POS} \quad v \\
\text{PHON} \langle ge \rangle + \boxed{2} + \langle t \rangle \\[1ex]
\text{INFL} \begin{bmatrix} \text{VINFL} \begin{bmatrix} \text{PART } pperf \end{bmatrix} \end{bmatrix}
\end{bmatrix} \\[4ex]
\text{MDTR} \quad
\begin{bmatrix}
perf - stem \\[1ex]
\text{MS} \begin{bmatrix}
\text{LME} \quad \boxed{1} \\
\text{POS} \quad v \\
\text{PHON} \boxed{2} \\
\text{INFL} \quad no - infl
\end{bmatrix}
\end{bmatrix}
\end{bmatrix}
$$

Applying this pattern to the perfect stem of *fragen* which differs from (22) only in belonging to the type *perf-stem* rather than *vroot*, yields the following morphological word:

(30) The pattern (29) applied to the perfect stem of *fragen*

$$
\begin{bmatrix}
pperf - vword \\[2ex]
\text{MS} \quad
\begin{bmatrix}
\text{LME} \quad \boxed{1}\langle fragen \rangle \\
\text{POS} \quad v \\
\text{PHON} \langle gefragt \rangle \\[1ex]
\text{INFL} \begin{bmatrix} \text{VINFL} \begin{bmatrix} \text{PART } pperf \end{bmatrix} \end{bmatrix}
\end{bmatrix} \\[4ex]
\text{MDTR} \quad
\begin{bmatrix}
perf - stem \\[1ex]
\text{MS} \begin{bmatrix}
\text{LME} \quad \boxed{1}\langle fragen \rangle \\
\text{POS} \quad v \\
\text{PHON} \boxed{2}\langle frag \rangle \\
\text{INFL} \quad no - infl
\end{bmatrix}
\end{bmatrix}
\end{bmatrix}
$$

A comparison of (30) and (18) shows that (30) is merely more specific than (18) in that it not only shows the output structure of the word but its morphological relation to the perfect stem from which the participial word is derived.

4 Morphological Patterns and Paradigms

At this point we have derived the two bold-faced words in the paradigm of the lexeme *fragen* in (10). Extending the system to cover the full paradigm is mostly a routine matter. For each of the other forms in the paradigm we will have to decide from which base they are derived by which operations. Each morphological pattern can thus be seen as specifying a general relation between four things: (i) a morphological input type, (ii) a morphological output type, (iii) the inflectional features of the newly created output, and (iv) the phonological operations that need to be applied to the phonology of the input to yield the phonology of the output. In this way, each pattern generates new morphological items that can either be fed into yet other morphological patterns or can be used to fill one of the morphological spell-out slots of a predicate in the sign module of the lexicon.

We will conclude this chapter by reflecting on an aspect of our morphological system that we have not mentioned yet but which it is important to appreciate: morphological patterns as types of morphological items which happen to be lexemically underspecified are types like all others. As such, they have the same privileges as other types which are not patterns. In particular, their types can be hierarchically organized into a multiple inheritance hierarchy where lower types can inherit information from their various supertypes. This property allows us to capture generalizations across morphological patterns that a traditional system with morphological rules is unable to capture, since the properties of one rule cannot be made dependent on the properties of another rule.[11]

Another look at the paradigm in (10) will suggest several applications of the availability of grouping morphological patterns together under more general morphological patterns. Note, for instance, that all six patterns creating the various person-number combinations for the past tense take the past tense stem as their input. We can capture this similarity between the six past tense patterns by postulating the *past-vword* pattern in (31) and the part of the inheritance hierarchy in (32).

By inheriting from their common mother type in (31), all the types at the bottom of the type tree in (32) are committed to using the same past tense stem as the base of the person-number word their pattern outputs (note that (31) fills in the TNS value for all six subpatterns but leaves the specification of PER and NUM to the individual subpattern).

---

[11]Note that this criticism does *not* apply to a system that encodes morphological patterns in lexical rules conceived of as typed feature structures that allows one lexical rule to be a subtype of other lexical rules. Copestake (1992) has developed such a system. The criticism is valid, though, for theories of grammar whose morphology fails to draw on typed feature structures organized in an inheritance hierarchy.

(31) The German *past-vword* pattern

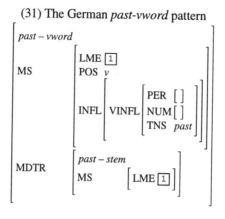

(32) A part of the German morphological hierarchy

past-vword

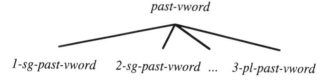

1-sg-past-vword   2-sg-past-vword   ...   3-pl-past-vword

5 Conclusion

In this chapter we have laid out the general structure of the morphological module of the lexicon. It consists of a fundamental morphological inventory which is a list of underived morphological items and a set of morphological patterns that may have various degrees of productivity. The application of the patterns to morphological items groups these items into paradigms. The grouping of patterns under more general patterns makes it possible to capture generalizations across subparadigms. Each morphological pattern creates a new morphological item which contains information about the item's phonological form combined with values for the morphosyntactic features LME, POS, and INFL which are selectable by predicates in the sign module via their various morphological spell-out slots. Any phonological operation or combination of phonological operations can be invoked by a morphological pattern in the derivation of a new type of morphological item. This makes it possible for violations of one-to-one mappings between morphosyntactic information and morpho-phonological operations of the kind that was illustrated in (3). Other morpho-phonological operations that our version of the word and paradigm model of morphology can handle but that are problematic for traditional morpheme-based systems include operations that change the phonology of the input rather than adding a phonologically constant string of segments, i.e., truncations, metathesis, and reduplication.

6

The Architecture of Our Theory of Predicates

In the previous five chapters we have motivated the need to recognize the construct predicate and introduced the fundamental representational apparatus for a lexicalist theory of predicates. Chapter 1 introduced the challenges we are concerned with in this book, in particular the challenge of designing a theory of predicates that is capable of capturing that certain contentive structures (where 'contentive' covers both meaning and the projection of grammatical function inventories) systematically recur in the world's languages even though they find a wide range of surface expressions. Crucially, these surface expressions comprise realizations of morphologically synthetic words and collocations of words (e.g., verb + auxiliary, verb + particle) lacking the morphological integrity of morphological words. It was shown that both classical versions and certain recent versions of lexicalist theories like LFG and HPSG are unable to provide a unified account of predicates that alternately can express their content synthetically or analytically. The source of the problem was shown to be due to the interaction of two theoretical commitments of these early lexicalist theories: on the one hand, they enforced the principle of Lexical Adicity which made it possible for the lexicon but withheld from the syntactic component the privilege to create new predicates with new argument structures. On the other hand, both LFG and HPSG imposed the principle of Morphological Expression which requires that every lexical entry be expressed by a single morphological word. The combination of these two principles made it impossible to account naturally for the systematic recurrence of predicates with equivalent content but different expression types: the contentively equivalent predicates could not all be represented in the lexicon because lexical entries were not allowed to be analytic but they could also not all be represented in the syntax because that would frequently have required the postulation of syntactically created argument structures.

In order to account for the wide-spread existence of analytically expressed predicates, recent HPSG [cf. Hinrichs and Nakazawa (1989, 1994)] and one strand of research in recent LFG [cf. Alsina (1993)] has abandoned the prohibition against syntactic predicate formation. As was shown in chapter 1, this amounts to an identification of lexicalism as a purely morphological concept: each lexical entry is expressed as one morphological word and only the lexicon but not the syntax is allowed to form morphological words. The other traditional component of lexicalism, namely the functional component which identified the lexicon as the exclusive grammatical component that creates and stores the units which function as the contentive heads of functional domains such as clauses, was simply abandoned.

Chapter 1 took the position that cleansing lexicalism of its traditional functional component and the inevitable syntacticization of predicate formation represent an unwarranted and unilluminating revision of classical lexicalism in the search of an analysis of analytically expressed predicates. We objected to this move on two grounds, both conceptual.

First, we believe that the principle of Lexical Adicity forms the conceptual heart of lexicalism according to a general theory design where the lexicon creates meaningful and f-structure bearing predicates and the syntax expresses these predicates in categorial structure and combines them with their arguments and modifiers. In our view, the nature of the argumentation for a lexicalist conception of grammar in early LFG bears this out. Most of the arguments that Bresnan and others brought forth in the late 70s and early 80s sought to present evidence that grammatical function changes or agreement/government phenomena which were handled with syntactic transformations in transformational grammar are better handled with lexical rules. Bresnan (1982b) is dominated by arguments of this kind from phenomena as diverse as passive, the dative alternation, clitics, causativization, long-distance agreement, secondary predicates, sluicing, and many more. A second strand of argumentation was morphological but can be seen as a consequence of the strongly functional orientation of lexicalism just discussed. By making lexically listed predicates the contentive heads of functional domains such as clauses and by mediating the relationship between a predicate and its arguments (theta marking, agreement, case government, etc.) via lexically specified grammatical functions that the arguments bear to the predicate, the theory had equipped the lexicon with all the information that was necessary to restrict all word formation to the lexicon. Thus, the push towards defining the function of syntax as the component which forms phrases but not words in our view was a natural byproduct of the development of more sophisticated lexical techniques originally designed to realize the conception of functional lexicalism. One kind of argument is virtually absent from the early argumentation for lexicalism: no empirical or conceptual arguments were presented that all lexical entries had to be expressed by single morphological words. With hindsight this asymmetry is very noticeable but presumably has the following simple explanation: while early LFG gave up the tool of transformations, it retained the use of phrase structure rules for the creation of syntactic phrase structure, including the conception that the phrase structure rules generate a tree with a set of word-size terminal nodes that must be filled by units from the lexicon. In the absence of any conflict on this issue between early LFG and the transformational theory it was trying to set itself apart from, it was presumably felt that there was no need to specifically motivate the restriction against lexically represented predicates that are categorially spelled out by several syntactically independent words. In sum, we believe that the functional aspect of lexicalism forms its conceptual heart and that the argumentation in early lexicalist theories bears that out. The arguments for the morphological aspects of lexicalism that were presented typically revolved around the prohibition against syntactic word formation and are the natural conceptual consequence of the powerful new lexical tools that had been designed to realize functional lexicalism. In contrast, the prohibition against multi-word lexical entries does not seem to have been, or to even have followed from, any *essential* aspect of lexicalism but was merely a function of LFG's adoption of classical phrase structure rules for the formation of syntactic phrases and the assumption that lexical insertion, as standardly construed, guided the interaction between the lexicon and the syntax. (See Jackendoff (1997) for a critical appraisal of "lexical insertion" within generative frameworks.)

In the light of the foregoing discussion it should become clear why we caution against the wholesale abandonment of the principle of Lexical Adicity in recent HPSG and some versions of recent LFG. We believe that this principle is the conceptual heart of lexicalism and that Morphological Integrity is a secondary consequence of functional lexicalism, whereas the restriction against analytically expressed lexical entries was never an essential aspect of lexicalism to begin with. By reducing lexicalism to its morphological aspects, one abandons its core motivation in favor of its secondary and non-essential aspects. As observed in chapter 1, we believe that this drastic move should only be made as a last resort, once all other alternatives of handling complex predicates that do maintain the core principle of lexicalism have demonstrably failed. Our claim is that the theory of predicates presented in this book maintains the core of lexicalism and yet is able to deal with the grammar of complex predicates.

In fact, this brings us to the second conceptual argument against abandoning functional lexicalism. By allowing predicate formation in the lexicon and in the syntax both recent LFG and recent HPSG are now able to handle both synthetically and analytically expressed predicates. However, because theories of this sort retain an arbitrary constraint against multi-word lexical entries, they still lose linguistically important generalizations when one and the same or obviously related predicates can be variously realized synthetically or analytically. Examples of this phenomenon are presented throughout this book. Here we will only remind the reader of one that was discussed in the previous chapter. At one stage in the history of German, perfect predicates in subordinate clauses could either be expressed by a participle-auxiliary combination or by the main verb in its participial form alone. In other words, the auxiliary was only an optional part of the surface realization of the predicate in subordinate clauses like (1):

(1)   – warum er geweint (hat)
        – why   he wept   has

'-- why he has wept'

As we explained in the previous chapter, the sentence in (1) has the same tense-aspect meaning, the same functional inventory, and the same valence whether the auxiliary is present in phrase structure or not. We also pointed out that a theory that abandons the functional restrictions on lexicalism can create the synthetic predicate *geweint* in the lexicon and the analytic predicate *geweint hat* in the syntax with exactly the same content. What such a theory is unable to do, however, is to *relate* the two predicates and thereby to capture naturally the intuition that we are dealing with one and the same predicate that can be expressed with an optionally present auxiliary.

We thus claim two conceptual advantages of our theory of predicates over the alternatives that we have discussed. First, our theory fully maintains the functional core principle of lexicalism and the attendant principle against syntactic word formation that is a natural consequence of a lexicon that handles the functional aspects of predicates. The alternatives sacrifice the functional core principle of lexicalism and reduce lexicalism to a combination of a secondary morphological principle and a weakly motivated constraint against analytically expressed lexical entries. The second advantage we claim is that by failing to restrict predicate formation to a single grammatical component and splitting it between the lexicon and the syntax, the alternatives to our theory still are unable to provide unified accounts for contentive heads that are intuitively felt to be predicates that happen to permit both synthetic and analytic surface expressions. In contrast, our theory can directly associate one predicate with both synthetic and analytic surface expressions and does not have to rely on the accidental coocurrence of one set of lexical rules and another set of syntactic rules that produce predicates in different components containing the same content.

Following the conceptual motivation of a theory of predicates in chapter 1 that separates the content of predicates from the way they are expressed, chapter 2 has presented a large number of empirical syntactic and morphological arguments for this general theory design. In chapters 3–5 we began to implement our theory by discussing the general structures for signs, both lexical and phrasal, and words that we employ. Finally, the previous chapter detailed the internal structure of the morphological module of the lexicon and how this module interacts with the lexicon's sign module. We emphasized that the morphological module consists of two parts, a fundamental morphological inventory and a set of morphological patterns (construed as types of derived morphological items) which interact to recursively create the paradigms of underived morphological items. Each member of such a paradigm is an individual morphological word that is specified for a phonological representation and characterized in terms of values for the three morphosyntactic attributes LEXEME, PART-OF-SPEECH, and INFLECTION through which predicates in the sign module of the lexicon constrain which morphological words can spell out their various morphological spell-out slots.

We have not yet discussed predicate formation patterns in the sign module of the lexicon in detail. We will start doing this in the following chapter. At this point it suffices to say that the sign module of the lexicon is isomorphic to the morphological module: as in morphology we draw a distinction between a fundamental predicate inventory and a general predicate inventory. The items in the fundamental predicate inventory are underived predicates (i.e., predicates that are not created by a pattern) whereas the items in the general predicate inventory are derived by the application of patterns to other predicates. These patterns have the same general structure as the morphological patterns but differ crucially in that the patterns in the predicate module of the grammar are predicate formation patterns. In other words, whereas morphological patterns map morphological items into other morphological items, predicate patterns map contentive units (i.e., units expressing meanings and bearing functional structures) into other contentive units. In the same way that several morphological patterns can create a morphological paradigm by being traceable to the same item in the fundamental morphological module (e.g., the patterns that collectively create the morphological paradigm of the lexeme *fragen* in (10) of the previous chapter), a number of predicate formation patterns can collectively create a predicate paradigm of a predicate in the sign module of the lexicon.

As we will show in the upcoming chapters, German has a basic predicate *küssen* 'kiss' and a number of predicate formation patterns that collectively create a predicate pattern for this predicate. A small part of this paradigm is shown in (2):

(2) A small fragment of the predicate pattern of the basic predicate *küssen*

Predicate Pattern	Surface Spell-out
3-sg-pres active	*küßt*
1-sg-perf active	*geküßt habe*
2-pl-future-perf active	*geküßt haben werdet*
2-sg-future active causative	*wirst küssen lassen*
1-pl-pres active causative	*küssen lassen*
3-sg-past werden-passive	*geküßt wurde*
3-pl-pres middle	*sich küssen*
...	...

On the left hand side we find the contentive characterizations of the predicates that the pattern creates and on the right the combination of morphological words that must appear together in the sentence in order for the output predicate's constraints on its morphological spell-out slots to be satisfied. Each predicate pattern thus does two things: it specifies the content of the output predicate (i.e., its functional-semantic content, its morphosyntactic content, and its functional structure) and for each of the morphological spell-out slots it determines whether the slot is filled and if so what LME, POS, and INFL values the word filling the slot must have. By allowing predicates to have several morphological spell-out slots (cf. (1) of the previous chapter), two predicates can belong to the same subparadigm of a predicate paradigm and yet be spelled out by a different number of morphological words. Several examples of this occur in (2): the first two predicates simply specify different slots in the tense-aspect paradigm of the predicate *küssen* (present vs. perfect) but the first predicate's pattern gives the predicate a synthetic spell-out whereas the second pattern requires an auxiliary-main verb combination for the perfect predicate.

The overall design of our theory thus sharply separates the content of predicates from their surface expression. This leads to the prediction that many different surface spell-out types can be functionally equivalent in that they are all capable of signaling predicates with equivalent contents. For instance, we would expect to find that instead of the auxiliary-main verb combination of German, other languages might use a particle-verb combination to express their perfects. Again other language might use synthetic spell-outs resulting from varying phonological operations: prefixation, suffixation, ablaut, reduplication, truncation, etc. This book and the literature in general provide systematic evidence for the morpho-phonological and syntactic variability of the same predicate notion.

However, while the morpho-phonological or syntactic spell-out type of an individual predicate is subject to Saussure's doctrine of the arbitrariness of the sign and hence in general unpredictable, one *can* specify a small number of predicate notions, arrangement types for predicates, and morpho-phonological operations that systematically recur in the world's natural languages. These recurring structures seem to be particularly natural components of natural language grammars, even if for most of them we cannot require that every language must instantiate them (unless we trivialize the issue by postulating them as observationally empty elements whose presence is not empirically verifiable). We find such recurrent patterns in each of the three domains we just mentioned: in the semantic domain we find such functional-semantic structures as active and passive predicates throughout the languages of the world as well as such morphosyntactic contents as tense-aspect; in the arrangement domain of predicates we find synthetically expressed predicates, auxiliary-verb combinations, and particle-verb combinations; in the morphology, we systematically find concatenative operations like prefixation and suffixation.

In order to capture the generalization that certain predicate contents, spell-out configurations for predicates, and morpho-phonological operations applying to the words that are part of the spell-out configurations of predicates systematically recur but are freely combinable with each other, we have postulated the existence of a number of archetypes in chapter 4. These archetypes are designed in an component-specific way, i.e., they don't cross the boundaries from one conceptual grammatical domain to any other. For instance, there are archetypes expressing contentive notions like passive or tense. Given their contentive nature, these archetypes do not refer to any other than contentive information, i.e., synthetic vs. analytic spell-out arrangements or morpho-phonological operations. The same is true for the other kinds of archetypes.

As explained in the previous chapter, the role of the archetypes is similar to the role of the various patterns that our theory postulates: they function as focal points in the vast space of potentially possible contents, arrangements, and morphological forms around which grammatical units must cluster in order to be valued highly by our evaluation metric. The postulation of grammatical archetypes is a compromise between the extreme nativist and empiricist positions which claim without serious empirical support that most features or no features of language are universal. In a sense, the archetypes represent the cautious null hypothesis about language typology because they allow us to avoid the blind leaps of faith that the rhetoric of extreme nativists ["All languages really have the same structure, we just can't demonstrate it (yet)."] and empiricists ["General cognitive and cultural properties conspire to motivate all recurring specific linguistic structures, we just can't demonstrate it (yet)."] demand from us. The archetypes represent empirically motivated classes of generalizations that all theories need to address. The large challenge, of course, is to provide analyses of these phenomena and then to motivate the elements of one's analyses in cognitively plausible ways. Our task is the modest one of trying to identify some important archetypes in the domain of predicates and to provide a vocabulary adequate to represent them and their language-particular instantiations. Questions concerning the possible cognitive underpinnings of the theory we propose are answerable mainly with respect to non-linguistic issues which we cannot address.

Diagram (3) at the end of this chapter represents the various modules that an individual grammar contains according to our theory of predicates as well as a characterization of how the modules interact with each other. The arrows indicate where units from one (sub-)component are put to use in another component. For instance, the two horizontal arrows specify that morphological words (whether derived or underived) have the role of filling spell-out slots in entries of the sign module, i.e., predicates (whether derived or underived).

From the formulation of the available syntactic patterns it follows that the syntax is unable to form new predicates *(Lexical Adicity)* or new morphological words *(Morphological Integrity)*. Their function is to create the phrase structure configurations in which predicates can realize their morphological spell-out slots and combine with their arguments and modifiers. The data structures associated with predicates require them to have a least one morphological spell-out slot for their categorial core and additional optional ones for auxiliaries and particles. This design makes it possible in principle for a predicate to be expressed by an indeterminate number of morphological words as its spell-out. A markedness convention on arrangement archetypes values non-auxiliated and non-particled predicate spell-outs more highly than spell-outs with auxiliaries and particles. The combined effect of the structure of predicates and these markedness conventions is that predicates can be spelled out by more than one word but preferably are spelled out synthetically (this is the principle of *Morphological Expression* from chapter 1).

With our grammar design now complete, we turn to the final part of the book which is dedicated to the case studies of various contentive archetypes and their realizations in different natural languages.

(3) The Architecture of the Theory of Grammar
Proposed in this Book

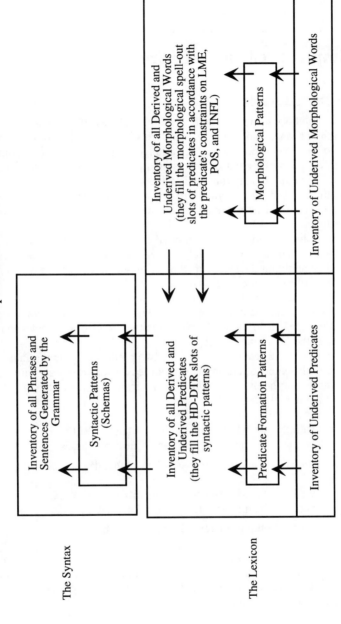

7

Simple Predicates Expressing Tense-Aspect

1 Introduction

In this chapter we will present analyses of predicates expressing notions of tense and aspect. Several tense-aspect archetypes will be introduced and associated with surface arrangements. We will sketch some representative parts of the tense-aspect paradigm of the German predicate *küssen* but will withhold many routine details from the reader. However, we believe that the analyses we provide will be detailed enough for the reader to see how they would be extended to a complete coverage of this predicate's paradigm.

It has already been mentioned in earlier chapters that German has predicates that can be alternately realized with or without a separable particle, depending on the syntactic context in which the predicate appears. One example of such a predicate is *an-rufen* 'call up.' Besides these particle-verb predicates, German of course also has simple predicates that don't come with a particle at all. The predicate *küssen* 'kiss' belongs to that class. In (1)–(5) we illustrate the difference between the two types of predicates that can be taken as their defining property.

(1) and (2) contain uses of the two predicates in subordinate clauses. Since both sentences are in the present tense, both predicates are expressed by single morphological words. The predicate in (2) is a compound consisting of the particle *an* and the word *ruft:*

(1)   weil   die Ministerin   ihren Mann   **küßt**
        because the minister(fem) her   husband kisses

        'because the minister kisses her husband'

(2)   weil   die Ministerin   ihren Mann   **anruft**
        because the minister(fem) her   husband up-calls

        'because the minister calls up her husband'

While (1) and (2) show that particle predicates like *anrufen* and simple predicates like *küssen* behave alike in subordinate clauses, (3) and (4) show that they part ways in main clauses, at least in those main clauses expressing the present or the past tense:

(3) Die Ministerin **küβt** ihren Mann
     the minister(fem) kisses her   husband

'The minister kisses her husband'

(4) Die Ministerin **ruft** ihren Mann **an**
     the minister(fem) calls her   husband up

'The minister calls up her husband'

German main clauses enforce the constraint that the part of the predicate which is realized by a morphologically finite word form must appear immediately after the first linear constituent of the sentence. This is why German is often called a "verb-second language." (3) and (4) show that simple predicates and particle predicates obey that constraint in different ways. The simple predicate in (3) appears in second position as a whole whereas the particle-predicate in (4) must leave its particle behind at the end of the sentence and move only the right-hand member of the sentence-final compound of (2) into the second linear position. (5) shows that it is impossible for the whole compound verb to front to second position:

(5) * Die Ministerin **anruft** ihren Mann
       the minister(fem) up-calls her   husband

'The minister calls up her husband'

We discuss the predicate paradigms of both simple and particle predicates in this book. In the present chapter we will start off with the less complex problems that the paradigms of simple predicates pose. For the remainder of this chapter we will pretend that the problem of particle predicates does not exist. In chapter 10 we will then turn our full attention to particle predicates and analyze them in the same detail in which simple predicates are handled here.

2   The Predicate Paradigm of the Simple Predicate *küssen* 'kiss'

Table (6) illustrates the tense-aspect paradigm of the simple active predicate *küssen* 'kiss.' We are only reproducing the indicative part of the paradigm, since an analysis of the subjunctive is a straightforward extension of the morphological and predicate patterns that are needed to generate the indicative paradigm. Passives are analyzed in their own right in chapter 8.

(6) The tense-aspect paradigm of *küssen* 'kiss'

Tense-Aspect Status	Surface Expression[1]
Basic (untensed)	*küß*
1-sg-present	*küsse*
2-sg-present	*küßt*
...	
1-sg-past	*küßte*
2-sg-past	*küßtest*
...	
1-sg-perfect	*geküßt habe*
2-sg-perfect	*geküßt hast*
...	
1-sg-pluperfect	*geküßt hatte*
2-sg-pluperfect	*geküßt hattest*
...	
1-sg-future	*küssen werde*
2-sg-future	*küssen wirst*
...	
1-sg-future-perfect	*geküßt haben werde*
...	
3-pl-future-perfect	*geküßt haben werden*

Together, the 36 cells in the complete predicate paradigm represent all the possible combinations of 6 tenses, 3 persons, and 2 numbers that a predicate can express. The internal structure of the paradigm is easily described:[2]

---

[1] The ss~β alternation in the various forms of *küssen* is due to an orthographic convention of German.

[2] The reader might want to take a minute and compare the paradigm of the predicate *küssen* 'kiss' in (6) with the morphological paradigm of the lexeme *fragen* 'ask' in (10) of chapter 5, in order to appreciate the use of paradigms in describing the systematic web of regularities that both predicates and words enter. Of course, while both kinds of conceptual entities enter into paradigms, their different 'values' in the grammatical system (in Saussure's parlance) determine that their paradigms express different relations among the members of each cell. In the case of morphological paradigms, the words filling the paradigm's cell are cross-classified by morphosyntactic features and the form differences that correlate with different features are morpho-phonological. In the case of signs, they are cross-classified by contentive features and the correlating form differences are constraints on the words that can fill the various morphological spell-out slots of the predicate.

One might say that both words and predicates are integrated into a web of functions (in the non-technical sense), but these functions represent different multidimensional logical spaces. The morphological module of the lexicon uses morpho-phonological operations to

(7) Description of the paradigm in (6)

Morphosyntactic content	Morphological form of the categorial core	Morphological form of the auxiliaries (from left to right)
Present	Present form	—
Past	Past form	—
Perfect	Part. Perfect	Pres. form of *haben*
Pluperfect	Part. Perfect	Past form of *haben*
Future	Bare infinitive	Pres. form of *werden*
Future Perfect	Bare infinitive	Pres. form of *werden* + Part. Perf. of *haben*

In the first column we find the six different points that German distinguishes within the tense-aspect dimension of the overall contentive logical space. The next two columns display the restrictions on the various spell-out slots that must be satisfied by predicates expressing one of the notions in the first column.[3] As we can see, the first two tenses are expressed synthetically. The remaining four tenses use various main verb-auxiliary combinations for their expression. The three perfect tense-aspects employ the auxiliary *haben,* the future uses the auxiliary *werden,* and the future perfect uses both auxiliaries at once.[4] The reader will presumably have noticed that

---

create word forms and assigns each word form to one point in the multidimensional morphosyntactic space defined by the different morphosyntactic dimensions LME, POS, and INFL. In contrast, the predicate module of the lexicon creates arrangements of morphological words and locates each such arrangement in a logical space with dimensions according to the content that predicates can express.

It is important to appreciate that despite the different forms and the different logical spaces defined by the two modules of the lexicon, they both have the function of recursively creating paradigms of surface forms and to associate each form with a point in some logical space they define. The design of our lexicon in (3) of the previous chapter directly accounts for both the parallelism and the differences in function between the two submodules of the lexicon.

[3] The reader should assume that all the predicates discussed before chapter 10 have empty particle lists unless a statement to the contrary is specifically made.

[4] Besides German verbs like *küssen* 'kiss' that form their perfect tenses with the auxiliary *haben,* there are also verbs that use the auxiliary *sein* instead. It is often claimed that the choice of auxiliary for a given verb is predictable from either its meaning, its functional inventory, or its argument structure. However, Fagan (1996, 1997a, 1997b) shows that even though there are subgeneralizations that can be accounted for in this manner, the amount of lexicalization of idiosyncratic choices makes it impossible to predict the auxiliary selection for all German verbs. In that light, it appears that the only descriptively adequate solution is to make use of default assignments of perfective auxiliaries that can be overridden by more specific statements in individual lexical entries that are exceptions to the generalizations that most other verbs follow.

We will skirt this issue in this book, since it doesn't seem to require any theoretical innovations beyond the tools which we are making use of in our analyses already. We previously used defaults in the statement of some syntactic patterns (= schemas) in chapter 3. With such defaults and overriding statements in the lexical entries of predicates, it is possible to define a *haben-type* of predicates and a separate *sein-type* and to assign each predicate to

either the categorial core of the predicate or the first auxiliary on the four non-empty auxiliary lists are filled with morphologically finite word forms. This is no accident: all six predicates of (7) are semantically finite and German requires that the categorial head of such a predicate be realized by a morphologically finite word that represents the person-number features of the predicate's subject (or a default third person singular if there is no subject).[5] The reader will recall that the six spell-out slots that are filled with finite word forms are the ones that represent the categorial heads of these predicates: in the first two cases, there is no auxiliary and this requires that the predicate's categorial core represent its categorial head as well and in the remaining four cases it is the first element on the auxiliary list which serves as the predicate's categorial head. The predicate formation patterns thus will ensure that the subject of a synthetic predicate morphologically agrees with the main verb but that the subjects of analytically expressed predicates agree with the auxiliary instead.[6]

3 Constructing the Tense-Aspect Paradigm of *küssen*

Predicate paradigms, like paradigms in the morphological module of the lexicon, are the result of the interaction of an underived lexical entry with a number of patterns that create new lexical entries, perhaps recur-

---

one of the two types (or to both types for those few predicates which can form their perfect with either auxiliary). Then we can define two versions of each of the predicate formation patterns for perfect tenses: the first one will require that its LEXDTR (the predicate that serves as input to the pattern) belong to the *haben-type* while the second one requires an input predicate of the *sein-type* and the pattern will add the appropriate auxiliary to the auxiliary list of the output. Features that the two versions of each perfect pattern have in common can be extracted from them and included into a more general supertype from which both perfect patterns inherit all information. In this way, all commonalities and differences between the classes of verbs taking one rather than the other auxiliary to form their perfect tenses are captured either via the default assignments of perfect auxiliaries, the statements of the predicate patterns and their inheritance grouping, and the overriding statements in the individual lexical entries of exceptional items.

We have implemented this strategy as part of the overall implementation of the ideas in this book (except for the default assignment of perfect auxiliaries which was not possible due to a lack of the default mechanism in the grammar development software that we used). To save space, we will therefore only deal with *haben* predicates here and trust it that the reader recognizes that the treatment of *sein* predicates is completely analogous.

[5]See (16) below and the discussion surrounding it.

[6]Note that because of our clean separation of the *contentive* information of predicates and their *morphosyntactic* spell-out, no inconsistency arises from the fact that a morphologically present tense form of the auxiliary *haben* is used to express the contentive notion of perfect of a predicate like *geküßt hat* 'has kissed.' We wonder how inconsistency can be avoided in theories like Chomsky's Minimalist Program that fail to draw that clean distinction but rely on a concept of 'feature checking' to "license" morphological features in the syntactic component. As we understand it, the present tense morphological features of the auxiliary *haben* in the German perfect would have to be checked against matching present tense features on a syntactically represented Tense head. We fail to see how this Tense head can contribute a perfect tense semantics to the Logical Form of the sentence if it must carry present tense features to license the presence of the present tense perfect auxiliary in the sentence.

sively, by allowing patterns to take each other's output as their input. In order to construct the tense-aspect paradigm of any German predicate, we thus will have to specify both its underived lexical entry and the tense-aspect patterns that it can feed either directly or indirectly.

3.1 The Underived Predicate *küssen* 'kiss'

We postulate the structure in (8) for the underived predicate *küssen* 'kiss.' We proceed to discuss how the information in this structure instantiates the various information types that we have introduced schematically until now.

The type of the whole data structure (8) identifies it as a lexical combinatorial item *(lci)*, i.e., a member of the predicate module of the lexicon. In particular, we are dealing with the predicate *küssen* which is an underived predicate, since it lacks the attribute LEXDTR beneath SYNSEM where its lexical derivational source would be specified if the item were derived.

Let us now look at the values this predicate takes in the three SYN(TACTIC)-SEM(ANTIC) dimensions for which predicates carry information: CSTRUC, ISTRUC, and VAL.

The CSTRUC (categorial structure) values require that the morphological spell-out slot of the predicate's core be filled by a verbal word from the morphological paradigm of the lexeme *küssen*. In addition, the predicate's core is identical to its head, since the underived predicate's auxiliary valence is empty. Comparing the morphological information associated with the core of (8) with a full-fledged morphological word as defined in chapter 5, we see that the information in (8) does not determine any particular morphological word as the filler of the core slot. Rather, it only identifies the paradigm from which the word must be drawn, namely the paradigm of the verbal lexeme *küssen* (note the type *vword* (= *verbal word*) on the value of the core!), leaving the specification of inflectional features unspecified. In other words, the underlying predicate, as one might expect, is itself uninflected and neutral between the various inflected word forms that might instantiate its core in inflected derivatives of its predicate paradigm. The various tense-aspect patterns in which the predicate can appear will place the inflectional features of the core in correspondence with the morphosyntactic content (tense, agreement) the pattern expresses and this will restrict which of the word forms of the morphological paradigm of *küssen* created by the morphological module of the grammar is compatible with the core spell-out slot of the predicate formed by this particular pattern.

The ISTRUC (information structure) associated with a predicate contains the predicate's semantic content in CONT, the grammatical functions (FSTRUC) it projects to the domain that it heads, and the semantic contribution each grammatical function makes to the semantic content of the predicate's domain. In the present case, the lci expresses a state of affairs of *kissing* involving a KISSER and a KISSED.

(8) The underived predicate *küssen* 'kiss'

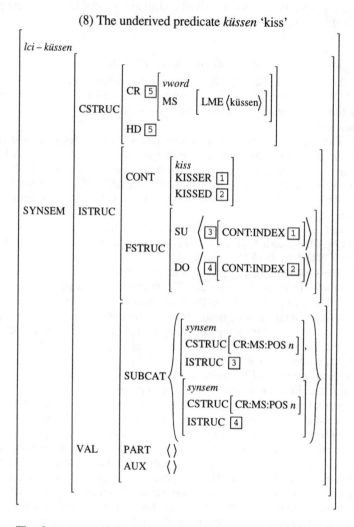

The f-structure of (8) contains two grammatical functions, a subject and a direct object.[7] Grammatical functions in an f-structure take as their values the information structures of the functional arguments of the predicate. This allows the predicate to identify the semantic contribution of

---

[7] All the other attributes in the f-structure take empty lists as their values in this case and have been suppressed, as will frequently be done to allow the reader to concentrate on information in any given representation that is crucial at this point in the exposition.

one of the grammatical functions it governs with a semantic role in its own content. In (8), the predicate requires that the semantic index of its subject function bear the semantic role of KISSER in the *kissing* state of affairs the predicate expresses. Analogously, the predicate assigns the semantic role of KISSED to its direct object grammatical function.

The third SYNSEM attribute is VAL(ENCE). Here we find information about aspects of the surface categorial spell-out of the predicate as well as the categorial spell-out of the predicate's grammatical functions, assuming that the predicate requires or allows its functional arguments to be categorially expressed. Starting at the bottom of the VAL value, we see that this predicate is both non-auxiliated and non-particled. It is non-auxiliated because all underived predicates (in German) are non-auxiliated. The only interesting things here happen in SUBCAT, the location where the predicate imposes categorial constraints on the expression of the grammatical functions it governs.

As inspection of the two members of the SUBCAT in (8) shows, what is subcategorized for in a categorial complement is a *synsem*. This makes categorial selection more powerful than selection in f-structure which is restricted to *istrucs* that cannot impose any c-structural constraints. A little reflection should bring out the motivation behind this difference. The f-structure has the primary function of bundling together many subtypes of the immense number of potentially existing semantic predicate argument types into a very small number of recurrent grammatical functions. These grammatical functions allow us to state binding, agreement, and case marking generalizations in a way that in principle is independent of the phrase structural spell-out of the predicate's f-structural arguments. For instance, uniform principles of anaphoric binding can be made sensitive to notions such as 'subject' whether this subject is expressed as a categorial constituent or as part of the morphological realization of the predicate ("pro drop").

By limiting the values of grammatical functions to (lists of) *istrucs,* we can give identical information structures to two predicates that only differ in whether their subject is categorially expressed: they will have the same contents and the same f-structures but will differ in that the subject *istruc* of one predicate is expressed by a subcategorized categorial complement in the predicate's valence whereas the subject is not categorially expressed in the other case. This captures the intuition that when an argument is "pro dropped," the predicate itself already contains all the *information* that the argument would express, were it expressed.

This natural account of "pro drop" would be lost if grammatical functions were *synsems* including categorial information, instead of purely informational *istrucs:* for a predicate with a "dropped" subject we would then not only have to specify the information that this subject bears but also its category, even though the subject is never expressed. In other words, we would in effect be postulating a phonologically empty category as the predicate's subject. Since there is no theory-neutral motivation for such empty categories and since we believe in any event that the use of such devices is proportional to a theory's lack of conceptual clarity, we resist the temptation to model grammatical functions as *synsems,* especially, since the more parsimonious solution as *istrucs* does everything we need done.

Since predicates obviously *can* select the categorial expression of the grammatical functions that they allow to be expressed in phrase structure, the values of the various valence attributes are (lists/sets of) *synsems.*[8] Our underived predicate *küssen* in (8) has two categorial complements in its subcategorization valence: both complements are specified as part of speech *noun* by the path CSTRUC:CR:MS:POS. The second line in each SUBCAT statement links the selected nominal to a grammatical function: the first selected *synsem* carries an information structure which is token-identical to the predicate's subject and the second *synsem* categorially expresses the predicate's direct object.

In sum, then, the underived predicate in (8) contains skeletal categorial information, non-temporal functional-semantic information, and valence information about the predicate's categorial surface spell-out as well as the categories that express the predicate's grammatical functions. This structure, either directly or indirectly, underlies all the members of the full predicate paradigm that is created by (recursively) applying a set of predicate patterns to this primitive predicate. Based on the "blueprint" in (8), the patterns will create new predicates with systematically related meanings, systematically related functional structures, and systematically related morphological surface spell-out arrangements. Some of these patterns are described in detail in the next sections.

3.2 Basic and Expanded Types

Besides the derived-underived distinction, we will make a second distinction that can be motivated on empirical grounds and also makes the statement of many predicate patterns easier to state. The distinction we have in mind is closely related to the inflectional-derivational distinction, except that inflection and derivation have strong morphological connotations and the distinction that we are after is a distinction between different relations among *predicates.* We illustrate this with the predicates in (9):

---

[8]This is sometimes denied, especially in GB approaches [see, for instance, Pesetsky (1982)], based on a limited number of cases where the category of an expression correlates with some other property it has. However, these cases don't generalize to all cases of categorial selection as is shown in Webelhuth (1992), Pollard and Sag (1987), and other works. A theory of grammar that does not allow lexical entries to select the categories of its dependents therefore is neither descriptively nor explanatorily adequate.

(9) Two types of patterns that the predicate *küssen* can appear in

	Causative Pattern	**Perfect Aspect Pattern**
Surface Form	adds auxiliary *lassen*	adds auxiliary *haben*
F-structure	changes the f-structure	does not change the f-structure
Content	changes the content non-monotonically	changes the content monotonically

As (9) shows, the primitive predicate *küssen* can appear in a causative formation pattern as well as a pattern for forming perfect tense-aspect predicates. Both of these patterns are highly productive and regular patterns of German. As the first row indicates, both patterns create analytically expressed predicates. From a contentive point of view, the two patterns differ, however. The causative pattern makes much more significant changes to the underlying predicate than the perfect pattern. It not only changes the f-structure by adding a new subject (to express the causer) and demoting the old subject but it also changes the content of the underlying predicate in a non-monotonic way. In contrast, the perfect pattern retains the f-structure of the underlying predicate and while altering the content, it does so by merely adding temporal information to the underlying content which was unspecified for tense-aspect.

Natural language grammars typically seem to have many patterns of both kinds: those like the German perfect pattern that retain the underlying predicate's functional inventory and only make its meaning more specific and on the other hand, those which change the meaning of the underlying predicate more drastically and consequently may also organize the new meaning with a different inventory of grammatical functions and links between the grammatical functions and semantic roles (what we have been calling functional-semantic information).

In order to capture this dichotomy, we will postulate a distinction between *basic* and *expanded* predicates which is different from the distinction between derived and underived predicates, as follows:

(10a) underived lci: an lci *without* a LEXDTR attribute;

derived lci: an lci *with* a LEXDTR attribute;

basic lci: an lci which may be derived or underived. If it is derived, then its f-structure and content do *not* need to be monotonic extensions of the values of the corresponding values of its LEXDTR;

expanded lci: an lci which is always derived from a basic lci whose functional inventory and functional-semantic links it cannot change. Its content must be a monotonic extension of its LEXDTR's content.[9]

(10b) contains a matrix with examples of each of the four types and how they combine to cross-classify predicates:

	Underived lci	**Derived lci**
(10b)		
Basic lci	the underived predicate *küssen*	the untensed causative predicate *küssen lassen* 'make kiss'
Expanded lci	none: expanded predicates by definition are derived	the perfect predicate *geküßt hat* 'has kissed' or the tensed causative predicate *küssen läßt* 'makes kiss'

The predicate in the upper left-hand corner represents the kernel of the predicate paradigm of *küssen:* it is the only member of this paradigm which is listed in the fundamental predicate inventory of the German lexicon (see the architecture of our theory of grammar at the end of the previous chapter), since it is not derived from any LEXDTR by any predicate pattern. In the column "Derived lci" we find the predicates which are derived from the kernel by some pattern either directly or indirectly. Among the derived predicates there are two kinds: those derived predicates which are not subject

---

[9]The similarity between the derived-underived and the basic-expanded distinction to the inflection-derivation distinction in morphology is the following. Both *bark* and *redden* are basic verbs in the sense that they are uninflected but their information can be expanded by inflecting them for various morphosyntactic features (e.g., adding *-ed* to express a past tense). Yet, *bark* is an underived verb, whereas *redden* has been derived from the adjective *red*. In this sense, *bark* is both underived and basic, *redden* is derived and basic, and *reddens* is derived and non-basic, since it carries inflection. The difference between the distinctions we are making in the text and the inflected-uninflected distinction is that the latter is a morphological distinction, whereas the distinction we are interested in making is one between different statuses of *predicates*.

to the functional and semantic constraints of expanded lci's and hence make new basic lci's out of old ones, perhaps by changing the functional inventory of the underlying basic lci and/or by changing the meaning or the functional-semantic links of the underlying predicate. Finally, in the lower right-hand corner, we find two predicates which are derived from the basic predicates in the first row. The perfect predicate *geküßt hat* takes the basic lci *küssen* in the upper left-hand corner as its input and adds temporal information to that predicate's content and does not alter its f-structure at all. Similarly, the tensed causative predicate *küssen läßt* expands the meaning of the basic untensed causative predicate *küssen lassen* (from the upper right-hand corner) by adding tense-aspect and agreement information to the output predicate for which the input predicate is unspecified.

To be precise about the changes that basic-lci's may and may not make to their underlying predicates, we specify the definition of this type in (11) and some constraints on it in (12):[10]

(11) The definition of the type expanded lci *(= exp-lci)*

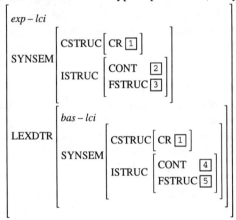

(12) Constraints on the type expanded lci *(= exp-lci)* in (11)

A.   The Functional Isomorphy Constraint

The f-structure of an expanded lci (③ above) is subsumed by the f-structure of its LEXDTR (⑤ above) whose type is minimal in the type ordering.

---

[10]We assume that the availability and the restrictions on this type are universal, i.e., that we are dealing with an archetype. This suffices to explain why so many different languages make use of predicate patterns that satisfy these particular restrictions.

B.   The Functional-Semantic Expansion Constraint

The content of an expanded lci (☑ above) and the content of its LEXDTR (☑ above) are isomorphic and ☑ subsumes ☑ . The functional-semantic links between the content and the f-structure in the expanded lci are isomorphic to equivalent links in the LEXDTR.

The constraint in (12A) prevents patterns of this type to change the functional inventory of the underlying predicate: the subsumption constraint ensures that all grammatical functions which are present in the daughter's f-structure are retained in the mother's f-structure. And since the daughter's f-structure belongs to a minimal type, the mother's f-structure cannot contain additional grammatical functions either.

The constraint in (12B) makes sure that the meaning of the output is structured in the same way as the meaning of the input: the pattern must not change the semantic adicity of the predicate. The pattern may, however, make the meaning of the predicate more specific, e.g., by adding tense or agreement/cross-reference information. Finally, the pattern must respect the links between semantic roles and grammatical functions that the input predicate has established.

3.3   Tense-Aspect   Archetypes

On the basis of the type *exp(anded)-lci,* we can now easily define contentive archetypes that express tense-aspect meanings and agreement patterns that recur systematically throughout the languages of the world. By declaring some of these archetypes (in the sense of chapter 4) and by configuring them according to the language-particular spell-outs surveyed in (7), German projects a tense-aspect paradigm from each of its underived predicates.[11]

(13) illustrates the fragment of the universal type hierarchy that contains the type *exp-lci* with some of its most important direct and indirect subtypes. We assume that a number of tense notions are encoded as contentive archetypes and that this accounts for why similar tense distinctions recur in the languages of the world. As indicated in the tree, we also assume the existence of archetypal agreement and case marking patterns. In particular, we assume a universally available pattern that creates agreement between a predicate and its subject, another one that creates agreement with both the subject and the predicate's object, etc. The frequency distribution of the various agreement patterns throughout the languages of the world suggests that the subject-only agreement type is less

---

[11]Recall that to declare an archetype means to effectively import this universal type into a language-particular grammar through the definition of a language-particular subtype of the archetype. Configuring an archetype means to add language-particular information to a type that declares the archetype, e.g., to add language-particular spell-out information to the information inherited from a contentive archetype.

marked than the type which enforces agreement with both the subject and the direct object, which in turn in less marked than potentially existing other universal and language-particular agreement patterns. In terms of an evaluation metric, this makes those grammatical representations least costly which are found attested most frequently in the languages of the world.[12]

(13) The type *exp-lci* and some of its subtypes

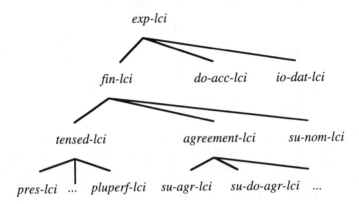

Case marking patterns are treated in the same way: we assume the existence of universally available subtypes of expanded predicates that code grammatical functions via certain cases: the subject of a finite verb is coded with nominative case, the direct and indirect objects of finite and non-finite verbs with accusative and dative case respectively. Postulating these as the universally unmarked case marking choices entails the prediction that if languages have overt case marking, then the distribution of the cases will typically be determined by grammatical functions.

---

[12]Some subject agreement patterns might more appropriately be analyzed as agreement with a bare NP with default case marking such as nominative or absolutive, rather than being keyed to the grammatical function the NP bears (e.g., the subject of an intransitive verb and the direct object of a transitive verb in certain ergative case marking systems or the nominative nominal in accusative systems when the SUBJ is non-nominative). We do not address this type of agreement nor ergative-absolutive case marking archetypes in this book, since we do not analyze data in detail that would depend on such archetypes. Obviously, in a fuller exposition, additional archetypes would be needed to account for different agreement and case marking types. The patterns that are defined below in the main text are geared towards our detailed analysis of German. We also emphasize that our system does *not* require that such notions as tense, aspect, and modality must always be expressed inflectionally in expanded predicates. Bybee (1985) specifically argues on typological grounds that these notions are expressed inflectionally in some languages but derivationally in others. Derivational formations of predicates expressing such notions are not subject to the constraints in (11) and (12) of the main text and can make changes to the underlying predicate that go beyond those licensed for expanded predicates. Some of the phenomena in section 3.6.1 of the present chapter may be of this derivational kind.

The definitions of the archetypes are straightforward, given the way we have structured our signs. (14) contains the structure of the type of finite lci's:

(14) The type *fin-lci*

$$
\begin{bmatrix}
\text{SYNSEM} \begin{bmatrix} \text{ISTRUC} & \begin{bmatrix} \text{CONT } \textit{timed} - \textit{nqsoa} \end{bmatrix} \\ \text{VAL} & \begin{bmatrix} \text{SUBCAT} \boxed{1} \end{bmatrix} \end{bmatrix} \\
\text{LEXDTR} \begin{bmatrix} \text{SYNSEM} \begin{bmatrix} \text{VAL} \begin{bmatrix} \text{SUBCAT} \boxed{1} \end{bmatrix} \end{bmatrix} \end{bmatrix}
\end{bmatrix}
$$

Recall that (14) is a subtype of the type *exp-lci* in (11) and hence inherits all the information in (11), including the constraints in (12). Adding the information of (14) to (11) means that (11)+(14) represent an expanded predicate that has been derived from a lexical daughter as follows. (12B) generally requires that the content of the derived predicate be identical or more specific than the content of the lexical daughter. Since (14) constrains the content of the derived predicate to expressing a timed (non-quantified) state of affairs, together the two constraints entail that a finite predicate expresses a timed version of the state of affairs expressed by the lexical daughter, with the exact time constraint (present vs. past vs. future, etc.) yet to be determined. In addition, finite predicates have the same subcategorization frames as their underlying predicates.

The various temporal subtypes of *tensed-lci* will now look like (15), where the particular choice *pres-nqsoa*, i.e., present tense (non-quantified) state of affairs, can be replaced by any other temporal type:

(15) The type *pres-lci*

$$
\begin{bmatrix}
\text{SYNSEM} \begin{bmatrix} \text{ISTRUC} & \begin{bmatrix} \text{CONT } \textit{pres} - \textit{nqsoa} \end{bmatrix} \end{bmatrix}
\end{bmatrix}
$$

Effectively, (15) further narrows down the choices of tense interpretation made available in (14).

The treatment of the agreement patterns is similar but requires particular care in the statement of the patterns. Each pattern adds some information to the generic expanded type (11) and thereby makes the enriched type available to individual grammars as a "cheap" pattern to incorporate via archetype declaration.

Defining a type which requires predicates to agree with their subjects misses the generalization that many languages have impersonal predicates that show a third person singular default agreement. The same is true for the case marking patterns to be introduced shortly: they should only apply to a predicate if it governs the relevant grammatical function. The agreement and case marking patterns thus need to be context-sensitive, i.e., they should state the conditions under which their constraints apply and should contain an "opt-out" clause for predicates that are exempt from the constraint because of their particular properties.

In (16), we illustrate how the typologically prevalent subject-only agreement pattern with third person singular default marking on the predicate can be captured:

(16) The type *subj-agr-lci*

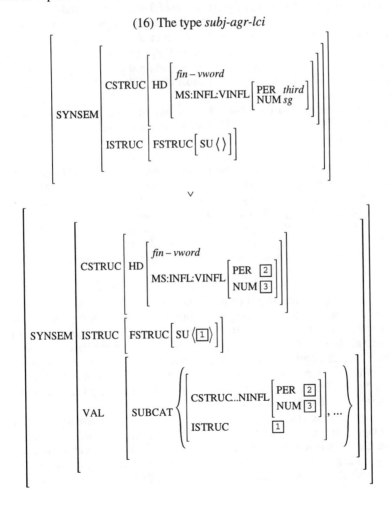

(16) is a subtype of (11) and it is a disjunctive type that an expression belongs to only if it satisfies the constraints in at least one of the type's disjuncts. Since the two disjuncts contain incompatible information in the present case (subject vs. no subject in the f-structure), each data structure belonging to this type must satisfy either the first or the second disjunct but cannot satisfy both. Let us look what information the second disjunct of (16) adds to (11): the predicate is required to have a finite verb as its categorial head (either the main verb or the leftmost auxiliary) and the person-number inflectional features of this categorial head are token-identical with the person-number inflectional features of that member of the predicate's subcategorization frame whose ISTRUC is interpreted as the predicate's subject. This is our formal way of requiring that the morphological form of the categorial head of this type of predicate correlates with the morphological form of the category that expresses the predicate's subject, or more simply, that this predicate must agree with its subject in person and number.

The first disjunct, now, represents the "opt-out" clause that we alluded to above: it represents the default case of third person singular features on the categorial head of the predicate just in case the predicate's f-structure fails to contain a subject.

Note that the design of our theory does not *force* languages to have agreement. The type (16), like all other archetypes, plays a role in evaluating the *markedness* of a predicate, not its grammaticality. Languages need not have any agreement and many don't, but *if* a language does make use of agreement between a predicate and any of its arguments, then the agreement pattern expressed by (16) is the pattern that is valued most highly in a natural language grammar. According to this system, agreement is preferably between the categorial head of a finite predicate and the predicate's subject. Alternative agreement patterns, i.e., agreement with something other than a subject or agreement involving a non-finite predicate, are claimed to be possible but less preferred and hence are predicted to occur less systematically in the languages of the world.

The case patterns are easy to state but will also involve a disjunction. Each one simply adds an inflectional requirement to the morphosyntactic features of the subcategorized argument that expresses the grammatical function that is coded by the case in question, *if that grammatical function is present in the predicate's f-structure*. (17) illustrates this for the *subj-nom-lci* which creates predicates that "assign" nominative case to their subjects. Since this type is a subtype of the type of finite predicates in (14), this case restriction will be predicted to be found typically on finite predicates in languages with overt case marking.

Accusative and dative cases will be optionally available to individual languages with case marking as well, but in contrast to the nominative, these cases are reserved for the direct object and indirect object respectively and they are "assigned" by a predicate to the categories expressing these grammatical functions whether the predicate is finite or not [note that these two types are located higher in the type hierarchy (13) than the nominative pattern].

(17) The type *subj-nom-lci*

$$\left[\text{SYNSEM} \left[\text{ISTRUC} \left[\text{FSTRUC} \left[\text{SU} \langle \rangle \right] \right] \right] \right]$$

∨

$$\left[\text{SYNSEM} \left[\begin{array}{l} \text{ISTRUC} \left[\text{FSTRUC} \left[\text{SU} \langle \boxed{1} \rangle \right] \right] \\ \\ \text{VAL} \quad \left[\text{SUBCAT} \left\langle \left[\begin{array}{ll} \text{CSTRUC..NINFL} \left[\text{CASE } nom \right] \\ \text{ISTRUC} \qquad \boxed{1} \end{array} \right], ... \right\rangle \right] \end{array} \right] \right]$$

3.4 Tense-Aspect Archetype Declaration and Configuration in German

In chapter 4, we laid out a vision of how universally available grammatical archetypes bias natural language grammars into taking on certain preferred shapes. We envision individual grammars to be evaluated by a procedure that attempts to minimize the amount of *independent information* in a given grammar, i.e., information that does not match (i.e., is not inherited from) information in one of the universal archetypes or at least a general language-particular type that the grammar defines. We referred to the process of defining a language-particular type as a subtype of an archetype as *archetype declaration* and the language-particular elaboration of such a type as *archetype configuration*. In the present section, we will apply both of these techniques. First, we will define a number of language-particular predicate types of German as subtypes of the tense-aspect, agreement, and case marking archetypes that we presented in the previous section. Since the archetypes are subtypes of the type *exp-lci* in (11), so will their German subtypes. As *exp-lci* is a type that derives a new predicate structure from an embedded LEXDTR, the newly defined German subtypes represent German-specific lexical patterns for the construction of predicates marked for tense-aspect information from underlying tenseless predicates. Together, the tense-aspect patterns serve to generate the tense-aspect predicate pattern of basic (derived or underived) predicates in the predicate module of the German grammar, as described in chapter 6.

The definition of German subtypes of archetypes illustrates the conceptual process of archetype declaration. This process involves the internalization and composition of universally recurring functional-semantic clusters and grammatical concepts such as agreement and case marking. It does not, however, yield complete predicate representations, since some aspects of language-particular tense-aspect representations are too idiosyncratic to plausibly be the result of a choice from a universal list. In particular, this holds of the information that fills the various morphological spell-out slots of predicates. This information is strongly subject to the Saussurean arbitrariness of the sign and must be determined by archetype configuration, the enrichment of a language-particular subtype of an archetype with language-particular information. The different spell-out configurations illustrated in (7) are a case in point.

As far as we can tell from a cursory examination of tense, aspect, passives, causatives, and middles, the relationship between Universal Grammar and individual grammars works in this fashion throughout, i.e., Universal Grammar defines types (like passive, causative, etc.) primarily in terms of contentive information and merely defines a range of permissible surface realizations of this content, governed by a markedness hierarchy. The building of morphological inventories (e.g., that German has a morphological item *werden* but no item *shall)* and the association of individual members or groups of members of that inventory with contentive information (what one might call "Saussurean sign formation") is the task of language-particular grammars and is something that language learners have to learn about their target grammars.

This hypothesized design of Universal Grammar and its relation to individual grammars is not a logical necessity because things might well have been otherwise. Rather than allowing individual grammars both to import archetypes and to refrain from doing so if that archetype is not desired in the grammar, UG could force all its archetypes onto all languages. Then all languages would be predicted to have passive, causative, and middle predicates in addition to all the other predicate types UG defines. UG could even have fully determined the surface spell-out of each of the predicate types it defines, thus in effect allowing for the existence of only one single language. But the Universal Grammar of the real world does neither of these things.

On the other hand, UG (granted that it exists) could have been designed in such a way that it only makes very low-level types available and doesn't compose lower-level information into higher-level types. One might compare this to a difference between relatively low-level and higher-level programming languages. The C language, for instance, does not contain the data type of a list and functions that operate on lists. A language like Lisp, on the other hand, does contain lists and functions that return the first member of the list, the list that remains if the first member is removed from the original list, etc. Lists can of course be defined as abstract data types in C and so can the functions just mentioned. This has to be done using the basic tools (e.g., arrays and pointers) made available by C and requires work that is not necessary in a language like Lisp that comes equipped with the higher-level tools because the developers of Lisp have already put in the labor of defining these concepts so that the end user of Lisp can take them for granted.

Our claim thus is that with respect to contentive information, UG behaves more like a higher-level programming language that makes available relatively internally complex and sophisticated tools to the user. Types like "expanded predicate" and "subject agreement predicate" contain many attributes and very specific information that can be imported into an individual grammar as a unit by reference to the type name rather than one attribute-value pair at a time. These types represent relatively rich information types equivalent to the sophisticated functions of higher-level programming languages.

With respect to surface realization on the other hand, our view is that UG behaves more like a low-level programming language. It just makes available the low-level components of the surface realization system one by one (e.g., *partld, auxd,* etc.) but does not seem to combine those into higher-level units that are universally associated with contentive information types as a whole.

This overall design predicts what indeed seems to be true impressionistically, namely that there is a relatively small core of contentive notions and grammatical relations/categories that are utilized by language after language but that there is a multiplicity of observable surface forms that different languages use to express these notions. As discussed at length in chapter 1, the only restraining force against this multiplicity of forms seems to be provided by the markedness preferences for surface spell-out (see section 5 of chapter 4) and those seem to have a relatively weak effect, since they can be easily overridden by the pragmatic pressure of having a means to express some notion at all. Their effects are thus mainly to be found in choosing directions for diachronic change which is an effect that speakers probably have no conscious awareness of at all.

3.4.1 Tense-Aspect Predicates in German

We are now well on our way to defining the patterns that will accept underived predicates like *küssen* 'kiss' in (8) as input and for each such input will return another predicate which expresses the same functional-semantic information as the input but enriched by morphosyntactic content information about tense-aspect.

In order to capture the fact that all German predicates expressing tense-aspect fall under the same agreement and case marking generalizations, we will first postulate the type *german-fin-lci* 'German finite lci' which declares typical agreement and case marking archetypes whose information it hands down to its various German subtypes expressing the different tense-aspects of this language:

(18) Declaring agreement and case marking archetypes via the language-particular type *german-fin-lci*

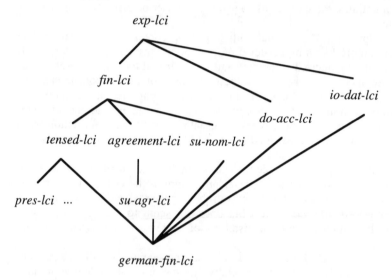

In concert with the subtypes of *german-fin-lci* that we will define momentarily, the archetype declaration in (18) has the following effect: by virtue of being a German finite predicate, an *lci* must (i) express a notional tense (because it is a subtype of *tensed-lci*), (ii) agree with its subject or lack a subject *(subj-agr-lci)*, (iii) be subject-less or have a nominative subject *(subj-nom-lci)*, (iv) have an accusative direct object or lack a direct object altogether *(do-acc-lci)*, and (v) govern a dative direct object or no direct object at all *(io-dat-lci)*. All of these structural components of German finite predicates are derived from archetypes and hence represent aspects of language-particular predicates that are valued highly by the evaluation procedure of our theory of predicates. We thus predict that many languages besides German, but not necessarily *all* natural languages, declare the same archetypes and this seems to be the situation confirmed by empirical typological studies. In this way, our theory provides an explanation of verifiable empirical data within the scope of theoretical linguistics that in our view is superior to the two "extremist" approaches that we criticized in the previous chapter: unlike the extreme nativist view, we can account for exceptions to universal tendencies without having to postulate multitudes of empirically non-verifiable empty categories; unlike the extreme empiricist view, we can account for universal tendencies in language for which no plausible general cognitive or language acquisition principles exist as sources, for example the use of third person singular default agreement on subject-less predicates as opposed to the equally general, cognitively natural, and conceivable choices of (i) not allowing subject-less predicates, or (ii) not realizing person-number features on the predicate when no subject is present.

With *german-fin-lci* at our disposal, we can now declare particular tense-aspect archetypes via subtypes of *german-fin-lci* that are also subtypes expressing specific tense-aspects:

(19) Declaring particular tense-aspect archetypes

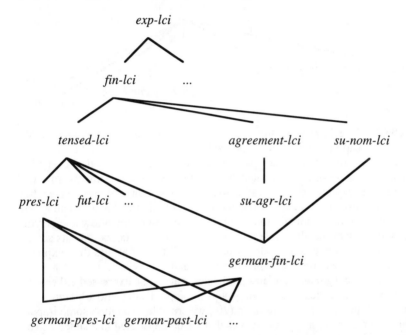

The important part of the graph is the line at the very bottom. Here we define German-specific subtypes of the various archetypal predicate patterns that the whole graph in (19) makes available to German and natural language grammars in general. For instance, the type *german-pres-lci,* the predicate pattern type that creates present tense versions of its LEXDTR inputs, combines the information of the *pres-lci* archetype and the information contained in the type *german-fin-lci* which is largely defined by archetypal means as well, as was just discussed. Consequently, all outputs of the present tense pattern must satisfy all the agreement and case marking constraints attached to the type *german-fin-lci,* the type capturing the generalizations that hold across all finite German predicates.

It is worth fleshing out further the structure of the type hierarchy below the type *german-fin-lci* in (19), because that type structure has interesting consequences. This is done in (20). Note that in the expanded graph, we not only represent the tense-aspect subtypes of *german-fin-lci* but also its person and number subtypes. In addition, we group the types that represent the same kind of information together and combine them with a disjunction operator (i.e., "v") to indicate that each group of subtypes partitions the type *german-fin-lci:*

(20) The subtypes of *german-fin-lci* and the partitioning they impose

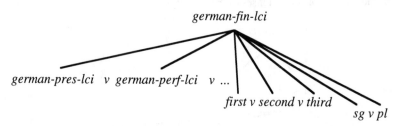

In chapter 4 we introduced the concept of partitions and explained how it allows us to capture important generalizations. What it means that each of the three groups of types in (20) partitions their mother type is that every instance of the mother type must belong to exactly one subtype in each group. This captures the generalization across German finite predicates that each one must express exactly one tense-aspect notion and that its categorial head must be inflectionally marked for exactly one of the allowable person types and one of the allowable number types. This generalization cuts across all German predicates no matter what kind of state of affairs they express, whether they are expressed synthetically or analytically, etc.[13]

In a theory that postulates predicates that can be expressed either synthetically or analytically and that groups these predicates into a hierarchy of types with possible partitions as in (20), we are able to capture some important generalizations across predicates that we demonstrated in chapter 2 to be inexpressible in theories whose lexicon is organized around *categorial heads* (as in HPSG and GB), rather than *predicates*. For instance, we cited data from Basque and Tzotzil that showed that finite predicates in these languages must express person-number agreement and aspect but that there is an important split. When the predicate is expressed synthetically, the single representative of the predicate will bear all this information. However, when the predicate consists of two verbs, then the agreement information must appear on one verb and the aspect information on the other.

---

[13]We wish to thank Andreas Kathol and Bob Kasper for discussing this issue with us. Bob Kasper emphasizes that the manner we use partitions here will only work in an open-world interpretation of the type hierarchy and that otherwise our specification using partitions is to be interpreted as an abbreviation for a hierarchy that contains the full cross-product of types.

It should be easy to see that if the predicates of Basque and Tzotzil are grouped into a type hierarchy structured like that in (20), the differences between synthetically and analytically expressed predicates can be expressed, *while it is still possible to capture the generalizations across all predicates which are lost in a category-based lexicon.* Since (20) is a hierarchy of *predicates,* the requirement that a choice must be made within each set of partitions (agreement, aspect) applies no matter whether a given predicate is expressed by a single word or more than one word. This ensures that every predicate, qua functional head of a clause, expresses the same kind of information. The various subtypes can then be further specified as to *how* this information is differentially spelled out on the categorial pieces realizing the predicate, i.e., which word of a multi-word predicate expresses which features (in Basque periphrastic predicates, for instance, person-number agreement for subjects appears on the auxiliary verb and aspect on the 'main' verb, whereas in Tzotzil we find the opposite distribution). In a category-based lexicon, in contrast, it remains mysterious in these cases and others that were presented in chapter 2 why some finite heads express both agreement and aspect while other finite heads in the same language express only one of these kinds of information but simultaneously obligatorily subcategorize for another verb that obligatorily bears the second kind of information.

Let us take stock of where we are in our analysis of the tense-aspect paradigm of the representative underived predicate *küssen* 'kiss' in (8). We have postulated a universal type *exp-lci* (expanded lci) in (11) as the basis of patterns that embed a predicate in the LEXDTR slot and expand the information in the input in accordance with the constraints in (12). Then we defined various subtypes of the universal pattern type in (13) that enrich it with tense-aspect, agreement, and case marking information that has archetypal status. We declared many of these archetypes as active in the grammar of German by postulating a German-specific type *german-fin-lci* in (18) which inherits crucial archetypal agreement and case marking information and transmits it to each of its subtypes illustrated in (19) and (20). (20), finally, ensures that each finite predicate in German, be it expressed synthetically or analytically, will be marked for exactly one of the available tenses, and that its categorial head bears one of the six possible tense-aspect combinations.

What remains to be captured, then, is the information we systematized in (7), namely which morphological category on the categorial core must cooccur with which auxiliaries (if any) in the surface expression of any specific tensed predicate. This is information that is not inherited from any more general source but must be stated in the local definitions of each type of German tensed predicate at the lower left of the type hierarchy in (20). That is the task we turn to in the next two subsections which discuss one synthetically and one analytically expressed tense-aspect pattern respectively.

3.4.2 The Present Tense Pattern of German

(21) contains the definition of the purely language-specific part of the German predicate pattern that expands basic input predicates like (8) to their present tense counterparts:[14]

(21) The type *german-pres-lci*

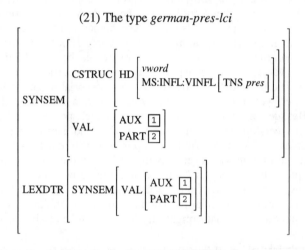

We learn two things from this representation about the language-particular fashion in which German expresses the present tense: the present tense does *not* add an auxiliary to the auxiliary list of the underlying predicate but instead requires that the categorial head of the predicate be expressed by a morphologically present tense form created by the morphological module of the grammar.[15] Assuming that (8) is representative of all basic predicates (of German) in having an empty auxiliary valence, (21) entails that the present tense member of the predicate paradigm of (8) will have an empty auxiliary valence as well. Our standard assumption that in the absence of an auxiliary the categorial head of a predicate is identical to its categorial core, together with (21), entails that the categorial core of the present tense derivative of (8) is a morphologically present tense form of the lexeme *küssen* [the categorial core of an expanded lci is structure-shared with the categorial core of its LEXDTR, cf. (11)]. Recall also that it follows from (20) that all finite predicates in German must have their categorial head specified for some person-number combination. Choosing a third person singular combination for

---

[14]The definition does not reflect any of the information that the type *german-pres-lci* inherits from its various supertypes. It focuses on the new information this type introduces. Further below, in (25) we merge all the local and inherited information of *german-pres-lci* to illustrate the overall informational structure of the German present tense predicate pattern. The reader might find it helpful to take a brief look at (25) before reading the paragraphs following (21).

[15]We also learn that the particle information does not change from input to output, but we are not dealing with particle predicates in this chapter.

purposes of illustration, we arrive at the following spell-out arrangement when the pattern in (21) is applied to the basic predicate in (8):

(22) The spell-out arrangement that results from applying the German present tense pattern (21) to the basic predicate *küssen* 'kiss' in (8); the remaining properties of the predicate are illustrated in (24)

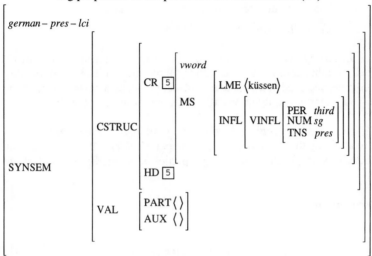

Assuming the existence of a basic morphological item *küssen* 'kiss' with a phonology value <küß> and a morphological pattern of German that suffixes <t> to the present stem of that item to derive its third person singular present tense form, we arrive at the following morphological word as the surface spell-out of the third person singular present tense variant of (8):

(23) The third person singular present tense morphological form of the lexeme *küssen* 'kiss'

Since the auxiliary and particle lists of the present tense predicate in (22) are both empty, (23) represents the complete surface realization of the information conveyed by (22). This is the form that appears in example sentence (1), repeated below for convenience, which was used at the beginning of this chapter to illustrate the synthetic expression of the present tense of simple predicates in German.

(1)   weil   die Ministerin   ihren Mann   **küßt**
        because the minister(fem) her husband kisses

        'because the minister kisses her husband'

In order to concentrate on the surface spell-out arrangement of (22), we left all other information out of the representation. But of course this is a predicate, and predicates contain information about subcategorization, content, and grammatical functions. (24) lays out those aspect of the sign (22):

(24) The subcategorization, content, and grammatical functions that result
     from applying the German present tense pattern (21) to the basic predicate
     küssen 'kiss' in (8); the remaining properties of the predicate are illustrated
     in (22)

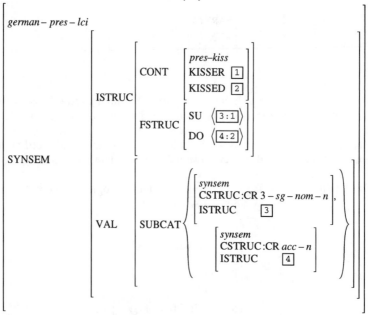

The content of this predicate refers to the same state of affairs of kissing as (8) but locates that state of affairs at the present time, as required by the supertype *pres-lci* (remember from (19) that *german-pres-lci* declares the archetype *pres-lci* and inherits all information from it, in this case the requirement that the content be a present state of affairs).

The predicate's functional structure ties the KISSER role to the grammatical function subject and the KISSED role to the direct object.

Finally, the subcategorization set ensures that the subject information structure is expressed by a third person singular nominative nominal and the direct object by an accusative nominal. Since the categorial head of the predicate is also third person singular, as shown in (22), the whole predicate represented by (22)+(24) agrees with its subject in person and number. Things could of course not be otherwise, since *german-pres-lci* is a subtype of *german-fin-lci* and this type declares the archetype *subj-agr-lci* in (19) which forces the categorial head of a predicate to agree with the predicate's subject [cf. (16)]. The case requirements on the nominals spelling out the subject and direct object in (24) are inherited from the two archetypal supertypes *subj-nom-lci* and *do-acc-lci* that were postulated in (18).

To conclude our discussion of the present tense predicate pattern of German, we provide the full pattern below and trace its components to the types where they originate:

(25) The German present tense pattern, i.e., the type *german-pres-lci*
   (= (21) except that all inherited information is included here)

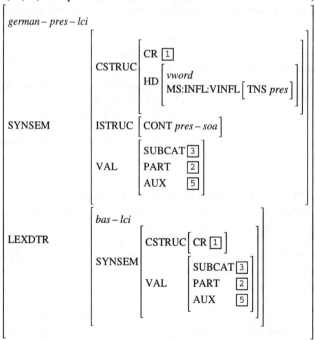

The identities of the auxiliary and particle lists of the input and output are part of the definition of the type *german-pres-lci* in (21) which also requires the categorial head of the predicate to be a morphologically present tense form. The content restriction of a present tense state of affairs for the output is inherited from the supertype *pres-lci.* The identity of the subcategorization frames of input and output comes from the supertype *fin-lci* in (14). The identity of the two categorial cores and the presence of a LEXDTR attribute are contributed by the original pattern archetype *exp-lci* in (11). This type also contributes the two constraints in (12) to the effect that the semantics of the output is an extension of the semantics of the input and that the f-structures of input and output are structurally isomorphic. This guarantees that inflectional patterns can only add morphosyntactic content to the underlying predicate but cannot change the underlying f-structure or the links between grammatical functions and semantic roles. Not shown in (25) are the agreement and case marking constraints internal to SUBCAT which are inherited via the supertypes *subj-agr-lci, subj-nom-lci,* and *do-acc-lci.* As an exercise, the reader might want to trace the relationship between the basic predicate in (8) and its derived present tense form in (22)+(24) to make sure that (25) indeed mediates between the two structures in the manner described here.

A look back to the overview in (7) shows that like the present tense, the past tense in German is expressed synthetically. A few simple changes to the treatment of the present tense suffice to extend our account to the past tense. We postulate another type *german-past-lci* which is equivalent to *german-pres-lci* in (21), except for two differences. The new type requires the categorial head to be spelled out by a morphologically past tense verb created by an appropriate word formation pattern in the morphological module of the lexicon. And secondly, *german-past-lci* of course declares the universal *past-lci* tense-aspect archetype instead of a present tense. This can be accomplished by obvious additions to the type hierarchy in (19). With this, we have productive patterns in place that will generate present and past tense predicates from (8) and from all other simple basic predicates in German.

3.4.3 The Perfect Tense Pattern of German

This brings us to an illustration of one of the four analytic predicate patterns in (7). The pattern that we will discuss, the perfect tense-aspect pattern in (26), applies to the same input predicate (8) as the synthetic present tense pattern. Like the previous pattern, (26) maps an underived predicate that is unmarked for tense-aspect into a predicate that has such a marking. Unlike the previous pattern, it associates its output predicate with an analytic surface expression.

Comparing (21) with (26), we see how the difference between synthetic and analytic expression of the same kind of content (in this case: tense-aspect) can arise: whereas (21) identifies the auxiliary lists of the LEXDTR and the mother, (26) specifies that the auxiliary list of the mother SYNSEM is the result of prefixing (the SYNSEM of) a morphologically present tense form of the auxiliary *haben* to the auxiliary list of the

LEXDTR. Simultaneously, the pattern requires that the categorial core of the new predicate take on the morphological perfect form of the lexeme specified by the underlying predicate.

(26) The type *german-perf-lci*

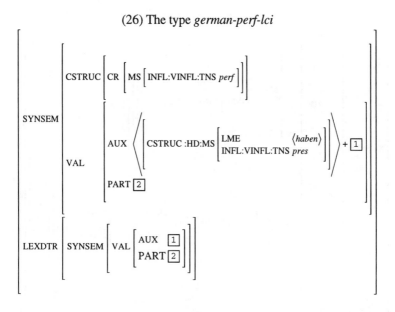

Applying this pattern to (8) by unifying (8) with the LEXDTR in (26) yields the result in (28) which should be compared with its present tense equivalent in (22).

Like its present tense counterpart in (22), this predicate expresses a tense-aspect of the underlying predicate (8) [the underlying predicate itself is unspecified for tense-aspect]. But in the perfect case, this tense-aspect information must be expressed by a combination of a morphologially present tense auxiliary *haben* and the participle of the perfect of the lexeme *küssen,* as in (27) which is the perfect tense-aspect counterpart to the present tense sentence in (1):

(27)   weil   die Ministerin   ihren Mann   **geküßt hat**
        because   the minister(fem)   her   husband   kissed   has

'because the minister has kissed her husband'

Of course, the lexical predicate in (28) depends on the morphological module of the grammar to generate the two morphological words the predicate requires in the two morphological spell-out slots that make up its surface arrangement. The patterns needed for this purpose introduce no new theoretical or practical problems.

(28) The spell-out arrangement that results from applying the German perfect tense-aspect pattern (26) to the basic predicate *küssen* 'kiss' in (8); the remaining properties of the predicate are illustrated in (29)

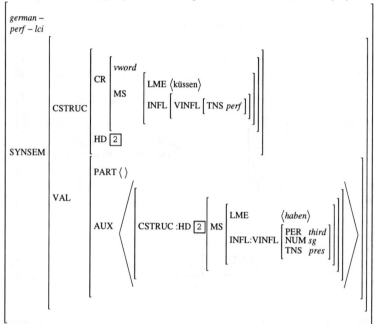

The reader should note that (26) expresses exactly the information in the third line of (7), in the same way that (21) expresses the information of the first line of that table. (21) and (26) serve the identical purpose of associating members of the German tense-aspect predicate paradigm with surface spell-outs, they just happen to differ in what kinds of spell-out arrangements they associate with particular tense-aspects.

Despite the difference in surface spell-outs, the present and perfect patterns are functionally equivalent as can be brought out by comparing the non-spell-out information in the two new predicates they generate. Note that with the exception of the tense-aspect difference, the perfect predicate in (29) is 100% identical to the present tense predicate in (24).

The contentive similarity of (24) and (29), despite their synthetic vs. analytic surface spell-outs in (22) vs. (28), is of course not surprising in the present context. After all, allowing equivalent predicate contents to be associated with varying modes of surface expressions is the major motivation behind the design of the theory of predicates proposed in this book. Our approach is guided by the principle of *Primacy of Function over Form:* since tense-aspect predicates *function* in the same way, they should also be analyzed in the same way, even if they differ in surface expression. Form is only a secondary determiner of the analysis of predicates.

(29) The subcategorization, content, and grammatical functions that result from applying the German perfect tense pattern (26) to the basic predicate *küssen* 'kiss' in (8); the remaining properties of the predicate are illustrated in (28)

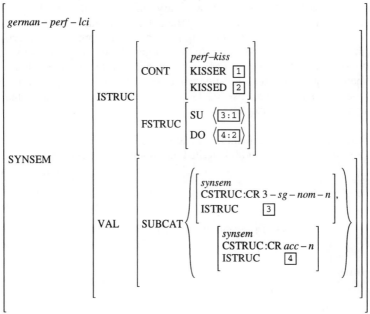

For completeness, in (30) we also present the fully spelled out perfect predicate pattern, i.e., the version of (26) which explicitly represents all information inherited from all supertypes of *german-perf-lci.*

Except for the spell-out information which is local to this type and the tense-aspect information which is inherited from the archetype *perf-lci,* all the information in this perfect pattern is identical to the information of the present tense pattern, because both patterns are subtypes of the type *german-fin-lci,* as can be verified in the type graph (20). Consequently, both predicate patterns inherit all the agreement and case marking constraints associated with this type which captures the generalization that synthetically and analytically expressed predicates agree and case mark in the same fashion.

The remaining three analytic tense-aspect patterns in (7) require only minor modifications from the treatment of the perfect pattern that we have discussed here in detail. Each pattern declares a different tense-aspect archetype and associates it with a different surface spell-out arrangement.

The future tense pushes a present tense version of the auxiliary *werden* 'become' onto the new predicate's auxiliary list and requires the categorial core to appear in the morphological form of the bare infinitive of the underlying lexeme. The pluperfect is identical to the perfect on the surface, except that it employs the morphological past tense (rather than the present tense) of the auxiliary *haben.* The future perfect, finally, differs from the perfect in surface spell-out by pushing two auxiliaries onto the new predicate's auxiliary list: the bare infinitive of the auxiliary *haben* preceded by the present tense of the auxiliary *werden,* making the latter act as the categorial head of all future perfect predicates. Defining these additional predicate patterns is routine, as is the definition of the additional morphological patterns that are required. Once all the patterns are in place, each simple, basic predicate of German is equipped with a full-fledged tense-aspect predicate paradigm that has one member for each tense that German predicates can express, including the appropriate surface expression.

(30) The German perfect tense pattern, i.e., the type *german-perf-lci*
    (= (26) except that all inherited information is included here)

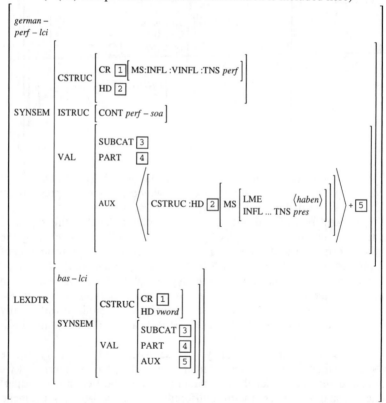

3.5 Tense-Aspect Predicates in the Syntax

Having gone through the trouble of defining predicate patterns and morphological patterns to create the tense-aspect versions of the simple basic untensed predicates of German, we naturally wish to use them in phrase structure. To this end, we need to take recourse to the syntactic schemas we defined in chapter 3. The synthetically expressed present tense predicate in (22)+(24) needs to undergo the argument schema twice in order to saturate its two SUBCAT requirements. Since its auxiliary and particle valences are both empty, it need not (and cannot) appear in the auxiliary and particle schemas.

(31) shows the crucial parts of the result of combining the present tense of *küssen* with its direct object in sentence (1).

The information flows as follows: the argument phrase on the left is identified with the second member of the predicate's SUBCAT on the right. The remainder of the predicate's SUBCAT is "percolated" to the mother for later saturation. From the indices on the arguments in the predicate's SUBCAT we can see that the first member of the set expresses the predicate's subject (and indirectly the KISSER) and the second one the predicate's direct object (and indirectly the KISSED). This is why in the mother node's content, the KISSED role bears the same index as the argument daughter on the left. By undergoing the argument schema a second time to saturate the remaining SUBCAT requirement, the phrase becomes saturated, functionally complete (it now has a subject), and semantically fully interpreted (the KISSER role is assigned to the subject index). After linearization, the result is a sentence like (1) whose subject is interpreted as the agent and whose direct object is the patient of kissing.

The perfect predicate spelled out as *geküßt hat* 'has kissed' goes through the argument schema twice in a completely analogous fashion, since its SUBCAT is identical to that of its present tense equivalent. However, it additionally has to undergo the auxiliary schema once in order to empty its auxiliary valence. The order of application of the three saturation steps is irrelevant, since all orders of application are guaranteed to yield the same result.[16] (32) shows the crucial parts of the result of combining the auxiliary *hat* with the perfect predicate (28)+(29), spelled out by the core *geküßt*, assuming that the predicate has not saturated any of its SUBCAT valences yet.

Given that the presence of the auxiliary and the correlation of its presence with a perfect interpretation of the predicate have already been determined by the perfect predicate formation pattern in the lexicon, the syntactic combination of the two pieces that spell out this predicate together

---

[16]This is so because word order is handled by separate linearization constraints and because each phrasal schema saturates one valence requirement at a time and carries all uncanceled information up to the mother for subsequent saturation. Eventually, all valences have to end up empty. Note, however, that the auxiliary and particle schemas take the right-most element off the lists they affect. The overall effect therefore is that where our system allows for alternative orders of saturation, all orders yield the same result.

(the core and the auxiliary) is completely anticlimactic: the only information in the auxiliary that matters at this point is its identity; the predicate on the left contributes its own categorial core to the linear-phonological structure of the sentence and makes sure that all the auxiliaries and particles that co-express the same predicate are present in the syntactic representation of the sentence. Particles and auxiliaries do not contribute any contentive information to the newly formed phrase as can be seen in (32): the mother's CONT and SUBCAT are completely determined by the predicate daughter which is the lexically created informational head of the mother phrase. The auxiliary plays no informational role in the syntactic component at all but at this point is merely present as a categorial piece of the surface spell-out of the predicate on the left.

At this stage, the phrase in (32) can undergo the two argument saturation steps we illustrated for the synthetically expressed present tense predicate earlier and so come to be fully saturated. The linear components of all the categorial constituents of the sentence can then be ordered to yield the word order of the perfect tense aspect-sentence in (27).

(31) The structure of 'ihren Mann küßt' (kisses her husband – acc)

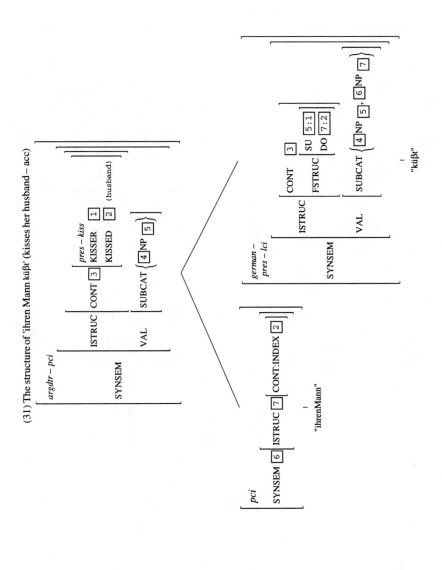

(32) The structure of 'geküßt hat' (has kissed)

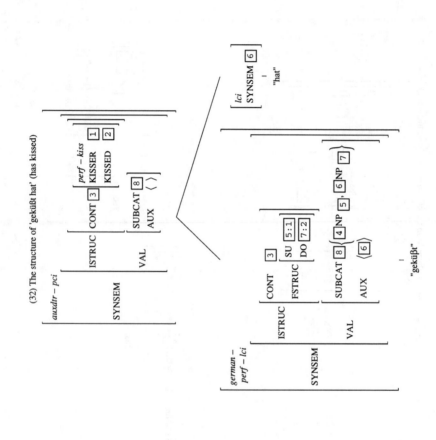

3.6 Interactions Between Tense-Aspect and Case Marking

In this final section, we leave German and look at some other languages. These show interesting interactions between different kinds of information that our theory locates in predicates, in particular tense-aspect, polarity, modality, and case government.

3.6.1 Georgian and Hindi Case Marking[17]

It is well known that Georgian (Kartvelian) and Hindi (Indo-European) possess surface case marking patterns that are sensitive to tense-aspect, or more generally, to what is commonly referred to as *morphosyntactic* information of various sorts. It is morphosyntactic information construed broadly that is relevant to our analysis of expanded predicates: these, it should be recalled, are predicates whose basic functional-semantic information is augmented by morphosyntactic information.

Turning first to Georgian, Anderson (1992: 104) observes that "the form of the case marking depends on the tense of its main verb." Harris (1981: 39–40) provides the following examples where there is observable variation in the case marking patterns for the SUBJ complement of a verb:

(33a)   nino   amtknarebs
               Nino-NOM she-yawns-I-I

               'Nino yawns'

(33b)   ninom   daamtknara
               Nino-ERG she-yawned-II-I

               'Nino yawned'

As can be seen, the verb form covaries with different patterns of case marking in Georgian: the tenses are indicated by capitalized Roman numerals and refer to so-called series I and II, while the Roman numeral in small capitals designates verb class. Georgian also exhibits another type of case marking pattern exemplified by (33c): [from Harris (1981: 135)]

(33c)   merabs   turme   daumtknarebia
               Merab-DAT apparently she-yawned-III-I

               'Merab apparently has yawned'

---

[17]The discussions and presentations of specific phenomena below are intended to be exploratory and suggestive of the way in which our approach finds natural extension beyond German: we ignore many of the challenging complexities of these phenomena and only highlight those aspects that are relevant to our limited purpose.

Such constructions are of note, since they reflect a morphosyntactic distinction not evident in German, namely, an evidential construal (with or without the appearance of an adverb such as *turme* 'evidently') for clauses containing a specific verb form and its DAT case governed complement. Evidentiality, like polarity, is one of the types of morphosyntactic content which we assume is lexically represented and will exhibit both synthetic and analytic expression in the languages of the world. In this respect, morphosyntactic content such as tense-aspect distinctions and evidentiality both have the lexical effects attributed to our lexical representations.

The case marking paradigm for Hindi resembles that of Georgian in certain respects. In particular, the case marking on the SUBJ varies between ERG in (34a) containing a predicate in the perfect tense and NOM in (34b) with a predicate in the synthetically expressed future tense and (34c) in the analytically expressed present progressive tense: [examples from Mohanan (1994: 8)]

(34a)   raam-ne   darvaazaa   k^{h}olaa
        Ram-ERG   door-NOM   open-PERF

        'Ram opened the door'

(34b)   raam   darvaazaa   k^{h}olegaa
        Ram-NOM   door-NOM   open-FUT

        'Ram will open the door'

(34c)   raam   darvaazaa   k^{h}oltaa   hai
        Ram-NOM   door-NOM   open-IMPERF   be-PRES

        'Ram is opening the door'

So far we have seen that different tense distinctions are determinative of different case marking patterns and that these correlations are keyed to distinct verbal forms. Given the morphological assumptions we have adopted, specifically concerning many-to-many mappings between forms and functions, we would also expect that there should be instances in the languages of the world where predicate forms are held constant while the functional aspects associated with relevant predicates determine different case markings. In fact, Hindi appears to possess such constructions as observed in Butt (1995: 16). This language contains analytic expressions to express modality whose precise interpretation, i.e., desire versus obligation, depends on the case marking of the SUBJ. This pattern is illustrated in (35a) and (35b), where the entity denoted by the DAT SUBJ in (35a) is interpreted as obligated to undertake the action denoted by the verb, while the ERG SUBJ in (35b) is interpreted as simply desirous of doing so.

(35a)   anjum-ko   xat   lik^h-naa   hai
        Anjum.Fem-DAT   letter.Mas.NOM   write-Inf.Mas.   be.Pres.3.sg.
        'Anjum has to write the letter'

(35b)   anjum-ne   xat   lik^h-naa   hai
        Anjum.Fem-ERG   letter.Mas.NOM   write-Inf.Mas.   be.Pres.3.sg.
        'Anjum wants to write the letter'

In sum, we see that both Georgian and Hindi display the type of interaction between morphosyntactic information, meaning determination, and case marking government that is hypothesized here to be diagnostic of lexical representations. The representations that we have developed for German can be adapted to address these grammatical phenomena as well. In the following section we will conclude with a different form of these interactions from Finnish.

3.6.2 Finnish

In chapter 2 we hypothesized that polarity in Finnish is appropriately included in the class of lexically represented analytically expressed predicates. Consider the following paradigm repeated from Figure 9 in chapter 2:

e-**n** lue	I don't read	e-**mme** lueneet	We don't read
e-**t** lue	You (sg.) don't read	e-**tte** lueneet	You don't read
e-**i** lue	S/he doesn't read	ei-**vät** lueneet	They don't read

Like tense-aspect, polarity is a type of morphosyntactic information which yields expanded predicates in the present theory. It is commonly observed that polarity determines case marking in Finnish: predicates that otherwise would permit either an accusative or partitive case marked object, like *lukea* 'read', allow only partitive objects when they appear in negative polarity. This distribution is illustrated below: [based on examples from Karanko-Pap et al. (1980: 103)]

(36a)   luin   kirjan
        read-1SG.PAST   book-ACC
        'I read (through) the book'

(36b)   luen   kirjaa
        read-1SG.PRES   book-PART
        'I am reading the book'

(36c)   en   lue   *kirjan/kirjaa
          NEG-1SG read book-ACC/book-PART

'I am not reading the book'

As can be seen, there are case restrictions depending on polarity. Positive polarity, exemplified in (36a) and (36b), is expressed synthetically in these instances and permits either ACC (36a) or PART (36b) OBJ marking, indicating a difference in aspect. Negative polarity, in contrast, is expressed analytically and prohibits ACC case marking of the OBJ, as indicated in (36c). In the theory developed here all of these forms would be variants of lexically represented predicates and therefore it is to be expected that case, being lexically determined, could be governed by such representations. Since lexical representations can have various surface manifestations in our theory, it is important to observe that Finnish has several tense distinctions that are expressed analytically. As seen previously, positive polarity can appear in various tenses and when these tenses are expressed analytically we find that ACC versus PART marking alternations obtain for OBJs, just like when positive polarity is expressed synthetically:

(37a)   olen   lukenut   kirjan
          COP-1SG read-PERF book-ACC

'I have read the book'

(37b)   olen   lukenut   kirjaa
          COP-1SG read-PERF book-PART

'I have been reading the book'

Similarly, when these analytically expressed tenses are negative in polarity the OBJ is restricted to being marked PART, as seen in (38):

(38)   en   ole lukenut   *kirjan/kirjaa
         NEG-1SG COP read-PERF book-ACC/PART

'I have not read/been reading the book'

In other words, the case government pattern of the basic predicate is maintained and modified according to whether it has the value positive or negative polarity in an expanded predicate: the case marking requirements are independent of the synthetic or analytic status of its surface expression.

The independence of case marking from surface expression and its dependence on functional-semantic properties of the predicate is dramatically displayed in connection with the case marking on many adverbs of "duration" and "frequency" in Finnish.[18] As has been seen, case government is specified as a property of predicates in our lexical representations: in fact, it is specified as independent of both semantic role and grammatical function. In this connection it is relevant, as observed in Maling (1993), that the object cases (NOM, ACC, PART) in Finnish which are associable with particular basic predicates are precisely the cases that appear on many adverbs of "duration" and "frequency." For example, the verb *lukea* 'read' takes either ACC or PART case for its OBJ complement: [examples from Maling (1993: 55)]

(39)   lapsi   luki   kirjaa/kirjan   illassa
          child-NOM read-3SG.PAST book-PART/ACC evening-IN

          'The child was reading/read the book'

In constructions where the "SUBJ" is specified for some case other than NOM, as in the analytically expressed modal construction in (40), then the OBJ can only appear in the NOM:[19]

(40)   lapsen   täytyy   lukea   kirja/*kirjan
          child-GEN must-3SG read-1st.INF book-NOM/ACC

          'The child must read the book'

On Maling's account this case marking pattern follows from a general convention stated previously in Zaenen, Maling, and Thráinsson (1985):

Case Assignment Generalization:

> The highest available GF is assigned NOM case, the next highest ACC.

In (39), the highest grammatical function is the SUBJ, and assuming the default assignment of case for a predicate such as 'read', it is assigned NOM, while the OBJ gets ACC case (or PART, since this paradigmatic opposition is meaningful in this language[20]). Depending on one's analysis, modal predicates either do not contain a SUBJ and are impersonal or contain "quirky" case marked SUBJs: in either instance, the highest GF in need of case is the OBJ and NOM is accordingly assigned to it.

---

[18]The following discussion represents a simplification of the complex and intriguing Finnish facts done in the interest of expediency: we do no more than provide the flavor of how data such as these are relevant for the theory proposed in this book. For a fuller presentation and an overview of the sort of lexically-based analysis we are adapting, see Maling (1993).

[19]The case marking effects of modality are also evident in the paradigm of synthetic versus analytic expression of Hungarian tense and modality presented as (12) in chapter 2.

[20]See Ackerman and Moore (forthcoming) for an analysis of such meaningful paradigmatic contrasts within a Dowty-type proto-property framework.

As noted in Maling (1993), to the degree that adverbs might observe the case marking conventions, this does not follow from the convention stated above since it is formulated in terms of GFs associated with a verb: adverbs are not generally assumed to bear GFs within the lexical representations of verbs.[21] We can see, however, that the relevant pattern obtains for Finnish adverbs when we compare (41) with (40) above: [Maling (1993: 55)]

(41)   lapsen   täytyy   lukea   koko päivä/*päivän
         child-GEN must-3SG   read-1st.INF   whole day-NOM/*ACC
         'The child must read the whole day'

In (41), the agentive argument bears GEN case, for the same reason as in (40), while the "true" OBJ complement of the verb does not occur: the adverbial thus bears NOM case, as did the true OBJ in (40). For our purposes what is important is the following: our lexical representations contain case specifications and these are expected to be affected, given our basic assumptions, by various properties of predicates such as their meaning, valence, semantic roles of arguments, and their grammatical function inventories. Since modal constructions in general modulate the meaning of basic predicates, they are good candidates for lexical representations in our theory and we would expect them to also alter typical lexical properties of basic predicates: we can see that in Finnish such analytic predicates yield different case assignments than the basic predicate (i.e., (39) above). These case assignments are in accordance with the general convention for lexical case government identified by Zaenen, Maling and Thráinsson (1985). In addition, this lexical case assignment pattern also applies to a lexically limited class of adverbials: their co-occurrence with a predicate provides a particular construal of the action denoted by that predicate. In effect, the co-occurrence of a basic predicate and an adverbial of a lexically specified sort is interpretable as representing a derived lexical predicate: the fact that case government obtains for such predicates would simply follow from the fact that lexical predicates are the locus of case assignment. An interpretation of this kind would seem circular in default of a class of predicates which must on their own be represented as selecting for the types of adverbs which play a role in modifying the meaning of verbs such as *lukea* 'read'. In fact, however, certain Finnish verbs denoting duration or extent such as *kestää* 'last', *viettää* 'spend', *viipyä* 'stay, remain' and *odottaa* 'wait', appear to semantically select for adverbs and these adverbs follow the pattern in the

---

[21]See Przepiórkowski (1997) for arguments that this type of data motivates the hypothesis that adverbs should be treated as complements.

case marking generalization. This pattern is evident in the following sentence from Karanko-Pap et al. (1980):

(42)   matka   kesti   tunnin
             trip-NOM last-3SG.PAST hour-ACC

'The trip lasted an hour'

Verbs such as these, as well as verbs such as *lukea* 'read' appearing with adverbs, require that these selected adverbs appear in the PART case when the predicate has a negative polarity value:

(43)   matka   ei   kestänyt tuntia-kaan
             trip-NOM NEG-3SG last-PERF hour-PART-NEG.EMPH

'The trip didn't (even) last an hour'

In other words, verbs in the class typified by *kestää* 'last' would seem to require lexical specification of adverbials, while the case marking pattern associated with such adverbials can be made to follow simply from the general case marking convention sensitive to the following hierarchy: [Maling (1993: 60)]

SUBJ > OBJ > MEASURE > DURATION > FREQUENCY

Finally, this case marking pattern interacts, as one would expect, with the polarity values of predicates (either underived or derived): this can be seen from the requirement that the duration adverb in (43) must appear in the PART case.

In sum, Finnish presents phenomena where many of the properties hypothesized to be associated with our lexical predicates interact in expected ways. We have seen here that tense is expressible either synthetically or analytically without affecting the core properties of basic predicates. On the other hand, case marking is affected by the polarity value of predicates. We have also seen that modality affects case marking and that modal predicates and simple predicates behave alike with respect to both the selection of certain adverbs and their case marking: the case marking of adverbials in these instances is likewise affected by polarity in the same way as it is affected when canonical arguments of predicates are at issue.

4 Conclusion

In this chapter, we have put all the pieces of our theory of predicates together in an analysis of the tense-aspect paradigms of underived German predicates like *küssen* 'kiss' in (8). Our goal was to formally capture the representative paradigm in (6) which groups together all the finite uses of *küssen,* where each use expresses a different tense-aspect and is represented by a different surface arrangement of words. According to the primacy of function over form, each of these different predicates should be analyzed in the same way, since they all function to locate the state of affairs of the underlying predicate in the time dimension. This functional criterion overrides the secondary formal criterion that some of these notions are expressed synthetically and others analytically.

We intentionally hid many routine details of the analyses from the reader to make those aspects of the analyses salient that are theoretically important while at the same time giving enough details of representative cases to allow the reader to conceive what a full-fledged analysis would look like.

In the final section, we looked at some interesting data from Georgian, Hindi, and Finnish where the case marking in a clause correlates with either its tense-aspect or its polarity. Since our theory locates each of these three kinds of information in the predicate, we expect such correlations to occur, no matter whether the predicate is expressed synthetically or analytically.

We have made crucial use of all the technical concepts that were introduced in the previous chapters: predicates, typed feature structures, type hierarchies, predicate patterns, morphological patterns, and type partitioning. We believe that each of these tools is a necessary prerequisite for capturing the important empirical and conceptual goals laid out and motivated in the previous chapters, especially chapters 1 and 2 where the need for a linguistic theory was demonstrated that can generalize across the contentive aspect of predicates independent of their synthetic or analytic surface expression.

8

Passive

1 Introduction

Passive is an empirically well-attested construction in the languages of the world. Since passive predicates typically differ from their active counterparts systematically in both form and surface function assignments of the predicates' arguments, active-passive pairs form a prototypical example of a grammatical function alternation. Moreover, since passives are believed to behave relatively similarly across different languages, they are also a good candidate for grammatical universals. It is presumably no accident that the framework of Relational Grammar paid much attention to passive in the early 1970s and that this framework's universal laws of sentence structure were strongly influenced by the analysis of passive. In their classic paper Perlmutter and Postal (1977) [henceforth referred to as "PP77"], the authors argued against the typical analyses of passive in the Standard Theory of Transformational Grammar of the mid to late 1960's which analyzed passive in terms of linear order-dependent transformations. These grammatical transformations, rather crude devices that ignored all but categorial information, applied to a linearly ordered input tree and transformed it into another linearly ordered output tree. PP77 demonstrated that a grammar based on such devices was unable to characterize passive in terms of one single operation applying in different languages, even though passive sentences seemed to have analogous differences from active sentences in these languages. Perlmutter and Postal's diagnosis of the problem was that transformational grammar was not equipped with the right primitives to provide an explanatory account of passives cross-linguistically. In their view, reiterated in much of the literature since the 1970s—including that of LFG—transformational grammar was too narrowly focused on phrase-structural explanations and its proponents were too unwilling to consider explanations involving other primitives, be they functional, semantic, or whatever. Our own criticism of the recent categorial excesses of transformational grammar in terms of empirically unverifiable functional heads is just a modern version of Perlmutter and Postal's (and others') earlier kinds of objections.

PP77 suggested that the generalizations lost in a phrase-structure based account can in fact be captured in a grammatical function based account, where subjects, objects, etc. are regarded as primitives of the theory. In particular, they suggested that (personal) passive be formulated as a universal rule that promotes the direct object of the active sentence into the subject of the passive and demotes the subject of the active clause into a grammatical function they called "chômeur" (the French word for "unemployed worker"). In addition, they postulated a relational hierarchy that such processes as case marking and agreement are sensitive to: the higher a grammatical function on the hierarchy, the more likely it is that the verb will agree with it, etc. Subjects were postulated to be higher on the hierarchy than both direct objects and chômeurs.

Not surprisingly, transformational grammarians sought to improve their theory in light of the more explanatory approach to grammatical function changes proposed by Relational Grammar. If transformational theory was to draw even or perhaps improve on Relational Grammar, then function changes needed to be statable without reference to linear order. Such approaches were developed in the early 1980s and have been part of GB theory and its off-shoots ever since. Soon we will consider this revised approach based on the absorption of abstract Case. It will be advantageous, however, to first discuss in some detail the descriptive facts of a number of passives in a language known as *passivfreudig* "positively inclined towards passives:" German.

2   Three German Passives

We will discuss three passive constructions in the present section.[1] It will be shown that they have much in common but that no two of them are exactly alike. All three constructions are expressed by an auxiliary-main verb combination, using one of the auxiliaries *werden, bekommen,* and *sein.* We will refer to the passives containing the first two auxiliaries as the "werden-passive" and the "bekommen-passive" respectively. Since the name "sein-passive" is already taken by a different passive construction involving this auxiliary which will not be discussed in the present chapter, we will need another name for this construction. Given that the construction we are interested in involves a combination of *sein* with the zu-infinitive of the main verb, we will refer to it as the "zuinf(initive)-passive."

In sections 2.1–2.6 we will document that the three constructions share a number of properties that set them apart from active sentences. In this sense it is justified to distinguish them from the active voice and to refer to them all as passive. Despite these similarities, however, we will show in sections 2.7–2.10 that no two constructions are completely alike in their grammatical behavior. This dualism concerning the striking similarities between the constructions and the fact that each one is unique is a challenge for any approach to passive.

---

[1]Additional passive constructions of German will be discussed in later sections of this chapter. The reader may also want to consult Brinker (1971) and Höhle (1978) which provide many additional details and insights.

2.1 All Three Constructions Are Passive

At this point we are ready to present the evidence that the constructions introduced in the last two paragraphs all differ from active ones with respect to a number of grammatical properties, and that any promising grammatical theory should express this generalization in some way. We will illustrate this claim with five distinctive grammatical features found in each construction.

2.2 The Logical Subject is Not the Grammatical Subject of the Passive Sentence

The argument structure of agentive transitive verbs is mapped into grammatical functions in such a way that in the unmarked case the agent argument of the verb, i.e., the logical subject, is realized as the grammatical subject of the sentence. For instance, in the following sentence the referent of *Maria* is the agent of the state of affairs of giving being described:[2]

(1) weil Maria dem Mann die Blumen schenkt
   because Maria the man the flowers gives

   'because Maria gives the man the flowers'

If we embed the verb *schenken* in each of the constructions under study, we find that the grammatical subject of the resulting sentence in no case refers to the agent of *schenken* (the subject of the sentence is underlined, the auxiliary appears in boldface):

(2) weil die Blumen dem Mann geschenkt **wurden**
   because the flowers the man given were

   'because the flowers were given to the man'

(3) weil die Blumen dem Mann zu schenken **sind**
   because the flowers the man to give are

   'because the flowers must be given to the man'

(4) weil der Mann die Blumen geschenkt **bekam**
   because the man the flowers given was

   'because the man was given the flowers'

In (2) and (3) the theme argument of *schenken* is the subject of the whole sentence and in (4) the subject expresses the beneficiary of the predicate. In this sense all the sentences (2)–(4) differ from the active sentence (1) in that

---

[2]The verb *schenken* is best translated as 'give as a present'. For convenience we gloss and translate it just as 'give'.

the surface subject of the whole sentence does not refer to the agent of the main verb.

2.3 The Logical Subject Can be Expressed in a *von*-phrase in the Passive

Next, we show that the constructions differ from active sentences in that they allow the agent of the active verb to be expressed by a prepositional phrase headed by the preposition *von*.[3] As (5) shows, this is of course impossible in regular active sentences:

(5) * weil die Blumen dem Mann <u>von</u> <u>Maria</u> **schenkte**
because the flowers the man by Maria gave

'because Maria gave the man the flowers'

However, if we take each of the sentences in (2)–(4) where the agent of the *schenken* state of affairs is left unexpressed and add a *von*-phrase to them, then the NP in the additional phrase can be interpreted as the agent of *schenken*:

(6) weil die Blumen dem Mann <u>von</u> <u>Johann</u> geschenkt **wurden**
because the flowers the man by Johann given were

'because the flowers were given to the man by Johann'

(7) weil die Blumen dem Mann <u>von</u> <u>Johann</u> zu schenken **sind**
because the flowers the man by Johann to give are

'because the flowers must be given to the man by Johann'

(8) weil der Mann die Blumen <u>von</u> <u>Johann</u> geschenkt **bekam**
because the man the flowers by Johann given was

'the man was given the flowers by Johann'

2.4 The Logical Subject is Omissible in the Passive

A third difference between the active and passive paradigms can be illustrated with reference to the finite passive sentences (2)–(4) without a *von*-phrase and their equivalents (6)–(8) with a *von*-phrase. Only the passive constructions allow the agent of the verb *schenken* not to be overtly

---

[3]Other prepositions can be used instead of *von* under conditions which are only partially understood. For instance, the more the thematic role of the demoted subject deviates from canonical agentivity [cf. Dowty (1991)] and approaches something resembling an instrument, the more likely it is that the oblique phrase can be headed by the preposition *durch*. Other prepositions are possible as well. The interested reader should consult the works cited in footnote 1 of this chapter.

expressed at all. The active construction in (1) prohibits such an omission, as shown in (9):

(9) * weil   dem Mann die Blumen schenkt
       because the   man   the flowers gives

'ø gives the flowers to the man'

2.5 The More Agentive the Active Verb, the More Likely it is that it Can Occur in the Passive Construction

Active sentences, as semantically unmarked, are typically indiscriminate concerning the semantic verb types they admit. Thus, although one occasionally finds a verb which can only occur in passive sentences (e.g., English *rumored)*, these gaps are accidental. In particular, active predicates are typically tolerant about the thematic role of their grammatical subject: they are as comfortable with non-agentive roles like those used below as with agentive roles:

(10)   weil   jeder   den Jungen **kennt**
        because everybody the boy   knows

'because everybody knows the boy'

(11)   weil   Peter dem Verein   **angehört**
        because Peter the   club(DAT) belongs

'because Peter belongs to the club'

In contrast, many languages systematically restrict their passive construction in that if there are any non-passivizable predicates in the language then they are non-agentive. All the German passive structures examined here follow this pattern. For instance, the werden- and zuinf-passives of the active sentence with the verb *kennen* in (10) are ungrammatical (or at least degraded):

(12) * weil   der Junge **gekannt wird**
       because the boy   known   is

'because the boy is known'

(13) * weil   der Junge zu **kennen ist**
       because the boy   to know   is

'because the boy has to be known'

Likewise, even though active sentences like (11) with the verb *angehören* are grammatical, and in general bekommen-passives are possible with verbs taking indirect objects, the following passive sentence with *angehören* is ungrammatical:

(14) * weil   der Verein **angehört bekam**
       because the club   belonged   got
       'because the club had members'

2.6 Each Passive Construction is Characterized by the Presence of an Auxiliary

Finally, we list a fifth property that distinguishes the German active predicative construction from all the structures we have contrasted it with. Each of the passive predicative constructions contains an obligatory auxiliary:

(15)   weil   die Blumen dem Mann geschenkt **wurden**
       because the flowers the man   given   were
       'because the flowers were given to the man'

(16)   weil   die Blumen dem Mann zu schenken **sind**
       because the flowers the man   to give   are
       'because the flowers must be given to the man'

(17)   weil   der Mann die Blumen geschenkt **bekam**
       because the man   the flowers given   was
       'because the man was given the flowers'

Active predicatively used predicates of course may or may not contain an auxiliary:

(18)   weil   Maria dem Mann die Blumen schenkt
       because Maria the man   the flowers gives
       'because Maria gives the man the flowers'

(19)   weil   Maria dem Mann die Blumen geschenkt **hat**
       because Maria the man   the flowers given   has
       'because Maria has given the man the flowers'

We have identified the following five properties of the passive constructions discussed in this section which systematically set them apart from active sentences:

(20)   Distinctive Properties of Passive Sentences in German

a.   The logical subject is not the grammatical subject of the passive sentence;
b.   the logical subject can be expressed in a *von*-phrase in the passive;
c.   the logical subject of the predicate is omissible in the passive;
d.   the construction has a preference for agentive predicates;
e.   the construction (when used predicatively) contains an auxiliary.

2.7 No Two Constructions are Precisely Alike

It is clear from the evidence presented in the last section that the three passive constructions are so strikingly similar that grammatical theory would miss a significant generalization if it failed to characterize them as a natural class distinct from active sentences.

The data to be discussed next disturb this clear picture, however. They show that despite the great similarity between the structures, there are also important differences between them. In fact, no two of the constructions behave completely alike. This renders the problem for grammatical theory somewhat more complex, for it will now be necessary to account for the fact that the constructions in some respects form a natural class and yet each one is partially autonomous from the others.

2.8 Idiosyncrasies of the bekommen-passive

The bekommen-passive differs from the werden-passive and the zuinf-passive in thematic roles and the grammatical functions affected by the operation of passive. Starting with the latter two, they both realize the following function changes:[4]

(21) a. SU --> ø/OBL
     b. DO --> SU

This schematic representation can be interpreted in the following fashion. Given an active three place predicate with both an indirect object and a direct object as exemplified in (22),

(22)   weil   Maria dem Mann   die Blumen   schenkt
        because Maria the man(IO) the flowers(DO) gives

        'because Maria gives the man the flowers'

the direct object of the active verb becomes the subject of the passive sentence:

---

[4]We focus here exclusively on the personal passives of transitive predicates.

(23)   weil   <u>die</u> <u>Blumen</u>   dem Mann   geschenkt **wurden**
because the flowers(SU) the man(IO) given   were

'because the flowers were given to the man'

(24)   weil   <u>die</u> <u>Blumen</u>   dem Mann   zu schenken **sind**
because the flowers(SU) the man(IO) to give   are

'because the flowers must be given to the man'

In each case the indirect object is barred from becoming the subject in the passive:

(25) *   weil   <u>der</u> <u>Mann</u>   die Blumen   geschenkt **wird**
because the man(SU) the flower(DO) given   are

'because the man is given the flowers'

(26) *   weil   <u>der</u> <u>Mann</u>   die Blumen   zu schenken **ist**
because the man(SU) the flowers(DO) to give   is

'because the man must be given the flowers'

The bekommen-passive, on the other hand, makes the indirect object into the new subject, leaving the direct object unaffected:

(27)   weil   <u>der</u> <u>Mann</u>   die Blumen   geschenkt **bekam**
because the man(SU) the flowers(DO) given   was

'the man was given the flowers'

The following sentence, parallel to (23) and (24), is consequently ungrammatical:

(28) *   weil   <u>die</u> <u>Blumen</u>   dem Mann   geschenkt **bekamen**
because the flowers(SU) the man(IO) given   were

'because the flowers were given to the man'

In sum, although the bekommen-structures share the properties in (20) with the other passives, they also differ from each of them in at least one way, namely, with respect to the alignment of thematic roles and the subject function.

2.9 Idiosyncrasies of the werden-passive

Since we have already demonstrated that the werden- and the bekommen-passives differ in at least one respect, we can concentrate here on the comparison of the werden- and the zuinf-structures. These two constructions systematically differ in the morphological form they select for the main verb. *Werden* requires a past participle but *zuinf* requires an infinitival form containing the element *zu:*

(29) weil   die Blumen   dem Mann   **geschenkt wurden**
      because   the flowers(SU) the man(IO)   given   were

      'because the flowers were given to the man'

(30) weil   die Blumen   dem Mann   **zu** schenk**en sind**
      because   the flowers(SU) the man(IO)   to give   are

      'because the flowers must be given to the man'

Neither predicate can be expressed with the morphological form of the main verb contained in the other.

2.10 Idiosyncrasies of the zuinf-passive

The zuinf-passive differs from both the werden-passive and the bekommen-passive. Unlike the first, it co-occurs with an infinitival verb form, while *werden* selects a participle. It differs from the bekommen-structures in that the former aligns the theme direct object of the active verb with the subject of the passive and leaves the beneficiary, if one is present, unaffected; the bekommen-passive, in contrast, aligns the indirect object with the subject of the passive and leaves the theme direct object of the base verb unaffected.

There is another way in which the zuinf-passive differs from the other two: the passive predicates containing zuinf are associated with a modal nuance which passives based on *werden* and *bekommen* lack. This difference can be seen in (6)–(8): (7) contains a semantic element of necessity that is not present in the modally neutral (6) and (8). This phenomenon is not particular to these example sentences but characterizes the three passives generally.[5]

2.11 Summary of Section 2

In this section we have suggested that all three of the constructions examined here should be analyzed as passives. Despite the overall similarities between the werden-, bekommen-, and zuinf-passives, no two of them display exactly the same set of grammatical properties. An optimal analysis of passive should account, in a principled manner, for as many of these

---

[5]The zuinf-passive can also express the modal notion of possibility. (7) thus is actually ambiguous and can also be translated as "It is possible for the flowers to be given to the man by Johann."

properties as possible. In the next section we will return to an evaluation of some current theories of passive and see how well they can handle the configuration of facts presented in the present section.

3 On Some Current Theories of Passive

3.1 Passive In GB

In section 1 we observed that Perlmutter and Postal (1977) found significant shortcomings in the analysis of function-changing operations in general and passive in particular within classical transformational grammar. By the early 1980s, transformational grammarians led by Chomsky had revised their theory to make grammatical function changing operations more abstract so as to make them independent of language-particular linear order. While transformational grammar has undergone a number of significant changes since then, its reliance on abstract Case to analyze passive structures still obtains. Since the formulation of this general approach in the form of Chomsky (1981) remains one of the clearest in the GB literature, we will base the following paragraphs on that book.

One of the central claims of Government and Binding Theory is that "constructions" in the sense of passive, raising, or unaccusativity are the products of the interaction of a small number of grammatical principles which affect different constructions of the same language and apply across languages as well.[6] In his discussion of passive, Chomsky (1981) stresses that Universal Grammar should not make reference to a "passive construction" for at least two reasons. First, the sentences classified as passive in a language often have properties which also need to be referred to in the analysis of non-passive constructions, e.g., raising. Chomsky argues, therefore, that what we call passive is composed of a number of recurrent primitive grammatical operations (e.g., NP-movement and Case absorption) and that the theory of grammar should concern itself with understanding these primitive operations and their interaction.[7]

---

[6]To be precise, *almost* alike, since the theory postulates that the principles can apply differently from language to language, depending on parametric choices.

[7]Note that Chomsky's argument loses its force in a construction-based theory that models constructions as types that can be grouped under supertypes which express generalizations across all their subconstructions. This kind of architecture, clearly not anticipated by Chomsky, *is* able to postulate descriptively adequate language-particular constructions while at the same time relating them to universal constructions (our archetypes) and types that capture generalizations across the various constructions.

In our view, this architecture is superior to Chomsky's Principles and Parameters (P&P) architecture because the construction+archetype architecture achieves analyses which are *both* descriptively and explanatorily adequate, whereas the P&P approach, in its program of finding ever more abstract explanations, has been reducing its descriptively adequate data coverage to a point where the theory really does not qualify as a *general* theory of language but rather as a theory of a highly idealized and regular subset of structures for which proposed principles provide partial analyses.

Second, the case for a compositional rather than a "primitive" theory of passive is strengthened by the observation that there is a cross-linguistic spectrum of construction types which are referred to by that name. Above we saw examples of this internal to German. In some languages passive exclusively affects the direct object; in some other languages indirect objects may be affected. Also, passive constructions cross-linguistically differ in whether the subject of the active verb can be expressed in the passive, whether only transitive but also intransitive verbs can undergo the process, and so forth. The argument then goes as follows: if there is no one set of grammatical properties which cause us to refer to a construction as passive, then passive itself is an epiphenomenon. The real phenomenon is the set of individual properties which we find recurring in the constructions that we have agreed to call "passive". At this point passive does not have the status of an operation made available or referred to as a whole construction by Universal Grammar. Rather it is the recurring result of the combination of primitive grammatical operations licensed by UG.[8]

Chomsky (1981) assumes that what "is usually called 'passive' seems to have two crucial properties":

(31) (I)   [NP,S] does not receive a theta role;
      (II) [NP,VP] does not receive Case within VP, for some
            choice of NP in VP.

He presents a theory of passive for constructions with passive morphology. It is claimed that "the 'core case' of passive involves passive morphology ..." (p. 127) and that "the unique property of the passive morphology is that it in effect 'absorbs' Case ..." (p. 124). Furthermore, "where there is passive morphology in a language, it must at least apply to the 'core case' of transitive verbs with objects ..." (p. 126). Finally, he invokes a "uniformity principle" applying to passive morphology (p. 126) which ensures that each morphological process either transmits, blocks, or assigns a new theta role uniformly.

In languages with a passive construction the lexicon contains a passive affix which has the properties of (i) combining with transitive verbs and (ii) absorbing one of the Cases the verb can assign. In English the passive affix absorbs the structural accusative Case. If the verb has an NP complement, then this NP will not be able to pass the Case Filter since it cannot be assigned Case by the verb and is outside of the government domain of other Case governors, in particular INFL. Therefore, it has to move into the subject position and will be spelled out as a nominative NP.

Government and Binding Theory has undergone a number of revisions since Chomsky (1981) and the theory of passive of course had to be adapted to these revisions. Also, being a family of related theories rather than just one theory, there are slightly different approaches to passive at any given

---

[8]For further discussion, cf. Chomsky (1981: section 2.7).

time. It is fair to say, though, that the theory just described is the canonical theory of passive in GB and that all influential alternatives maintain its claim that passive is driven fundamentally by a process that prevents a verb from assigning one of its Cases VP-internally, even though these theories may derive this property in different ways.[9]

How well does this revised transformational theory of passive account for the portion of the German paradigm presented in the previous section? Clearly, it represents a considerable improvement over the classical trans-formational approach criticized by Perlmutter and Postal. Since passiviza-tion is triggered by an absorption of abstract Case, it is now in principle in-dependent of linear order and can apply uniformly to languages with different base orders. The revised theory arguably also has a better handle on the dif-ferences in case marking, agreement, etc. between active and passive sen-tences than its predecessor. Given that the direct object's Case is absorbed in the passive structure, the remainder of the grammatical system will ensure that this NP ends up in the subject position. Tying case marking, agree-ment, etc. to different phrase structure positions will then make it possible in principle to account for the phenomena under discussion.[10]

Despite these significant improvements over earlier transformational theories of passive, the current transformational family of theories actually

---

[9]Some authors, e.g., von Stechow (1990) attribute the absorption to the auxiliary that must appear in predicative passive constructions. This account cannot, however, be generalized to attributively used passives, since those don't contain auxiliaries.

Baker (1988), elaborating on earlier proposals by Jaeggli (1986) and Baker et al. (1989) claims that the passive affix invoked in Chomsky's theory actually *is* the verb's agent argument and that in languages like German or English, this argument is base-generated in INFL and requires accusative Case. This requirement forces the verb to incorporate into INFL to Case-mark the affix and bind it morphologically. Being forced to spend its ac-cusative Case in INFL, the verb is unable to Case-mark the direct object within the VP which is consequently forced to move into the subject position to receive nominative Case assigned by INFL. German poses considerable problems for Baker's approach. We will mention only a few here. Since in predicative passive structures German obligatorily employs an auxiliary, this auxiliary is predicted to bear the passive affix, since it is closer to INFL than the main verb and by the head movement constraint should have priority over the main verb with regard to movement into the INFL node bearing the passive affix. Second, as we showed in the main text, the agent can be overtly expressed in a syntactically free prepositional phrase. This should lead to a violation of the theta criterion in Baker's theory, since the patient theta role is assigned to two arguments, the passive affix and the prepositional phrase. Baker addresses this problem by claiming that the passive affix is a clitic and the prepositional phrase doubles that clitic, similar to the clitic doubling phenomenon in some of the Romance languages/dialects. This flies in the face of the fact that (i) German does not have Romance-style clitics nor (ii) do its overtly observable pronouns display doubling phenomena of any kind comparable to that found in Romance. Applying Baker's theory of passive to German thus necessitates a considerable "normalization" of the language.

As we will show in connection with our own analysis, the generalizations of German passive can actually be captured elegantly (i) *without* any prior typological reengineering of the language and (ii) *without* considerable phrase-structural "normalization" like the main verb's moving across the auxiliary to be adjacent to the affix it needs to bind.

[10]Although it must be clearly recognized that the relationship is not direct, given that GB only has universal principles affecting abstract Case and none governing the distribution of observable *morphological* case. Since there is no universal connection between abstract Case and morphological case [see Marantz (1992)], GB's supposedly explanatory Case Theory actually makes no empirically verifiable predictions about case at all.

explains little about German passive, at least we are not aware of anything this approach can explain that is missed in non-transformational theories of the same data. In terms of capturing actual generalizations across different passives of German—generalizations which are clearly language-particular in nature—we feel that the transformational approach is actually inferior to the most elegant non-transformational alternatives.

To begin with, the transformational approach has no more of a universal explanation for why German has a passive construction (and that it has several passives with different properties) but many other languages have no passive [see Keenan (1985: 247)]. In GB this is dependent on the accident of whether to include a Case-absorbing affix in the lexicon of the language. In the approach we will lay out later there is also a choice but a different one: does the language choose to postulate a lexical type that inherits from the universally available passive archetype? If yes, the language will have passive, if no, then it will not.

GB also does not have an explanatory edge with respect to the differences between active and passive sentences in languages that do choose to instantiate passive. That languages prefer personal over impersonal passives does not follow from independent principles of GB but must be stated separately in the evaluation metric. The same is true in our approach. That most passives in the world's languages promote the active direct object rather than the indirect object or some other grammatical function is also a matter of markedness rather than a universal principle. Finally, that the promoted constituent takes on the properties of a surface subject is claimed to follow from independent principles constraining movement. Some of these principles face very serious empirical difficulties, however, which have been known for more than a decade since the theory was originally proposed and have not been solved in a principled manner. Among these principles is *Burzio's Generalization* which is supposed to derive the Case absorption effect in passives. There are well-known counterexamples to this generalization. One is mentioned in the following paragraph from Sobin (1985: 649) which discusses Chomsky (1981):

Chomsky claims that a morphological passive verb will block Case assignment to one NP that it governs so that unless that NP is moved to a position where it can be assigned Case, the sentence containing it is ruled ungrammatical by the Case Filter [footnote omitted; the authors]. This "Case-absorption" property of passive (Chomsky's property (II), p. 124) is treated as the "core property" of passive, presumably a part of Universal Grammar. Contrary to this thesis, certain Ukrainian passive constructions such as (1) indicate that if such a Case-absorption property exists at all, it is not universal:

(1)   Stadion   bulo   zbudovano   v   1948 roc'i
       stadium-acc.masc be-past-neu   build-part-neut   in 1948

       'The stadium was built in 1948'

I shall argue that the nonassignment of theta-role to subject (Chomsky's property (I)) is a more consistent property of morphological passive constructions and a better candidate for being designated the core property of passives. The question of how Case is assigned to NPs in passive constructions is still open.

The question raised by Sobin in the last sentence of the quotation remains open within GB thirteen years later. Sobin's proposal to make demotion of the active subject rather than absorption of objective Case the primary criterion for passive has been essentially ignored within the GB community. It will, however, be one of the cornerstones of our universal definition of passive.

Another principle which the GB approach to passive crucially depends on is that part of the *Projection Principle* which requires all complement positions to be theta-marked, thus ruling out movement into a complement position and ensuring that all NPs whose Case has been absorbed are forced to move to a subject position. As Chomsky (1981) notes, this also predicts that expletive pronouns are never found in object positions. This claim is known to be empirically false as well, as the examples (32)–(34) taken from Postal and Pullum (1988: 643) show:

(32)   They never mentioned *it* to the candidate that the job was poorly paid
(33)   We demand *it* of our employees that they wear a tie
(34)   I blame *it* on you that we can't go

While some attempts have been make in the GB community to explain away these and similar examples as idioms [including Webelhuth (1992: 136, footnote 13)], this is really just a way of addressing the problem by declaring it solved because it now has a name: idioms are as much a problem for the *Projection Principle* as are expletives.[11]

The transformational approach to German passive does not provide any explanations of this data that cannot be provided by a suitable non-transformational alternative, and these alternatives are both more precise and more coherent than the Case absorption theory of passive. Moreover, there are a number of language-particular generalizations that our approach will be shown to capture which are not easily captured by the transformational approach.

How, for instance, can the transformational approach uniformly characterize the three passive constructions we introduced in the previous section as passives while at the same time capturing the differences between them?

There is no one observable morpheme that occurs in all and only passive constructions: while each passive construction involves an auxiliary, the auxiliary is different each time. And it cannot be argued that the mere

---

[11]Chomsky (1981: 327) refers to idiom chunks as "quasi-arguments" which Ruwet (1991: 300, footnote 24) comments on as follows: "this notion seems to me to be empty—it is a purely terminological way of sweeping a serious question under the rug."

presence of an auxiliary is a distinctive signal of passive, since we saw in the previous chapter that German *active* verbs use auxiliaries to express their perfect tense-aspect and their future tense.

There is also no *affix* that occurs in all and only passive structures. While the werden- and the bekommen-passive require the main verb to bear the "participial" affix, the zuinf-passive has the main verb appearing in the morphological form of the zu-infinitive. Worse yet, main verbs in both of these morphological forms occur in non-passive sentences as well:

(35)   weil   Maria **geraucht**   hat
        because Maria smoked-pperf has

        'because Maria smoked'

(36)   [Ein Buch **zu lesen**] ist erlaubt
        a   book to read   is   allowed

        'Reading a book is allowed'

In (35), the participle is part of the surface realization of an active perfect predicate, in (36) the zu-infinitive is the predicate of an active sentential subject.

Since German fails to provide for a constant piece of observable form that can be said to be responsible for the passive effects in the three passives discussed so far, it would seem that Government and Binding Theory will have to "normalize" the language in terms of yet another empirically unobservable category that appears in all German passive constructions, in addition to the invisible agreement markers that have already been postulated in some analyses of this language.

However, given that it can be demonstrated that no two of the three passives have identical properties, it would appear that postulating only one such invisible passive affix is not enough. Recall that German passives differ in whether the active direct object or the active indirect object takes on the function of the subject in passive sentences and that this correlates in part with the choice of auxiliary: the werden- and zuinf-passives are direct object passives whereas the bekommen-passive is an indirect object passive. We would seem to need at least two different invisible affixes, one for each objective Case to be absorbed and constrained to appear with only a subset of the possible passive auxiliaries.[12] Yet if there are two such affixes which carry the universal force of passive but differ in language-particular properties, how does the theory capture *language-particular* generalizations that cut across the different German passives. For instance, it was demonstrated in section 2 of this chapter that all German passives allow the agent to be ei-

---

[12] A potential way around this is to assume that the auxiliary regulates which Case is absorbed. This, however, would leave the invisible passive affix with little else to do than to "signal" passivehood in a phonologically invisible manner. The proposal of a linguistic signal that is necessarily imperceivable by the hearer strikes us as conceptually strange at best.

ther omitted freely or to be expressed as an oblique marked with the German-specific preposition *von*. If the transformational theory is forced to postulate two different invisible passive affixes for German to capture the language-particular properties of different passives, then it has no principled explanation for why these distinct affixes happen to have many of the same language-particular properties.

The linguistically significant generalizations mentioned in the previous paragraph are also missed if instead of postulating Case-absorbing affixes the absorption is relegated to the auxiliaries appearing in the passive constructions. Since minimally three different such auxiliaries must be postulated as the source of the passive effects in the three different constructions, it is not obvious how generalizations across them can be expressed.

Worse yet, two of the three German passives discussed here not only can be used predicatively but attributively as well. Their surface expression in that use differs crucially from their surface expression in the predicative use: *no auxiliary is part of the exponence of the attributive predicate*. This is shown with the examples below:

(37)   das dem Jungen geschenkte   Buch
         the the boy   given-attr-pperf book

         'The book which was given to the boy'

(38)   das dem Jungen zu schenkende Buch
         the the boy   give-attr-zuinf book

         'The book which must be given to the boy'

(37) is an attributively used werden-passive and (38) an attributively used zuinf-passive. Clearly, in light of the above examples whose meanings and function assignments are identical to those of their predicative counterparts despite the absence of an auxiliary, the passive effect in the predicative constructions cannot be attributed to the individual auxiliaries or even the presence of an auxiliary.

Nor can the passive nature of the synthetic predicates in (37)–(38) be associated with any one single component form of the predicates occurring in these structures, independently of the other parts of the realization of the predicate. We demonstrated in (35) and (36) that the participle of the perfect and the zu-infinitive by themselves can have active force. This leaves only the attributive inflection at the right margin of the words **geschenkte** and **zu schenkende** in (37)–(38). That this is not a candidate for a passivizing force is shown by (39a) which displays an attributive adjective with the same inflection,

(39a)   der **freundliche** Mann
          the friendly   man

          'the friendly man'

and by (39b) which contains an attributive participle of the present, also
with the same morphological ending. The predicate has an unambiguous active voice interpretation:

(39b)   der dem Jungen das Buch   **schenkende** Mann
          the the boy-dat the book-acc give-attr-ppres book

          'the man who is giving the book to the boy'

We sum up the conclusions of this chapter so far. Individual natural languages can contain more than one passive construction. German is a language with a large number of passives that share a number of empirically
testable properties but also differ from each other in certain respects. The
challenge for linguistic theory is to relate the various passives in German to
each other and to the passive constructions in other languages in search of a
universal theory of passive without loosing the ability to state what is language-particular and even construction-particular. No one single surface feature marks all and only passive predicates or passive sentences in German.
Instead, we find three predicative constructions whose predicates are analytic
configurations of an auxiliary and a non-finite form of the main verb and
two attributive constructions in which the predicate is synthetically expressed and bears the attributive morphology required by all predicates used
in adnominal function. Despite the observed variability with respect to the
surface realization of these predicates, there are strong functional-semantic
generalizations that cut across them and across the passive constructions that
are found in other languages of the world, no matter how that information is
expressed morphologically or syntactically. For instance, all the German
constructions involve a demotion of the active subject to an oblique in the
passive, this oblique can optionally remain unexpressed or be expressed in a
prepositional phrase headed by *von,* both passive constructions formed with
the zu-infinitive of the main verb contain the modal nuance of neces-
sity/possibility that the passives built on the participle of the perfect uniformly lack, etc.

    The purpose of this book is to develop an information-based formal-
ism that allows the informational overlap between different predicates to be
modeled in terms of their participation in the same lexical inheritance hierarchy. The system is intentionally designed to allow predicates informationally related in this way to have non-identical and perhaps radically different
surface expressions. That the German passives seem to contain very similar
functional and semantic information whereas their surface expressions do not
contain a uniform signal of that shared information is not an unexpected
configuration on our account. In particular, that the surface realization of

some passives is a single morphological word and that of others a combination of an auxiliary and a main verb is not remarkable either. The systematic availability of these two surface realization types for predicates expressing all kinds of contents is documented throughout this book.

In the remainder of this chapter we will present an analysis of the German passives mentioned up to this point and some impersonal passives in that language as well. Towards the conclusion of the chapter we will show that our general approach to passives generalizes easily to constructions in other languages where the passive exponence involves some more unusual morphological surface effects, e.g., passive words formed through vowel fronting, reduplication, etc.

4 Systematizing the German Passive Types

Counting passives with an expressed agent (= long passives) separately from equivalent ones that omit the agent (= short passives),[13] this chapter will analyze altogether 14 different German passive constructions. In this section we give an example of each construction and provide an overview table that allows for an easy comparison of their respective properties. We encourage the readers to refer to the examples and the table whenever they are unsure which construction is being talked about later in the text or what the exact properties are that some particular construction instantiates.

Each of the 14 passives can be uniquely identified by how they behave with respect to the following nine properties:

---

[13]We need to postulate different types for them, given that they contain different information.

(40) Properties entering into the characterization of German passives

1.	do (direct object)	the active direct object is the subject of the passive.
2.	io (indirect object)	the active indirect object is the subject of the passive.
3.	imp (impersonal)	the passive has no subject.
4.	long	the passive expresses the demoted agent in a *von*-phrase.
5.	short	the demoted agent is implicit.
6.	modal	the meaning of the passive involves the modal notion of necessity/possibility.
7.	werden	the categorial head of the predicate is the auxiliary *werden*.
8.	bek. (bekommen)	the categorial head of the predicate is the auxiliary *bekommen*.
9.	sein	the categorial head of the predicate is the auxiliary *sein*.

For mnemonic reasons, the type names identifying the passive pattern types reflect certain crucial properties of the construction. To keep the names from filling a whole typographical line, we are employing a number of abbreviations which are explained in (41):

(41) Abbreviations used in the type names of German passives

Abbreviation	Stands for
pers	personal passive
imp	impersonal passive
zuinf	the main verb bears the verbal inflection of a zu-infinitive
attrpart	the passive is used attributively and the main verb bears the verbal inflection of a participle of the perfect
attrzuinf	the passive is used attributively and the main verb bears the verbal inflection of a zu-infinitive.

The table (42) lists these 9 distinguishing properties at the top and the 14 passives they are used to characterize on the left.

(42) The empirical properties of 14 different passives

Passive		do	io	imp	long	short	modal	werden	bek.	sein
P1	german-short-pers-werden-pas-lci	✓				✓		✓		
P2	german-long-pers-werden-pas-lci	✓			✓			✓		
P3	german-short-imp-werden-pas-lci			✓		✓		✓		
P4	german-long-imp-werden-pas-lci			✓	✓			✓		
P5	german-short-pers-zuinf-pas-lci	✓				✓	✓			✓
P6	german-long-pers-zuinf-pas-lci	✓			✓		✓			✓
P7	german-short-imp-zuinf-pas-lci			✓		✓	✓			✓
P8	german-long-imp-zuinf-pas-lci			✓	✓		✓			✓
P9	german-short-pers-bekommen-pas-lci		✓			✓			✓	
P10	german-long-pers-bekommen-pas-lci		✓		✓				✓	
P11	german-short-attrpart-pas-lci	✓				✓				
P12	german-long-attrpart-pas-lci	✓			✓					
P13	german-short-attrzuinf-pas-lci	✓				✓	✓			
P14	german-long-attrzuinf-pas-lci	✓			✓		✓			

Each of the passives identified in this table is illustrated with an example carrying the same numerical and type identifiers used in the table:

P1 *german-short-pers-werden-pas-lci*

(43)　weil　　die Blumen dem Mann geschenkt **wurden**
　　　　because the flowers the man given were

'because the flowers were given to the man'

P2 *german-long-pers-werden-pas-lci*

(44)　weil　　die Blumen dem Mann von Johann geschenkt **wurden**
　　　　because the flowers the man by Johann given were

'because the flowers were given to the man by Johann'

P3 *german-short-imp-werden-pas-lci*

(45)　weil　　dem Mann geholfen **wurde**
　　　　because the man helped was

'because the man was helped'

P4 *german-long-imp-werden-pas-lci*

(46)　weil　　dem Mann von seinen Nachbarn geholfen **wurde**
　　　　because the man by his neighbors helped was

'because the man was helped by his neighbors'

P5 *german-short-pers-zuinf-pas-lci*

(47)　weil　　die Blumen dem Mann zu schenken **sind**
　　　　because the flowers the man to give are

'because the flowers must be given to the man'

P6 *german-long-pers-zuinf-pas-lci*

(48)　weil　　die Blumen dem Mann von Johann zu schenken **sind**
　　　　because the flowers the man by Johann to give are

'because the flowers must be given to the man by Johann'

P7 _german-short-imp-zuinf-pas-lci_

(49)   weil   dem Mann zu helfen **war**
          'because the man to help   was

          'because the man had to be helped'

P8 _german-long-imp-zuinf-pas-lci_

(50)   weil   dem Mann von seinen Nachbarn zu helfen **war**
          because the man by his   neighbors to help   was

          'because the man had to be helped by his neighbors'

P9 _german-short-pers-bekommen-pas-lci_

(51)   weil   der Mann die Blumen geschenkt **bekam**
          because the man the flowers given   was

          'the man was given the flowers'

P10 _german-long-pers-bekommen-pas-lci_

(52)   weil   der Mann die Blumen von Johann geschenkt **bekam**
          because the man the flowers by Johann given   was

          'the man was given the flowers by Johann'

P11 _german-short-attrpart-pas-lci_

(53)   die dem Mann geschenkten Blumen
          the the man given   flowers

          'the flowers given to the man'

P12 _german-long-attrpart-pas-lci_

(54)   die dem Mann von Johann geschenkten Blumen
          the the man by Johann given   flowers

          'the flowers given to the man by Johann'

P13 _german-short-attrzuinf-pas-lci_

(55)   die dem Mann zu schenkenden Blumen
          the the man to give   flowers

          'the flowers that must be given to the man'

P14 *german-long-attrzuinf-pas-lci*

(56)   die dem Mann von Johann zu schenkenden Blumen
       the the man   by Johann to give   flowers

       'the flowers that must be given to the man by Johann'

5   The Type Hierarchy for Passive Predicates

We will now proceed as we did in the previous chapter. We will analyze two predicate patterns in detail and demonstrate how the general design
of our theory of predicates allows us to capture contentive generalizations
across them, even though one is realized synthetically and the other one by a
main verb-auxiliary combination.[14] The remaining twelve instances of the
passive construction in German will then be seen as variations of the two
representative cases and their analyses as routine extensions of the analyses
presented here.

The two representative cases we have chosen are the long personal zu-
infinitive passive in its predicative and attributive versions. We repeat
examples of these constructions below to allow the reader to see them side
by side:

P6 *german-long-pers-zuinf-pas-lci*

(57)   weil   die Blumen dem Mann von Johann zu schenken sind
       because the flowers the man   by Johann to give   are

       'because the flowers must be given to the man by Johann'

P14 *german-long-attrzuinf-pas-lci*

(58)   die dem Mann von Johann zu schenkenden Blumen
       the the man   by Johann to give   flowers

       'the flowers that must be given to the man by Johann'

Based on the overview in (42), we get the following comparative profile of
the two constructions:

---

[14]The German infinitive marker *zu* is orthographically treated like a separate word when it
combines with a simple verb. As will be discussed in chapter 10, when it comes to stand
between a verb stem and a particle of a verb-particle predicate, conventional German
orthography spells these three units as one word. The infinitive marker follows the
generalization that it must never be separated from the verb stem that is part of the predicate
that it marks. It thus has the typical profile of a morphological prefix that follows from the
morphological integrity of words that our theory of predicates is committed to (cf. the
discussion in chapter 1).

(59) A comparison of the predicative and attributive versions of the long personal zu-infinitive passive

		Predicative Version [= (57)]	Attributive Version [= (58)]
(i)	Personal vs. impersonal	Personal	Personal
(ii)	Function that is promoted	Direct Object	Direct Object
(iii)	By-phrase expressed	Yes	Yes
(iv)	Modal nuance	Yes	Yes
(v)	Form of categorial core	zu-infinitive	zu-infinitive
(vi)	Auxiliated vs. non-auxiliated	Auxiliated	Non-auxiliated
(vii)	Auxiliary involved	*sein*	n/a

Both passives represent personal predicates. The subject function of the predicative version (57) is realized as the nominative NP *die Blumen* which agrees with the verb in person and number. The attributive predicate modifies the head noun *Blumen* in (58) via its subject function and agrees with it in gender, number, case, and declension class.[15]

A comparison of (57) and (58) with their active equivalent in (60) shows that the subject of both passive versions is realized as the direct object of the corresponding active sentence:

(60)　　weil　　Johann dem Mann　　die Blumen　　schenkt
　　　　because Johann the　man-IO the flowers-DO gives

　　　'because Johann gives the man the flowers'

The two zu-infinitive passives under discussion share an additional three properties: both express a by-phrase, both express a modal notion of necessity/possibility, and both require their categorial core to be in the form of the German zu-infinitive. Despite this striking overlap in contentive proper-

---

[15]That the attributive predicate's SUBJ function is involved in the modification can be seen more clearly in examples like the following where the adnominal (active) predicate takes the reflexive *sich* as its direct object:

(i)　　der *sich*ᵢ　　rasierende Mannᵢ
　　　the himself shaving　man

　　　'the man shaving himself'

In (i), the reflexive is interpreted as bound by the head noun *Mann* which its predicate modifies. In the next chapter, we will present evidence that this reflexive must be bound by its predicate's subject. This condition can only be met in (i) if the adnominal predicate has a subject whose index it identifies with the index of the nominal it modifies. This conclusion is further supported by the fact that only personal predicates can be used attributively. Impersonal passives and idiosyncratically impersonal predicates are systematically barred from attributive use.

ties and the similar morphological restriction on the categorial core, the two predicates nevertheless differ in that the predicative version—like all predicative passives in German—requires the presence of an auxiliary in its surface expression, in particular the auxiliary *sein*. In contrast, the attributive version is expressed without an auxiliary but—like all adnominally used adjectival and verbal predicates in German—has to bear an attributive inflection expressing gender, number, case, and declension class.

The challenge we face is that of capturing the generalizations that hold across the two versions of the zu-infinitive passive while simultaneously associating the predicative version with an auxiliated surface spell-out involving the auxiliary *sein* and the attributive version with a different, single-word spell-out expressing the right morphological features. We are not aware of any prior linguistic theory that is able to accomplish this.

We begin by postulating the types that we need for our analysis of passives and a corresponding hierarchy of inheritance relations between the types. A number of passive predicate constructions recur systematically in the languages of the world. This motivates the postulation of several passive archetypes whose semantic and grammatical information is universally available to individual languages as one chunk via archetype declaration. In particular, personal passives that promote the underlying predicate's direct object are found around the globe, as are impersonal passives. Both of these passive constructions typically occur in short and long forms, depending on whether the predicate's agent argument is expressed or not. These typological considerations support the existence of the following archetypes of passive:

(61) Passive archetypes

univ-pas-bas-lci

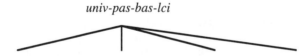

univ-do-pas-lci   *univ-long-pas-lci*   *univ-short-pas-lci*   *univ-imp-pas-lci*

We will define the types we need for our analysis later. First, however, we will determine which German-specific passive types we need in order to capture the two versions of the zu-infinitive passive and, in particular, which of the German-specific types inherit from the archetypes in (61). To that end, we present two more type hierarchies. The first one extends the universal hierarchy in (61) by adding contentive German passive types, i.e., types which inherit contentive but not spell-out information from the archetypes in (61). This hierarchy appears in (62) and is designed to illustrate the functional-semantic identity of the predicatively and attributively used zu-infinitive passives:

(62) The contentive identity of the two long zu-infinitive passives

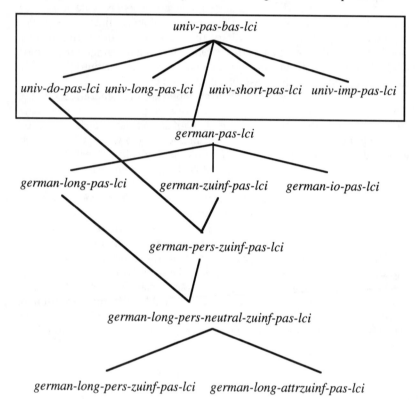

The archetypes have been boxed to make them easily distinguishable from the language-specific types that inherit from them and to bring out graphically how the functional-semantic content of the language-specific types is largely defined in terms of the universal chunks of information contained in the archetypes.

The types whose composition we are interested in appear all the way at the bottom. What is important to recognize is the overlap in supertypes between the two versions of the zu-infinitive passive. This type structure captures the semantic and grammatical-functional generalizations across the two types at the bottom, in light of the contributions of their shared supertypes tabulated in (63):

(63) The shared supertypes of the two zu-infinitive passives

Type Name	Contribution
univ-pas-bas-lci	requires that the predicate's logical subject bear an oblique GF
univ-do-pas-lci	promotes the active direct object to the passive subject
univ-long-pas-lci	provides for the surface expression of the logical subject
german-pas-lci	declares the universal passive type
german-long-pas-lci	spells out the logical subject in a German-specific *von-* phrase
german-zuinf-pas-lci	specifies the core of the passive predicate as a *zu* infinitive and adds a modal nuance to the predicate's meaning
german-pers-zuinf-pas-lci	declares *univ-do-pas-lci*
german-long-pers-zuinf-pas-lci	combines the information in its two supertypes.

The type structure illustrated here is sufficient to capture all the five properties that were specified in (59) as having to fall out from the analysis as properties belonging to both versions of the zu-infinitive passive: (i), (ii) that both are personal passives and personal passives based on the promotion of an underlying direct object in particular is a consequence of their common supertype *univ-do-pas-lci*; (iii) the spell-out of the by-phrase is accomplished by *univ-long-pas-lci* and the choice of the preposition *von* in this function derives from *german-long-pas-lci;* (iv), (v) the modal nuance in meaning that appears in both passives and the requirement that the categorial core be a morphological zu-infinitive originate in their supertype *german-zuinf-pas-lci.*

Even though we won't go into the details of the analysis of the remaining 12 German passives we surveyed earlier, it should be obvious that many of the types that we have postulated in (62) and (63) will be involved in capturing further generalizations across the two zu-infinitive passives and the other passives. For instance, as we showed in table (42), there are direct object passives and long passives in German outside the zu-infinitive passives. (43) illustrates a personal *werden* passive and (52) is a long passive spelled out with the auxiliary *bekommen.* The properties that hold across *all* direct object passives and across all long passives, whatever other differences there may be between the constructions, are captured by making all the passives that share a given property subtypes of the same universal or language-specific type whose definition contains that property.

Once the type hierarchy in (62) is completed to contain all the 14 passive types and once all these types are linked upwards to the supertypes from which they inherit the information that (42) attributes to them, the result is an immense network of type relationships that collectively define (i) what is common to all passives in German, (ii) what is unique to each of the 14 passives, and (iii) how these 14 passives form various alliances in behavior (e.g., all the long passives, all the impersonal passives, all the direct object passives, all the indirect object passives, etc.).[16]

The existence of such immense overlap between the many German passive constructions makes sense against the background of our speculations of the functional utility of archetypes and type hierarchies in chapter 4. There we suggested that language learners attempt to minimize the amount of "independent" grammatical units in their grammars, i.e., grammatical units that don't share linguistic properties with large classes of other grammatical units. We suggested that the degree of independence of a grammatical unit was to be measured in terms of the amount of information it contains which is not inherited from supertypes that also transfer their information to other grammatical units. Moreover, we speculated that this kind of linguistic economy principle applies "all the way up," in the sense that it affects all types in a type hierarchy. We took this as a plausible motivation for why we not only find that various construction types *within* one language typically show an overlap of properties but why this is also true *across* languages. If the "Minimize independence" economy principle applies all the way up, then even the most general language-particular types are subject to it. The way that these types can reduce their relative amount of independence is to inherit information from a source that acts as an umbrella over all language-specific type systems, namely the *archetypes* of Universal Grammar.

Assuming, then, that both language-particular and cross-linguistic recurrence of properties is a function of the economic design feature of natural language to reduce the amount of independent information in a grammar, we may speculate further as to why natural language grammars are shaped by such a principle. One imaginable answer is that human memory and the human mind in general are organized to work in an associative fashion: when the organism receives new information, an attempt is made to automatically match this information against information in the memory of the organism in order to determine whether the new information bears on information that is already available. It is not hard to see why in many cases it will be desirable for the organism to bundle new types of information together with old types of information, for instance all situation types representing danger to the organism, all foods, all tools that are useful to complete a certain task, etc. Extensive informational "bundling" of this kind of

---

[16]In fact, there is such a rich cross-classification of types in the completed network that looking at the overall network is very confusing. That is the reason we postulated the representation in (42) which is more user-friendly.

course has precisely the effect of minimizing the information independence of memory units that we have argued plays such a formative role in the design of natural language grammars. While we are well aware that these ideas are highly speculative and programmatic, we feel that there is sufficiently strong empirical support for the notions (i) that natural language grammars systematically attempt to minimize independent information, and (ii) that human memory is associative, to warrant further research into the question of whether these two factors are related.

After these remarks about the more general significance of the type overlap we see in (62) and even more so in (42), we now return to the two differences between the predicative and the attributive versions of the zu-infinitive passive that are mentioned in the last two lines of (59): the predicative version of the predicate has an analytic surface expression consisting of the zu-infinitive of the categorial core and a form of the auxiliary *sein* whereas the attributive version is spelled out by a single morphological word realizing the categorial core in the form of the zu-infinitive bearing additional attributive inflection. Recall from (63) that both passives under discussion are subtypes of the type *german-zuinf-pas-lci* which is responsible for requiring the predicate's categorial core to instantiate the morphological category of the zu-infinitive. This means that the only spell-out differences that remain to be captured are the presence of the auxiliary in the predicative version and the presence of the attributive inflection in the attributive version. This is accomplished with the configuration in (64) and the definitions of the types appearing in that configuration.

The boxed types in (64) represent the two arrangement archetypes *auxd-lci* and *nauxd-lci* that are relevant in the current context: *auxd-lci* is the class of predicates which have a non-empty auxiliary list, whereas *nauxd-lci* means that a predicate is synthetically expressed (*adnom-lci* also is an archetype, but it is not an arrangement archetype). As is indicated in (64), all German predicative passives are auxiliated, with each subtype of *german-pred-pas-lci* determining the particular auxiliary involved: two types require *werden* and *bekommen* to be the first auxiliary on the predicate's auxiliary list respectively. The type *german-pred-zuinf-pas-lci* which represents all predicative zu-infinitive passives (personal vs. impersonal, short vs. long) introduces the auxiliary *sein* and its subtype representing the long, personal version of the predicative zu-infinitive passive inherits this constraint.

The attributive version of the zu-infinitive passive belongs to a different part of the type hierarchy responsible for spell-out, however. The attributively used passives all assimilate to adnominally used verbs which in turn behave like adnominally used predicates in German; in particular, all adnominally used predicates bear the attributive inflection illustrated in (39). As the hierarchy indicates, all instances of this type *german-adnom-lci* (a subtype of the functional-semantic archetype *adnom-lci)* are non-auxiliated.

In combination, the two type hierarchies in (62) and (64), including the definitions of the types in the hierarchies, derive the comparative profile of the two zu-infinitive passives laid out in (59). The five properties that are shared by the predicative and attributive versions of the zu-infinitive passive follow from (62), along the lines sketched in (63). The differences in surface expression between the two passives is orthogonal to their contentive identity and is handled in another part of the German type hierarchy, one segment of which is graphed in (64).

(64) The spell-out contrast between the two long zu-infinitive passives

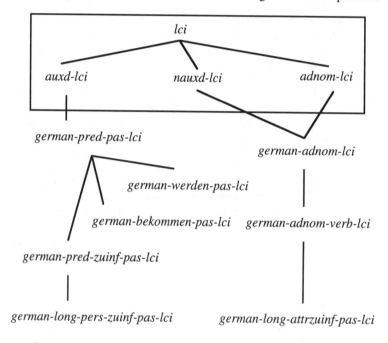

By systematically extending these two type hierarchies in accordance with the demands of the empirical data, it becomes possible to capture all the generalizations, sub-generalizations, and idiosyncrasies of the German passives systematized in (42). Moreover, by drawing on the passive archetypes in (61), our analysis expresses the structural components which German passives share with passives in other languages of the world and is able to explain/motivate why German makes use of clusters of linguistic information that recur as wholes in many other languages as well.

6   Definitions of the Passive Types and Illustrations

In this section we will provide the representation of the underived German predicate *schenken* 'give as a present' and will lay out the details of the structure of the two productive predicate formation patterns that create the predicative and attributive uses of this predicate in (57) and (58). Since both of these patterns instantiate a number of other types, the details of these other types will be discussed as well.

We start at the top of the type hierarchy in (62). Here is our definition of the universal passive archetype:

(65) The passive archetype *(univ-pas-bas-lci)*

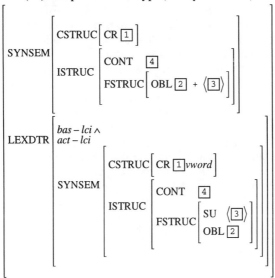

The definition creates a new basic lci from an embedded one.[17] The embedded daughter must be an active lci to prevent double passivization.[18] The in-

---

[17]Since the passive predicate formation operation changes grammatical functions, it violates the constraint (12A) on expanded lci's in the previous chapter. That is why passive creates a new *basic* predicate from an input basic predicate whereas the tense-aspect operations map basic predicates to expanded predicates (for the basic~expanded distinction, refer to section 3.2 in chapter 7). However, the newly formed passive basic predicates can be expanded via the tense-aspect patterns like any other basic predicate as well. Thus, when the predicative zu-infinitive passive predicate appears in the future pattern, its surface expression will consist of the zu-infinitive of the categorial core and two auxiliaries: the auxiliary *sein* which is part of the expression of the zu-infinitive passive, and the auxiliary *werden* which is part of the expression of the future tense, as we already know from our last chapter. The future equivalent of the predicate in (57) thus would have the following surface expression:

(i)   zu schenken sein   werden
       to give-inf   be-inf will-3-pl

       'will have to be given'

[18]Double passivization perhaps exists in Turkish and Lithuanian but we have not studied the issue of whether the examples Baker (1988: 33) quotes from Timberlake and Knecht might merely involve multiple exponence of a single passive signifier rather than authentic double passivization. This type of passive, if it exists at all, seems to be so rare and unusual,

put predicate must have a subject and its categorial core must be verbal. The output of the pattern type preserves the categorial core of the input but differs functionally from the input in the way we take to be characteristic of all passive predicates (see the discussion following (31) above, in particular Sobin's evidence from Ukrainian in favor of a demotion account of passive over an approach in terms of Case absorption): the information structure associated with the subject of the active predicate is demoted to an oblique in the passive output; in particular, since the value of OBL is a list whose left to right ordering we take to reflect increasing degrees of obliqueness, the demoted agent of the passive predicate is the most oblique element on the mother's list of oblique grammatical functions.[19]

With (65), we have postulated a property that all passives universally and all German passives share: passive predicates are derived from active predicates whose grammatical subject takes on an oblique grammatical function in the passive. Since this universal property is a functional one, we do not necessarily expect to find any constant categorial or morphological reflex of passivization either universally or in all the passives of any one language. This empirical predication is borne out but causes awkward empirical and conceptual problems for the Case absorption theory, as we have shown.

Returning to (62), we define the next passive type needed for our two zu-infinitive passives in German, the archetype responsible for the promotion of the direct object in the most widely attested passives [the general type (65) leaves open which GF is promoted to subject, if any]:

---

however, that we assume it not to be an instantiation of the universal passive type. Turkish and Lithuanian thus would be analyzed as having created language-particular passive types without declaring any of the passive archetypes from UG. This is a highly marked situation which is predicted to be very rare cross-linguistically, as it seems to be.

[19](65) accomplishes this by defining the list of obliques of the passive output as the result of suffixing the (information structure of) the embedded subject to the list of obliques of the underlying active verb. Following much work in Relational Grammar, LFG, and HPSG we assume that binding theory is sensitive to relative obliqueness. In this way, it can be derived that demoted agents, like other obliques more generally, typically cannot bind arguments bearing a term grammatical function (= subject, indirect object, direct object).

(66) The direct object passive archetype *(univ-do-pas-lci)*

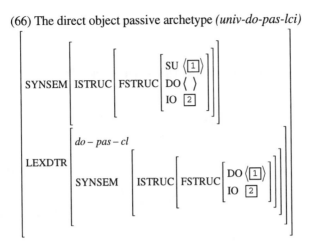

We see that this type promotes the information structure that serves as the direct object of the input predicate to the subject of the passive output. As a result, passive predicates of this type do not govern direct objects. Additionally, the type transfers any information about the embedded indirect object to the output predicate's indirect object.[20]

The type *univ-long-pas-lci* achieves the result that the information structure which the passive demotes from a subject to an oblique is still spelled out categorially by the newly created passive predicate. The passive oblique may be spelled out by a different part of speech, however (e.g., PP rather than an NP).[21] (67) accomplishes this by requiring that both the LEXDTR and the mother have a SUBCAT element corresponding to the passive oblique (the rightmost element on the mother's list of obliques), but failing to further constrain the part of speech features of these corresponding SUBCAT elements:[22]

---

[20]We are unaware of any 'domino' style passive constructions where the indirect object of the embedded predicate advances into the direct object function of the passive predicate that has been vacated by the advancement of the original direct object to the subject function. If there are no or few such constructions cross-linguistically, this would constitute another empirical challenge for those who claim that the structure of language can be derived from general cognitive principles alone. It is hard to see what general cognitive principle could be forceful enough to have this effect, or how the choice between one or another of the object grammatical functions (direct vs. indirect) could have any strong relevance for any general cognitive principle.

[21]If (67) did not separate the spell-out of the passive oblique from the other SUBCAT elements and simply identified the SUBCAT of the mother and the daughter, then the passive oblique would have to belong to the same part of speech as the subject of the underlying active verb. This would rule out a change in category from NP to PP which is found in many languages of the world.

[22]The equivalent type for short passives differs from (67) in that it sends all the SUBCAT members of the embedded predicate to the new passive predicate, except, naturally, for the category that spells out the passive oblique.

(67) The long passive archetype *(univ-long-pas-lci)*

$$
\begin{bmatrix}
\text{SYNSEM} & \begin{bmatrix}
\text{ISTRUC} & \left[\text{FSTRUC}\left[\text{OBL}[\ ]\ +\ \langle \boxed{1}\rangle\right]\right] \\
\text{VAL} & \left[\text{SUBCAT}\left\{\left[\text{ISTRUC}\,\boxed{1}\right]\right\}\cup\boxed{3}\right]
\end{bmatrix} \\
\text{LEXDTR} & \left[\text{SYNSEM}\left[\text{VAL}\left[\text{SUBCAT}\left\{\left[\text{ISTRUC}\,\boxed{1}\right]\right\}\cup\boxed{3}\right]\right]\right]
\end{bmatrix}
$$

(68) The German long passive type *(german-long-pas-lci)*

$$
\begin{bmatrix}
\text{SYNSEM} & \begin{bmatrix}
\text{ISTRUC} & \left[\text{FSTRUC}\left[\text{OBL}[\ ]\ +\ \langle \boxed{1}\rangle\right]\right] \\
\text{VAL} & \left[\text{SUBCAT}\left\{\begin{bmatrix}\text{CSTRUC:CR:MS} & \begin{bmatrix}\text{POS} & p \\ \text{INFL :PINFL}\langle\text{von}\rangle\end{bmatrix} \\ \text{ISTRUC} & \boxed{1}\end{bmatrix}\right\}\cup\boxed{3}\right]
\end{bmatrix} \\
\text{LEXDTR} & \left[\text{SYNSEM}\left[\text{VAL}\left[\text{SUBCAT}\left\{\left[\text{ISTRUC}\,\boxed{1}\right]\right\}\cup\boxed{3}\right]\right]\right]
\end{bmatrix}
$$

Since (67) leaves open *how* the passive oblique is spelled out categorially, each language that declares this archetype will have to configure it by providing a language-particular spell-out for the "by-phrase." As we know,

German uses a PP headed by the preposition *von* for this purpose.[23] This is captured in definition (68) which is structurally identical to (67), since it simply fills in the categorial features of the passive oblique which (67) leaves unspecified.

Up to this point we have defined the universal passive archetype (65), the direct object archetype (66), the long passive archetype (67), and its German subtype (68) which fixes the German-specific spell-out of the passive oblique. Next, we will define the type *german-pas-lci* which declares the universal passive archetype to be active in German, followed by the subtypes of this type which are responsible for the properties characterizing all the German zu-infinitive passives.

The type *german-pas-lci* is easily defined:

(69) The German passive type *(german-pas-lci)*

$$\left[\text{SYNSEM} \left[\text{VAL} \left[\text{PART} \langle \, \rangle \right] \right] \right]$$

What (69) says is that no German passive predicate is formed by means of a particle. As far as spell-out is concerned, no other generalizations cover all German passive constructions: some use an auxiliary and some don't, and there is also no one morphological category that must be present on the categorial core of all passive predicates in German, as we argued in detail earlier in this chapter.

This does not, however, mean that there aren't any generalizations across all passives in German, just that they don't need to be stated in the German-specific type in (69), because they follow from archetypes or the structure of the type hierarchy. For instance, since (69) is a subtype of the universal passive type, it follows that all German passives are characterized by a demotion of the subject argument of the underlying agent. By assuming that the long and short passive subtypes of (69) partition their mother type, we predict that each passive can occur in both long and short versions, etc.

Let us now turn specifically to the type *german-zuinf-pas-lci* of the two zu-infinitive passives whose details we wish to analyze in this chapter. In (63) we had decided that this type is the source of the commonalities that all zu-infinitive passives share, be they personal, impersonal, long, short, predicative, or attributive [cf. P5–P8 and P13–P14 in (42)]: all these passives are formed with the zu-infinitive of the categorial core and all of them have the same modal nuance in their meaning. This can be expressed as follows:

---

[23]See footnote 3, however. We are simplifying here.

(70) The German zu-infinitive passive type *(german-zuinf-pas-lci)*

$$\left[\text{SYNSEM} \left[\begin{array}{l} \text{CSTRUC} \left[\text{CR } \textit{zuinf} - \textit{vword} \right] \\ \text{ISTRUC} \left[\text{CONT } \textit{zuinf} - \textit{modal} - \textit{psoa} \right] \end{array} \right] \right]$$

As desired, the categorial core of this type of predicate must be realized by a morphological verb that is a zu-infinitive. Below, when we will encode the predicative and attributive subtypes of (70), we will further specify that the predicative subtypes' categorial cores be *predicative* vs. *attributive* zu-infinitives respectively. Together with the relevant morphological patterns, this will yield the correct morphological forms for the categorial cores of the predicates in (57) and (58).

The second line of (70) equips all zu-infinitive passives with a zu-infinitive modal nuance (= zu-infinitive modal state of affairs) which has two subtypes that partition the type, one expressing necessity and one expressing possibility. Each passive of this kind thus is forced to express one of these two modal notions in any of its uses.

The bottom four zu-infinitive passives in (62) are now straightforward. The type *german-pers-zuinf-pas-lci* only bundles the information in (70) and (66), i.e., it simply combines the semantic/morphological information complex in (70) with the function change in (66). Similarly, *german-long-pers-neutral-zuinf-pas-lci* merely merges the information in the previous type with that in (68) as a result of which the passive oblique is spelled out in a *von* -phrase.

The two types at the bottom of (62) both inherit all this information and thereby are predicted to have the contentive information in (59) in common, as well as the commonality of calling on the zu-infinitive as the spell-out of the predicate's categorial core.

By defining the German-specific types in (64), we can account formally for the differences in spell-out between the two passives in (59). The type *german-pred-pas-lci* declares the archetype *auxd-lci* and thereby captures the generalization that all predicative passives in German are formed with an auxiliary. Its subtype *german-pred-zuinf-pas-lci* makes sure that the auxiliary *sein* appears, rather than the auxiliaries *werden* or *bekommen* which German uses in passives with other functional-semantic information. As promised above in connection with (70), (71) also fixes the categorial core of the predicative use of the zu-infinitive passive as a morphologically predicative zu-infinitive:[24]

---

[24]The morphology creates the form *zu schenken* as the predicative zu-infinitive of the lexeme *schenken* in the following steps: it first creates the bare infinitive of the lexeme by

(71) The German predicative zu-infinitive passive type
(*german-pred-zuinf-pas-lci*)

$$
\begin{bmatrix}
\text{SYNSEM}
\begin{bmatrix}
\text{CSTRUC}\begin{bmatrix}\text{CR } \textit{pred–zuinf – vword}\end{bmatrix} \\[4pt]
\text{VAL}\begin{bmatrix}
\text{AUX}\left\langle\begin{bmatrix}\text{CSTRUC:HD}\begin{bmatrix}\text{MS}\begin{bmatrix}\text{LEX}\langle \textit{sein}\rangle\end{bmatrix}\end{bmatrix}\end{bmatrix}\right\rangle + \boxed{1}
\end{bmatrix}
\end{bmatrix} \\[20pt]
\text{LEXDTR}\begin{bmatrix}\text{SYNSEM}\begin{bmatrix}\text{VAL}\begin{bmatrix}\text{AUX }\boxed{1}\end{bmatrix}\end{bmatrix}\end{bmatrix}
\end{bmatrix}
$$

These type definitions account for all the contentive and spell-out properties of the predicate of (57) which we listed in (59). (63) gives an overview of how its various supertypes contribute to its functional and semantic information and (62) shows graphically how the types' relationship to each other in the type hierarchy captures the relevant generalizations. The surface spell-out of the predicative zu-infinitive passive in (57) is due to its being a subtype of (71) which creates the surface arrangement of a predicative zu-infinitive of the categorial core which is supported by a word form of the auxiliary *sein*.

As a result, the type *german-long-pers-zuinf-pas-lci* is a predicate formation pattern that takes predicates with a subject and a direct object as input and derives a predicative zu-infinitive predicate which has all the properties mentioned in its local type definition and its various supertypes. In order to illustrate the overall effect of the system we have designed, we need to postulate a lexical entry for the active predicate *schenken* that will serve as the input to the predicate pattern. This is done in (72).

The structure of this underived predicate is very similar to the structure of the predicate *küssen* 'kiss' we used to illustrate tense-aspect patterns in the previous chapter. The CSTRUC this time of course specifies the morphological lexeme *schenken* as the paradigm from which the spell-outs of the categorial core must come. The subcategorization frame contains three nominal expressions which each spell out one of the grammatical functions governed by the predicate. The number after the colon in each grammatical function constitutes the semantic index of the grammatical

---

suffixing *en* to the present tense stem *schenk*. Then, a predicative zu-infinitive morphological pattern prefixes the infinitive marker to the result to yield *zu schenken*.

function which allows us to trace how the grammatical functions are related to the semantic roles in the predicate's content.

(72) The underived predicate *schenken* 'give as a present'

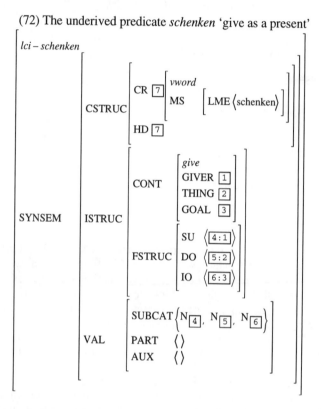

Applying the *german-long-pers-zuinf-pas-lci* predicate pattern to (72) yields the new predicate in (73). We invite the reader to convince herself that this follows from the definitions of the types and their hierarchical organization that we have proposed.

This predicate representation captures all the properties listed under "Predicative Version" in (59): (i) the passive is personal, since the f-structure of (73) contains a subject; (ii) comparing (73) with (72) we see that the direct object of the active predicate in (72) has been promoted to the subject function of the passive in (73); (iii) (73) associates the passive oblique with the categorial spell-out of a prepositional phrase headed by *von;* (iv) the passive predicate's CONT expresses the modal nuance associated with all zu-infinitive passives in German; (v) the categorial core of (73) is specified as a zu-infinitive; (vi), (vii) the predicate in (73) is auxiliated and uses the auxiliary *sein* as its categorial head.

(73) The predicative zu-infinitive pattern that results from the application of the pattern type *german-long-pers-zuinf-pas-lci* to the basic predicate in (72)

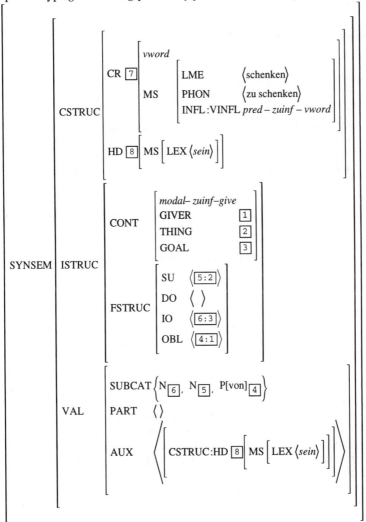

Since (73) is a basic predicate, it qualifies as an input to any of the tense-aspect patterns that the previous chapter has made available. In (57) we see the predicate that results when the German present tense predicate formation pattern is applied to (73), given a choice of third person plural for the inflectional features of the categorial head. The result is the analytic spell-out *zu schenken sind* with the morphological third person present tense form of the passive auxiliary *sein* which of course agrees with the subject *die*

Blumen in accordance with the requirement captured in the last chapter that in German the categorial head of a finite predicate agrees with the predicate's subject in person and number. The distribution of cases on the two NPs in (57) is accounted for as well: the system of inflection developed in the previous chapter requires that all finite personal predicates in German govern the nominative case on their subject and all expanded predicates govern the dative case on their indirect objects. The representation (73) thus accounts for all the contentive properties of (57), as well as its surface spell-out properties. This completes our analysis of the predicative version of the German zu-infinitive passive.

We now turn to our analysis of the attributive version of this passive. Before we can proceed, we need to develop some general assumptions about attributively used predicates universally and in German. The attributive passive predicates of German can be shown to inherit most of their specifically attributive properties from more general regularities.

First, we need to extend our data structures for signs to allow one sign to modify another. This is done by introducing the archetype *mod-lci* below:

(74) The archetype *mod-lci*

$$\begin{bmatrix} mod-lci \\ \\ \text{SYNSEM} \begin{bmatrix} \text{ISTRUC} \begin{bmatrix} \text{MOD–CONT } mod-cont \end{bmatrix} \\ \\ \text{VAL} \quad \begin{bmatrix} \text{MOD} \langle [\ ] \rangle \end{bmatrix} \end{bmatrix} \end{bmatrix}$$

The universal predicate type in (74) differs in two ways from the non-modificational predicates we have seen up to this point. First, instances of this type have a valence attribute MOD via which they select a single constituent to modify. Secondly, modifiers have an information-structural attribute MOD-CONT which non-modificational predicates lack. The value of this attribute is used to combine the CONT of the modifier with the CONT of the modified expression and is then transferred to the phrase formed from the modifier and the constituent it modifies by a syntactic modification schema.[25]

---

[25]This treatment of the semantics of modification is an adaptation of Kasper (to appear). We would like to thank Bob Kasper for discussing his work on modification with us at length.

Like in Pollard and Sag (1994), our syntactic modification schema treats the modifier as the semantic head of its phrase but the modified element as its syntactic head. Thus when an adjective modifies a noun, the nominal part of speech will be projected to the phrase resulting from the modification. However, the content of the newly formed phrase will be determined by the modifier which integrates the meaning of the modified element into its MOD-CONT. That MOD-CONT is then identified with the mother's CONT. In this way, our theory, like Kasper's, can handle both intersective adjectives (a "red car" is both red and a car) and

Adnominal predicates are one type of modifier. Two things are special about adnominals: (i) they select a nominal in their MOD valence; and (ii) they semantically modify their noun via the index of their subject grammatical function (cf. footnote 15). This is a consequence of the definition of the type *adnom-lci* in (75):

(75) The archetype *adnom-lci* [subtype of (74)]

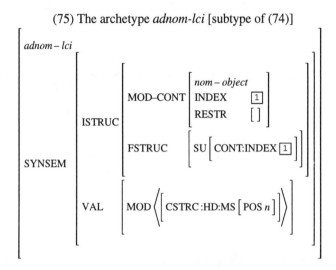

The semantic type of the value of MOD-CONT is a nominal object which introduces an index and a set of restrictions on the index. How the CONT of the modifier and the CONT of the modified enter into the restriction on the output index depends on the meaning of the particular adnominal modifier.

Intersective nominal modifiers restrict their index as in (76): the MOD-CONT of the modifier refers to the same index as the subject in the modifier's f-structure and the noun that the predicate modifies. The restriction on that index is provided by the modifier's CONT and the restrictions on the index of the modified noun. From this it follows that *red car* means "a thing which is a car and is red."

As (64) shows, German adnominal modifiers declare the archetype in (75) and inherit all its contentive aspects. Via (77), German configures this archetype by enforcing agreement between the modifier and the modified noun in gender, number, case, and declension class.

---

operator adjectives (a "former senator" is someone who used to be a senator rather than someone who is both former and a senator).

(76) The archetype *intersect-adnom-lci* [subtype of (75)]

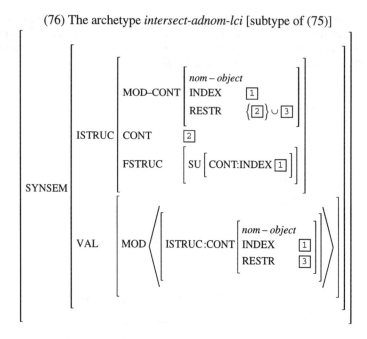

The type in (77) is a supertype of the type *german-adnom-verb-lci* which, naturally, introduces the restriction that its categorial core must be a verb with attributive inflection. *german-long-attrzuinf-pas-lci,* finally, i.e., the type at the lower right end of the contentive type tree in (62) and the spell-out type tree in (64), is the predicate formation pattern that applies to basic predicates like (72) to derive an attributive zu-infinitive passive predicate from them.

From a spell-out point of view, an attributive zu-infinitive thus is required to lack an auxiliary, since it is a subtype of the archetype *nauxd-lci* [cf. (64)]. Moreover, its categorial core must be a morphologically attributive zu-infinitive based on the lexeme specified in its categorial core.[26]

---

[26]The core of an attributive zu-infinitive can be derived with the following morphological patterns. To derive the form *zu schenkenden* in (58) of the main text, we first derive the bare infinitive *schenken* as described in connection with the derivation of the predicative zu-infinitive in footnote 24. Then we input this form into an attributive zu-infinitive pattern which circumfixes *zu ... d* to the bare infinitive. Finally, a pattern which realizes the morphological features of gender, number, case, and declension class will suffix *-en* to this result to create the final surface spell-out needed for the predicate in (58).

Note that the morphological patterns for the creation of the predicative and attributive zu-infinitives differ in that the first has a purely prefixal morpho-phonological effect whereas the second is circumfixal. This kind of absence of a one-to-one mapping between the morphosyntactic features and their morpho-phonological spell-outs was one of the reasons cited in chapter 5 of incorporating a word and paradigm morphology into our overall theory of predicates. This decision thus allows us to capture generalizations that otherwise would be missed.

(77) The type of German adnominal predicates *(german-adnom-lci)*
[subtype of (75), see (64) for further supertypes]

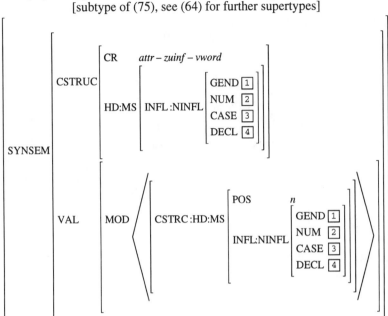

   With this, we finally have all the contentive and surface spell-out features in place to illustrate what output is created when the basic predicate in (72) is fed into the long attributive zu-infinitive passive pattern in German. We will give the representation in two pieces, starting out in (78) with the surface spell-out of the derived predicate.

   The representation in (78) underlies the surface-grammatical features listed under "Attributive Version" in (59): (v)–(vii) this attributive zu-infinitive passive has an empty AUX list but, like the predicative version, involves a zu-infinitive as its categorial core. It therefore is a synthetically expressed predicate, one that bears attributive inflection through which it agrees with the head noun that it modifies. (78) is also responsible for the existence of a dative NP,[27] a PP headed by *von* (which is property (iii) from (59), and a head noun that agrees with the passive predicate in (58): the agreeing head noun is present because of the predicate's MOD value; the NP and the PP are present because they appear in the predicate's SUBCAT.[28]

---

[27]The dative case on the predicate's indirect object is a result of the inflectional expansion of this predicate in accordance with the case marking rules of German which require dative case on all indirect objects. Cf. (13) in the previous chapter.

[28]There is one discrepancy between (78) and the expression (58): the predicate's SUBCAT in (78) contains an NP category for the spell-out of the predicate's subject. No such NP

(78) The spell-out of the attributive zu-infinitive passive that results from the application of the pattern type *german-long-attrzuinf-pas-lci* to the basic predicate in (72)

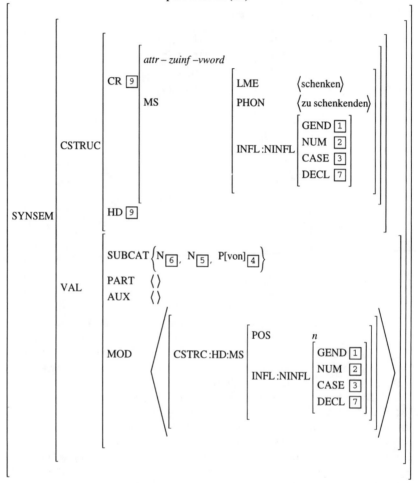

occurs in (58) and the expression would become ungrammatical if another NP were added. The "extra" NP is of course the result of the subject function (in particular, the subject's index) being used to turn a non-modificational predicate into a modifier (cf. footnote 15). There are two straightforward ways to solve this problem: (i) the modification schema which saturates the predicate's MOD list simultaneously saturates the SUBCAT element that is coindexed with the member of MOD; (ii) the SUBCAT of a phrase's modifier daughter counts as saturated if it is a singleton set whose member's ISTRUC is the predicate's subject.

The predicate expressed by the spell-out features in (78) bears the following contentive features:

(79) The contentive features of the attributive zu-infinitive passive that results from the application of the pattern type *german-long-attrzuinf-pas-lci* to the basic predicate in (72)

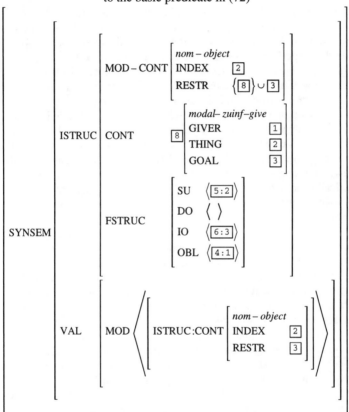

Contentively, i.e., as far as the predicates' ISTRUC is concerned, this attributive predicate differs from its predicative equivalent in (73) only in those values that reflect the general attributive-predicative contrast. As a modifier, (79) has a MOD-CONT attribute but the non-modificational predicate (73) does not. The values of CONT and FSTRUC in both predicates are identical, however: both predicates refer to a modalized form of a state of affairs of giving, both predicates govern the same grammatical functions, and those functions are linked to the same semantic roles in both predicates.

The properties of the "Attributive Version" in (59) which were not already taken care of by (78) now follow from the representation in (79):

(i) the predicate in (79) is personal, since its f-structure contains a subject; (ii) the subject ISTRUC in (79) has been promoted from the direct object function in the underlying predicate (72); (iv) the modal nuance is a consequence of the type to which the predicate's CONT belongs.

By deriving (59) we have achieved the goal we had set ourselves for this chapter with respect to the minimal pair (57)–(58): our theory captures the contentive generalizations that hold across the predicative version of the zu-infinitive passive in (57) and the attributive version of the same passive in (58). According to our analysis, the two predicates in these expressions express the same CONT, govern the same grammatical functions, and link their grammatical functions to semantic roles in identical fashion. Despite this contentive similarity, the predicate in (57) is expressed analytically and the predicate in (58) synthetically. In the approach to predicates proposed in this book, this surface difference between predicates is secondary and does not prevent the predicates from appearing in the same lexical type hierarchy and inheriting their contentive features from the same supertypes to the effect that they are contentively identical (modulo the predicative-attributive contrast). In theories that give primacy of form over function by requiring synthetically and analytically expressed predicates to be generated in different components of the grammar, it is impossible to achieve the same amount of linguistic generalization.

We have presented detailed analyses of only two of the fourteen German passives tabulated in (42) and exemplified in (43)–(56). The two passives are representative, however, of synthetically and analytically expressed passives in German and many other languages in general. Predicate representations for the remaining passives can be obtained through modifications to the types that we have defined in this chapter, e.g., by swapping the auxiliaries *werden* and *bekommen* in for the auxiliary *sein* in the types defining the spell-outs of the werden-passive and the bekommen-passive. Similarly, other passives require a different morphological form for the categorial core of the passive predicate, employ different function changes, existentially quantify over the index of the passive oblique rather than having it spelled out in a *von*-phrase etc. All of these changes are routine extensions of the general type structures for the synthetically and analytically expressed passives that we have already made available in the analyses in this chapter.

7 Conclusion

In this chapter, we have surveyed fourteen passive constructions in German and shown that they have many of the properties of passives found to be typical of this construction cross-linguistically. Even within German it could be shown that rather than being autonomous from each other, all passives are related by a very rich network of cross-classifying grammatical properties.

We examined at some length why a theory of passive in terms of the absorption of abstract Case in a GB framework is unable to account for this rich network of interrelations among passive constructions that nevertheless are all distinct pairwise. There is no one piece of form, e.g., an auxiliary or an observable affix, that occurs in all and only passive constructions. Hence, in order to capture the properties which all passive constructions share, a GB framework would have to take recourse to the postulation of an empirically non-verifiable affix. However, since each of the passive constructions can also be shown to be distinct from all of the others, postulating one such empty affix is not sufficient. Rather, several empirically non-verifiable affixes will have to be postulated in order for all the differences between the various passive predicates to fall out. In discussing the GB approach to passive, we promised that our theory would be able to account for both the similarities and the differences between the passives *without* postulating any phonologically non-overt material. We have made good on that promise.

Like in the previous chapters, we also took issue with theories of grammar that force synthetically and analytically expressed predicates to be generated in different components of the grammar. We consider any linguistic theory to be non-optimal if its general design forces separate analyses in separate grammatical components of contentively identical constructions like the German predicative and attributive zu-infinitive passives merely because one passive is expressed synthetically and the other one analytically.

The alternative theory that we are proposing in this book does not suffer from this flaw. By invoking predicates, typed feature structures, type hierarchies, predicate patterns, morphological patterns, and type partitioning, it is possible to give unified analyses of the contentive structures of corresponding passive predicates and to associate them with synthetic or analytic surface expressions, as empirically appropriate.

Beyond the surface expression types needed for the German passives, there are additional ones for passive constructions in other languages of the world that can be defined easily to configure the same passive archetypes that German defines. We will conclude this chapter by illustrating some of these.

The table in (80) contains some of the different means that languages use to spell out their passive predicates:

(80) Expression forms of passive in the world's languages[29]

Synthetic vs. Analytic	Subtype	Language
Synthetic expression:	Circumfixation	German
	Infixation	Mayan
	Reduplication	Hausa
	Vowel fronting	Singhalese
Analytic expression:	Main verb + Aux	German

(81) illustrates the use of reduplication in the formation of passive predicates in Hausa [cf. Haspelmath (1990: 31)]:

(81) Active   Passive

| dá-f-àa | 'cook' | dà-f-á-ff-ée | 'cooked' |
| nèe-m-áa | 'look for' | nèe-m-á-mm-ée | 'sought' |

In contrast, Singhalese forms its morphological passives by fronting all the vowels of the phonology of the underlying stem (cf. Haspelmath 1990: 31):[30]

(82) Active   Passive

bala-	'see'	bäle-	'be seen'
hura-	'scratch'	hire-	'be scratched'
soda-	'wash'	sede-	'be washed'

Our theory would postulate patterns for the above passive predicates that associate the passive archetype with language-particular arrangement information of the following schematic form:

(83) The spell-out of passive in Hausa/Singhalese (schematic)

$$\left[\text{SYNSEM} \left[\begin{array}{l} \text{CSTRUC} \left[\text{CR } pas-vword \right] \\ \text{VAL} \quad \left[\text{AUX} \langle \rangle \right] \end{array} \right] \right]$$

---

[29]This table is based in large part on information in Haspelmath (1990).
[30]We are omitting the marks of vowel length in the following examples.

Both constructions would lack an auxiliary, because both languages use morphology on the predicate's categorial core to signal its passivehood. Where the languages differ from each other and from the synthetically expressed predicates in German is the morpho-phonological operations they employ to derive passive word forms in the morphological module of the lexicon. Where German uses circumfixation, Hausa uses reduplication, and Singhalese uses vowel fronting.

Despite the surface differences between all the passive constructions discussed in this chapter, they all have similar semantic and functional properties that distinguish them in a unified manner from active constructions. The theory of predicates in this book can capture the contentive generalizations across these constructions and yet respect their widely diverging surface realizations. It is able to do so without a need to enrich the primary linguistic data with empirically unobservable affixes or 'functional' heads to make the data fit into the theory.

9

Causatives

Causatives have presented perennial puzzles for formal linguistic theories since the beginnings of generative grammar. They raise issues concerning the determination of grammatical functions, clause boundaries, and the borderline between syntax and morphology, among others. It has proven difficult to provide adequate analyses for them in theories of grammar that are designed to maintain a strong version of lexicalism. In that light, it is not surprising that recent analyses of analytically expressed causatives in LFG [Alsina (1993), Butt (1995)] and HPSG [Abeillé et al. (in press)] find it necessary to allow the syntax to create causative predicates with new argument structures, in violation of the principle of *Lexical Adicity* stated in chapter 1.

Throughout this book we have taken the view that *Lexical Adicity* is a sine qua non of lexicalism. We have argued that while there can be no doubt that in light of the difficulties posed by complex predicates, classical lexicalism needs to be revised, there is a conceptually and empirically superior way of reforming classical lexicalism than that of abandoning *Lexical Adicity* and by so eliminating the core functional component of lexicalism reducing this concept to the much more trivial claim that only the lexicon can compose morphological words.

In this chapter we will demonstrate that the properties of causatives no more require a weakening of functional lexicalism than do the tense-aspect and passive predicates treated in the previous two chapters. In fact, the clear differences between simple predicates and their causative counterparts with respect to meaning, grammatical function inventories and, most commonly, valence, demand a lexical treatment for these predicates, given our guiding principles. The same crucial assumptions that were invoked in the analyses of these other types of predicates will yield elegant and explanatory analyses of the cross-linguistic properties of causatives: (i) grammars contain predicates and patterns for the productive creation of new predicates from old ones; (ii) the contentive aspect of these predicates can be inherited as a cluster from universal predicate archetypes and need not be recomposed from primitives language by language; (iii) predicates with the same or similar contentive aspects can be expressed as single morphological words or as combinations of several words, depending on the preferences of individual languages. All of these assumptions use "primacy of function over form" as a crucial guiding principle in the analysis of predicates and leave the core assumptions of functional lexicalism fully intact, as explained in chapter 1.

1 Three Types of Causatives

In this section we will show that like other predicates causatives traverse the syntax-morphology boundary. Their contentive aspects can be expressed synthetically in one construction but analytically in another. In fact, in causatives the situation is quite involved, since a few things are going on simultaneously in their grammatical behavior. One issue that arises with these predicates is that causatives semantically express two states of affairs. As it will turn out, this bipropositional structure motivates why some causatives behave as biclausal structures in certain respects, e.g., the binding of anaphoric pronouns. This is not always so, however: in many languages causative predicates consistently behave as if they project one single clause. Surprisingly, there is even a third class of causatives, namely constructions which simultaneously evince monoclausal and biclausal properties. We will refer to these constructions as "mixed" causatives.

While expressing these differences in clausality between the various constructions is a significant challenge for a lexicalist theory of grammar, the hurdle is put even higher by the fact that examples of each of these three types of causatives are reported to be found with synthetic and analytic expressions of the causative predicate. The table below provides an overview of the languages whose causatives we will look at in more detail:

(1) Causative types according to clausality and syntheticity

	Analytic	Synthetic
Monoclausal	German I	Malayalam
Biclausal	German II	Chi-Mwi:ni
Mixed	Italian	Turkish

The first row contains causative constructions that display only monoclausal and no biclausal effects according to a number of pretheoretical diagnostics which we will introduce shortly. "German I" therefore is a causative construction that shows only monoclausal effects and whose predicate is expressed analytically, i.e., with more than one morphological word. Malayalam also has a causative construction with consistently monoclausal behavior, but unlike German it expresses its causative predicate in one single morphological word. The languages listed in the remaining two rows of the table have causative constructions which have been reported to consistently show biclausal and mixed effects respectively.

Although we will analyze the six constructions above as complex predicates associated with lexical representations, it is important to observe that we are *not* claiming that all apparent instances of causative constructions should necessarily be treated in this way. For example, the English causative construction discussed in the next subsection may well represent an instance of a construction with two syntactically distinct predicates which are merely connected through "subject to object raising" (induced by the lexical properties of the higher predicate) and which *don't* share a lexical representation. In fact, it may be the case that such two-predicate raising constructions represent a pathway for the diachronic evolution of complex predicates from co-occurring but lexically still separate predicates that together express the same or similar meanings as the newly evolving single predicate. In our opinion, the causative constructions in (1) have already undergone this sort of development.

2   Terminology and Pretheoretical Diagnostics for Clausality

It will be best to agree on some terminological conventions and some pretheoretical diagnostics for monoclausality vs. biclausality before we approach different causative constructions and compare them. It should be recalled that the diagnostics yield inconsistent results in the case of mixed causatives which are identified as monoclausal by some and biclausal by other tests. The results from each individual diagnostic therefore should not be seen as an absolute value but should be considered relative to the outcome of all the other diagnostics. It should be the diagnostic profile of the whole construction rather than one individual diagnostic that determines the clausality of the construction. Once such an overall profile leads us to assign the construction either to the monoclausal or the biclausal group, the data that the diverging diagnostics are based on must be explained in terms that do not depend on clausality.

Our choice of diagnostics in determining clausality is obviously important. Unfortunately it has been influenced by such accidental factors as what kind of information we have available about the languages whose causative constructions we are interested in. Clearly, if additional factors are taken into account or if the diagnostics we employ don't really show what we take them to show, then the typology of causatives will have to be revised. Fortunately, these are empirical matters that can be addressed in future linguistic inquiry. We hope to have taken at least a few important steps in the right direction.

Since we will primarily be dealing with causatives formed from transitive verbs, the resulting causative predicate will contain information about up to three semantic arguments. Our terminology will be based on causatives that embed a predicate with a clearly distinguished active human agent argument and a non-human patient argument:

(2)   **Sue**Human eats the **fish**Non-human

In a causative construction like (3) we have an additional argument:

(3) **Mary**Causer causes **Sue**Causee to eat *fish*Patient

We will refer to *Mary* as "the causer," to *Sue* as "the causee" and to *fish* as "the patient," "the patient of the lower verb," or "the lower patient." In constructions where the lower predicate's arguments are not clearly distinct in terms of agentivity or humanness, we will apply the terms "causee" and "patient" in analogy with the behavior of similarly expressed predicates that draw the distinctions clearly. As an added typographic signal, we will underline the causee and italicize the patient in all the causative examples in this chapter.

We will apply three pretheoretical diagnostics of monoclausality and four diagnostics of biclausality in the creation of clausality profiles for different causative constructions.

The first diagnostic of monoclausality is that the causative predicate has the grammatical functional profile of a generic monoclausal three-place predicate that denotes a single state of affairs. The prototype of such a verb is *give* which in many languages governs three distinct functions: a subject, a direct object, and an indirect object/oblique. If causative predicates behave like typical verbs *give* in this respect, this diagnostic will identify them as monoclausal.

Second, there are many empirical reasons for postulating that some semantic and/or grammatical arguments of a predicate are in some sense more closely related to the predicate than others.[1] This can be reflected in phrase-structural differences, e.g., the verb in English forms a phrase with its objects which the subject argument is external to, making the subject argument less closely related to the verb than its objects. It can also be reflected in terms of idiom formation in that patient arguments typically form idioms more easily with verbs than agent arguments, etc. As a whole, these criteria converge on an ordering that establishes agentive subjects as being less closely bound to the predicate than patient objects. From this point of view, the three arguments of causativized predicates can be ranked as follows: the patient is the innermost argument, the causee is less closely bound to the embedded predicate, since it is an agent, and the causer is least closely bound, since it is not even a semantic argument of the embedded predicate.

The two arguments farthest away from each other on this hierarchy are the causer (an argument of CAUSE) and the lower patient (the innermost argument of the embedded predicate). We will use the possibilities of binding-theoretic interaction between these two arguments as another diagnostic. Since anaphoric binding is typically constrained to applying to arguments of the same clause in the world's languages, if in a causative construction the two arguments of the causative that are most distant from each other can enter into an anaphoric binding relationship, then we will take this to be a symptom of monoclausality. (4) illustrates this case:

---

[1] See Kiparsky (1987), Bresnan and Kanerva (1989), and the use of obliqueness hierarchies in Pollard and Sag (1987, 1994).

(4) [Clause-1 **NPCauser-i** V **NPCausee** (V) **NPPatient-i**]

Assuming the rightmost NP to be an anaphor that is bound by the causer across the intervening causee, this is tentative evidence that all three NPs appear in one and the same clause.

Finally, recall from the previous chapter that passive is universally defined as the demotion of the underlying subject. In the unmarked case, the underlying direct object is promoted to the surface subject of the passive predicate. In other words, the unmarked passivization construction acts on a single clause and creates another single clause. Consider a causative construction like (4) in this light: if the causative in (4) can be passivized with the consequence that the causer is demoted from a subject to an oblique and the patient is promoted to the new surface subject, then this is evidence that all three arguments of the original causative predicate appear in one clause.

These, then are our three diagnostics for monoclausality. We will sum them up in a table once we have discussed the tests for biclausality. If each of these diagnostics returns a positive result for a causative construction, we take that to be strong evidence that the construction is monoclausal.

The first of the four diagnostics of biclausality acts as a counterpart to the first diagnostic for monoclausality: if we find doubled grammatical functions in the causative predicate, e.g., two direct objects or two indirect objects, then we will take that to be an indication that two clauses are present, under the assumption that each clause contains only a single instantiation of each non-oblique grammatical function. According to this diagnostic, the English construction in (5) would be biclausal, because both the causee and the patient can be shown to behave like direct objects:

(5) I made **her** read *it*

(5) is an instance of the two-predicate raising-to-object construction, in which the subject of the underlying predicate *read* is structure-shared ("has been raised") with the object function of the causative predicate. While the two clauses overlap because of this functional identification, they have not been collapsed into a single clause and the lower "caused" clause contains a subject distinct from the subject of the "cause" clause.

The presence of such a biclausal structure with a discrete subject in the lower clause may also be indicated by binding-theoretic facts. Thus, if in a structure similar to (4) the causer is unable to bind the patient argument, then the reason is possibly that the structure needs to be parsed into two clauses as in (6) rather than just one as in (4):

(6)

[Clause-1 **NP Causer-i** V [Clause-2 **NP Causee-k** (V) **NP Patient-*i/k**]]

Since binding is typically clause-bound, the structure in (6) is one way of naturally accounting for the inability of the causer to bind the patient. We thus again get the picture typical of subject-to-object raising sentences:

(7) * The woman$_i$ made John call herself$_i$

Moreover, recall that the upper surface direct object of such clauses appears both in the higher and the lower clause. We are therefore not surprised if it can enter into binding-theoretic relationships with elements in both clauses, since no clause boundaries need to be crossed to maintain such relationships. The English construction type illustrated in (5) and (7) displays the expected behavior again. The surface direct object (the causee) in the causative construction can be bound by the surface subject (the causer), because subjects can always bind direct objects in English:

(8) The woman$_i$ made herself$_i$ call John

Simultaneously, the primary direct object (the causee) can bind the secondary direct object (the patient), because the primary direct object also acts as the subject of the lower clause which contains the patient:

(9) John made the woman$_i$ criticize herself$_i$

The English causative construction thus behaves biclausally both with respect to the doubling of grammatical functions and the binding theory.

The third diagnostic for biclausality is the counterpart of the third diagnostic for monoclausality. Recall that we argued that passivization is clause-bound and hence that if the patient as the innermost argument of the causative predicate can become the surface subject of the passivized causative, this suggests that the causative predicate projects all its semantic arguments into a single clause. Conversely, if that patient argument *cannot* become the surface subject of the passivized causative, then one reason for this may be that there really are two clauses and what is being passivized is the upper clause. Since the patient does not bear a grammatical function in the upper clause, it is barred from promoting to the subject of the passivized causative.

We can illustrate this feature again with the English subject-to-object raising causative construction. Compare the following three examples:

(10)   Mary made Sue$_{Causee}$ criticize Helen$_{Patient}$
(11)   Sue$_{Causee}$ was made to criticize Helen$_{Patient}$

(12) * Helen_Patient was made Sue_Causee to criticize

Passivization of the active causative (10) yields the result in (11) rather than (12): the causee and not the patient of the embedded predicate becomes the surface subject of the passivized causative. Postulating a biclausal structure for (10) immediately accounts for this paradigm: since the causee but not the patient bears the grammatical function of direct object in the upper clause, it will become promoted to the subject function if the upper clause is passivized. Finding a paradigm of this kind in a causative construction thus is another diagnostic for biclausality.

The fourth and final diagnostic for biclausality comes from binding theory once again. Recall from our earlier discussion that subjects make very good binders cross-linguistically. Consequently, there are languages in which subjects are the only grammatical function that can antecede anaphors in constructions where there is no doubt about how many clauses are present or what grammatical functions the arguments present in the sentence bear. Dalrymple (1993: 11) cites the Marathi reflexive *swataah* as an example of an anaphor requiring a subject as its antecedent.

Assume, then that we have a language with an anaphor that must be anteceded by a subject and we lexicalize the lower patient argument of a causative construction with that anaphor. If only the causer can antecede the anaphor, then we will assume that only one clause is present and that the causer is the subject of that clause. On the other hand, if either only the causee or both the causee and the causer can antecede the anaphor in the innermost argument position, then we have reason to believe that the causee is a subject. Since the causer is always a subject of active causative constructions, the construction must thus have two subjects. Since we are assuming that non-oblique grammatical functions cannot be doubled within clauses, this state of affairs indicates the presence of two clauses, with the causer the subject of the higher clause and the causee the subject of the lower one.

(13) and (14) sum up the pretheoretical diagnostics of monoclausality and biclausality that we will attempt to apply to each of the causative constructions discussed in the next sections:

(13) Diagnostics of monoclausality: (= 1CLP)

a. No doubled term grammatical functions, i.e., SUs, IOs, DOs;
b. the causer can bind the patient of an embedded transitive verb;
c. the patient can become the surface subject when the causative verb is passivized.

(14) Diagnostics of biclausality: (= 2CLP)

a.   doubled term grammatical functions;
b.   the causer cannot bind the patient of an embedded transitive verb but the causee can;
c.   the patient, even though it has the form of a DO, cannot become the subject of the passivized causative because it is the DO of the embedded clause and not the DO of the causative clause;
d.   in languages where otherwise only subjects can bind, the causee can bind the patient.

From here on, we will frequently abbreviate "monoclausal property" as "1CLP" and "biclausal property" as "2CLP."

The following three sections will be concerned with purely monoclausal, purely biclausal, and mixed causatives respectively. It will be shown that the functional property of clausality is independent of surface realization, since for each of the three clausality types we can find languages that express that type through a synthetic predicate and other languages that express the type analytically.

3   Purely Monoclausal Causatives

This section has two subsections that both deal with a purely monoclausal causative construction. They differ in that in German the predicate of this construction is expressed through an auxiliary-main verb combination whereas Malayalam uses a single synthetic verb form that is morphologically identified as a causative word form.

3.1   German I

Compare the regular non-causative transitive sentence (15) with the causativized counterpart in (16) which is one of the two German causative constructions:

(15)   Ellen hat den Jungen gekämmt
          Ellen has the boy   combed

          'Ellen combed the boy'

(16)   Ellen ließ *den Jungen* <u>von</u> <u>seiner</u> <u>Schwester</u> kämmen
          Ellen caused the boy   by   his   sister   comb

          'Ellen had the boy combed by his sister'

According to our terminological convention, *Ellen* is the causer, *von seiner Schwester* is the causee, and *den Jungen* is the lower patient. (Recall that the causee is underlined throughout and the lower patient is italicized.) (16) has the grammatical-functional profile of a three-place verb: the mapping from semantic roles to grammatical functions is as in (17):

(17) SUCauser OBLCausee OBJPatient (= **1CLP**)

The absence of any doubled grammatical function in a causativized transitive is a monoclausal property.

In all other respects, the construction in (16) behaves like a single clause as well. We illustrate this with anaphoric binding. As Reis (1976) has shown, the German anaphor *sich* must be anteceded by the subject of the minimal clause containing it:[2]

(18)
    *Maria glaubt   [daß √Ellen   *die Frau
    Maria believes that Ellen-SU the woman-DO

    *sich   gezeigt hat]
    herself-IO shown has

    'Maria believes that Ellen showed the woman herself'

(19)
    *Maria glaubt   [daß √Ellen   *der Frau
    Maria believes that Ellen-SU the woman-IO

    *sich   gezeigt hat]
    herself-DO shown has

    'Maria believes that Ellen showed the woman herself'

(18) and (19) both contain the ditransitive predicate *zeigen* 'to show.' In the first example, we have lexicalized the indirect object of this predicate with the reflexive *sich*. Of the three underlined functions in (18), only the subject of the embedded clause can be understood as binding *sich,* whereas the direct object of the lower clause as well as the subject of the main clause are not possible antecedents. In (19) we reflexivized the direct object of the predicate of the lower clause and like before, only the subject of its own clause can antecede the anaphor. Assuming that the anaphor *sich* obeys Reis' Generalization, this data is immediately accounted for: the two objects in (18) and (19) cannot antecede the reflexive because the reflexive must be bound by a subject and the main clause subject cannot do so because it is not contained in the same minimal f-structural clause that contains the re-flexive.

---

[2]Reis notes some exceptions to the domain restriction (but not the antecedent restriction) when *sich* is embedded within a prepositional phrase or occurs in certain word orders in subject-to-object raising constructions. Both of these circumstances will be carefully avoided here; all our examples are therefore expected to fall under Reis' Generalization.

Armed with this generalization about *sich,* we can now return to the causative construction and see what happens when we lexicalize the lower patient with *sich:*

(20) Ellen$_i$ ließ *sich$_{i/*k}$* <u>von ihrer</u> <u>Schwester</u>$_k$ kämmen
      Ellen caused herself by her sister comb

      'Ellen caused her sister to comb herself'

(21) Ellen$_i$ ließ <u>von ihrer</u> <u>Schwester</u>$_k$ *sich$_{i/*k}$* kämmen
      Ellen caused by her sister herself comb

      'Ellen caused her sister to comb herself'

Independently of the word order we choose for the causee and the lower patient, only the causer can antecede *sich.* According to our diagnostics, this is double evidence for a monoclausal analysis of this construction: since the causer *Ellen* can bind *sich,* these two expressions must occur in the same clause if *sich* behaves in causatives as it does elsewhere. Secondly, the fact that the causee *her sister* cannot antecede *sich* suggests that the causee is not a subject because otherwise it would have to be the subject of the minimal sentence containing *sich* in (20)–(21). The binding facts thus unambiguously favor a monoclausal analysis of this German causative construction.

In sum, the causative construction we have called German I passes two tests for monoclausality and none for biclausality. We therefore take it to be an instance of a purely monoclausal causative construction. As all the examples show, this construction is formed by a combination of the auxiliary *lassen* and the bare infinitive of the predicate's categorial core (alias "the main verb"). Moreover, the auxiliary and the main verb can be separated from each other in phrase structure, for instance when the auxiliary that serves as the categorial head of the predicate appears in the second position of a main clause, as in (20)–(21).

3.2 Malayalam[3]

Malayalam has a purely monoclausal causative construction as well. Interestingly, in this language the causative predicate is expressed by one single morphological word.

In (22) we provide an example of a simple transitive sentence:

(22) kutti   annaye   nulli
      child-NOM elephant-ACC pinched

      'The child pinched an elephant'

---

[3]The Malayalam data is cited from Mohanan (1983), pages 59, 61, 63 and Marantz (1984), page 282.

As in the German construction just discussed, the causative predicate formed from the predicate of (22) governs three distinct grammatical functions, namely a subject, a direct object, and an oblique. This is a monoclausal property:

(23)   amma   kuṭṭiyekkoṇte *aanaye*   ṇulliccu
        mother child-INST   elephant-ACC pinch-CAUSE-PAST

'Mother made the child pinch the elephant'

Secondly, the causative predicate can be passivized and under passivization the lower patient rather than the causee becomes the subject of the passive predicate. This is illustrated by the grammaticality of (24a) and the ungrammaticality of (24b):

(24a)   ammayaal   *aana*   ṇuḷḷikkappeṭṭu
        mother-INST elephant-NOM pinch-CAUSE-PASS-PAST

'The elephant was caused by mother to be pinched'

(24b) *   ammayaal   *kuṭṭi*   aanaye   ṇuḷḷikkappeṭṭu
          mother-INST child-NOM elephant-ACC pinch-CAUSE-PASS-PAST

'The child was caused to be pinched by mother'

Since the lower patient, the innermost argument of the embedded predicate, can become the subject of the passive clause and we assume in general that passive is clause-bound, this is further evidence for the monoclausal nature of the Malayalam causative construction.

    Finally, like German, Malayalam has an anaphor *(swaṇtam)* that is subject-oriented [see Mohanan (1983: 55)]. In the non-causative sentence (25), the possessive reflexive can only take the subject *Johnny* as its antecedent and cannot be bound by the direct object *Mary:*

(25)   jooṇi   meeṙiye swaṇtam wiiṭṭil   wecca umma weccu
        Johnny Mary   self's   house-LOC at   kiss   put

'Johnny kissed Mary at Johnny's/*Mary's house'

(26)   amma   kuṭṭiyekkoṇte *aanaye*   swaṇtam wiiṭṭil wecca
        mother child-INST   elephant-ACC self's   house at

        ṇulliccu
        pinch-CAUSE-PAST

    'Mother made the child pinch the elephant at
    mother's/*child's/*elephant's house'

The binding facts in (26) fall out from the subject orientation of the possessive reflexive and the assumption that the causative consists of only one clause with only one subject which expresses the causer *mother*. Neither the causee nor the lower patient can antecede the possessive reflexive because the single clause cannot have more than one subject and the subject function is already taken by the causer.

The Malayalam causative construction thus displays only mono-clausal properties. Functional-semantically it behaves like German I, but there is one crucial difference between the two constructions: in Malayalam the causative predicate is expressed by a single morphologically integrated word form whereas German uses a combination of two phrase-structurally independent word forms.

4 Purely Biclausal Causatives

Now we will encounter causative constructions that behave in all respects as if they contain two clauses. They show the typical properties of raising-to-object constructions which identify the object of the higher clause with the subject of the clause immediately embedded under the higher clause. We will refer to the higher clause as the "cause clause" and the lower one as the "caused clause." An analytic version of this construction is presented in 4.1. and a synthetic version in 4.2.

4.1 German II

German has a second causative construction apart from the one we saw in section 3.1.[4] Like the first construction, however, the present one expresses its predicate with the auxiliary *lassen* and the bare infinitive of the main verb.

Note the difference between (27) and the earlier example (16), both of which are causatives based on the predicate of the simple non-causative sentence (24):

(27) Ellen ließ den Vater *den Jungen* kämmen
      Ellen made the father the boy   comb

      'Ellen made father comb the boy'

---

[4]As pointed out previously, there are certain causative constructions that may admit of a two-predicate subject-to-object raising analysis. Our motivation for treating the present variant of the German causative as a complex predicate derives from its parallel behavior with other complex predicates, in particular the tense-aspect predicates analyzed in chapter 7 and the passive predicates discussed in chapter 8. Specifically, it falls under some of the same word order, topicalization, and postposing generalizations as these other complex predicates. See chapter 11 for examples.

Unlike (16), (27) expresses both the causee and the lower patient as noun phrases [(16) expresses the causee as an oblique PP] which is a first hint that these two elements both bear the same grammatical function, albeit in different clauses. Secondly, both NPs in (27) are accusative, the case typical of direct objects in German. The double-accusative pattern is found in many languages in subject-to-object raising constructions and also appears in German sentences containing predicates that appear to involve subject-to-object raising, e.g., the perception predicate in (28):

(28)   Ellen sah den Vater den Jungen kämmen
        Ellen saw the father the boy   comb

        'Ellen saw father comb the boy'

Like other direct objects, the two accusatives in (27) can appear before the subject of their clause in a subordinate clause but this order is dispreferred if the direct object is non-pronominal:

(29)   weil   ihn ihn niemand$_{SUBJ}$ kämmen lieβ
        because him him nobody   comb   made

        'because nobody make him comb him'

(30) ? weil   den Vater den Jungen niemand$_{SUBJ}$ kämmen lieβ
        because the father the boy   nobody   comb   made

        'because nobody make the father comb the boy'

All this evidence suggests that this causative construction contains two direct objects, one that expresses the causee and one for the lower patient. Assuming that each clause can have at most one direct object, this is evidence of the presence of two clauses in this construction, with the clauses being related by the functional-semantic analog of subject-to-object raising.

If the conclusion in the previous paragraph is correct, then the subject-oriented anaphor *sich* should behave differently in the construction we are calling German II than in the previously discussed construction German I. For, if the overt direct object of the cause clause really is identified with the subject of the caused clause, then the subject of the minimal clause containing *sich* in the lower object position should be the causee rather than the causer. In other words, the construction should behave like (7)–(9) with the lower patient anteceded by the surface direct object but not the surface subject which functionally is "one clause too far away" from the anaphor. This prediction is borne out:

(31)   Hans$_i$ lieβ den Jungen$_k$ sich$_{k/*i}$ kämmen
        Hans   made the boy   himself   comb

        'Hans made the boy comb himself'

Compare (31) with (20) and (21) where the binding facts were just the opposite: the causer could bind the lower patient but the causee could not. This is further strong evidence that the second German causative construction is purely biclausal, as compared to the purely monoclausal behavior of the first German construction.

4.2 Chi-Mwi:ni[5]

The Chi-Mwi:ni causative is interesting because functional-semantically it behaves exactly like the purely biclausal construction from German we just saw but differs from it in that the predicate of the Chi-Mwi:ni construction is expressed as one single morphological word. As we understand it, the components of this word are not separable under any syntactic or phrase-structural conditions.

As a first indication of biclausality, note that the causee and the lower patient are both expressed as simple noun phrases in the causative (32):

(32)   Mwa:limu ø-wa-ándik-ish-iz-e   <u>wa:na</u> xaṭi
         teacher   SP-OP-write-CAUSE-T/A children letter

         'The teacher made the children write a letter'

This is compatible with (32) being an instance of subject-to-object raising in which the causee is expressed as the direct object of the cause clause and the lower patient as the direct object of the caused clause.[6] Further evidence for this structure is provided by passivization. As the difference between (33) and (34) indicates, only the causee but not the lower patient can become the subject when the predicate in (32) is passivized:

(33)   <u>Wa:na</u> wa-ándik-ish-iz-a: xaṭi na mwa:limu
         children SP-write-CAUSE-PASS-T/A letter by teacher

         'The children were made to write a letter by the teacher'

(34) * Xaṭi a-ándik-ish-iz-a <u>wa:na</u>   na mwa:limu
       letter write   children by teacher

       'The letter was made to be written by the children by the teacher'

---

[5]The Chi-Mwi:ni data is cited from Marantz (1984), pages 267, 270, 271. In an effort to provide an analysis of all relevant clausality effects, we rely on Marantz's arguments for a purely biclausal analysis of this construction.
[6]Following Marantz (1984), these two identically marked NPs bear two identical grammatical functions, implicating two separate clauses. On the other hand, Polinsky (1995) has demonstrated that in some languages identically case-marked arguments in causative constructions bear different grammatical functions.

(32)–(34) are parallel to the English sentences (10)–(12) whose grammaticality judgments we had assumed to follow from the presence of two clauses with identity between the object of the higher and the subject of the lower clause. Passivization thus provides powerful evidence for the biclausality of the Chi-Mwi:ni causative construction.

The binding theory, finally, falls into place as well. In both (35) and (36) we have lexicalized the lower patient with an anaphor that reportedly follows the same binding principle as the German reflexive *sich:* it must be bound by the subject of the minimal clause containing it. In a sentence such as (35), only the surface direct object causee which acts as the subject of the minimal clause containing the anaphor can be interpreted as anteceding the reflexive. The surface subject is "one clause too far away:"

(35) Mi_i [ni-m-big-ish-iz-e] $mwa:na_k$ $ru:hu\text{-}y\text{-}é*_{i/k}$
      I-SUBJ SP-OP-hit-CAUSE-T/A child-OBJ himself

      'I made the child hit himself'

If we replace the third person anaphor in (35) with a first person anaphor to make it featurally compatible only with the first person subject of the cause clause and incompatible with the third person direct object of the cause clause, then the sentence becomes ungrammatical:

(36) Mi_i [ni-m-big-ish-iz-e] Ali_k $ru:hu\text{-}y\text{-}á*_{i/*k}$
      I-SUBJ SP-OP-hit-CAUSE-T/A Ali-OBJ myself

      'I made Ali hit myself'

The reason is obvious: *mi* bears the right features to bind the anaphor but is not close enough structurally to bind it; *Ali,* on the other hand, is structurally in the right position to bind the anaphor [cf. (35)] but conflicts with it featurally.

In sum, like the second German causative construction, the Chi-Mwi:ni causative construction discussed in the present section behaves biclausally in every respect. Interestingly, however, the predicate that projects these two clauses is expressed by one single morphological word.

5 Mixed Causatives

The causative constructions whose data are introduced in this section are very interesting as well. Both constructions differ from the previous four in that they simultaneously evince monoclausal and biclausal properties. But like the previous two clausality types, this mixed type can be expressed analytically or synthetically.

5.1 Italian[7]

The Italian causative, like Romance causatives in general, is very complex and consists of a number of different constructions with different properties. The reader should be aware that our goal here is not to provide anything like a comprehensive analysis of these constructions. Our much more modest interest is in showing that there exist *some* causative constructions which display a mixture of monoclausal and biclausal behaviors, i.e., that this construction type exists and has to be recognized as one type of complex predicate. It will be self-evident to anybody familiar with the complexity of Romance causatives that we are addressing only a tiny portion of this construction type and that the sketch we provide for the Italian causative discussed here needs to be filled in with an analysis of those aspects of the construction that go beyond the very limited theoretical questions we are pursuing in this chapter.

The Italian causative under discussion behaves biclausally with respect to the binding theory but monoclausally in all other respects. Thus, note that the functional profile of the causative sentence in (37) is similar to that of a sentence headed by a ditransitive verb of the *give* type. The causer is expressed as a subject (as part of the verbal inflection), the causee as an indirect object marked by the preposition *a,* and the lower patient is expressed as a direct object:

(37)   Farà   riparare *la macchina* <u>a</u> <u>Giovanni</u>
         he will make repair   the car   to Giovanni

         'He will make Giovanni repair the car'

The absence of functional doubling is a monoclausal property. Moreover, the patient direct object becomes the subject when the predicate of (37) is passivized:

(38)   *La macchina* sarà   fatta riparare <u>a</u> <u>Giovanni</u>
         the car   will be made repair to Giovanni

         'The car will be made to be repaired by Giovanni'

In this respect, the Italian construction patterns with the purely monoclausal causative construction of Malayalam [cf. (24)] and against the purely biclausal causative of Chi-Mwi:ni [cf. (33)–(34)].

Despite this evidence from relational uniqueness and passivization, however, there is evidence for the biclausality of the construction from binding theory. The argument is based on the anaphor *se stesso* (which varies in form as a function of its inflectional features). This element occurs in the following non-causative sentence that we use as a control. (39) is of the

---

[7]The Italian data is cited from Burzio (1986), pages 225, 254, 264 and Rosen (1990), page 107.

subject-to-object raising type and the inability of the subject of the main clause to bind the anaphor suggests that this anaphor must find an antecedent within the minimal f-structural clause containing it:

(39) * Maria$_i$ considerava [Giovanni orgoglioso di se stessa$_i$]
        Maria considered   Giovanni proud   of herself

      'Maria considered Giovanni proud of herself'

Lexicalizing the lower patient position of our Italian causative with the inflectionally correct form of *se stesso* shows that the causative construction behaves like the biclausal raising-to-object construction (39) with respect to the binding of this anaphor:

(40) * Con le minacce   fecero accusare *se stessi$_i$* a Giovanni
        with threats-   (they$_i$) made accuse   themselves to Giovanni

      'With threats they made Giovanni accuse themselves'

(41)   Con le minacce   fecero accusare *se stesso$_i$* a Giovanni$_i$
        with threats-   (they) made accuse   himself   to Giovanni

      'With threats they made Giovanni accuse himself'

In both sentences, the subject causer is left unexpressed and signaled through the finite morphology on the causative auxiliary. (40) shows that this understood subject is unable to antecede *se stessi* and (41) shows that once the anaphor is put into the singular, it *can* be anteceded by the causee which is expressed as an indirect object on the surface.

    (40) and (41) thus repeat the binding paradigm that we saw in the English subject-to-object raising sentences (7)–(9), the example illustrating the German biclausal causative (31), and the same types of example for the purely biclausal causative in Chi-Mwi:ni [(35)–(36)].

    In sum: Italian has a causative construction that behaves monoclausally with respect to non-binding theoretic properties but biclausally with respect to at least one binding theoretic property.[8]

    Finally, note that this Italian mixed causative is expressed analytically by the combination of the auxiliary *fare* and the bare infinitive of the main verb.

---

[8]Since it is well-known that in languages with more than one anaphor these do not all need to have the same binding domains [cf. Dalrymple (1993)], we cannot exclude that other anaphors in Italian will behave differently. This is immaterial to our theoretical point, however, that this Italian causative in at least some respects behaves monoclausally and in at least some other respects behaves biclausally.

5.2 Turkish[9]

This brings us to the final empirical option we will illustrate here: a mixed causative construction whose predicate is expressed by a single synthetic word form. This case is found in Turkish which has a causative construction that behaves very similarly to the Italian construction we just examined.

(42) provides a simple non-causative transitive sentence of this language:

(42) Hasan bavul-u   açtɨ
      Hasan suitcase-ACC opened

      'Hasan opened the suitcase'

The causativized version of (42) in (43) expresses the causee as an indirect object marked by dative case and the lower patient by a direct object marked by accusative case. The presence of three distinct grammatical functions in this causative is a monoclausal property:

(43) Mehmet <u>Hasan-ɨ</u>   *bavul-u*   aç-tɨr-dɨ
      Mehmet Hasan-DAT suitcase-ACC open-CAUSE-PAST

      'Mehmet had Hasan open the suitcase'

In further support of a monoclausal analysis, the lower patient can become the surface subject when (43) is passivized, but the causee cannot:

(44) *Bavul*   Mehmet tarafɨndan <u>Hasan-a</u>
      suitcase Mehmet by   Hasan-DAT

      aç-tɨr-ɨl-dɨ
      open-CAUSE-PASS-PAST

      'The suitcase was caused by Mehmet to be opened by Hasan'

(45) * <u>Hasan</u> Mehmet tarafɨndan *bavul-u*
       Hasan Mehmet by   suitcase-ACC

       aç-tɨr-ɨl-dɨ
       open-CAUSE-PASS-PAST

       'Hasan was caused by Mehmet to open the suitcase'

---

[9]The Turkish data is cited from Aissen (1979), pages 11, 14, 15, 131, 132.

As in Italian, some binding-theoretic facts spoil a purely monoclausal picture of the Turkish causative. For some speakers the first person anaphor *kendim* cannot be bound by an indirect object:

(46) * Hasan bana$_i$ kendim-i$_i$ anlatti
     Hasan me-DAT myself-ACC explained

     'Hasan explained me to myself'

Yet, apparently even those speakers who find (46) ungrammatical accept both (47) and (48):

(47)   Ben$_i$ <u>Hasan-a$_i$</u>   kendim-i$_j$ yika-t-ti-m
      I   Hasan-DAT myself-ACC wash-CAUSE-PAST-1SG

      'I made Hasan wash me'

(48)   <u>Bana$_i$</u>   kendim-i$_i$ anlat-tir-di
       me-DAT myself-ACC explain-CAUSE-PAST

       'He made me explain myself'

(47) is expected under a monoclausal analysis. If there is only one clause, then the causer should be its subject and as a subject should be able to antecede the anaphor in the direct object position of the same clause.

  (48) presents a problem, however. Here the causee in the grammatical function of an indirect object binds the lower patient, even for speakers who do not allow indirect objects to bind that same anaphor in non-causative environments like (46). One obvious way of explaining the difference between (46) and (48) is that in (46) the dative phrase is a pure indirect object whereas in (48) it is an indirect object identified with a subject of a lower clause. If *kendim* can take any subject as its antecedent, then both the surface subject and the indirect object causee in the causative construction qualify as possible binders. For this explanation to succeed, the construction has to be biclausal, however, in contradiction to the arguments for monoclausality from surface grammatical functions in (43) and passivization in (44)–(45).

  The Turkish causative thus displays a mixed clausality profile, like the Italian causative discussed in the previous subsection. In contrast to that construction, however, the Turkish causative expresses its predicate as one single morphological word.

6   Variation in Causative Constructions

  In the previous three sections we have illustrated that with respect to clausality, the world's languages contain at least three different causative construction types: (i) those with only monoclausal properties, (ii) those with only biclausal properties, and (iii) those with both monoclausal and bi-clausal properties. Moreover, each of the three clausality types is instanti-ated with both analytic and synthetic surface expressions for the predicate in some language.

A third parameter of variation that could be observed in the examples we presented but that we have not drawn any attention to is the variation in surface grammatical functions found in the various constructions. The only functional feature that remains constant throughout all the constructions is that in active causative sentences the causer is expressed as the subject of the construction. The causee's and the patient's grammatical function fluctuates, however, as the following table documents for monoclausal causatives:

(49)   The grammatical functions in monoclausal causatives of transitive verbs

	Causer	Causee	Patient
German	SU	OBL	DO
Malayalam	SU	OBL	DO
Italian	SU	IO	DO
Turkish	SU	IO	DO
Chamorro	SU	DO	OBL

The causee can appear as an oblique, an indirect object, or a direct object; the lower patient may serve as a direct object and sometimes in other functions as well, even though we have to go outside the set of languages we have been dealing with to show that. Gibson (1992) shows that in Chamorro the lower patient appears in a grammatical function called "2-chômeur" in her framework, which would translate into a kind of oblique under our assump-tions. The causee appears as a direct object in this Chamorro construction.

As long as the causer is realized as the subject, almost all logically possible relational choices are thus instantiated in monoclausal causatives. Moreover, while there seem to be some functional preferences, there does not seem to be a principled way of predicting which relational spell-out a language will choose. We will capture the preferences through a set of de-fault assumptions in the definitions of our archetypes and some additional markedness statements.

7   Causative Archetypes and Their Declarations

Our analytical strategy will not be unexpected at this point: we will proceed in the customary manner by defining a number of archetypes for causatives that Universal Grammar makes available to individual grammars. These types express what the various causative constructions that are found frequently in the world's languages have in common, which is a set of functional-semantic characteristics. In a second step, we allow individual natural languages to define pattern types in their grammars that declare these causative archetypes to form language-particular types whose autonomous information content is minimized because much of their information is inherited from archetypes that the causative types of most other natural languages use as 'role models' as well. Given that the causative archetypes leave their surface spell-out underspecified, each incorporating grammar will have to configure the archetype with language-specific spell-out information that may give the causative predicates a wide variety of surface realizations, including synthetic and analytic surface appearances.

We begin by postulating the three causative archetypes in (50):

(50) The causative archetypes

univ-caus-bas-lci

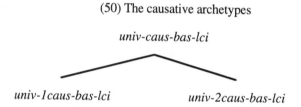

univ-1caus-bas-lci   *univ-2caus-bas-lci*

The archetype *univ-caus-bas-lci* encodes what all causative predicate constructions have in common semantically and functionally. It leaves the issue of whether the causative predicate governs one or two f-structural clauses to be decided by its two archetypal subtypes: the monoclausal causative subtype *univ-1caus-bas-lci* will project the grammatical functions of the underlying causativized verb into a single f-structural clause whereas its companion type *univ-2caus-bas-lci* will create a biclausal f-structure. The six causative constructions that are the topic of this chapter will then be shown to have their properties determined by declaring the archetypes in (50) as in (51).

Compare (51) with the survey table in (1): for each language with a biclausal causative (German, Chi-Mwi:ni) in (1), (51) postulates a type (i.e., *german-2caus-bas-lci, chi-mwi:ni-2caus-bas-lci*) which declares the biclausal causative archetype *univ-2caus-bas-lci*. On the other hand, the two languages which have monoclausal causative constructions (German, Malayalam) declare the monoclausal causative archetype. This archetype is also declared by Italian and Turkish whose causatives (i.e., the causatives discussed in this book) the table in (1) categorizes as mixed. As we suggested earlier, these causatives behave like monoclausal causatives in all respects except for binding theory. In a later section of this chapter these binding-theoretic biclausality effects will be shown to be derivable without the postulation of two f-structural clauses. (51) therefore contains four language-particular subtypes of the monoclausal causative archetype and two instantiations of the biclausal causative archetype. The hierarchy postulates the additional type *german-caus-bas-lci* as a supertype of both the monoclausal and biclausal German causatives. This is done to capture the German-specific generalizations that hold across these two German predicate types, in particular the generalizations with respect to surface spell-out: as mentioned in sections 3.1 and 4.1, the German causative predicates have identical surface spell-outs, i.e., a combination of the bare infinitive of the categorial core and a form of the auxiliary *lassen.* The type *german-caus-bas-lci* expresses this information. As it is neutral between monoclausality and biclausality, it declares the most general causative archetype *univ-caus-bas-lci* which is likewise neutral with respect to clausality.

(51) The causative type hierarchy

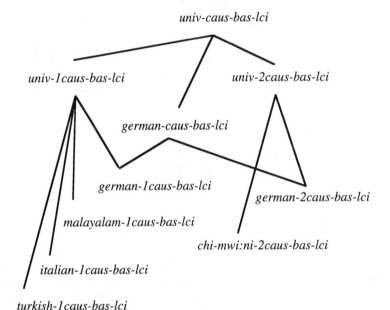

We proceed to define the archetypes. In (52) we find the type *univ-caus-bas-lci* which expresses the universal contentive core of causative constructions that language-particular causatives typically instantiate.[10]

All the instantiations of this predicate formation type will have a basic lci as their LEXDTR whose categorial core is identical to the categorial core of the causative expression which is formed by this pattern.

---

[10]The hedge indicated by "typically" is a function of the possibility left open by our theory that some language may develop a parochial causative construction in marked circumvention of the universal "precompiled" causatives. Examples of this might be Finnish and Hindi whose causative constructions have the typologically unusual property of not necessarily increasing the valence of the underlying verb. See Mohanan (1994) and Ackerman and Moore (1994).

The mother is a basic rather than an expanded lci, because this pattern creates non-inflected forms which can then be expanded inflectionally with tense-aspect patterns like those developed in chapter 7. This is the same methodology we applied to passives in the previous chapter.

(52) The causative archetype *(univ-caus-bas-lci)*

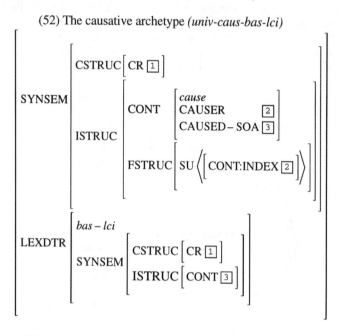

As (52) shows, we analyze the content of the archetypal causative construction as a two-place causation relation between a causer and a caused state of affairs. The causer is semantically identified with the index of the subject function in the output f-structure. This captures the generalization that in active causative constructions, whether monoclausal [cf. (49)] or bi-clausal, the causer is always expressed as the causative predicate's subject. The value of the second attribute of the causative predicator, i.e., CAUSED SOA, is identified with the CONT of the LEXDTR. In other words, seman-tically the causative archetype adds (i) a causer index and (ii) a causation rela-tion to the meaning of the underlying verb.

The two universal subtypes of the general causative archetype have the primary function of representing the difference between monoclausal and biclausal causative f-structures and related differences in categorial subcatego-rization.

The required distinction is best modeled through the introduction of a grammatical function that is reserved for the expression of f-structural clauses. We call this grammatical function COMPLEMENT CLAUSE (CCL) and demonstrate how its different behavior is responsible for many of

the crucial differences between monoclausal and biclausal causative constructions. A look ahead for the purposes of comparison between the representation of the monoclausal causative in (53) and the biclausal causative in (54)
reveals the following difference in the structures with respect to the grammatical function CCL. (53) identifies the value of CCL of the LEXDTR
with the value of CCL in the causative output and thereby keeps the number
of f-structure clauses in the input and the output constant and will create a
monoclausal causative predicate if given a monoclausal predicate as input. In
contrast, (54) tags the whole f-structure of the input and embeds it as a new
complement clause in the output predicate's f-structure. As a result, the
causative predicate that is formed will have one more f-structural clause than
the input from which it is derived. In particular, if the input was a simple
predicate governing a monoclausal f-structure, then the output will by necessity be biclausal. The crucial differences between monoclausal and biclausal causatives that we surveyed earlier in this chapter can all be shown
to be a consequence of this representational difference.

(53) displays the internal structure of the monoclausal causative
archetype.

(53) The monoclausal causative archetype *(univ-1caus-bas-lci)*

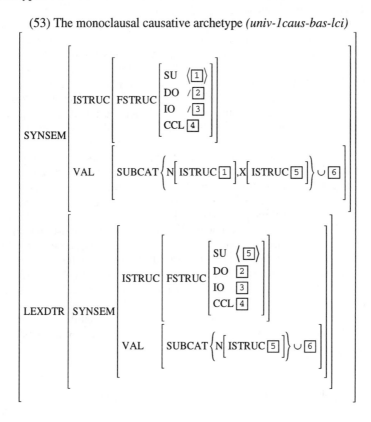

We will move through the information in (53) from top to bottom to illustrate its consequences. (53), like its biclausal counterpart below, says nothing about CONT, since it inherits its CONT specification from its general causative mother type. It does, however, make changes in grammatical functions: (i) it adds a new grammatical subject and thereby ejects the original subject from this function (note that the input and output subjects are not identical and that by (52) the new subject represents the new semantic role *causer*); (ii) moreover, it contains two statements that by default the causative output preserves the direct and indirect object information of the input; in other words, the direct and indirect objects of the underlying predicate will retain those grammatical functions in the causativized output predicate, everything else being equal (i.e., unless a subtype overrides these function assignments);[11] in conjunction with several markedness principles we state shortly, these defaults derive the unmarked function assignments of monoclausal causatives illustrated partially in (49); finally, as was already mentioned, the monoclausal causative preserves the number of complement clauses of the underlying predicate rather than increasing the clausal valence.

The grammatical function changes of (53) typically lead to changes in subcategorization. In particular, because of the additional grammatical function for the new causer argument, the SUBCAT of the causativized verb will typically have an extra NP argument whose ISTRUC represents the new subject. In addition, the underlying subject may still be expressed by the derived predicate but may change its part of speech, in particular if it takes on an indirect object or oblique function which is spelled out as a PP in many languages. A comparison of the input and output SUBCATs reveals the changes that are responsible for these categorial alternations.

This brings us to the structure of the biclausal causative archetype in (54). Like the previous type, this type introduces a new subject for the causer and therefore the subjects of the input and output are not identical. Otherwise, however, this biclausal type creates a raising-to-object structure which is reflected by three properties of the representation: (i) the f-structure of the LEXDTR predicate is embedded as a complement clause into the f-structure of the causativized output predicate; and (ii) the primary clause in the mother contains a direct object whose information structure is identical to the information structure of the lower subject. As a result, a causativized predicate derived from a transitive verb will govern three grammatical functions: a subject (for the causer), a direct object (which expresses the subject of the underlying predicate), and the whole f-structure clause of the underlying, non-causative verb (with a subject and a direct object, since the underlying verb was assumed to be transitive).

---

[11] These defaults are intended to capture similar effects as Gibson & Raposo's (1986) *Inheritance Principle*.

(54) makes one additional change: it adds a nominal element to the LEXDTR's subcategorization that allows the new subject to be expressed categorially.

(54) The biclausal causative archetype *(univ-2caus-bas-lci)*

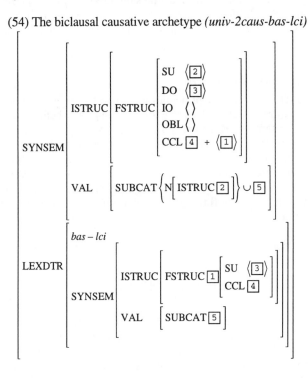

The patterns in (53)–(54) yield different numbers of functional clauses when applied to an underlying monoclausal predicate (i.e., a predicate whose CCL is the empty list of complement clauses): (53) preserves the number of clauses in its input predicate and will map the new subject function as well as all the input predicate's grammatical functions into a single clause in the causativized predicate; in contrast, (54) will create at least two clauses, i.e., a functional matrix clause containing the new subject, a direct object, and a complement clause consisting of the f-structure of the underlying predicate (whose subject is identified with the direct object function in the main clause).

The three archetypes in (52)–(54) play a crucial role in the next sections which are dedicated to capturing the differences and similarities between the six causative constructions surveyed in (1) in our theory of predicates.

8   Purely Monoclausal Causatives

The present section is concerned with the question of how German and Malayalam customize the monoclausal causative archetype in (53). In preparation of this discussion, we will have to state some preference principles for causative constructions that will help us capture some cross-linguistic generalizations.

8.1   Preference Principles

Two sets of preference principles will be stated: (i) general preferences for all f-structures of clausal information structures, whether causative or not; (ii) one preference principle for all causatives.

The preference principle for causatives interacts with some more general preference principles for all f-structures. The general preferences are based on wide-spread claims in the literature on what types of clausal structures are found most typically in the world's languages.

First, languages definitely seem to prefer clauses with subjects to clauses without subjects:[12]

(55) Personal f-structures are preferred over impersonal f-structures

$$\left[\text{SU} \langle [\ ] \rangle \right] <_\text{m} \left[\text{SU} \langle \rangle \right]$$

This is reflected, among others, in the fact that languages typically have fewer impersonal predicates than predicates with a subject.

Second, languages typically seem to have many more predicates governing direct objects than predicates that select indirect objects or obliques. This is expressed by (56) and (57):

(56) Direct objects are preferred over indirect objects

$$\begin{bmatrix} \text{DO} \langle [\ ] \rangle \\ \text{IO} \langle \rangle \end{bmatrix} <_\text{m} \begin{bmatrix} \text{DO} \langle \rangle \\ \text{IO} \langle [\ ] \rangle \end{bmatrix}$$

(57) Direct objects are preferred over obliques

$$\begin{bmatrix} \text{DO} \langle [\ ] \rangle \\ \text{OBL} \langle \rangle \end{bmatrix} <_\text{m} \begin{bmatrix} \text{DO} \langle \rangle \\ \text{OBL} \langle [\ ] \rangle \end{bmatrix}$$

---

[12]The expression "A $<_\text{m}$ B" is intended to convey that A is less marked than B.

Finally, one preference principle for all causatives. Comrie (1976) claims that in general there are far more languages in the world whose causative constructions behave monoclausally than there are languages with biclausal causatives. This can be made to follow from making the universal type for monoclausal causatives less marked than the universal type for biclausal causatives:

(58) Monoclausal causatives are preferred over biclausal causatives

$$univ - 1caus - bas - lci \quad <_m \quad univ - 2caus - bas - lci$$

8.2 The Effects of the Preference Principles and the Defaults of the Monoclausal Causative

The above markedness principles interact with the defaults in the monoclausal causative (53) to predict that some function changes in monoclausal causatives should be found more frequently in the world's languages than others. Let us go through a number of cases. Assume that we embed a one-place intransitive predicate like *dance* in the monoclausal causative construction. What function array is the resultant predicate predicted to have in most languages of the world, everything else being equal? The answer is <SU$_{causer}$, DO$_{causee}$> and the reasons are the following. The causativized predicate will have two arguments, the causer and the causee. The universal causative construction always makes the causer into the subject. This leaves the causee. Which function assignment to the causee would be valued most highly by (55)–(57)? (55) has already been satisfied, because the predicate already has a subject. According to (56) and (57), predicates in general prefer direct objects over indirect objects and obliques. The best choice of grammatical function for the causee thus is the direct object which will create <SU$_{causer}$, DO$_{causee}$> as the most unmarked function set associated with monoclausal causatives formed from intransitive predicates. In order to yield this optimal result, individual grammars must override the direct object default in (53) to change the subject of an underlying intransitive verb into the direct object of the monoclausal causative. According to the typological study in Comrie (1976), this is the correct typological result.

Assume, then, that the underlying predicate is transitive instead. The most unmarked function set is predicted to be <SU$_{causer}$, DO$_{lower\ patient}$, X$_{causee}$>, where X is either an indirect object or an oblique. The subject is again assigned to express the causer by the universal causative itself. Since the underlying predicate is transitive, the direct object default applies this time and prefers that the direct object of the underlying predicate retain this function in the newly formed causative predicate. This prevents the causee from appearing in that function which will have to appear either as an indirect object or an oblique.

Looking back at (49), we see that our system of defaults and preferences predicts the language types in the first four rows of this survey to be instantiated more frequently than the type of Chamorro. The Chamorro causative is the only example in the table that violates the direct object default by failing to preserve the direct object status of the lower patient in the causativized predicate. Since there is no preference principle that enforces this default override, this change is unmotivated. Everything else being equal, we would expect predicates with unmotivated structures to be found less frequently than predicates whose internal structure is motivated by archetypes or universal preference principles. In the present case, this prediction appears to be correct, as the monoclausal causative in Chamorro indeed seems to be typologically less usual than the other causatives that appear in (49).

On the other hand, it is well-known that many languages display alternative encodings of the causee both with respect to grammatical functions and case marking. The regularities underlying alternative encodings are not reflected in the preference principles proposed here, since they are in many cases motivated semantically, e.g., the realization of the causee may reflect the difference between direct and indirect causation, etc. There have been several efforts in the literature to explain variable encodings of the causee, e.g., Comrie (1975), Cole (1983), Marantz (1984), Gibson and Raposo (1986), Baker (1988), and Alsina (1992).

Having captured the most likely functional inventories of monoclausal causatives cross-linguistically, we now turn to the specifics of these causative constructions in German and Malayalam.

8.3 German

Recall that German instantiates both the monoclausal and the biclausal causative and that it uses the same surface configuration to express the respective predicates: a form of the auxiliary *lassen* combined with the bare infinitive of the underlying predicate. As we discussed in connection with the type hierarchy in (51), this shared information should be extracted from the definitions of the two language-particular causative types and stated in a language-particular supertype they both share. This is done in (59).

As the reader can see, this type also requires the particle valences of the mother and the daughter to be empty, since no causatives in German can ever contain a separable particle.

The definition of the German monoclausal causative predicate formation pattern is now straightforward,[13] since most crucial information is inherited from this type's supertypes. For instance, all information about

---

[13]We only present the pattern that applies to transitive predicates. The pattern for intransitive predicates is identical, except that it overrides the direct object default and makes the causee into the direct object of the causative predicate, in order to satisfy the preference principles (56) and (57), as discussed earlier. We will follow the same procedure throughout this chapter.

the spell-out of the predicate is inherited from *german-caus-bas-lci;* the meaning of the output predicate is inherited from *univ-caus-bas-lci* as is the presence of a new subject to express the causer. The monoclausality of the construction is determined by *univ-1caus-bas-lci* and its two functional defaults are also adopted, meaning that underlying direct and indirect objects retain these grammatical functions in the causativized predicate.

(59) The German causative type *(german-caus-bas-lci)*

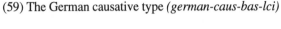

$$\begin{bmatrix} \text{SYNSEM} & \begin{bmatrix} \text{CSTRUC} \begin{bmatrix} \text{CR } \textit{pred--bareinf } - \textit{vword} \end{bmatrix} \\ \text{VAL} \begin{bmatrix} \text{PART} \langle \rangle \\ \text{AUX} \left\langle \begin{bmatrix} \text{CSTRUC:HD} \begin{bmatrix} \text{MS} \begin{bmatrix} \text{LEX} \langle \textit{lassen} \rangle \end{bmatrix} \end{bmatrix} \end{bmatrix} \right\rangle + \boxed{1} \end{bmatrix} \end{bmatrix} \\ \text{LEXDTR} \begin{bmatrix} \text{SYNSEM} \begin{bmatrix} \text{VAL} \begin{bmatrix} \text{PART} \langle \rangle \\ \text{AUX } \boxed{1} \end{bmatrix} \end{bmatrix} \end{bmatrix} \end{bmatrix}$$

The only two properties that the supertypes do not fix is the grammatical function of the causee and its categorial expression. This is the only thing left for (60) to do.

As we can see, the causee of a causativized transitive predicate in German bears the grammatical function of an oblique (the underlying subject has been appended to the end of the list of obliques of the input predicate) and its corresponding SUBCAT element is a prepositional phrase headed by *von,* the same as the passive oblique in long passives.[14]

---

[14]The identity of the expression of the passive oblique and the causee of causativized transitive predicates in a *von* phrase suggests that the monoclausal causative pattern in fact applies to predicates which have already been passivized or that the German monoclausal causative construction is actually a hybrid construction that is causative in some respects and passive in others. On the other hand, there are verbs like *sehen* 'see' which can be passivized but cannot appear in the monoclausal causative, but this might be due to different degrees of agentivity that the monoclausal causative and the German passives impose on the underlying predicate. In any event, as inspection of the passive and causative archetypes shows, both involve a demotion of the underlying subject and from that point of view it is perhaps not surprising that there are languages that express this demoted underlying subject in the same fashion.

(60) The German monoclausal causative type *(german-1caus-bas-lci)*

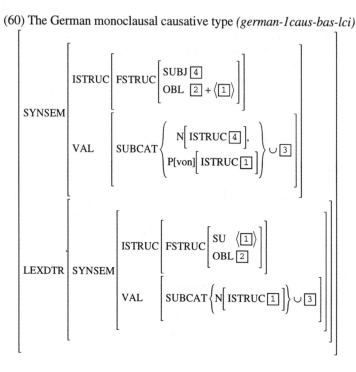

Feeding a transitive predicate like *küssen* 'kiss' into the predicate pattern in (60) therefore yields the output predicate in (61).

As expected, this causative predicate has the categorial representation of all German causative constructions consisting of a morphological form of the auxiliary *lassen* in combination with the predicative bare infinitive of *küssen* [cf. (59)]. The predicate's content is a relation between a causer and a caused state of affairs of kissing, following the general causative meaning in (52).

Since the underlying predicate does not govern a complement clause and the monoclausal causative pattern does not add a clause, all the grammatical functions of the causativized transitive appear in one clause. The f-structure contains three grammatical functions: a subject for the causer, a direct object for the lower patient [in accordance with the direct object default in (53)], and an oblique for the causee, as determined by (60). Each of these grammatical functions is spelled out: the subject and the direct object as NPs which will be assigned nominative and accusative case by the case marking principles for expanded predicates postulated in chapter 7. The oblique causee is linked to a SUBCAT element that must be realized by a prepositional phrase headed by the preposition *von*.

(61) The *bas-lci-küssen* in the German monoclausal causative pattern

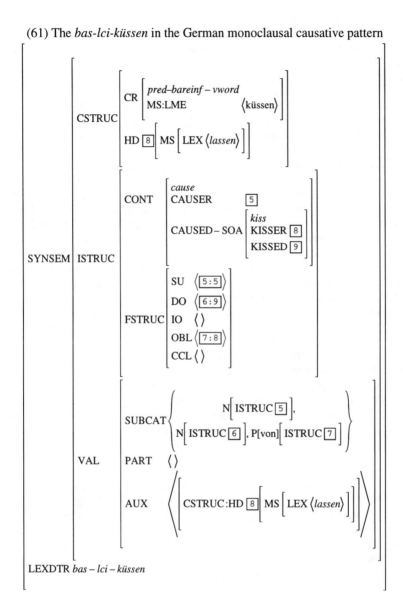

The representation in (61) can be shown to account for the purely monoclausal effects found in the German causative construction surveyed in section 3.1 of this chapter. First, as was shown in (16), its predicate governs three different grammatical functions and in this respect it behaves like a simple three-place predicate. The causer in (16) is expressed as a subject, the lower patient as a direct object, and the causee as an oblique. This functional profile follows directly from the lexical entry of the predicate of (61) given immediately above, in particular the fact that the entry has only a single f-structure which contains exactly these three grammatical functions and no others.

Secondly, we diagnosed the causatives under discussion as monoclausal on the basis of the binding theory. In particular, on the basis of examples like (18)–(19) we had observed that the German reflexive *sich* obeys the following binding-theoretic constraint outside of causatives:

(62) *sich* is bound by the subject of the minimal f-structure containing it.

(20)–(21) showed that in monoclausal causatives, *sich* can be bound by the causer but not the causee. These grammaticality judgments are predicted correctly by (62) and the lexical representation (61) of the predicate of sentences like (20)–(21). In all the monoclausal causatives, the causer is the subject of the single f-structure, but the causee is an oblique. If *sich* occurs as the lower patient in such a structure and hence bears the grammatical function of direct object, it can only be understood as bound by the causer, since that element is represented by the subject of the minimal f-structure containing the grammatical function representing *sich*. The causee, however, is correctly predicted not to be a possible binder, since it bears a grammatical function that is unable to bind *sich,* following (62).

The representation in (61) thus explains why the construction we referred to as "German I" in (1) displays purely monoclausal effects. (61) is the result of applying the German monoclausal causative pattern type to the underived predicate *küssen* which inherits its purely monoclausal profile from the universal monoclausal causative type in (53). This concludes our discussion of the German monoclausal causative.

8.4 Malayalam

With this, we turn to the other monoclausal causative that was discussed in section 3, that of Malayalam. The causative in Malayalam has the same functional-semantic structure as its German counterpart discussed in the previous subsection. In particular, it also carries the direct and indirect objects over from the underlying predicate to the causative predicate (at least for underlying transitives) and it also demotes the causee to an oblique (which is expressed as an instrumental nominal):

(63) The Malayalam monoclausal causative type *(malayalam-1caus-bas-lci)*

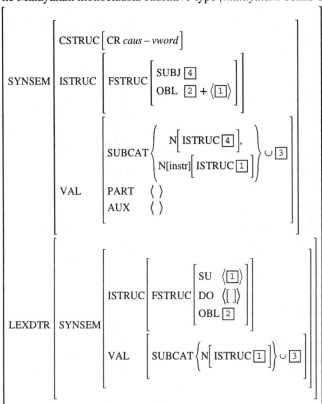

There is one crucial difference between German and Malayalam: whereas German lexicalizes its causative with a combination of the auxiliary *lassen* and the bare infinitive of the main verb, Malayalam has a morphological-derivational category *caus-vword* (= causative verb word). This word represents the functional-semantic information of the Malayalam causative all by itself, given the empty auxiliary valence of the causative type.

We had diagnosed Malayalam causatives like (23) as monoclausal in section 3.2 on the basis of three properties which can now be seen to follow from the functional-semantic aspects of the representations of the causativized predicates that (63) outputs (compare the ISTRUC of the German predicate (61) which is structurally identical in that respect): (i) the causer, the causee, and the lower patient in (23) bear three distinct grammatical functions; (ii) when the causativized predicate is passivized as in (24), the lower patient rather than the causee becomes the subject of the passivized causative—this follows from the fact that the lower patient but not the causee bears the direct object function which contributes the subject function in Malayalam passive; (iii) in sentences like (26), anaphors interpreted as the lower patient must be anteceded by the causer and not the causee—this follows from the requirement illustrated with (25) that these anaphors must be anteceded by a subject and the subject in Malayalam causatives is interpreted as the causer and not the causee.

Despite these functional-semantic similarities between the German and the Malayalam monoclausal causatives, the first is expressed as a syntactically separable combination of an auxiliary and a main verb and the second as a single morphological word. This follows from the language-particular spell-out differences between the German type (61) and the Malayalam type (63) which otherwise inherit practically identical functional-semantic information from the universal causative archetypes.

9 Purely Biclausal Causatives

The biclausal causatives we have seen are more uniform from both a functional and the semantic perspective. The universal biclausal type contains more information than its monoclausal counterpart and leaves less information to be filled in by individual languages.

9.1 German

The German biclausal causative pattern need not state any information beyond that contained in the type hierarchy in (51): it inherits its functional-semantic information from its universal biclausal supertype and its spell-out information from its supertype *german-caus-bas-lci* which fixes the spell-out of both the monoclausal and biclausal causatives in German.

Consequently, when given the underived predicate *küssen* 'kiss' as an input, the *german-2caus-bas-lci* pattern creates the causativized predicate in (64).

The categorial expression of this biclausal predicate is inherited from the same supertype as that of its monoclausal counterpart in (61) and hence is identical to it. Their CONTs are also identical, since the CONT of both monoclausal and biclausal causatives is fixed by the common supertype *univ-caus-bas-lci*.

Where the two predicates differ is in their f-structures and their SUBCATs. The f-structure of (64) is biclausal: it consists of a matrix clause and an embedded clause which are connected by "raising to object." Consequently, the matrix clause has a subject that realizes the causer and a direct object that bears no semantic role with respect to the semantic *cause* functor but instead is identical to the subject of the embedded clause. In the embedded clause we find the f-structure of the underlying predicate *küssen* which has a subject interpreted as the KISSER and a direct object interpreted as the KISSED. In the two clauses combined we find a total of four term grammatical functions, two subjects and two direct objects.

(64) The *bas-lci-küssen* in the German biclausal causative pattern

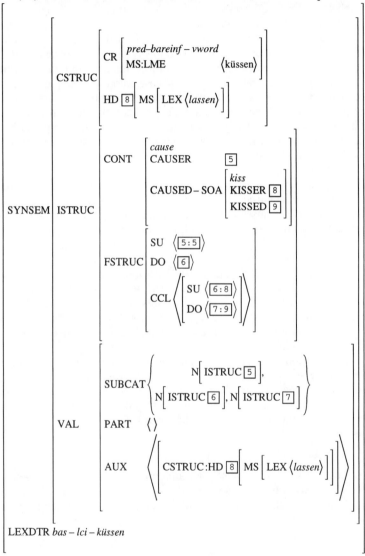

However, since the upper direct object is identical to the lower subject, the SUBCAT of this predicate contains only three elements, one NP for the subject of the higher clause and two for the two direct objects.[15]

The representation (64) is responsible for the properties on the basis of which we had categorized the construction "German II" as biclausal. First, unlike in the German causative discussed earlier, the present one expresses both the causee and the lower patient of an underlying transitive verb as accusative noun phrases, as in (27). This follows from our representations because both of these elements bear direct object functions in their respective f-structures and the generalized accusative case marking principle referred to in footnote 15 marks all subcategorized categories expressing direct objects with accusative case. Since the predicate of (27) is biclausal with each clause containing its own direct object, the accusative case marking rule has a chance to apply twice with the consequence that this sentence contains two accusative NPs on the surface.

Our representation also explains why the biclausal causatives show exactly the mirror image binding-theoretic behavior of the monoclausal causatives. In the biclausal causative (31), a lower patient *sich* anaphor can be anteceded by the causee but not the causer. In concert with the binding-theoretic constraint on *sich* in (62) it follows from (64) that only the causee qualifies as a binder. The causee bears two grammatical functions, the direct object of the primary clause and the subject function of the secondary clause, the clause that contains *sich*. The causee therefore satisfies the binding constraint on *sich*. The causer, on the other hand, is a subject but crucially, because there are two f-structural clauses in this causative, it is the subject of the wrong clause. It does not occur in the *minimal* clause containing the direct object function which is borne by *sich* and hence is unable to meet the locality condition in (62).

At this point we have derived the properties of the two German causatives we set out to capture, both the properties they share (e.g., the causer is the subject of both, their meanings, the analytic surface expression of the predicate) and the properties in which they differ (surface expression of the causee, different binding-theoretic behavior).

9.2   Chi-Mwi:ni

The Chi-Mwi:ni biclausal causative merely configures the biclausal causative archetype by associating it with a synthetic surface spell-out. Chi-Mwi:ni simulates the situation in Malayalam in that this language expresses its causative predicate with morphological means and does not make

---

[15]Note that the presence of biclausal predicates requires a trivial revision of the case marking principles of chapter 7. The principles stated there only assigned accusative and dative case to SUBCAT elements that spell out grammatical functions in the topmost f-structure. The generalized version will assign these cases no matter whether the grammatical function appears in the topmost or an embedded f-structure clause.

use of an auxiliary. The categorial core of the causative predicate thus is required to appear in the morphological shape of a causative verb word:

(65) The Chi-Mwi:ni biclausal causative pattern *(chi-mwi:ni-2caus-bas-lci)*

$$
\begin{bmatrix}
\text{SYNSEM}
\begin{bmatrix}
\text{CSTRUC}\begin{bmatrix} \text{CR } caus\ -vword \end{bmatrix} \\
\text{VAL}\begin{bmatrix} \text{PART}\langle\rangle \\ \text{AUX }\langle\rangle \end{bmatrix}
\end{bmatrix}
\end{bmatrix}
$$

From a functional-semantic point of view, Chi-Mwi:ni causative predicates are structurally identical to German biclausal causative predicates like the one presented in (64).

Following Marantz (1984), we had diagnosed this causative in Chi-Mwi:ni as biclausal on the basis of three properties, all of which can now be seen to follow from our representation of causatives in this language [cf. the relevant features of (64)]. First, in sentences like (32) the causee and the lower patient both appear as simple noun phrases rather than being marked by adpositions, since Chi-Mwi:ni expresses direct objects as noun phrases.[16] Second, when the causative predicate above is passivized, the causee and not the lower patient becomes the subject of the resulting passive predicate, as in (33)–(34). Under the assumption that Chi-Mwi:ni passive instantiates the universally most unmarked passive type that we have defined, this follows as well. The passive should be clause-bound and should make the direct object into the subject of the new predicate. In (64), the direct object of the primary clause is semantically identical to the subject of the secondary clause and hence is interpreted as the causee. Even though the lower patient is a direct object as well, the clause boundary between it and the subject position of the primary clause makes it "too far away" to become the subject of the new passive predicate. Third, an anaphor of sentences like (35)–(36) that must be anteceded within its own clause can be bound by the causee but not the causer. This follows by parity of reasoning with the German example on the basis of the biclausal f-structure we are postulating for both constructions.

The similarities between the German and Chi-Mwi:ni constructions analyzed in the present section thus follow from the fact that they both instantiate the universal biclausal causative construction. Interestingly, this functional-semantic similarity is not disturbed by the fact that these two languages impose crucially different surface realizations on the expression of their shared functional-semantic structure: German expresses this causative

---

[16]Note that our theory is not committed to claiming that the two direct objects behave alike in *every* respect. One is clearly structurally more prominent than the other and this might be reflected in differential behaviors with respect to agreement or other properties.

through an analytic combination of an auxiliary and a main verb but Chi-Mwi:ni has a morphological category "causative verb form" and employs this word form without any attendant auxiliary. The result is a predicate that expresses the informational equivalent of two clauses in one single word.

10   Mixed Causatives

Having handled the purely monoclausal and purely biclausal causatives, we now turn to the unusual causatives that simultaneously behave monoclausally in most respects but show biclausal binding-theoretic effects.

The first such case comes from Italian. There are two pieces of evidence for the monoclausality of the relevant construction: (i) there is no doubling of grammatical functions, and (ii) the lower patient can become the subject of the passivized causative, which should only be possible if it is the direct object of the same clause that contains the causer. Since these two arguments are farthest apart in terms of grammatical relations and they are in the same clause, we assume that there is only one clause in the causative f-structure. This leads us to postulate a monoclausal causative type for Italian in (66) that is a subtype of the universal monoclausal causative.

In accordance with the direct object default of the monoclausal causative archetype in (53), the direct object of the underlying verb retains that grammatical function in the causative predicate. The causee is mapped into the indirect object of the causativized predicate which is spelled out in a prepositional phrase headed by *a*. The type also indicates that the causativized predicate is realized on the surface by a combination of the auxiliary *fare* and the bare infinitive of the main verb.

(66) The Italian monoclausal causative type *(italian-1caus-bas-lci)*

$$
\begin{bmatrix}
\text{SYNSEM} & \text{ISTRUC} & \begin{bmatrix}
\text{CSTRUC}\begin{bmatrix}\text{CR } bareinf - vword\end{bmatrix} \\[2pt]
\text{FSTRUC}\begin{bmatrix}
\text{SUBJ } \boxed{4} \\
\text{DO} \quad \boxed{5} \\
\text{IO} \quad\ \boxed{1} \\
\text{OBL } \boxed{2} \\
\text{CCL } \boxed{7}
\end{bmatrix} \\[2pt]
\text{VAL}\begin{bmatrix}
\text{SUBCAT}\left\langle \begin{matrix} \text{N}\begin{bmatrix}\text{ISTRUC}\boxed{4}\end{bmatrix}, \\ \text{P[a]}\begin{bmatrix}\text{ISTRUC}\boxed{1}\end{bmatrix} \end{matrix} \right\rangle \cup \boxed{3} \\[2pt]
\text{PART } \langle\,\rangle \\[2pt]
\text{AUX } \left\langle \begin{bmatrix} \text{CSTRUC:HD }\boxed{8}\begin{bmatrix}\text{MS}\begin{bmatrix}\text{LEX }\langle fare\rangle\end{bmatrix}\end{bmatrix}\end{bmatrix} \right\rangle \cup \boxed{9}
\end{bmatrix}
\end{bmatrix} \\[6pt]
\text{LEXDTR} \quad \text{SYNSEM} \begin{bmatrix}
\text{ISTRUC} \quad \text{FSTRUC}\begin{bmatrix}
\text{SU} \quad \langle\boxed{1}\rangle \\
\text{DO} \quad \boxed{5}\langle[\ ]\rangle \\
\text{IO} \quad \langle\,\rangle \\
\text{OBL}\ \boxed{2} \\
\text{CCL}\ \boxed{7}
\end{bmatrix} \\[2pt]
\text{VAL}\begin{bmatrix}
\text{SUBCAT}\left\langle \text{N}\begin{bmatrix}\text{ISTRUC}\boxed{1}\end{bmatrix}\right\rangle \cup \boxed{3} \\[2pt]
\text{AUX} \quad \boxed{9}
\end{bmatrix}
\end{bmatrix}
\end{bmatrix}
$$

Applying this pattern type to the transitive predicate *riparare* "to repair" yields the following monoclausal causative predicate:

(67) The *bas-lci-riparare* in the Italian monoclausal causative pattern

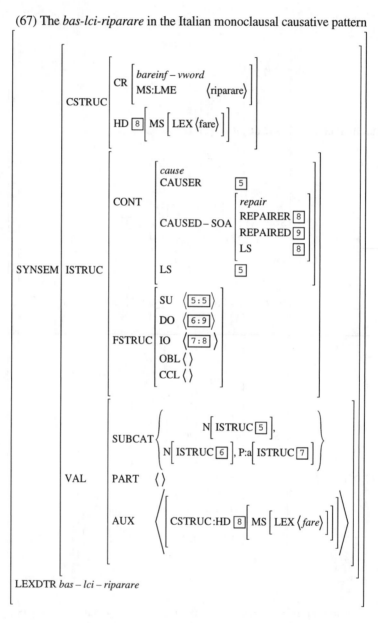

(67) governs three different grammatical functions: its direct object is interpreted as the REPAIRED, i.e., the lower patient, which will bring this
element into the subject position when the predicate is passivized. The

representation we have assigned thus accounts for the monoclausal properties of the causative exemplified by (37)–(38).

This brings us to the binding theory. We repeat the facts that must be accounted for:

(68) * Con le minacce   fecero accusare *se stessi$_i$*   a   <u>Giovanni</u>
with threats-   (they$_i$) made accuse   themselves to Giovanni

'With threats they made Giovanni accuse themselves'

(69)   Con le minacce   fecero accusare *se stesso$_i$* a   <u>Giovanni$_i$</u>
with threats-   (they) made   accuse   himself   to Giovanni

'With threats they made Giovanni accuse himself'

The anaphor *se stesso* (as well as its inflectional variants) generally needs to be bound within its own clause. In both of the sentences above, it lexicalizes the lower patient which has two potential antecedents within the same clause, i.e., the only clause we are postulating for this causative: the subject causer which is expressed by the verbal morphology in the examples above, and the indirect object causee *a Giovanni*. In fact, however, only (69) is grammatical and therefore only the indirect object causee can antecede the anaphor and the subject causer cannot.

We must create a binding domain for the anaphor *se stesso* that will exclude the causer in (68)–(69) as a possible binder, even though it is the subject of the clause containing the anaphor. Cross-linguistically, it is unusual for a subject to be unable to bind an anaphor in the same clause and elsewhere in Italian subjects are able to enter into such binding relationships. We hypothesize that monoclausal causatives sometimes behave in this special fashion because they are marked by a "bracketing paradox" that is not found in most other predicates: on the one hand, the preference principle in (58) prefers monoclausal predicates over biclausal predicates; against that, the universal causative archetype in (52) gives causatives a bipropositional semantic structure. We believe that even though binding theory in the normal case is sensitive to grammatical functions, it can under marked circumstances also refer to the semantic structure of a predicate. In particular, Dalrymple (1993: 8) presents evidence that reflexives may require a logical as opposed to a grammatical subject as their antecedent, where the logical subject of a predicate is defined as the semantic role that is highest on a thematic role hierarchy [Kiparsky (1987), Bresnan and Kanerva (1989), Alsina (1993)]. One of the reflexive pronouns in Marathi must be bound by the grammatical subject if it appears in an active sentence but by the passive oblique in passive sentences. This antecedent requirement cannot be given a unified treatment in terms of grammatical functions but it can be captured at the level of thematic structure because the subject of active sentences and the passive oblique both serve as the logical subject of the predicate in the same clause as the reflexive.

Anticipating this discussion, we have explicitly marked the logical subject as the value of an additional attribute LS in the causativized Italian predicate (67). The CAUSER is the logical subject in the matrix proposition and the REPAIRER is the logical subject of the caused state of affairs. Given this representation, the binding-theoretic condition in (70) will account for the grammaticality contrast between (68) and (69):

(70)   Binding-theoretic requirements of the Italian anaphor *se stesso:*

se stesso is bound by a term grammatical function within the minimal f-structure containing it; it cannot be bound by a logical subject other than the logical subject of the minimal state of affairs containing its index.

The presence of (70) in the grammar of Italian thus explains why the binding theory gives us a false positive for biclausality of Italian causatives like those in (68)–(69): even though there is only one functional clause that is projected by each of these causatives and only one subject, the anaphor *se stesso* can take both subjects and logical subjects as antecedents and must prefer the closest logical subject if there is a potential ambiguity. The subject causer of (68) and (69) and the indirect object causee both are potential antecedents for the anaphor interpreted as the lower patient and expressed as the predicate's direct object. For the subject this is obvious and for the indirect object this follows because it is the logical subject of the minimal state of affairs containing the index of the lower patient. By the disambiguation condition, the semantically closest logical subject wins out and the grammatical subject is excluded as a possible binder. These are exactly the facts in (68) and (69).

It is clear that the Turkish causative with mixed clausality effects can be handled in an analogous fashion. It differs from the Italian case in that the predicate's surface expression is synthetic rather than analytic. A trivial modification of the Italian representation in (67) captures this difference.

The monoclausal nature of the Turkish representation will account for the lack of relational doubling in (43) and the fact that its three arguments bear nominative (causer), accusative (lower patient), and dative (causee) case respectively. The direct objecthood of the lower patient will also account for the fact that it rather than the causee becomes the subject when the predicate is passivized, as in (44)–(45).

Recall, however, that one binding-theoretic diagnostic presents evidence for the biclausality of the construction. As before, we must assume that this diagnostic reports a false positive and that the binding facts have a different explanation than the presence of two clauses.

In particular, for some speakers the first person anaphor *kendim* cannot be bound by an indirect object, except in causatives:

(71) Ben₁ Hasan-a₁ *kendim-i*₁ yïka-t-tï-m
       I   Hasan-DAT myself-ACC wash-CAUSE-PAST-1SG

      'I made Hasan wash me'

(72) Bana₁ *kendim-i*₁ anlat-tïr-dï
       me-DAT myself-ACC explain-CAUSE-PAST

      'He made me explain myself'

In (71) the lower patient is anteceded by the subject causer. This is unproblematic. In (72), however, the indirect object causee antecedes the lower patient, even for those speakers of Turkish who do not allow indirect objects to antecede this kind of anaphor outside causatives.

The relevant Turkish binding facts follow from (73):

(73) Binding-theoretic requirements of the Turkish anaphor *kendim:*

      kendim is bound by the subject of the minimal f-structure containing
      it or the logical subject of the minimal state of affairs containing its
      index, provided that logical subject bears a term grammatical func-
      tion.

(73) differs from the analogous Italian constraint in (70) in dropping the disambiguation condition: whereas in Italian only the closest logical subject can bind *se stesso,* in Turkish both the closest subject and the closest logical subject qualify as possible binders of the anaphor *kendim.*

With this we have accounted for the intriguing mix of properties found in the Italian and Turkish causative constructions surveyed in section 5 of this chapter.

11 Summary of this Chapter

Causatives represent one of the most complex predicate constructions in natural language. Not only do we find variation from language to language (and even within one and the same language) with respect to how many functional clauses a given causative predicate projects, but there is also considerable cross-linguistic variation in the grammatical-functional alternations involved in causative - non-causative predicates. Cutting across all these differences, we find that the same or equivalent causatives can be expressed synthetically or analytically.

Our general approach to complex predicates allows us not only to relate causatives to other types of predicates but also to relate all of the causative constructions discussed here to a small number of universally available causative archetypes that express the semantic similarity between the various language-particular constructions and some of their grammatical-functional properties as well. Other functional properties were fixed at the level of language-particular causative constructions, because the amount of variation involved makes it impossible to predict the full inventory of grammatical functions in many causatives on universal grounds. Cross-linguistic preferences were captured through markedness principles and defaults in the statement of the monoclausal causative archetype.

As with the other predicate types discussed in this book, causative predicates can be expressed either as a single morphological word or as a combination of several such words. As mentioned in chapter 1 and reiterated at the beginning of this chapter, several influential works in recent LFG and HPSG have argued (explicitly or implicitly) that the functional component of classical lexicalism cannot be maintained in analyses of analytically expressed causatives and that predicate formation has to be distributed across both the lexicon and the syntax, thereby reducing the concept of lexicalism to a purely morphological constraint against word formation in the syntactic component.

Our analyses in this chapter have demonstrated that this was a theoretical overreaction: the functional-semantic similarities across causatives *can* be captured in a grammatical theory that postulates the lexicon as the single component of predicate formation, provided that (i) the lexicon is a lexicon of *predicates* as opposed to single morphological words, (ii) these predicates are structured so that they can be lexically associated with either a synthetic or analytic surface expression, and (iii) the predicates can participate in a type hierarchy of predicates that include the causative archetypes defined in this chapter.

We have introduced two innovations in our analysis of causatives that go beyond the theoretical concepts we had made use of prior to the present chapter. First, the concept of logical subject and its application in binding theory. We cited Dalrymple's discussion of a Marathi reflexive as evidence that precisely the same theoretical concept is fruitful outside of the analysis of Italian and Turkish causatives. Secondly, we have made use of functionally complex predicates, i.e., single predicates that are lexically associated with complex f-structures in the sense that one f-structure is embedded within another. The utility of this concept has been demonstrated elsewhere as well, in particular in the LFG literature. (See Abaitua (1988), Dahlstrom (1991), Ishikawa (1985), O'Connor (1992), and Simpson (1991) for representative work on this issue.)

Both of the conceptual innovations in this chapter can thus be shown to have motivation that is independent of the particular uses that we have put them to here. Beyond that, we have simply applied the generic tools that our theory of predicates makes available and that were already familiar from our analyses of tense-aspect and passive predicates in previous chapters.

10

Predicates with Separable Particles

1 The Problem

In chapters 1 and 2 we illustrated the challenge presented to standard lexicalist assumptions by the behaviors of Hungarian, Estonian, Fox, and German phrasal predicates consisting of a verb and a separable particle. Employing the terminology of the previous chapters, many phrasal predicates exhibit functional-semantic properties which suggest that they should be represented in the sign module of the lexicon as single units separate from, but often relatable in regular ways to, non-particle predicates: they appear to be derived predicates. On the other hand, there are also many phrasal predicates that are not relatable in transparent ways to non-particle predicates: these are more "idiomatic" and therefore cannot be legitimately analyzed as derived, though they do exhibit all of the same formal characteristics as regular (derived) phrasal predicates.

From the perspective of morphology, the particle and verb often serve as a single unit for purposes of category changing operations and other types of morphological derivation. Finally, from the perspective of phrasal structure, when these predicates are not expressed as a single morphological object, they appear to be composed of two syntactic atoms, with the distribution of these pieces being determined by syntactic principles.

In this chapter we examine several aspects of certain phrasal predicates in German. In addition, we will extend the assumptions and patterns necessary to create a complete tense-aspect paradigm for every simple predicate (i.e., predicates not containing particles) of the language, developed in Chapter 7, to German predicates with separable particles: the tense-aspect analysis was restricted in Chapter 7, it should be recalled, to simple predicates.

As previously mentioned, the existence of phrasal predicates is well-attested and wide-spread cross-linguistically. Phrasal predicates in other languages display the same essential behavioral profile as those in German and are therefore, in principle, amenable to the same sort of analysis as that proposed here. On the other hand, in languages like Hungarian, Estonian, and Fox there are, as in German, many regular subclasses of predicates represented by combinations of verbs and particles as well as numerous language-specific conditions on the syntactic distribution of the pieces of phrasal predicates. Given all of these particularities, we will forego developing our basic proposal to apply beyond the class of primarily "idiomatic" German phenomena treated in this chapter: it will be obvious, however, that the analytic assumptions relevant to the treatment of these "idiomatic" variants can easily be extended to account for instances where phrasal predicates can be analyzed as derived because patterns of regularity between the particled predicates and a simple predicate can be identified. We begin by presenting some representative examples which serve to illustrate why these predicates are of immense theoretical interest.

The basic phenomenon is exemplified by the following pair of sentences containing the representative predicate *an-rufen* 'call up.' These sentences illustrate the crucial combination of two properties of particle predicates in German: (i) the predicate *an-rufen* is always realized by two pieces: the particle *an* and the verb *rufen;* and (ii) in some constructions the particle and the verb appear as a compound word displaying all effects of *Morphological Integrity* as in (1); but in constructions like (2) they are syntactically separable:

(1)   weil   Peter Maria an-ruft
        because Peter Maria up calls

        'because Peter calls Maria up.'

(2)   Peter ruft Maria an
        Peter calls Maria up

        'Peter calls Maria up.'

(1) and (2) are contentively identical except that (1) is a subordinate clause and (2) a main clause. Observe the well-known difference in word order between these two clause types in modern German: in subordinate clauses the finite verb (in our examples the verbs *anruft* and *ruft)* appears at the end of the sentence whereas in main clauses it appears in second position, thereby satisfying the so-called "verb-second constraint."

The verb and the particle in (2) can be separated by an arbitrary number of constituents as long as the verb stays in second position and the particle stays at the end of the sentence (except for "extraposable" constituents which can follow the particle). This situation contrasts sharply with the state of affairs in (1). Here the particle and the verb show the intonational profile of compounds and like compounds cannot be separated by any syntactically independent constituents from each other, be they arguments, adjuncts, or anything else. In other words, they obey the principle of *Morphological Integrity.*

The distribution of particles that form a predicate together with a verb is peculiar from one point of view but quite natural from another. Let us trace the predicate *anrufen* "to call up" through all six tenses in both subordinate and main clauses. We start with subordinate clauses:

(3)   weil   die Ministerin   ihren Sekretär   **anruft**
because the minister(fem) her   secretary(masc) up-calls
'because the minister calls up her secretary'

(4)   weil   die Ministerin   ihren Sekretär   **anrief**
because the minister(fem) her   secretary(masc) up-called
'because the minister called up her secretary'

(5)   weil   die Ministerin   ihren Sekretär   **angerufen hat**
because the minister(fem) her   secretary(masc) up-called   has
'because the minister has called up her secretary'

(6)   weil   die Ministerin   ihren Sekretär   **angerufen hatte**
because the minister(fem) her   secretary(masc) up-called   had
'because the minister had called up her secretary'

(7)   weil   die Ministerin   ihren Sekretär   **anrufen wird**
because the minister(fem) her   secretary(masc) up-call   will
'because the minister will call up her secretary'

(8)   weil   die Ministerin   ihren Sekretär
because the minister(fem) her   secretary

angerufen haben wird
up-called   have   will
'because the minister will have called up her secretary'

As can be seen above, in subordinate clauses the particle and the verb invariably appear in their compounded form where they may never be separated. This is not true for main clauses where we find two patterns, depending on whether the tense of the clause is expressed synthetically or analytically:

(9)   Die Ministerin   **ruft** ihren Sekretär   **an**
the minister(fem) calls her   secretary(masc) up
'The minister calls up her secretary'

(10)   Die Ministerin   **rief** ihren Sekretär   **an**
the minister(fem) called her   secretary(masc) up
'The minister called up her secretary'

(11)   Die Ministerin   **hat** ihren Sekretär   **<u>angerufen</u>**
         the minister(fem) has her   secretary(masc) up-called
         'The minister has called up her secretary'

(12)   Die Ministerin   **hatte** ihren Sekretär   **<u>angerufen</u>**
         the minister(fem) had   her   secretary(masc) up-called
         'The minister had called up her secretary'

(13)   Die Ministerin   **wird** ihren Sekretär   **<u>anrufen</u>**
         the minister(fem) will her   secretary(masc) up-call
         'The minister will call up her secretary'

(14)
         Die Ministerin   **wird** ihren Sekretär
         the minister(fem) will her   secretary(masc)

         <u>angerufen</u> haben
         up-called   have

         'The minister will have called up her secretary'

No alternative expressions of these tenses are possible, i.e., in the two synthetic tenses, exemplified in (9) and (10), the verb and the particle are syntactically independent whereas in the four analytic tenses, shown in (11)–(14), they form a compound. That the difference between synthetic and analytic encoding is criterial is also demonstrated by the fact that when the present or past tense must be expressed analytically, the compound form of the verb-particle predicate must appear. This situation arises, for example, when there is a modal auxiliary in the present or past tense:

(15)   Die Ministerin   **muß** ihren Sekretär   **<u>anrufen</u>**
         the minister(fem) must her   secretary(masc) up-call
         'The minister must call up her secretary'

(16)   Die Ministerin   **wollte** ihren Sekretär   **<u>anrufen</u>**
         the minister(fem) wanted her   secretary(masc) up-call
         'The minister wanted to call up her secretary'

The generalization concerning the separability of a verb and a particle which together express one predicate is thus the following:

(17)   The Verb-Particle Separability Generalization

      a.   A verb and a particle that constitute the surface realization of a predicate must be expressed as two syntactically separate and morphologically non-compound items if (a) the predicate heads a main clause and (b) the surface expression of the predicate does not contain an auxiliary.

      b.   Elsewhere, i.e., in all subordinate clauses and in main clauses with an auxiliary, the verb and the particle appear as a compound word that is subject to the morphological integrity of words.

From one point of view, the condition in (17) is a rather strange one, since it simultaneously refers to clausality and the absence of an auxiliary. This is not a combination of structural conditions known to frequently govern empirical phenomena throughout the world's languages. Towards the end of the chapter we will argue that in the context of other structures of German grammar (17) is not as peculiar as it looks in isolation.

    The behavior of the particle-verb combinations in the representative examples (1) and (2) shows that a large number of predicates in German systematically have both syntactic and morphological realization alternatives. This creates analytic difficulties for any theory of the syntax-morphology interface but takes on even greater urgency for lexicalist approaches. Recall from the discussion in chapter 1 that several conceptions of lexicalism can be distinguished. Despite differences among various lexicalist frameworks, they all maintain the principle of *Morphological Integrity* which was stated as follows:

(18)   *Morphological Integrity*

    Syntactic mechanisms neither make reference to the daughters of morphological words nor can they create new morphological words in constituent structure.

(1) and (2) present a serious problem for this principle once we try to capture the properties of the predicate *an + rufen* with one single lexical representation.[1] For, while it is clear that the surface form of the predicate should mention the two forms *an* and *rufen,* whichever form we choose will lead to a violation of *Morphological Integrity* in the generation of either sentence (1) or sentence (2). This is easily illustrated. Assume first that we postulate

---

[1] Section 2 below discusses why it is uninsightful to postulate two separate lexical entries for the predicates in (1) and (2), no matter whether these entries are unrelated or one is derived from the other by a lexical rule.

the compound [[an] [rufen]] as the surface form of the predicate *anrufen*. Then the separation of the component parts of this compound in the main clause (2) violates the prohibition of *Morphological Integrity* against syntactic mechanisms making reference to the daughters of morphological words. It is clear that to get the linear order of this sentence right, the linearization rules must be able to refer to the morphological parts of the compound rather than to the compound as a whole. On the other hand, assume that—in clear violation of the principle of *Morphological Expression* from (21) in chapter 1—we find some way of associating the predicate *anrufen* with both the exponents [an] and [rufen] where those two forms do *not* form a compound. Now we have the means to separate the two items in the main clause in (2) but we have no way of creating the compound in the subordinate clause (1) without violating the other half of *Morphological Integrity:* syntactic mechanisms cannot create new morphological words— including, of course, *compound* words—in constituent structure.

The existence of optionally separable particles thus poses a serious challenge for *Morphological Integrity* and by association for all presently prominent versions of lexicalism which would like to address the lexicality of these and other constructions consisting of syntactically independent elements.

Other properties of particle-verb predicates like *an+rufen* add to the sense that their behavior is paradoxical. We will mention two here: the notion that the particle and the verb in principle are morphologically independent of each other is supported by the fact that they can be separated by morphological material whose presence is arguably governed by syntactic well-formedness conditions. Compare the way that morphologically simplex verbs express their zu-infinitive and their participle of the perfect forms in (19)–(20) with how particle-verb "compounds" form the equivalent categories in (21)–(22):[2]

(19)   *zu* tanzen
       to   dance

       'to dance'

(20)   *ge*   tanzt
       PERF danced

       'danced'

(21)   an *zu* rufen
       up to call

       'to call up'

---

[2]We have analyzed the examples (19)–(20) into the component parts that are the subject of our present theoretical discussion. Conventional German orthography spells (20)–(22) as one word but (19) as two separate words.

(22)   an *ge*   rufen
            up PERF called

            'called up'

Despite the differences between these pairs of examples, note that they both follow the same generalization: in each case the infinitive marker *zu* and the perfect marker *ge* appear immediately before the verb stem. Accordingly, the marker is word-initial in simplex words but has to intervene between the particle and the verb in particle-verb compounds. Since the presence or absence of the infinitive marker *zu* is arguably determined by the syntactic environment, the data just presented seem to lend further support to the notion that the particle and the verb are really composed in constituent structure by syntactic mechanisms, for how else could they be separated by morphemes whose presence is regulated syntactically?[3]

The following considerations seem to force the analytical pendulum back to the lexical side again. Not only do verb-particle combinations show the intonational and cohesive properties of (compound) words, but they also behave like simplex verb units in that they can undergo processes of morphological derivation. In lexicalist theories of grammar this is taken to be an unmistakable sign of lexicality because it is standardly assumed that any item which can be input to a lexical process has been created in the lexicon itself.[4] In this light, consider the following examples:

(23) ein   kaufen   Ein   kauf   *Ein kaufung
       in   purchase   in   purchase
       'do shopping'   'shopping'

(24) ein   laden   Ein   ladung   *Ein lad
       in   load   in   loading
       'invite'   'invitation'

---

[3]With this formulation of the problem, we have in effect anticipated our solution: what the syntax regulates is nothing more than the *presence of a morphosyntactic feature!* In a theory that draws a sharp distinction between morphosyntactic features and the morpho-phonological mechanisms that spell out these features, there is no paradox between the syntax requiring a particular feature and the morphology creating the word forms in the lexicon that have the appropriate feature matrixes. The success of this solution of course depends on maintaining a theoretically clean division between morpho-phonological forms/operations and morphosyntactic features. Allowing that distinction to be blurred leads to much confusion. We suspect that the lack of a theory of morphological spell-out in Baker (1988) which is rightly lamented in Spencer (1991) is not in small part due to the fact that Baker (1988) breaks down the barrier between morphology and syntax with precisely the consequence that his theory now lacks a strict enough separation of primitives and operations to formulate a theory of morphological spell-out that in combination with his theory of syntactic structures yields an elegant *overall* theory of the morphology and syntax of grammatical function changing effects.
[4]For this type of argument, see Lapointe (1985) and Bresnan (1982a).

(25) aus   tausch   aus   tauschbar
     out   exchange   out   exchangeable
     'exchange'   'exchangeable'

The two particle-verb combinations *ein + kaufen* and *ein + laden* can both be nominalized. The nominalization of the first verb consists of the particle followed by the form *kauf* which is identical to the root form of the verb *kaufen*. The verb in (24) however, cannot nominalize with its root form, it must add the affix *ung* instead. The final column shows that neither verb can nominalize with the form the other one uses. This test is of course one of the standard diagnostics Chomsky (1970) used for determining the lexical status of a form: if the formal change it undergoes is irregular, then this is an argument that it is not produced by a syntactic process because syntactic processes are assumed to be regular while lexical processes tolerate exceptions much more easily. (25) shows that particle-verb combinations can convert to the category adjective. Note that the spelling in (23)–(25) is deceptive in that we have separated the particle from the rest of the word (standard German orthography spells all of these compounds as single words). This should not obscure the fact that these words fully obey *Morphological Integrity*, i.e., no syntactic material can ever intervene between the particle and the second part of the compound.

Our goal in this chapter is to provide a unified analysis of particle-verb predicates like those appearing in (1) and (2). We will show that the theory of predicates that was developed in the first six chapters of this book and that was then applied to simple tense-aspect, passive, and causative predicates in the previous three chapters is capable of capturing the intuition that particle-verb predicates, like simplex predicates, have one unified lexical entry with one semantics and one set of f-structural information that are expressed no matter whether the exponent of this lexical entry is one compound morphological item as in (1) or a combination of a verb and a c-structurally independent particle as in (2).

The next section will present more evidence for the lexicality of particle-verb predicates. Then we will lay the morphological ground work for our analysis by making available to the sign module of the lexicon all the morphological items that are needed for both the synthetic and analytic surface expressions of these predicates. Finally, we will turn to the structure of the lexical entries of the particle-verb predicates and the predicate formation patterns that allow them to have full-fledged tense-aspect paradigms.

2 Further Evidence for the Lexicality of Particle-Verb Predicates

The following two subsections will address two issues. Section 2.1 presents arguments that the particle *an* and the verb *rufen* in sentences like (2) should be analyzed as the analytic realization of one single lexical predicate, just as the compound *anrufen* in (1) is analyzed as the realization of such a single lexical predicate. Section 2.2 will go one step further and argue that sentences like (1) and (2) contain *the same lexical predicate* but realize it differently depending on the construction in which the predicate finds itself. An alternative analysis according to which there are two separate lexical entries for the two predicates in (1) and (2), whether or not they are related by a lexical rule, is rejected as unexplanatory on both conceptual and empirical grounds.

2.1 Arguments for a Lexicalist Analysis of Particle-Verb Predicates

Drawing on arguments in Chomsky (1970) in favor of the Lexicalist Hypothesis as well as standard arguments for lexical as opposed to syntactic operations, it can be shown that verb-particle predicates belong to the lexical component and are not created in the syntax, no matter whether the verb and the particle appear as one word as in (1) or as two words as in (2).

We begin by showing that verb-particle predicates display lexical idiosyncrasies like predicates with non-separable prefixes of the kind which led Chomsky (1970) to place derived nominalizations in the lexicon rather than in the syntactic component.

First, like predicates formed with prefixes, particle-verb predicates frequently display a non-compositional semantics, i.e., the semantic relationship between the whole predicate and the semantics of its constituent pieces is idiosyncratic and must be listed. (26) illustrates this, where "=" symbolizes a separable particle and "-" an inseparable prefix:

(26)	nehmen	'to take'	an=nehmen	'to suppose'
	rufen	'to shout'	an=rufen	'to phone'
	kaufen	'to buy'	ver-kaufen	'to sell'
	fahren	'to drive'	ver-fahren	'to lose one's way'

Second, often there is no systematic relationship between the valences of a predicate with a prefix/particle and the predicate based on the verbal element by itself:

(27)	gehen (Intr)	'go'	ein=gehen (Tr)	'enter (contract)'
	treffen (Tr)	'meet'	ein=treffen (Intr)	'arrive'
	dauern (Intr)	'last'	be-dauern (Tr)	'regret'
	deuten (Tr)	'interpret'	be-deuten (Intr)	'mean'

Finally, some particle-verb combinations simply must be listed as a unit because the verbal part by itself does not exist. The same phenomenon exists for prefix predicates as well:

(28)   *[[deutsch]en]   [[ein=deutsch]en]   'to Germanize'

       *[[frisch]en]   [[er-frisch]en]   'to refresh'

We reemphasize that these lexical diagnostics yield positive results even for the particle-verb predicates whose particle and verb can be separated syntactically. The effects of lexical idiosyncrasy and grammatical function changes thus obtain independently of whether the surface realization of the predicate is one morpho-phonological word obeying *Morphological Integrity* or multiple syntactically independent words that each satisfy *Morphological Integrity* individually but do not obey the principle collectively.[5]

2.2   Arguments against Multiple Lexical Entries

We believe that the evidence above unambiguously argues against any attempt to compose particle-predicates in the syntactic component. It does not, however, decide the issue of whether in sentences like (1) and (2) we are dealing with one predicate whose surface realization is a function of the syntactic context the predicate finds itself in or whether the predicates of (1) and (2) have separate yet almost identical lexical entries.

In light of the systematic evidence presented throughout this book for the concept *predicate* which can be expressed either synthetically or analytically, we believe that it is both conceptually and empirically uninsightful to postulate two separate lexical entries for particle-verb predicates, no matter whether these separate entries are assumed to be unrelated or to be related by a lexical rule.

First, there are hundreds of pairs of predicates in German that would have to be listed doubly, even though the two members of each pair are virtually identical contentively, with the one predictable difference of usage in main clauses vs. subordinate clauses. This argues against the postulation of unrelated separate entries.

Second, if there are two separate lexical entries for each of the hundreds of predicates under discussion, then both members of each pair must be

---

[5]While the grammar of particle-verbs is riddled with lexical idiosyncrasies, there are also many semi-regular and very regular processes involving particles. Stiebels (1996) emphasizes the productivity of some particle-verb predicates and on that basis proposes a syntactic treatment of these predicates. This leaves her without a unified account of particle-verb predicates, since many have to be listed in the lexicon because of idiosyncratic properties they have. In contrast, our unified treatment of particle-verb predicates can handle *all* the data, namely in the lexical component. Our theory lists the irregular cases but derives the regular ones through productive predicate formation patterns of the kind we have employed elsewhere in this book in the analysis of productive tense-aspect, passive, and causative constructions.

assumed to have paradigms which are defective in a way that is typical of the whole class of particle-verb predicates. For instance, the compound predicate which appears in the subordinate clause in (1) cannot appear in the main clause (2'), because in synthetically expressed main clauses the verb and the particle must be separated:

(2') * Peter <u>an</u>-<u>ruft</u>   Maria
      Peter up-calls Maria
      'Peter calls Maria up.'

And the separated version which occurs in the main clause (2) cannot appear in subordinate clauses like (1'). In subordinate clauses, the verb and the particle can never be separated by syntactically permutable material:

(1') * weil   Peter <u>an</u> Maria <u>ruft</u>
      because Peter up Maria calls
      'because Peter calls Maria up.'

So, while the separated version only has main clause forms in the present and past tense, the compound version has all subordinate clause forms and in addition main clause forms in all but the present and the past tense. Remarkably, even though each predicate by itself is defective, both predicates together have the complete predicate paradigm of forms and uses of a regular simple predicate, e.g., the predicate *küssen* 'to kiss.' The systematicity of this situation across the large class of particle-verb predicates argues against the postulation of two lexical entries, whether these are assumed to be unrelated or related by lexical rule. The two-entry theory simply fails to capture the insight that the two versions of the particle-verb predicates collaborate to function as a system of uses that is identical to the system of uses of a regular non-particle predicate in German.

   Even if one entry were derived from the other by a productive lexical rule, the resultant analysis would lack insight and be quite ad hoc. The lexicon would be said to contain hundreds of predicates which all happen to have the same kind of defective paradigm. In addition there happens to be a lexical rule that happens to apply only to these defective predicates and which derives predicates which not only happen to be contentively identical (modulo the main vs. subordinate clause difference) to their inputs but also happen to have all and only those paradigm slots which the input predicate is missing. This is a suspicious collection of coincidences!

   Compare this to the conceptual elegance of the theory of particle-verb predicates that we will develop in this chapter. It postulates one single lexical entry for the predicate in (1) and (2) and associates an ambiguous surface spell-out with this predicate so that the particle and the verb realizing the predicate must appear separately in main clauses without an auxiliary and as a morphological compound everywhere else. From this it follows that the two predicates in (1) and (2) and all similar pairs express identical information, since we are dealing with *the same predicate* in different syntactic environments. Moreover, none of these predicates are defective, since they all have a complete predicate paradigm like any regular non-particle verb as well. They merely differ in that depending on the syntactic context, the predicate is expressed in different ways. All of the coincidences of the two-entry theory are thus avoided. Note, however, that the elegant one-entry approach is dependent on the availability of predicate structures whose content can be expressed alternately by a single word or a combination of words.

The two-entry theory fails in one other respect. Given how the grammar of particle-verb predicates is riddled with lexical idiosyncrasies, one would expect to find at least some instances where two hypothetical entries forming a particle-verb pair would drift away from each other in the lexicon. That is not the case. As far as we are aware, the separated and the compound versions of a given particle-verb predicate always have exactly the same meaning, govern exactly the same grammatical functions, govern exactly the same subcategorized elements with identical case marking, agreement, etc. This follows as a theorem from the one-entry theory: we are dealing with two surface realizations of one predicate with one meaning, one f-structure, and one SUBCAT. There is no lexical drift because no two representations exist which can drift apart. On the other hand, the systematic absence of lexical idiosyncrasies between the purported two lexical entries of related predicates is an accident, since the same grammatical domain is characterized by a large amount of lexical idiosyncrasy otherwise.

We believe that the evidence presented in this and the previous subsection makes a very strong case (i) that all particle-verb predicates should be associated with lexical entries and none should be composed in the syntax, and (ii) that each particle-verb predicate has no more than a single lexical entry which associates the predicate with alternative synthetic and analytic spell-outs as a function of the syntactic context in which the predicate appears. In the next two sections we will show that both of these demands can be met in the general approach to predicates argued for in this book.

3 The Division of Labor between the Sign Module and the Morphological Module in the Analysis of Particle-Verb Predicates

The goals spelled out in the last paragraph suggest that the grammatical properties of particle-verb predicates should be approached by the following division of labor between the two modules of our lexicon. For each particle-verb predicate the sign module contains a single lexical entry that defines the contentive features of both synthetic and analytic uses of the predicate. Moreover, the predicate's lexical entry requires a particle and a

verb to be present in the predicate's morphological spell-out but, by crucially stating this requirement disjunctively, allows the particle and the verb
to alternately be realized either as a morphological compound acting as the
predicate's categorial core or as an analytic configuration where the verb by
itself acts as the predicate's categorial core and the particle is selected in the
predicate's particle valence. These two realization options are illustrated in
(29) and (30) below for the predicate *an+rufen* in sentences (1)–(2).

(29) The synthetic realization of the predicate *an+rufen*

$$
\left[
\text{SYNSEM}
\left[
\begin{array}{l}
\text{CSTRUC} \left[\text{CR} \left[\begin{array}{l} \textit{vword} \\ \text{MS} \left[\text{LME} \langle \textit{an, rufen} \rangle \right] \end{array} \right] \right] \\
\\
\text{VAL} \quad \left[\text{PART} \langle \rangle \right]
\end{array}
\right]
\right]
$$

Recall that the morphosyntactic attribute LME (LEXEME) of a word form
determines the morphological paradigm from which the word form must be
taken. The partial lexical entry (29) in the sign module of the grammar thus
imposes the following constraints on its spell-out slots: the categorial core
slot has to be filled by a word form from the paradigm of the internally
complex lexeme <an, rufen>; in contrast, the particle spell-out slot is not
instantiated in this version of the predicate. Consequently, since the particle
and the verb together constitute one morphological word, the word unit they
form is subject to the cohesion requirements of the principle of
Morphological Integrity. This is sufficient to explain why in this usage
they can never be separated by syntactically commutable material.

The crucial features of the analytic realization option are displayed in
(30). (30) differs from (29) in two ways: first, the predicate's categorial core
is based on the verbal lexeme *rufen* alone; and second, the predicate's particle
valence forces this lexical entry to syntactically combine with a sister
constituent that is morphologically realized by a word form of the particle
an. Unlike the representation in (29), the predicate representation in (30)
neither requires nor allows the two word forms spelling out the predicate's
categorial core and the predicate's particle valence to form one compounded
morphological word. As a result, in realizations of (30) these two words are
each required to display the effects of *Morphological Integrity* individually
but they do not need to do so as a unit. Syntactic material is therefore able
to intervene between them, as for instance in example sentence (2).

(30) The analytic realization of the predicate *an+rufen*

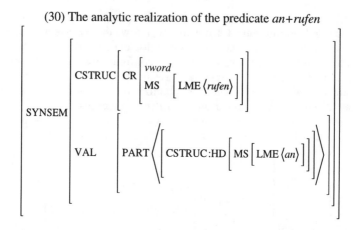

It is possible to collapse the representations in (29) and (30) in such a way that the new representation can be realized as either (29) or (30), depending on the syntactic context in which the predicate finds itself. This is done in (31).

What is special, then, about particle-verb predicates in comparison with more regular predicates is that both their categorial core and their particle valences have more than one realization option. The two realization options differ from each other in that one is created as a morphological compound in the morphological module of the lexicon whereas the other one consists of two morphologically independent words in the syntax. This flexible spell-out constellation creates the illusion that these predicates violate the principle of *Morphological Integrity* and that the syntax either can accomplish compounding or that it can break up compounds. This appearance gives these predicates their considerable theoretical interest. However, the apparent paradox these predicates pose disappears when they are given disjunctive lexical entries like the one in (31).[6]

Two things remain to be done now to complete the analysis of particle-verb predicates. We need to design the morphological module in such a way that it will make available all the morphological word forms that are needed in the two surface realizations made possible by (31). And secondly, we need principles that govern the choice of the disjuncts that appear in the

---

[6]Note that we have already used disjunctive type specifications elsewhere in this book. For instance, in chapter 7 we disjunctively specified each finite predicate in German for one of the six tense-aspects that it must bear and simultaneously for one of six person-number combinations. Thus, the simultaneous disjunctions in the lexical entries of the particle-verb predicates are not remarkable from a conceptual point of view. Many types must specify a limited range of choices in more than one part of their definition. Particle-verb predicates are peculiar, however, in two respects. (i) the choice made in one dimension (i.e., whether the core is compound or simplex) has consequences for the choices that are available in other dimensions (i.e., whether or not there is a particle). (ii) The alternation crosses the syntax-morphology boundary in a non-trivial manner. These peculiarities will be discussed further towards the end of the chapter.

lexical entries of the particle-verb predicates. The next two sections deal with these issues respectively.

(31) The realization of the predicate *an+rufen* that is neutral between the synthetic spell-out in (29) and the analytic spell-out in (30)

$$
\begin{bmatrix}
\text{SYNSEM} & \begin{bmatrix}
\text{CSTRUC} & \begin{bmatrix} \text{CR} & \begin{bmatrix} vword \\ \text{MS} & \begin{bmatrix} \text{LME} \langle rufen \rangle \vee \langle an, rufen \rangle \end{bmatrix} \end{bmatrix} \end{bmatrix} \\
\\
\text{VAL} & \begin{bmatrix} \text{PART} \left\langle \begin{bmatrix} \text{CSTRUC:HD} \begin{bmatrix} \text{MS} \begin{bmatrix} \text{LME} \langle an \rangle \end{bmatrix} \end{bmatrix} \end{bmatrix} \right\rangle \vee \langle \ \rangle \end{bmatrix}
\end{bmatrix}
\end{bmatrix}
$$

4   The Morphology of Particle-Verb Predicates

The infrastructure to create the morphologically separate pieces of the analytic realization option in (30) is already in place. If we add underived lexical entries for the simplex verbal lexeme *rufen* and the particle *an,* the morphological patterns invoked in the analysis of the present and past tense-aspect paradigms of non-particle predicates in chapter 7 will derive all the word forms of *rufen* that are needed to lexicalize the categorial core of the analytical usage illustrated in (30).[7] Since the particle does not inflect, all that is needed for its morphological analysis is a standard underived lexical entry like that in (32):

(32) The lexical entry of the German particle *an*

$$
\begin{bmatrix}
part\text{--}word \\
\text{MS} \quad \begin{bmatrix}
\text{LME} & \langle an \rangle \\
\text{PHON} & \langle an \rangle \\
\text{POS} & p \\
\text{INFL} & no-infl
\end{bmatrix}
\end{bmatrix}
$$

---

[7]Recall from (9)–(14) that the verb and the particle can only be separated in synthetically expressed tenses, i.e., in the present and past tense.

The morphological analysis of the particle-verb compounds that realize the categorial core of (29) is far more interesting. Among others, the analysis will have to deal with the data in (19)–(22) which show that simplex verbs and particle-verb compounds differ in the positioning of the markers for the zu-infinitive and the perfect: whereas simplex verbs take these two inflectional signals as prefixes, they appear in-between the particle and the verb in particle-verb compounds.

What is the best analysis of this phenomenon within our strong theory of lexicalism?[8] The following two sets of empirical data point in the direction of a solution. The table in (33) juxtaposes a number of simplex verbs in the second column with a number of particle-verb compounds formed from the same verbs on the right. Note that throughout the word forms of the participles of the perfect in both columns are identical, even though most verbs in the table form their perfects irregularly:

(33)

Simplex	Perfect of simplex		Perfect of particle compound	
teilen	**geteilt**	'divide'	ein-**geteilt**	'divide up'
schlafen	**geschlafen**	'sleep'	ein-**geschlafen**	'fall asleep'
schließen	**geschlossen**	'close'	ein-**geschlossen**	'lock in'
ziehen	**gezogen**	'pull'	ein-**gezogen**	'move in'
streichen	**gestrichen**	'stroke'	ein-**gestrichen**	'collect'
reißen	**gerissen**	'tear'	ein-**gerissen**	'tear down'
werfen	**geworfen**	'throw'	ein-**geworfen**	'throw in'
binden	**gebunden**	'bind'	ein-**gebunden**	'integrate'
brechen	**gebrochen**	'break'	ein-**gebrochen**	'break in'
gehen	**gegangen**	'go'	ein-**gegangen**	'perish'

Secondly, some verbs in German undergo certain vowel changes in some of their present tense forms (compare the vowels in the infinitives on the left with the vowels in the two boldfaced columns). These vowel changes occur whether the verb is used as part of a simplex word or as part of a compound:

---

[8]Stiebels and Wunderlich (1992) argue for a lexicalist analysis of particle-verb compounds. However, in order to account for the separability of the particle and the verb their analysis resorts to "relativizing" the principle of *Morphological Integrity* as follows: "No syntactic rule has access to a part of a word unless all parts are words themselves." Our analysis, in contrast, does not compromise this key morphological principle.

(34)

Simplex	3sg-pres of simplex		3sg-pres of particle compound	
laden	**läd**	'load'	ein-**läd**	'invite'
geben	**gibt**	'give'	ein-**gibt**	'enter data'
fahren	**fährt**	'drive'	ein-**fährt**	'carry in'
fallen	**fällt**	'fall'	ein-**fällt**	'remember'
brechen	**bricht**	'break'	ein-**bricht**	'break in'

The systematic formal identity between the inflected word forms of simplex verbs and their use in particle-verb compounds clearly indicates that the same lexeme is present in both. It is important to appreciate, however, that what recurs in (33)–(34) is a *lexeme* rather than a *sign*. Recall the difference: a lexeme is a morphological paradigm whose members are combinations of morphophonological and morphosyntactic information but which do not intrinsically bear meanings or grammatical functions. This latter information is borne only by signs in the sign module of the lexicon and not by lexemes or word forms in the morphological module of the lexicon. The lexemes and word forms ultimately will be related to meanings and grammatical functions indirectly, by filling one of the morphological spell-out slots of a predicate in the sign lexicon.

This distinction is crucial for a proper understanding of the data in (33) and (34). Note that there are pairs of simplex and compound words in these tables which systematically behave alike from the point of view of morphological form even though they realize predicates that are completely unrelated from a contentive point of view. For instance, the meaning of the particle verb *eingehen* 'perish' in the last line of (33) is not compositionally derived from the meaning of the particle *ein* 'in' and the verb *gehen* 'go.' Nevertheless, morphologically all forms of the simplex irregular verb *gehen* are identical to the corresponding forms of the verbal part of the compound verb *eingehen*. The same is true for the pair *fallen* ~ *einfallen* in (34): they govern different grammatical functions, cases and have the completely unrelated meanings 'fall' and 'remember.' Yet, all their verbal forms are 100% identical.

We now have considered two problems. First, if the inflected compound verbs in (21)–(22) are morphologically derived from an underlying compound verb like

(35) [$_V$ [$_P$ an] [$_V$ ruf]]

that lacks the inflectional signal, then we need to postulate an infixation operation that will infix the inflectional signal between the particle and the verb stem to generate the two surface forms (21)–(22). Postulating such an operation is suspicious on two counts. As (19)–(20) document, in simplex verbs these inflectional signals are simply prefixes and not infixes. Moreover German is in general not a language that uses infixes in its morphology.

The second problem that an underlying representation like (35) causes is the systematic morphological identity between the simplex word forms in (33)–(34) and the verbal parts of the compound word forms in the same row. We showed that this identity is clearly not due to the presence of the same meaningful sign. How is it, then, that the word in (35) shows exactly identical inflectional behavior as the simplex verb *rufen* in (36)?

(36) [$_V$ ruf]

Technically speaking, (35) and (36) are two independent lexical entries with different meanings, etc. and there is no reason to expect that any morphological idiosyncrasies of one would extend to the other. Yet, that is precisely what we find with respect to inflection.

There is a simple proposal that will solve both of these problems simultaneously. Instead of assuming that words like *anrufe* are bracketed as in (37), they are assumed to be bracketed as in (38):

(37) * [[$_V$ [$_P$ an] [$_V$ ruf]] e]   (call-up, 1st-sg-present)

(38)   [$_V$ [$_P$ an] [$_V$ [ruf] e]]   (call-up, 1st-sg-present)

The difference is the following: in (37) we start out with the hypothesized underlying compound stem *anruf* and then suffix the first person singular present tense marker to it. This does not explain why the compound stem behaves inflectionally like the simplex stem outside compounds.

In (38), on the other hand, we assume that the right-hand member of a particle-verb compound is a fully formed word rather than a verb root or a verb stem. This means that before the verb stem *ruf* can compound with the particle *an,* it first has to combine with an inflectional ending, in this case the 1st-sg-present ending *e.*

Both of the problems with the analysis in (37) disappear as soon as we choose the analysis in (38) instead. The reason that we find the same inflectional behavior throughout (33)–(34) is that in particle-verb compounds the particle only enters the picture *after* the right-hand member of the compound has already been fully inflected. But this right-hand member is *the same lexeme* as the verb whose inflected form appears in the simplex examples on the left-hand side in (33)–(34). The systematic inflectional identities now follow directly.

The putative infixation problem in (21)–(22) disappears under this analysis as well. Since the zu-infinitive of *anrufen* is formed by compounding the particle *an* with the already inflected zu-infinitive *zu rufen* of *rufen,* the infinitive signal ends up in the middle of the compound, even without a suspicious infixation operation:

(39)   [v [p an] [v [*zu* [[**ruf**] en]]]]   (call-up zu-infinitive)

We can cite additional support for this solution and against the infixation solution from a restriction on the formation of German participles of the perfect. While many verbs in German form their participle by prefixing *ge* to the verb stem, not all of them do. In particular, verbs like those in (40) with non-initial main stress omit the participial "prefix" (the syllable bearing main stress is underlined):

(40)

Simplex	Perfect of simplex		Perfect of particle compound	
berufen	**be<u>ru</u>fen**	'summon'	<u>ein</u>-**berufen**	'summon'
betonieren	**beto<u>niert</u>**	'pour concrete'	<u>ein</u>-**betoniert**	'set in concrete'
beziehen	**be<u>zog</u>en**	'cover with'	<u>ein</u>-**bezogen**	'consider'

Note, crucially, that the participial *ge* is not only obligatorily absent in the simplex verbs on the left but also in the particle-verb compounds on the right, even though the verbs on the right bear main stress on the particle and hence the first syllable of the complex word.

The data in (40) fall out immediately from our assumption that particle-verb compounds are compounds of fully inflected words. In that case, the word *einberufen* in the first line of (40) is compounded from the particle *ein* and the participle *berufen*. The simple participle *berufen* lacks the *ge* prefix, since the stem underlying it does not bear word-initial stress. Consequently, the particle-verb compound *einberufen* must likewise lack *ge-*, since it is formed from the participle *berufen*. On the other hand, an analysis of inflected particle-verb compounds that combines the particle with a verb stem and then adds inflection is unable to naturally account for the fact that the compound verbs in the right-hand column of (40) behave like their corresponding simplex verbs in the left-hand column, since one type of verb has non-initial stress and the other one bears stress on its initial syllable.

On the basis of the three advantages discussed in this section, we therefore postulate the following relationship between particle-verb compounds and the particles and the simplex verbs that occur in them. In chapter 5 we developed general data types for morphological words and patterns. We applied these data types to the simplex words that are involved in the surface spell-out of non-particle predicates in German. For instance, we postulated a morphological pattern that creates third person singular present tense word forms like that in (41) from underlying present tense stems:

(41) The morphological word *ruft* 'calls up'

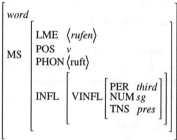

(41) is the word form that spells out the categorial core of the predicate *an-rufen* in (2). The particle in (2) which forms the second part of the analytical spell-out of the predicate of that sentence has the lexical entry (32).

This means that we have all the morphological material that we need to spell out the analytic version of particle-verb predicates. In fact, as was mentioned earlier, this was already accomplished at the end of chapter 7.

For reasons already discussed above, we will *not* postulate any morphological representations for particle-verb compounds below the fully inflected word level. In particular, these expressions have no roots and stems and hence are unable to undergo the inflectional morphological operations of simplex lexemes which do have paradigmatic members at those morphological ranks.

Consequently, the only way that a fully inflected third person singular present tense particle-verb compound like *anruft* of sentence (1) can be created is by compounding the particle in (32) with the fully inflected word form *ruft* in (41) which bears these same inflectional features. This is accomplished by the morphological pattern in (42).

Observe how the information from the two morphological daughters flows to the compound word in (42): the LME value of the top MS (morphosyntax) attribute is bi-lexemic as one would expect of a compound word and consists of the concatenation of the unit lexeme values of the particle daughter and the verb daughter of the compound. The phonology of the mother is the result of concatenating the phonologies of the two daughters. Here is where the influence of the particle ends: both the part of speech and the inflectional features of the compound are contributed by the right-hand member of the compound alone, i.e., the verb. This is what makes it possible to first inflect the right-hand member before it enters into the compound: its inflectional features will be carried up to the whole word by the pattern in (42) anyway.

(42) The German particle-verb compounding
morphological pattern

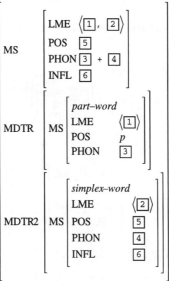

Applying the morphological compounding pattern in (42) to the particle in (32) and the simplex verb in (41) yields the particle-verb compound in (43). This is the word that spells out the synthetic particle-verb predicate in (1) which displays all the effects of *Morphological Integrity.*

(43) The particle-verb compound *anruft* formed
from (32) and (41)

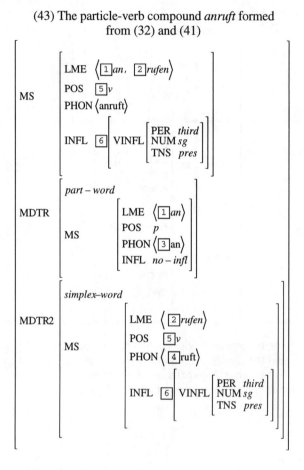

5   Completing the Analysis

We take stock of where we are in our analysis at this point. We began with the two sentences in (1) and (2) and showed in section 2.2 that they are best seen as containing two different surface realizations of the same lexical predicate, rather than the result of two separate lexical entries. In (29) and (30) we presented the alternative synthetic and analytic spell-outs that would be needed for this single predicate and we collapsed these representations into the lexical entry (31) with disjunctive spell-out slots.

The synthetic spell-out version accounts for the surface structure of the predicate in sentence (1). In the previous section we derived the compound morphological item (43) as the kind of filler of the categorial core

spell-out slot in (29).[9] That means that we have the morphological structures to spell out the synthetic version of the predicate in (31).

The analytic spell-out version in (31) underlies the surface structure
in (2) where the same predicate as in (1) is represented by two separate
words, as is indicated by the categorial core in (30) and the non-empty particle valence. We have morphological representations for these two words at
our disposal as well, in the form of (32) and (41).

These are all the morphological resources that are needed to lexicalize
both the synthetic and the analytic predicates in (1)–(2) in accordance with
(31).

At this point our analysis is almost complete. The predicate that appears in (1)–(2) is associated with the lexical representation in (44):

(44) The lexical entry of the particle-verb compound *an+rufen*
(underived and uninflected)

$$
\begin{bmatrix}
\text{SYNSEM} & \begin{bmatrix}
\text{CSTRUC} & \begin{bmatrix} \text{CR} & \begin{bmatrix} \textit{vword} \\ \text{MS:LME} \langle \text{rufen} \rangle \vee \langle \text{an,rufen} \rangle \end{bmatrix} \end{bmatrix} \\[4ex]
\text{ISTRUC} & \begin{bmatrix}
\text{CONT} & \begin{bmatrix} \textit{call} - \textit{up} \\ \text{CALLER} \; \boxed{1} \\ \text{CALLED} \; \boxed{2} \end{bmatrix} \\[3ex]
\text{FSTRUC} & \begin{bmatrix} \text{SU} & \langle \boxed{3:1} \rangle \\ \text{DO} & \langle \boxed{4:2} \rangle \end{bmatrix}
\end{bmatrix} \\[6ex]
\text{VAL} & \begin{bmatrix}
\text{SUBCAT} & \{ \text{N}_{\boxed{3}}, \text{N}_{\boxed{4}} \} \\
\text{AUX} & \langle \rangle \\
\text{PART} & \langle \begin{bmatrix} \text{CSTRUC:HD} & \begin{bmatrix} \text{MS} \begin{bmatrix} \text{LME} \langle \textit{an} \rangle \end{bmatrix} \end{bmatrix} \end{bmatrix} \rangle \vee \langle \rangle
\end{bmatrix}
\end{bmatrix}
\end{bmatrix}
$$

---

[9]We say "kind of filler" because the representation in (31) does not specify the inflectional
features of the word spelling out the categorial core. But (31) of course can undergo the
inflectional expansions of chapter 7.

The predicate combines with two NPs, a subject and a direct object. The subject is interpreted as the CALLER and the direct object as the CALLED. Contentively, the two sentences in (1) and (2) are exactly identical. They only differ in the number of words that spell out the predicate.

To complete the analysis, we need to take care of two more things. On its own, (44) will overgenerate in two respects. Since the disjunctions in its two spell-out slots are as yet independent of each other, there are four logically possible combinations of choices:

(45)   Core   Particle

a.   <an, rufen>   <>
b.   *   <an, rufen>   <an>
c.   *   <rufen>   <>
d.   <rufen>   <an>

Of these four logically possible choices, only the first and the last are desirable. The choice in (45a) is represented by (29) and (45d) represents (30). (45b) is undesirable because it spells out the particle twice and (45c) is inappropriate because it drops the particle altogether.

Thus, our first order of business is to rule out (45b–c). This is easily done by making the following assumptions:

(46) Assumptions about particle-verb predicates I

a.   Particle-verb predicates in German belong to the type *pv-lci;*
b.   the types *compound-lci* and *partld-lci* partition the type *pv-lci.*

The partition statement in (46b) requires that every particle-verb predicate in German either have a compound categorial core *(compound-lci)* or a non-empty particle valence *(partld-lci),* but not both. (45b–c) are incompatible with this constraint: (45b) has a compound core as well as a particle and (45c) has neither. In a moment we will speculate on why particle-verb predicates might be subject to the constraint in (46b).

Before we do this, we will make sure that the two legitimate realization options in (45a) and (45d) are applied under the right circumstances, i.e., we will derive the *Verb-Particle Separability Generalization* in (17).

This is easily done with another type partition declaration:

(47) Assumptions about particle-verb predicates II

a.   The type *second-lci* is defined as a predicate whose categorial core is finite and linearized in the second linear slot of the linear structure of German main clauses;
b.   the types *compound-lci* and *second-lci* partition the type *pv-lci.*

The type definition in (47a) and the partition declaration in (47b) entail that the separated option in (45d) is only available when the predicate's categorial core appears in the second position of a main clause and that the compound option in (45a) is mandatory otherwise.

We will spell out in some more detail how this follows. At this point, the four type partitions in (48) are relevant:

(48)　Each of these pairs of types partition the type of particle-verb predicates

　　a.　*partld-lci* v *npartld-lci;*
　　b.　*compound-lci* v *simplex-lci;*
　　c.　*compound-lci* v *partld-lci;*　　　[= (46b)]
　　d.　*compound-lci* v *second-lci.*　　　[= (47b)]

The last two partitions were just defined. The first partition simply says that on each usage, a predicate either has a particle or it does not, but not both. The second one says that on each usage the categorial core of a predicate either is morphologically a compound or it is simplex, but not both. This is a matter of logic, given the general structure of signs.

Note, now, that there are only two ways for a particle-verb predicate to simultaneously satisfy all four constraints in (48). We illustrate this by showing that once we make a choice in (48a), all the remaining choices are forced upon us:

(49)　The consequences of choosing *partld-lci* in (48a)

　　a.　*partld-lci* v ~~*npartld-lci;*~~
　　b.　~~*compound-lci*~~ v *simplex-lci;*
　　c.　~~*compound-lci*~~ v *partld-lci;*　　　[= (46b)]
　　d.　~~*compound-lci*~~ v *second-lci.*　　　[= (47b)]

By choosing the first disjunct in (49a), we commit the particle-verb predicate to having a particle in its particle valence. Since (49c) says that a predicate cannot simultaneously be particled and a compound, the compounding option is eliminated throughout. Consequently, a particled lci must also belong to the types *simplex-lci* and *second-lci.* In sum, a predicate that takes the particled option in (48a) must have a morphologically simplex categorial core (this follows from *simplex-lci*) and must appear in the second position of a German main clause [as a function of the definition of *second-lci* in (47a)].

Assume, then, that a predicate instantiates the second choice in (48a):

(50)   The consequences of choosing *npartld-lci* in (48a)

    a.   ~~*partld-lci*~~-v *npartld-lci;*
    b.   *compound-lci* v ~~*simplex-lci;*~~
    c.   *compound-lci* v ~~*partld-lci*~~-   [= (46b)]
    d.   *compound-lci* v ~~*second-lci.*~~   [= (47b)]

This time, the various constraints can only be resolved if the particle-verb predicate is non-particled and its categorial core is a morphological compound.

The configuration in (49) underlies the generalization in (17a). The type *partld-lci* identifies the predicate as being realized by two words, a verb and a particle, that are syntactically separable. The type *second-lci,* as defined in (47a), forces the categorial core of the predicate to contribute the finite verb in the second position of a main clause. This is only possible if the predicate does not have an auxiliary, because in auxiliated predicates, the auxiliary would have to carry the finite inflection.

(50), on the other hand, underlies the second half of the generalization in (17). Since (50) says that the categorial core of the predicate is a compound and by (50d) a compound categorial core cannot appear in the second position of a main clause, the predicate in (50) either occurs in a subordinate clause, i.e., a clause where the verb-second constraint is inapplicable, or the predicate contains an auxiliary which can satisfy the verb-second constraint in main clauses. These are exactly the states of affairs described in (17b).

This completes our demonstration that the four constraints in (48) collectively derive the empirical generalizations in (17) and (45) and thus that the lexical entry in (44) does not overgenerate. We end this discussion with a short speculation about the rationale of each of the four constraints. We already mentioned that the two constraints in (48a–b) are natural: by definition, every predicate must have a categorial core which is either simplex or compound but not both and every predicate must have a particle valence which is either empty or non-empty, but not both.

The remaining two constraints in (48c–d) are not as straightforward. But we believe that they can be motivated as well. Since particle-verb predicates have to satisfy both (48c) and (48d), they are subject to the conjoined constraint in (51):

(51) (*compound-lci* v *partld-lci*) & (*compound-lci* v *second-lci*)

(51) is logically equivalent to (52):

(52) *compound-lci* v (*partld-lci* & *second-lci*)

Since all disjunctions are interpreted as exclusive, (52) again says that a particle-verb predicate either lacks a particle and has a compound core in non-second position or it has both a particle and realizes its non-compound core in second position.

We speculate that the constraint in (52) is operative because the type of particle-verb predicates in German has developed as a compromise between the two simpler types of predicates schematized in (53):

(53)   a.   [$_{\text{Main Clause}}$ X Verb (Clitics) ..... Particle]

       b. [$_{\text{Sub. Clause}}$ .... [$_{\text{V}}$ Particle Verb]]

Some particles derive historically from adverbial modifiers which have lost their semantic and adverbial independence and have grammaticalized into a particle of an analytically expressed particle-verb predicate. Before the adverbial modifier became part of the predicate, it could be separated from the main verb of the sentence. One circumstance where such linear separation would occur frequently is in main clauses like (53a): the main verb appears in second position and often is separated from the particle by nominal clitics which typically appear closer to the second position than modifiers of all kinds.

On the other hand, many particle-verb predicates are back-formations from nominal compounds. For instance, the verb *schlaf-wandeln* 'sleepwalk' is a back-formation from the noun *Schlaf-wandler* 'sleepwalker.' In other words, the second part of the compound which originally had to be a noun now could also be a verb. Many of these particle-verb predicates originally could only appear in the syntactic configuration shown in (53b). They were banned from (53a) because their status as morphological compounds with respect to the principle of *Morphological Integrity* did not allow the linear separation of the two pieces of the compound that would be required by (53a).

We would like to suggest that the peculiar mix of morphological and syntactic properties of the synchronic German particle-verb predicates is a result of these predicates simultaneously realizing the two constructions in (53). Against this background, the constraint in (52), which is rather unnatural in isolation, begins to make sense.

Take a predicate that can only be used in the configuration (53b) because its morphological structure does not allow the two pieces of its categorial core to be linearly separated. In order to assimilate this predicate to the predicates that can appear with the properties described by (53a), the requirement that its categorial core is a compound in non-second position has to be replaced by the requirement that the particle and the verb now are syntactically independent of each other and that the verb has to appear in second position. In other words, a predicate that starts out instantiating the first disjunct of (52) becomes more flexible by being given the choice of taking on the conjoined properties in the second disjunct of (52).

On the other hand, assume that we start out with a predicate that can occur in the context (53a) and we want to generalize its lexical properties by analogy with the compound predicates in (53b). Clearly, the crucial change that needs to be made is that the syntactic independence of the particle and the verb in second position have to be traded in for a morphological compound that can only occur in non-second position. From the point of view of (52), this means that a predicate that started out instantiating the second conjunct gains the option in the first conjunct as well and therefore now has both realization options typical of synchronic German particle-verb predicates.

6 Conclusion

This concludes perhaps the most challenging and most diverse case of alternately synthetic and analytic predicates that we have analyzed in this book. In this chapter we have argued that the particle-verb predicates of German exemplified in (1) and (2) should be given unique lexical entries with a single information structure. The lexical entry of this kind of predicate specifies that it can be realized either as a morphological particle-verb compound that obeys *Morphological Integrity* as a whole unit or as a particle and a verb which are projected into phrase structure as two independent syntactic atoms which have to satisfy *Morphological Integrity* individually but do not have to do so as a unit and hence can be linearly separated by syntactic material.

Our general theory of predicates thus makes possible an analysis of optionally separable particles that avoids the analytical problem this class of predicates has represented for classical lexicalist theories of grammar. As was discussed in connection with our overview of lexicalism in (18) of chapter 1, the classical theories of lexicalism simultaneously sought to enforce (i) the principle of *Morphological Integrity* which prohibits the manipulation of pieces of morphological words by syntactic operations and (ii) the principle of *Morphological Expression* which requires each lexical predicate to be expressed by one and only one morphological word. We showed at the beginning of this chapter that under these assumptions the existence of predicates with optionally separable particles creates an analytical paradox: if the lexical entry of these predicates obeys *Morphological Expression* and consists of a verb-particle compound, then syntactic linearization rules have to refer to the pieces of this compound in a main clause like (2) where syntactic material intervenes between the two pieces that constitute the hypothetical compound. This violates the principle of *Morphological Integrity*. On the other hand, if the lexical entry is spelled out by a particle and a verb which do not form one morphological unit, then this lexical entry violates *Morphological Expression* and additionally *Morphological Integrity* in contexts like (1) where syntactic rules would need to form the particle and the verb into a morphological compound.

This analytical paradox disappears in our theory of predicates, since we depart from classical lexicalism by demoting *Morphological Expression* from a principle that cannot be violated to a preference principle. This means that while the preferred spell-out of predicates is in terms of a single morphological word, the marked choice of a spell-out in terms of more than one independent word is dispreferred but possible. Predicates with separable particles make use of this marked realization option of *Morphological Expression* and this allows them to be in full compliance with *Morphological Integrity* in both of their possible surface realizations: when they are realized as a compound, this compound as a whole is inseparable in the syntactic component, and when it is realized analytically, then each of the words contained in its surface spell-out satisfies *Morphological Integrity* individually but they do not form one morphological unit that needs to satisfy this principle. For this reason, these words can be separated by other syntactic material under this realization option without any violation of *Morphological Integrity*.

We presented the morphological items and patterns that are necessary to lexicalize the spell-out slots of particle-verb predicates and showed that the most explanatory morphological analysis derives the inflected forms of particle-verb predicates not from underlying roots and stems but by compounding a particle with a verb that is already fully inflected. This kind of analysis is only possible within a word and paradigm model of morphology.

Finally, we postulated lexical entries for particle-verb predicates which contain spell-out disjunctions and a number of partitioning constraints which collectively entail that particle-verb predicates signal their contentive aspects in exactly one of two ways: in main clauses without auxiliaries, the verb and the particle must be separated, but everywhere else they must be compounded and the compound appears in non-second position.[10] We speculated that the disjunctions in the lexical entries of the synchronic particle-verb predicates and the type partitionings are the result of the reciprocal assimilation in constructional behavior of two classes of predicates, one of which was synthetically expressed and the other one analytically. The resultant predicate acts as the functional head of a sentence that has a choice between these two realization options, depending on the syntactic and morphological context in which the predicate finds itself.

---

[10]Note that the elsewhere class contains the important case of category-changed morphological derivatives of particle-verb predicates. Thus, the agent nominalization of *anrufen* 'call up' is *Anrufer* 'caller' and the *-able* adjective is *anrufbar* 'able to be called up.' Since nouns and adjectives can never occur in the second position of German main clauses, these non-verbal particle predicates do not have the option of the second disjunct in (52). This ensures that the particle must always be present in category-changing morphological derivatives formed from particle-verb predicates. There is thus no reason for any category-changing derivational predicate formation rules to treat particle-verb predicates different from simplex verbs.

11

Reprise and Evaluation

In chapter 1 we observed that a number of analytically expressed predicate constructions did not find a satisfactory analysis in the traditional strongly lexicalist theories of generative grammar. The reason proposed was that while these theories did not allow new predicates to be formed in the syntax, they simultaneously assumed that every lexical entry must be spelled out by at most one morphological word in the syntactic component. The treatment of some of these phenomena led to variants of both LFG and HPSG that weakened the classical constraints of lexicalism. In each case, the lexicon's privileged relation to predicate formation was given up and the syntax was allowed to form new predicates by composing the relevant information in phrase structure. As a consequence, the conception of the lexicon as the locus for the interplay between contentive and formal information associated with "words" was effectively reduced to a primarily morphological concept.

In contrast, we have suggested that the conceptual core of lexicalism is its functional aspect and that its morphological aspect is secondary. In line with this hypothesis of the primacy of function over form we argued that recent moves within lexicalist frameworks represent a weakening of empirically motivated and theoretically useful core assumptions. We argued that a less radical reform of classical lexicalism was sufficient to account for the grammar of analytically expressed predicates: the principle of *Morphological Expression* which requires every lexical entry to be expressed by exactly one morphological word can be weakened from a "hard" constraint to a preference principle which prefers single-word lexical entries but allows for analytically expressed lexical entries as a marked option. In the remainder of the book we have set out to develop such a theory in detail and to apply it to a number of analytically expressed predicate constructions that have challenged strong theories of lexicalism (as well as non-lexicalist theories of grammar).

Our theory of predicates is built on the following crucial proposals:

I. The bearers of lexical information structures are lexical predicates rather than morphological words. The information carried by these predicates, i.e., their semantic content and their f-structures, can be expressed via three types of lexically specified morphological spell-out slots: the predicate's categorial core, the predicate's auxiliary valence, and the predicate's particle valence. Only the first slot is filled obligatorily. If the remaining two slots are unfilled, then the predicate is synthetic, otherwise it is analytic. The predicate's semantic content, its f-structure, its valence, and the filling of its spell-out slots must all be fixed before syntactic phrase formation schemas can apply to it. This means that the syntax can neither form new predicates nor new morphological words. Rather, all predicate formation and word formation happens in one single component, the lexicon. This retains what we consider the core guiding principles motivating classical lexicalism. The resulting system postulates what we believe to be a very natural and intuitive division of labor between the lexical and the syntactic components: the lexicon forms predicates and the syntax saturates their valences (including the auxiliary and particle valences of analytic predicates).

II. The lexicon consists of two submodules, one for signs and one for morphological items. As a result, morphological items do not directly bear semantic contents and f-structures but only become indirectly associated with such contentive aspects by filling one of the morphological spell-out slots of a predicate in the sign module of the lexicon. Both modules of the lexicon are designed to be intelligent in the sense that they contain productive patterns for the formation of new predicates and words from items that are already present in the relevant module. The result is a very powerful lexical engine with two parallel productive systems that interact via the morphosyntactic information in morphological words that predicates can select for in their various morphological spell-out slots. The data structures in both parts of the lexicon do not require one-to-one mapping between information and form: just like one predicate may be spelled out by one or more words, one morphosyntactic feature may have any number of morphophonological reflexes. The morphological system therefore instantiates a word and paradigm morphology that avoids the disadvantages that are typical of a morpheme-based morphology, particularly the proliferation of null morphemes and the problem of dealing with non-concatenative morphological operations such as reduplication, circumfixation, and truncation.

Clearly one should account for preferred patterns of correspondence between the elements in the two submodules. Our focus has been primarily on developing the types of representations that permit a principled explanation to be given for cross-linguistically recurring patterns of correspondence between the contentive and formal aspects of predicates. We have addressed this issue by positing archetypes and language-particular multiple inheritance type hierarchies. This leads to the third type of proposal we have made.

III. As in HPSG, all linguistic units are modeled as typed feature structures that can be organized into a multiple inheritance hierarchy. According to this conception, a grammar is a system for recursively defining types of expressions. Generalizations across types can be captured by grouping them under common supertypes from which they inherit the information they share. For any given type, one can determine how much independent information it contains, in the sense that its information is not inherited from any super-types which also transfer this information to other subtypes. The degree of independent information in a type therefore is a measure of its informational isolatedness in the grammar. We have proposed that natural language grammars are designed to keep the amount of independent information in grammatical units to a minimum, perhaps as a result of a general cognitive principle that attempts to associate new information human beings acquire to information already stored in the person's memory. As a consequence of this design, natural language grammars attempt to weave their types into dense networks of cross-classifying inheritance relationships. We went one step further and proposed that the bias against independent information holds across the board for all language-particular types and that this motivates the postulation of universal clusters of grammatical information which we referred to as archetypes. These archetypes are no different in kind from any other grammatical types, they exist to group even the most general language-particular types under more general types in a universal type hierarchy which allows all the types in any natural language to reduce their amount of independent information by matching the information in a supertype.

The archetypes interact with our evaluation metric by motivating the structure of language-particular types. Since they are assumed to be available to all language learners, they make possible a kind of innately guided learning. Since they only represent highly valued structures rather than structures that a language must instantiate, they represent the kind of phenomena that we would expect to find attested most frequently in the world's languages, but not necessarily. We suggested that such a "soft" theory of universals is a common sense compromise between extremist nativist and extremist empiricist positions on language learning which respectively claim that almost all linguistic knowledge is innate or that almost all of it is gained via induction guided by general cognitive mechanisms. We believe that the extremist nativist claim significantly overstates the similarities between natural languages and that on the other hand the extremist empiricist view by far overstates the heterogeneity of natural languages. In contrast, we have proposed a system which motivates why a number of structures seem to recur from language to language, i.e., because of archetypes, while permitting particular languages to display departures from these archetypes in many ways.

The postulation of archetypes provides an explanatory mechanism suited to the nature of our representations in much the manner that principles and parameters are appealed to within the structuralist tradition that favors tree-theoretic representations. However, based on several opportunities in this book to compare the performance of principles and parameters with our own theory of archetypes we have come to the conclusion that there is a sharp contrast between the *claimed* advantages of the principles and parameters approach in theory and its comparative failure to provide explanation of the kind available in our theory *in practice*. This is particularly evident when the criteria characteristic of good work in unification-based approaches are considered: theory unity, explicitness in analysis, empirical coverage, and theory-independent verifiability of claims.

We applied our theory of predicates to four empirical domains in chapters 7 through 10. Each chapter presents evidence that predicates expressing the same kind of information can alternately be expressed by single words or by combinations of a number of words, either an auxiliary-main verb combination or a combination of a verb and a particle. In each case it can be shown that linguistically significant generalizations are captured in a theory of grammar designed in accordance with I-III above, but that these generalizations are lost in theories making other assumptions, for instance, theories with category-based rather than predicate-based lexicons, theories that allow predicate formation both in the syntax and the lexicon, etc. The crucial components that enabled the capturing of the generalizations were the postulation of both synthetically and analytically expressed predicates in one component of the grammar where both predicates can be grouped under common supertypes in a lexical type hierarchy and their shared information be associated with variably synthetic or analytic surface expressions.

For instance, in chapter 7 which dealt with tense-aspect predicates, we argued that it is counterintuitive and inelegant to generate the present and past tenses of German predicates in the lexicon simply because these predicates are expressed synthetically while forming the remaining four tenses in the syntax because their expression involves an auxiliary-main verb combination. Instead, we proposed that all six tenses are the result of German predicate formation patterns in the lexicon which enrich the meaning of an underlying untensed predicate with tense-aspect information and fill in the derived predicate's morphological spell-out slots as required to yield a synthetic or analytic surface spell-out. According to this theory, it is a predicate that bears tense information and not the morphological word that spells out the predicate. According to the alternative category-based approach, the untensed predicate must be embedded under an auxiliary category in the syntax in order for a new tensed predicate to be formed syntactically. We showed that our theory but not its category-based competitor can handle data such as the following where the same tense-aspect meaning is expressed whether or not the optional auxiliary is present on the surface:[1]

(1)   daß er noch nicht gekommen (ist)
        that he yet not come   has

        'He has not come yet'

(2)   – warum er geweint (hat)
        – why he wept   has

        '-- why he has wept'

---

[1]These sentences were actually discussed in footnote 3 in chapter 5.

By attaching information content to predicates and having predicates spelled out via one or more morphological spell-out slots, we can directly capture the intuition that the predicate with and without the auxiliary expresses the same information, by postulating a predicate formation pattern that adds an optionally expressed auxiliary to the newly formed tensed predicate. The category-based alternative theory will have to postulate two radically different structures for the predicates with and without auxiliaries, since in this theory, the tense will be contributed by the auxiliary when it is present and by the main verb otherwise.

   In chapter 8 we discussed passives like the ones in (3) and (4) which are contentively equivalent but differ in that the predicative predicate in (3) is formed with the predicative zu-infinitive of the main verb and an accompanying auxiliary *sein* whereas the attributive predicate in (4) is based on the zu-infinitive bearing attributive inflection.

(3)   weil   die Blumen dem Mann von Johann zu schenken sind
       because the flowers the man by Johann to give   are

       'because the flowers must be given to the man by Johann'

(4)   die dem Mann von Johann zu schenkenden Blumen
       the the man by Johann to give   flowers

       'the flowers that must be given to the man by Johann'

As was shown in detail, it is possible to capture the contentive generalizations across these predicates if they are generated in one and the same lexical component that (i) allows them to belong to a common supertype that expresses their shared meaning; but (ii) at the same time allows them to specify their morphological spell-out slots differentially. In a category-based lexicon or a theory where predicate formation is spread across the lexicon and the syntax, this amount of generalization is beyond reach.

   Chapter 9 surveyed the kinds of causative constructions that can be found in the world's languages and documented that with respect to clausality there are three kinds of causatives (which we were able to reduce to two kinds through a reanalysis later in the chapter). Crucially, for each of the different kinds of causative predicates, we were able to cite a languages which expresses them synthetically or analytically:

(5) Causative types according to clausality and syntheticity

	Analytic	Synthetic
Monoclausal	German I	Malayalam
Biclausal	German II	Chi-Mwi:ni
Mixed	Italian	Turkish

By postulating monoclausal causative archetypes which determine the meaning and the f-structures of causatives, both monoclausal and biclausal, we were able to make these predicate structures available to all natural language grammars. Using defaults and some preference principles, we were able to make predictions which types of causatives are typologically most frequently instantiated. By allowing individual grammars to declare these contentive archetypes and associate them with language-particular spell-outs, our theory is able to capture the generalization documented in (5) that all types of causative predicates can in principle be expressed both synthetically and analytically.

Chapter 10, finally, dealt with the theoretically interesting phenomenon of predicates with separable particles. We discussed the alternation illustrated in (6)–(7):

(6)   weil   Peter Maria an-ruft
        because Peter Maria up calls

        'because Peter calls Maria up.'

(7)   Peter ruft Maria an
    Peter calls Maria up

    'Peter calls Maria up.'

We presented evidence that the same predicate appears in (6) and (7) rather than two different predicates which happen to have identical information structures, whether or not these putative two predicates have autonomous lexical entries or one is derived from the other one by a lexical rule. This analysis allowed us to account for the unusual mix of morphological and syntactic properties of these predicates which we attributed to their being a blend of two construction types: on the one hand, the particle and the verb can be syntactically separated under special syntactic circumstances, but on the other hand, they must form a compound that obeys *Morphological Integrity* and can even participate in category-changing derivational predicate formation operations which must take place in the lexicon in any lexicalist approach to grammar.

The success of our individual analyses of tense-aspect, passive, causatives, and separable particles in terms of a unified and formally precise conception of lexically represented complex predicates leads us to believe that grammars must adhere to the theoretical ideas described above in I-III in order for them to be maximally explanatory in capturing linguistically significant generalizations. A similar degree of generalization across all four types of predicate constructions is difficult to achieve with either the argument attraction mechanism or the syntactic co-head and predicate composition techniques of HPSG and LFG, since the properties of verb-particle constructions cannot be captured with mechanisms designed to address the properties of predicates consisting of an auxiliary and a verb. In addition, a uniform lexical treatment of these constructions of the sort offered here provides an explanation for well-attested patterns of morphologization (i.e., grammaticalization) in the domain of complex predicate formation that all four constructions display in many languages.

One aspect of our analyses which we have not focused on in the present book is evidence internal to German that confirms the treatment of these different constructions (and others we haven't discussed) as uniformly belonging to the general type *predicate*. In fact, there is strong evidence of this kind: as is shown in Webelhuth and Ackerman (1998), it is possible to formulate word order generalizations over the whole class of constructions which we have identified as complex predicates in the present book. These word order generalizations unify them into a single class and distinguish them from other classes of grammatical elements. The identical treatment of these entities with respect to syntactic phenomena such as word order is both expected under an analysis that treats them as representing a natural class and further supports the theory of predicates developed here.

In chapter 2 we informally discussed many other phenomena which we believe to argue for the conception of predicates that is developed in this book. Formal analyses of these phenomena and many others remain to be worked out. However, we believe that the success of the representative applications to which we have put our theory in chapters 7–10 makes it initially plausible that the phenomena presented in chapter 2 fall within the scope of our theory of predicates as well.

In sum, we have articulated a lexicalist theory guided by the principle of the primacy of function over form. We believe that this heuristic has yielded insightful and plausible analyses of the phenomena examined in this book. It is clear that an enriched conception of the lexicon is central to the explanation of many recurring grammatical phenomena. In contrast, the lexicon conceived as a repository of idiosyncratic information or listed stipulations associated with words deprives linguistic research of alternative analyses that permit the statement of large generalizations across classes of predicates and the identification of more nuanced, smaller generalizations that exist across classes and languages as well as within classes and languages: these lexicalist analyses also hold promise for fruitful interaction with cognitive science. Restricted to a limited view of the lexicon, transformational grammarians have typically sought explanation in the syntactic component and have exerted relatively little effort in developing tools for the lexical component that are as powerful, productive, and creative as the various tools that enter the syntactician's toolbox on a regular basis. The development of powerful lexical operations in LFG and of lexical type hierarchies in HPSG worked against this trend in the early to mid-1980s, but, as previously suggested, the lexicon ceded explanatory ground to the syntax in several influential versions of these two theories in the early 1990s as well.

It is our belief that a predicate-based lexicon that includes a powerful lexical engine like the one we have introduced in this book is the central component of grammar.

On the one hand, via its storage function, such a lexicon *is* able to model the immense amount of idiosyncratic lexical information that Saussure referred to as the arbitrariness of the sign.

On the other hand, via the type hierarchy and predicate formation patterns of varying degrees of productivity, the lexicon is likewise able to express patterns of regularity across predicates at every level of generality, including the generalizations that are due to the effects of the archetypes made available by Universal Grammar.

The results flowing from these architectural assumptions and representational tools set strongly lexicalist theories apart favorably from the recent state of the art in the transformational paradigm, where a purely theory-dependent proliferation of categorial heads and syntactic movements has made the promise of a unified, concrete, and empirically contentful theory of syntax and morphology a matter of faith against all evidence.

References

Abaitua, Josepa. 1988. *Complex Predicates in Basque: From Lexical Forms to Functional Structures.* Doctoral dissertation, University of Manchester.

Abeillé, Anne, Danièle Godard, and Ivan A. Sag. In press. Two Kinds of Composition in French Complex Predicates. In Erhard Hinrichs, Andreas Kathol, and Tsuneko Nakazawa, eds., *Complex Predicates in Nonderivational Syntax.* New York: Academic Press.

Abney, Steven. 1996. Statistical Methods and Linguistics. In Judith L. Klavans and Philip Resnik, eds., *The Balancing Act: Combining Symbolic and Statistical Approaches to Language.* Cambridge, Mass.: MIT Press, 2–26.

Ackerman, Farrell. 1984. Verbal Modifiers as Argument Taking Predicates: Complex Verbs as Predicate Complexes in Hungarian. *Groningen Working Papers in Linguistics.* Groningen: University of Groningen, 23–71.

Ackerman, Farrell. 1987. *Miscreant Morphemes: Phrasal Predicates in Ugric.* Doctoral Dissertation, University of California, Berkeley.

Ackerman, Farrell and Philip LeSourd. 1994a. Preverbs in Hungarian and Fox. Unpublished manuscript, University of California at San Diego.

Ackerman, Farrell and Philip LeSourd. 1994b. Preverbs and Complex Predicates: Dimensions of Wordhood. *Proceedings of West Coast Conference of Linguistics,* 1–16.

Ackerman, Farrell and Philip LeSourd. 1997. Toward A Lexical Representation of Phrasal Predicates. In Alex Alsina, Joan Bresnan, and Peter Sells, eds., *Complex Predicates : Structure and Theory.* (CSLI Lecture Notes No. 64.) Stanford, Calif.: CSLI Publications, 67–106.

Ackerman, Farrell and John Moore. 1994. Valence and the Semantics of Causativization. In *Proceedings of the Twentieth Annual Meeting of the Berkeley Linguistics Society.* Berkeley: Berkeley Linguistics Society, 1–13.

Ackerman, Farrell and John Moore. Forthcoming. *Proto-properties and Grammatical Encoding.* Stanford, Calif.: CSLI Publications.

Ackerman, Farrell and Gert Webelhuth. In press. The Composition of (Dis)continuous Predicates: Lexical or Syntactic? *Acta Linguistica Hungarica.*

Adams, Douglas Q. 1987. *Essential Modern Greek Grammar.* New York: Dover Publications.

Aissen, Judith. 1979. *The Syntax of Causative Constructions.* New York: Garland. [1974. Doctoral dissertation, Harvard University.]

Aissen, Judith. 1987. *Tzotzil Clause Structure.* (Studies in Natural Language and Linguistic Theory, Vol. 7.) Dordrecht: D. Reidel.

Aissen, Judith. 1994. Tzotzil Auxiliaries. *Linguistics* 32.4/5, 657–690.

Aissen, Judith L. and David M. Perlmutter. 1983. Clause Reduction in Spanish. In David M. Perlmutter, ed., *Studies in Relational Grammar 1.* Chicago: University of Chicago Press, 360–403.

Alsina, Alex. 1992. On the Argument Structure of Causatives. *Linguistic Inquiry* 23.4, 517–555.

Alsina, Alex. 1993. *Predicate Composition: A Theory of Syntactic Function Alternations.* Doctoral dissertation, Stanford University.

Alsina, Alex. 1996. Resultatives: a Joint Operation of Semantic and Syntactic Structures. In Miriam Butt and Tracy Holloway King, eds., *On-line Proceedings of the First LFG Conference, Rank Xerox, Grenoble, August 26–28, 1996.* <http://www-csli.stanford. edu/ publications/LFG/lfg1.html>.

Andersen, Henning. 1980. Morphological Change: Towards a Typology. In Jacek Fisiak, ed., *Historical Morphology.* The Hague: Mouton, 1–50.

Anderson, Stephen R. 1992. *A-Morphous Morphology.* (Cambridge Studies in Linguistics 62.) Cambridge: Cambridge University Press.

Andersson, Anders-Borje and Östen Dahl. 1974. Against the Penthouse Principle. *Linguistic Inquiry* 5, 451–453.

Aronoff, Mark. 1976. *Word Formation in Generative Grammar.* Cambridge, Mass.: MIT Press.

Aronoff, Mark. 1994. *Morphology by Itself: Stems and Inflectional Classes.* Cambridge, Mass.: MIT Press.

Austin, Peter and Joan Bresnan. 1996. Non-configurationality in Australian Aboriginal Languages. *Natural Language and Linguistic Theory* 14.2, 215–268.

Bach, Emmon. 1983. On the Relationship between Word-grammar and Phrase-grammar. *Natural Language and Linguistic Theory* 1.1, 65–89.

Baker, Mark C. 1988. *Incorporation: A Theory of Grammatical Function Changing.* Chicago: University of Chicago Press.

Baker, Mark, Kyle Johnson, and Ian Roberts. 1989. Passive Arguments Raised. *Linguistic Inquiry* 20.2, 219–251.

Beard, Robert. 1981. *The Indo-European Lexicon: A Full Synchronic Theory.* (North Holland Linguistics Series. no. 44.) Amsterdam: North Holland.

Beard, Robert. 1995. *Lexeme-Morpheme Base Morphology.* (SUNY Series in Linguistics.) Albany: State University of New York Press.

Behagel, Otto. 1932. *Deutsche Syntax: Eine Geschichtliche Darstellung.* Heidelberg: Carl Winters Universitätsbuchhandlung.

Behrens, Leila. 1995/1996. Lexical Rules Cross-Cutting Inflection and Derivation. *Acta Linguistica Hungarica* 43.1/2, 33–65.

Bell, Sarah J. 1983. Advancements and Ascensions in Cebuano. In David M. Perlmutter, ed., *Studies in Relational Grammar 1.* Chicago: University of Chicago Press, 143–218.

Benmamoun, Elabbas. 1992. *Functional and Inflectional Morphology: Problems of Projection, Representation, and Derivation.* Doctoral dissertation, University of Southern California.

Besten, Johannes Bernardus den. 1989. *Studies in West Germanic Syntax.* Amsterdam: Rodopi.

Bierwisch, Manfred. 1990. Verb Cluster Formation as a Morphological Process. *Yearbook of Morphology* 3, 173–199.

Bittner, Maria and Ken Hale. 1996. The Structural Determination of Case and Agreement. *Linguistic Inquiry* 27.1, 1–68.

Blevins, James P. 1995. Syncretism and Paradigmatic Opposition. *Linguistics and Philosophy* 18.2, 113–152.

Bloomfield, Leonard. 1925–1927. Notes on the Fox Language. *International Journal of American Linguistics* 3, 219–232; 4, 181–219.

Bochner, Harry. 1993. *Simplicity in Generative Morphology*. Berlin: Mouton de Gruyter.

Bodomo, Adams B. 1996. Complex Verbal Predicates: The Case of Serial Verbs in Dagaare and Akan. In Miriam Butt and Tracy Holloway King, eds., *On-line Proceedings of the First LFG Conference, Rank Xerox, Grenoble, August 26–28, 1996*. <http://www-csli. stanford.edu/publications/LFG/lfg1.html>.

Bodomo, Adams B. 1997. *Paths and Pathfinders: Exploring the Syntax and Semantics of Complex Verbal Predicates in Dagaare and Other Languages*. Doctoral dissertation, Norwegian University of Science and Technology.

Booij, Geert. 1990. The Boundary between Morphology and Syntax: Separable Complex Verbs in Dutch. *Yearbook of Morphology* 3, 45–63.

Börjárs, Kersti, Nigel Vincent, and Carol Chapman. 1996. Paradigms, Periphrases and Pronominal Inflection: A Feature-based Account. *Yearbook of Morphology* 155–180.

Bowers, John. 1993. The Syntax of Predication. *Linguistic Inquiry* 24.4, 591–656.

Bresnan, Joan. 1982a. The Passive in Lexical Theory. In Joan Bresnan, 1982b, 3–86.

Bresnan, Joan. 1982b, ed., *The Mental Representation of Grammatical Relations*. Cambridge, Mass.: MIT Press.

Bresnan, Joan. 1994. Locative Inversion and the Architecture of Universal-Grammar. *Language* 70.1, 72–131

Bresnan, Joan. 1995. Category Mismatches. In Akinbiyi Akinlabi, ed., *Theoretical Approaches to African Linguistics*. Trenton, N.J.: Africa World Press, 19–46.

Bresnan, Joan. To appear a. Explaining Morphosyntactic Competition. In Mark Baltin and Chris Collins, eds., *Handbook of Contemporary Syntactic Theory*. Blackwell Publishers. <http://www-csli.stanford.edu/~bresnan/download.html>.

Bresnan, Joan. To appear b. Optimal Syntax. In Joost Dekkers, Frank van der Leeuw, and Jeroen van de Weijer, eds., *The Pointing Finger: Conceptual Studies in Optimality Theory*.

Bresnan, Joan. Forthcoming. *Lexical Functional Syntax*.

Bresnan, Joan and Jonni M. Kanerva. 1989. Locative Inversion in Chichewa: A Case Study of Factorization in Grammar. *Linguistic Inquiry* 20.1, 1–50.

Bresnan, Joan, and Sam A. Mchombo. 1995. The Lexical Integrity Principle: Evidence from Bantu. *Natural Language and Linguistic Theory* 13.2, 181–254.

Brinker, Klaus. 1971. *Das Passiv im heutigen Deutsch: Form und Funktion.* München: Hueber.

Burzio, Luigi. 1986. *Italian Syntax: A Government-Binding Approach.* Dordrecht: D. Reidel.

Butt, Miriam. 1995. *The Structure of Complex Predicates in Urdu.* (Dissertations in Linguistics.) Stanford, Calif.: CSLI Publications.

Butt, Miriam, Maria-Eugenia Niño, and Frederique Segond. 1996. Multilingual Processing of Auxiliaries in LFG. In Dafydd Gibbon, ed., *Natural Language Processing and Speech Technology: Results of the 3rd KONVENS Conference.* Berlin: Mouton De Gruyter, 111–122.

Bybee, Joan L. 1985. *Morphology: A Study of the Relation between Meaning and Form.* Amsterdam: John Benjamins.

Bybee, Joan L., Revere D. Perkins, and William Pagliuca. 1994. *The Evolution of Grammar: Tense, Aspect, and Modality in the Languages of the World.* Chicago: The University of Chicago Press.

Carstairs, Andrew. 1987. *Allomorphy in Inflexion.* London: Croom Helm.

Chomsky, Noam. 1957. *Syntactic Structures.* The Hague: Mouton.

Chomsky, Noam. 1965. *Aspects of the Theory of Syntax.* Cambridge, Mass.: MIT Press.

Chomsky, Noam. 1970. Remarks on Nominalization. In Roderick A. Jacobs and Peter S. Rosenbaum, eds., *Readings in English Transformational Grammar.* Waltham, Mass.: Ginn, 184–221.

Chomsky, Noam. 1981. *Lectures on Government and Binding.* Dordrecht: Foris.

Chomsky, Noam. 1982. *Some Concepts and Consequences of the Theory of Government and Binding.* Cambridge, Mass.: MIT Press.

Chomsky, Noam. 1995. A Minimalist Program for Linguistic Theory. In Noam Chomsky, *The Minimalist Program*. Cambridge, Mass.: MIT Press, pp. 167–217.

Chomsky, Noam. 1996. Some Observations on Economy in Generative Grammar. Unpublished manuscript, MIT.

Clark, Andy. 1993. *Associative Engines: Connectionism, Concepts, and Representational Change*. Cambridge, Mass.: MIT Press.

Clements, George N. and Samuel Jay Keyser. 1983. *CV Phonology: A Generative Theory of the Syllable*. Cambridge, Mass.: MIT Press.

Cole, Peter. 1983. The Grammatical Role of the Causee in Universal Grammar. *International Journal of American Linguistics* 49.2, 115–133.

Collins, Chris and Höskuldur Thráinsson. 1996. VP-Internal Structure and Object Shift in Icelandic. *Linguistic Inquiry* 27.3, 391–444.

Comrie, Bernard. 1975. Causatives and Universal Grammar. *Transactions of the Philological Society* 1974, 1–32.

Comrie, Bernard. 1976. The Syntax of Causative Constructions: Cross-Language Similarities and Divergences. In Masayoshi Shibatani, ed., *The Grammar of Causative Constructions*. (Syntax and Semantics, Vol. 6.) New York: Academic Press, 261–312.

Comrie, Bernard. 1981. *Language Universals and Linguistic Typology: Syntax and Morphology*. Chicago: University of Chicago Press.

Copestake, Ann. 1992. *The Representation of Lexical Semantic Information*. (Cognitive Science Research Papers 280.) Brighton: University of Sussex.

Corver, Norbert. 1997. *Much*-Support as a Last Resort. *Linguistic Inquiry* 28.1, 119–164.

Curry, Haskel. 1961. Some Logical Aspects of Grammatical Structure. In Roman Jacobson, ed., *Structure of Language and its Mathematical Aspects: Proceedings of the 12th Symposium in Applied Mathematics*. Providence: American Mathematical Society, 56–68.

Dahlstrom, Amy. 1987. Discontinuous Constituents in Fox. In Paul D. Kroeber and Robert E. Moore, eds., *Native American Languages and Grammatical Typology: Papers from a Conference at the University of Chicago, April 22, 1987*. Bloomington, Ind.: Indiana University Linguistics Club, 53–73.

Dahlstrom, Amy. 1991. *Plains Cree Morphosyntax.* New York: Garland. [1986. Doctoral dissertation, University of California, Berkeley.]

Dalrymple, Mary. 1993. *The Syntax of Anaphoric Binding.* (CSLI Lecture Notes No. 36.) Stanford, Calif.: CSLI Publications.

Davies, William and Carol Rosen. 1988. Unions as Multi-predicate Clauses. *Language* 64.1, 52–88.

Davis, Anthony. 1997. *Lexical Semantics and Linking and the Hierarchical Lexicon.* Doctoral dissertation, Stanford University.

Décsy, Gyula. 1966. *Yurak Chrestomathy.* (Indiana University publications. Uralic and Altaic series, v. 50; Indiana University. Uralic and Altaic series 50.) Bloomington: Indiana University.

Di Sciullo, Anne-Marie, and Edwin Williams. 1987. *On the Definition of Word.* Cambridge, Mass.: MIT Press.

Dixon, R.M.W., ed., 1976. *Grammatical Categories in Australian Languages.* (Linguistic Series No. 22.) Canberra: Australian Institute of Aboriginal Studies.

Dowty, David R. 1979. *Word Meaning and Montague Grammar: The Semantics of Verbs and Times in Generative Semantics and in Montague's PTQ.* Dordrecht: Reidel.

Dowty, David. 1991. Thematic Proto-roles and Argument Selection. *Language* 67.3, 547–619.

Dowty, David. 1996. Towards a Minimalist Theory of Syntactic Structure. In Harry C. Bunt and Arthur van Horck, eds., *Discontinuous Constituency.* Berlin: Mouton, 11–62.

Fagan, Sarah M. B. 1996. Tests for Unaccusativity Revisited. Paper presented at the Second Germanic Linguistics Annual Conference, University of Wisconsin, Madison.

Fagan, Sarah M. B. 1997a. Split Intransitivity in German and the Unaccusative Hypothesis. Paper presented at the Third Germanic Linguistics Annual Conference, University of California, Los Angeles.

Fagan, Sarah M. B. 1997b. Unaccusativity in German. Unpublished manuscript, University of Iowa.

Falk, Yehuda N. 1984. The English Auxiliary System: A Lexical-Functional Analysis. *Language* 60.3, 483–509.

Fillmore, Charles and Paul Kay. 1996. *Construction Grammar.* Unpublished manuscript, University of California at Berkeley.

Frank, Anette. 1996. A Note on Complex Predicate Formation: Evidence from Auxiliary Selection, Reflexivization, and Past Participle Agreement in French and Italian. In Miriam Butt and Tracy Holloway King, eds., *On-line Proceedings of the First LFG Conference, Rank Xerox, Grenoble, August 26–28, 1996.* <http://www-csli. stanford.edu/publications/LFG/lfg1.html>.

Freidin, Robert. 1997. Review Article: The Minimalist Program. *Language* 73.3, 571–582.

Friederich, Wolf. 1976. *Moderne Deutsche Idiomatik.* Ismaning: Max Hueber.

George, Leland and Jaklin Kornfilt. 1977. Infinitival Double Passives in Turkish. *Proceedings of the Annual Meeting of the North Eastern Linguistic Society,* 65–79.

Gibson, Jeanne D. 1992. *Clause Union in Chamorro and in Universal Grammar.* New York: Garland. [1980. Doctoral dissertation, University of California at San Diego.]

Gibson, Jeanne and Eduardo Raposo. 1986. Clause Union, the Stratal Uniqueness Law and the Chomeur Relation. *Natural Language and Linguistic Theory* 4.3, 295–331.

Ginzburg, J. and Ivan Sag. Forthcoming. *English Interrogative Constructions.*

Goddard, Ives. 1987. Fox Participles. In Paul D. Kroeber and Robert E. Moore, eds., *Native American Languages and Grammatical Typology: Papers from a Conference at the University of Chicago, April 22, 1987.* Bloomington, Ind.: Indiana University Linguistics Club, 105–118.

Goddard, Ives. 1988. Post-transformational Stem Derivation in Fox. *Papers and Studies in Contrastive Linguistics* 22, 59–72.

Goddard, Ives. 1990a. Paradigmatic Relationships. *Proceedings of the Sixteenth Annual Meeting of the Berkeley Linguistics Society, February 16–19, 1990: Special Session on General Topics in American Indian Linguistics.* Berkeley: Berkeley Linguistics Society, 39–50.

Goddard, Ives. 1990b. Primary and Secondary Stem Derivation in Algonquian. *International Journal of American Linguistics* 56.4, 449–483.

Goldberg, Adele E. 1995. *Constructions: a Construction Grammar Approach to Argument Structure.* (Cognitive Theory of Language and Culture.) Chicago: University of Chicago Press.

Gould, James L. and Peter Marler 1987. "Learning by Instinct": Reply. *Scientific American* 256.4, 62–73.

Green, Georgia M. 1997. Modeling Grammar Growth: Universal Grammar without Innate Principles or Parameters. Paper presented at GALA97 conference on language acquisition, Edinburgh, April 4–6, 1997. <http://lees.cogsci.uiuc.edu/~green/>.

Greenberg, Joseph H. ed. 1978. *Universals of Human Language.* Stanford, Calif. : Stanford University Press.

Grimshaw, Jane. To appear. Extended Projection and Locality. In Peter Coopmans, Martin Everaert, and Jane Grimshaw, eds., *Lexical Structure.* Erlbaum.

Gross, Maurice. 1979. On the Failure of Generative Grammar. *Language* 55, 859–85.

Hajdú, Péter. 1968. *Chrestomathia Samoiedica.* Budapest: Tankönyvkiadó.

Hajdú, Péter. 1982. The Negative Auxiliary in Samoyed. In Ferenc Kiefer, ed., *Hungarian Linguistics.* (Linguistic and Literary Studies in Eastern Europe, Vol. 4.) Amsterdam: Benjamins, 109–130.

Hale, Ken. 1983. Warlpiri and the Grammar of Non-configurational Languages. *Natural Language and Linguistic Theory* 1.1, 5–47.

Harris, Alice C. 1981. *Georgian Syntax: A Study in Relational Grammar.* Cambridge: Cambridge University Press.

Harris, Alice C. and Lyle Campbell. 1995. *Historical Syntax in Cross-linguistic Perspective.* Cambridge: Cambridge University Press.

Haspelmath, Martin. 1990. The Grammaticization of Passive Morphology. *Studies in Language* 14.1, 25–72.

Hawkins, John A. 1983. *Word Order Universals.* New York : Academic Press.

Heine, Bernd. 1993. *Auxiliaries: Cognitive Forces and Grammaticalization.* New York: Oxford University Press.

Helbig, Gerhard and Wolfgang Schenkel. 1980. *Wörterbuch zur Valenz und Distribution deutscher Verben.* Leipzig: VEB Bibliographisches Institut.

Hendrick, Randall. 1991. The Morphosyntax of Aspect. *Lingua* 85, 171–210.

Hinrichs, Erhard and Tsuneko Nakazawa. 1989. Flipped Out: AUX in German. *CLS 25: Papers from 25th Annual Regional Meeting of Chicago Linguistic Society.* Chicago: Chicago Linguistic Society, 193–202.

Hinrichs, Erhard and Tsuneko Nakazawa. 1994. Linearizing Finite AUX in German Verbal Complexes. In John A. Nerbonne, Klaus Netter, and Carl Jesse Pollard, eds., *German in Head-Driven Phrase Structure Grammar.* Stanford: CSLI Publications, 11–38.

Höhle, Tilman N. 1978. *Lexikalistische Syntax: Die aktiv-passiv Relation and andere Infinitkonstruktionen im Deutschen.* Tübingen: Niemeyer Verlag.

Hoeksema, Jack. 1991. Complex Predicates and Liberation in Dutch and English. *Linguistics and Philosophy* 14.6, 661–710.

Hooper, Joan B. 1972. The Syllable in Phonological Theory. *Language* 48, 525–540.

Hopper, Paul J. and Elizabeth Closs Traugott. 1993. *Grammaticalization.* Cambridge: Cambridge University Press.

Ishikawa, Akira. 1985. *Complex Predicates and Lexical Operations in Japanese.* Doctoral dissertation, Stanford University.

Jackendoff, Ray. 1975. Morphological and Semantic Regularities in the Lexicon. *Language* 51, 639–671.

Jackendoff, Ray S. 1987. *Consciousness and the Computational Mind.* Cambridge, Mass.: MIT Press.

Jackendoff, Ray. 1995. The Boundaries of the Lexicon. In Martin Everaert, Erik-Jan van der Linden, Andre Schenk, and Rob Schreuder, eds., *Idioms: Structural and Psychological Perspectives.* Hillsdale, N.J.: Erlbaum. 133–166.

Jackendoff, Ray. 1997. *The Architecture of the Language Faculty.* Cambridge, Mass.: MIT Press.

Jaeggli, Osvaldo A. 1986. Passive. *Linguistic Inquiry* 17.4, 587–622.

Jaeggli, Osvaldo and Kenneth J. Safir. 1989. The Null Subject Parameter and Parametric Theory. In Osvaldo Jaeggli and Kenneth J. Safir, eds., *The Null Subject Parameter.* (Studies in Natural Language & Linguistic Theory. Series No: 15.) Dordrecht: Foris, 1–44.

Jartseva, V. 1963. Ob Analticheskix Formax Slova. In Viktor Maksimovich Zhirmunskii and O.P. Sunik, eds., *Morfologicheskaia Struktura Slova V Iazykakh Razlichnykh Tipov.* Moscow: Izd-vo Akademii nauk SSSR, 52–60.

Johns, Alana. 1992. Deriving Ergativity. *Linguistic Inquiry* 23.1, 57–88.

Johnson, Kyle. 1991. Object Positions. *Natural Language and Linguistic Theory* 9.4, 577–636.

Jones, William. 1904. Some Principles of Algonquian Word Formation. *American Anthropologist* 6, 369–411.

Jones, William. 1911. Algonquian (Fox): An Illustrative Sketch. In Franz Boas, ed., *Handbook of American Indian Languages. Part 1.* (Smithsonian Institution, Bureau of American Ethnology, Handbook of American Indian languages; Bulletin 40, Part 1.) Washington, D.C.: Government Printing Office, 735–873.

Jusczyk, Peter W. 1993. From General to Language-Specific Capacities: The WRAPSA Model of How Speech Perception Develops. *Journal of Phonetics* 21.1–2, 3–28.

Jusczyk. Peter W. 1997. *The Discovery of Spoken Language.* Cambridge, Mass.: MIT Press.

Jusczyk, Peter W. and Josiane Bertoncini. 1988. Viewing the Development of Speech Perception as an Innately Guided Learning Process. *Language and Speech* 31.3, 217–238.

Kahn, Daniel . 1976. *Syllable-based Generalizations in English Phonology.* Doctoral dissertation, Massachusetts Institute of Technology.

Kálmán, C. G., et al. 1989. A Magyar Segédigék Rendszere. [The Hungarian Auxiliary System]. *Általános Nyelvészeti Tanulmányok* 17, 49–103.

Kamp, Hans and Uwe Reyle. 1993. *From Discourse to Logic. Introduction to Modeltheoretic Semantics of Natural Language, Formal Logic and Discourse Representation Theory.* Dordrecht: Kluwer.

Kaplan, Ronald M. 1989. The Formal Architecture of Lexical-Functional Grammar. In Chu-Ren Huang and Keh-Jiann Chen, eds., *Proceedings of the Republic of China Computational Linguistics Conference (ROCLING II)*. Taipei: Academia Sinica, 3–18. [1995. Mary Dalrymple, Ronald M. Kaplan, John Maxwell, and Annie Zaenen, eds., *Formal Issues in Lexical-Functional Grammar*. Stanford: Center for the Study of Language and Information, 7–27.]

Kaplan, Ronald M. and Joan Bresnan. 1982. Lexical-Functional Grammar: A Formal System for Grammatical Representation. In Joan Bresnan, 1982b, 173–281. [1995. In Mary Dalrymple, Ronald M. Kaplan, John Maxwell, and Annie Zaenen, eds., *Formal Issues in Lexical-Functional Grammar*. Stanford, Calif.: Center for the Study of Language and Information, 29–130.]

Karanko-Pap, Outi, Maria Vilkua, and László Keresztés. 1980. *Finn Nyelvkönyv*. Tankönyvkiadó, Budapest.

Karmiloff-Smith, Annette. 1992. *Beyond Modularity: A Developmental Perspective on Cognitive Science*. Cambridge, Mass.: MIT Press.

Kasper, Robert T. To appear. The Semantics of Recursive Modification. *Journal of Linguistics*.

Kathol, Andreas. 1994. Passives Without Lexical Rules. In John Nerbonne et al., eds., *German in Head-Driven Phrase Structure Grammar*. Stanford, Calif.: CSLI Publications, 237–272.

Kathol, Andreas. 1995. *Linearization-Based German Syntax*. Doctoral dissertation, Ohio State University.

Keenan, Edward L. 1985. Passive in the World's Languages. In Timothy Shopen, ed., *Language Typology and Syntactic Description, Volume 1, Clause Structure*. Cambridge: Cambridge University Press, 243–281.

Keenan, Edward and Timberlake, Alan. 1985. Predicate Formation Rules in Universal Grammar. In Jeffrey Goldberg et al., eds., *West Coast Conference on Formal Linguistics* 4, 123–138.

Kenstowicz, Michael J. 1994. *Phonology in Generative Grammar*. Cambridge, Mass.: Blackwell.

Keresztés, László. 1990. *Chrestomathia Morduinica*. Budapest: Tankönyvkiadó.

Kim, Dae-Bin. 1992. *The Specificity/Non-Specificity Distinction and Scrambling Theory.* Doctoral dissertation, University of Wisconsin, Madison.

King, Tracy Holloway. 1995. *Configuring Topic and Focus in Russian.* (Dissertations in Linguistics.) Stanford, Calif.: CSLI Publications.

Kiparsky, Paul. 1973. Abstractness, Opacity, and Global Rules. In *Three Dimensions of Linguistic Theory.* Tokyo: TEC, 57–86.

Kiparsky, Paul. 1987. Morphology and Grammatical Relations. Unpublished manuscript, Stanford University.

Kiss, Katalin É. 1987. *Configurationality in Hungarian.* Dordrecht: D. Reidel.

Kneale, William Calvert and Martha Kneale. 1962. *The Development of Logic.* Oxford: Clarendon Press.

Kroeger, Paul. 1993. *Phrase Structure and Grammatical Relations in Tagalog.* (Dissertations in Linguistics.) Stanford, Calif.: CSLI Publications.

Kulonen, Ulla-Maija. 1989. *The Passive in Ob-Ugrian.* Helsinki: Suomalais-Ugrilainen Seura.

Lapointe, Steven. 1985 *A Theory of Grammatical Agreement.* New York: Garland. [1980. Doctoral dissertation, University of Massachusetts, Amherst.]

Levin, Beth and Malka Rappaport-Hovav. 1997. From Lexical Semantics to Argument Realization. In Hagit Borer, ed., *Handbook of Morphosyntax and Argument Structure.* Dordrecht: Kluwer.

Levin, Juliette. 1985. *A Metrical Theory of Syllabicity.* Doctoral dissertation, Massachusetts Institute of Technology.

Lieber, Rochelle. 1992. *Deconstructing Morphology: Word Formation in Syntactic Theory.* Chicago: University of Chicago Press.

Mahajan, Anoop Kumar. 1990. *The A/A-bar Distinction And Movement Theory.* Doctoral dissertation, Massachusetts Institute of Technology.

Maling, Joan. 1993. Of Nominative and Accusative: The Hierarchical Assignment of Grammatical Case in Finnish. In Anders Holmberg and Urpo Nikanne, eds., *Case and Other Functional Categories in Finnish Syntax.* Berlin: Mouton de Gruyter. 50–74.

Manandise, Esméralda. 1988. *Evidence from Basque for a New Theory of Grammar.* New York: Garland.

Mandler, Jean M. 1992. How to Build a Baby II: Conceptual Primitives. *Psychological Review* 99.4, 587–604.

Manning, Christopher D. 1996. *Ergativity: Argument Structure and Grammatical Relations.* Stanford, Calif.: CSLI Publications. [1994. Doctoral dissertation, Stanford University.]

Marantz, Alec. 1984. *On the Nature of Grammatical Relations.* Cambridge: MIT Press.

Marantz, Alec. 1992. Case and Licensing. In German F. Westphal, Benjamin Ao, and Hee-Rahk Chae, eds., *ESCOL '91: Proceedings of the Eighth Eastern States Conference on Linguistics.* Columbus: Ohio State University, 234–253.

Marantz, Alec. 1995. The Minimalist Program. In Gert Webelhuth, 1995a, 349–382.

Marler, Peter. 1990. Innate Learning Preferences: Signals for Communication. *Developmental Psychobiology* 23.7, 557–568.

Matsumoto, Yo. 1992. *On the Wordhood of Complex Predicates in Japanese.* Doctoral dissertation, Stanford University.

Matsumoto, Yo. 1996. *Complex Predicates in Japanese: A Syntactic and Semantic Study of the Notion 'Word'.* (Studies in Japanese Linguistics.) Stanford, Calif.: CSLI Publications.

Matthews, P. H. 1972. *Inflectional Morphology: A Theoretical Study Based on Aspects of Latin Verb Conjugation.* Cambridge: Cambridge University Press.

Matthews, Peter H. 1991. *Morphology.* 2nd. ed. Cambridge: Cambridge University Press.

Mayerthaler, Willi. 1981. *Morphologische Natürlichkeit.* (Linguistische Forschungen, Bd. 28.) Wiesbaden: Akademische Verlagsgesellschaft Athenaion.

Mehler, Jacques and Emmanuel Dupoux. 1994. *What Infants Know: The New Cognitive Science of Early Development.* Cambridge, Mass.: Blackwell.

Meshchaninov, I. I. 1982 [1948]. *Glagol.* Leningrad: "Nauka," Leningradskoe otd-nie.

Michaelson, Truman. 1917. Notes on Algonquian Languages. *International Journal of American Linguistics* 1, 50–57.

Michaelson, Truman. 1925. Accompanying Papers. *Bureau of American Ethnology Annual Reports* 40, 21–658.

Mohanan, K. P. 1982. Grammatical Relations and Clause Structure in Malayalam. In Joan Bresnan, 1982b, 504–589.

Mohanan, K. P. 1983. Move NP or Lexical Rules? Evidence from Malayalam Causativization. In Lori Levin, Malka Rappaport and Annie Zaenen, eds., *Papers in Lexical-Functional Grammar.* Bloomington, Ind.: Indiana University Linguistics Club, 47–111.

Mohanan, Tara Warrier. 1994. *Argument Structure in Hindi.* Stanford, Calif.: CSLI Publications. [1990. *Arguments in Hindi.* Doctoral dissertation, Stanford University.]

Mohanan, Tara. 1995. Wordhood and Lexicality: Noun Incorporation in Hindi. *Natural Language and Linguistic Theory,* 13.1, 75–134.

Mugane, John Muratha. 1996. *Bantu Nominalization Structures.* Doctoral dissertation, University of Arizona.

Napoli, Donna Jo. 1989. *Predication Theory : A Case Study for Indexing Theory.* Cambridge: Cambridge University Press.

Nash, David. 1982. Verb Roots and Preverbs. In S. Swartz, ed., *Papers in Warlpiri Grammar: in Memory of Lothar Jagst.* (Work Papers of SIL-AAB. Series A, Vol. 6.) Darwin: Summer Institute of Linguistics, Australian Aborigines Branch, 165–216.

Neeleman, Ad. 1994. *Complex Predicates.* Doctoral dissertation, Utrecht University.

Neeleman, Ad and Fred Weerman. 1993. The Balance Between Syntax and Morphology: Dutch Particles and Resultatives. *Natural Language and Linguistic Theory* 11.3, 433–475.

Nevis, Joel Ashmore. 1988. On the Development of the Clitic Postposition Category in Estonian. *Finnisch-Ugrische Forschungen: Zeitschrift fur finnisch-ugrische Sprach- und Volkskunde* 48.2-3, 171–197.

Nichols, Johanna. 1986. Head-marking and Dependent-marking Grammar. *Language* 62.1, 56–119.

Niño, Maria-Eugenia. 1995. A Morphologically-based Approach to Split Inflection in Finnish. Unpublished manuscript, Stanford University.

Niño, Maria-Eugenia. 1997. Split Inflection and the Architecture of Grammar: The Case of Finnish Verbal Morphology. Unpublished manuscript, Stanford University.

Nordlinger, Rachel. 1995. Split Tense and Mood Inflection in Wambaya. In *The Twenty-First Annual Meeting of the Berkeley Linguistics Society, February 17–20, 1995.* Berkeley, Calif.: Berkeley Linguistics Society, 226–236.

Nordlinger, Rachel and Joan Bresnan. 1996. Nonconfigurational Tense in Wambaya. In Miriam Butt and Tracy Holloway King, eds., *On-line Proceedings of the First LFG Conference, Rank Xerox, Grenoble, August 26–28, 1996.* <http://www-csli.stanford.edu/publications/ LFG/lfg1.html>.

O'Connor, Mary Catherine. 1992. *Topics in Northern Pomo Grammar.* New York: Garland. [1987. Doctoral dissertation, University of California, Berkeley.]

Orgun, Orhan. 1995. Sign Based Morphology. Unpublished manuscript, University of California, Berkeley.

Orgun, Cemil Orhan. 1996. *Sign-Based Morphology and Phonology with Special Attention to Optimality Theory.* Doctoral dissertation, University of California at Berkeley.

Perlmutter, David. 1979. Predicate: A Grammatical Relation. In Philip Hubbard and Peter M. Tiersma, eds., *Linguistic Notes from La Jolla,* 127–150.

Perlmutter, David M. and Paul M. Postal. 1977. Toward a Universal Characterization of Passivization. In *Proceedings of the 3rd Annual Meeting of the Berkeley Linguistics Society.* Berkeley: Berkeley Linguistics Society, 394–417.

Pesetsky, David Michael. 1982. *Paths and Categories.* Doctoral dissertation, MIT.

Pesetsky, David. 1989. Language-Particular Processes and the Earliness Principle. Unpublished manuscript, Massachusetts Institute of Technology.

Plunkett, Kim and Virginia Marchman. 1991. U-shaped Learning and Frequency Effects in a Multi-layered Perceptron: Implications for Child Language Acquisition. *Cognition* 38.1, 43–102.

Plunkett, Kim and Virginia Marchman. 1993. From Rote Learning to System Building: Acquiring Verb Morphology in Children and Connectionist Nets. *Cognition* 48.1, 21–69.

Polinsky, Maria. 1995. Double Objects in Causatives: Towards a Study of Coding Conflict. *Studies in Language* 19.1, 129–221.

Pollard, Carl and Ivan A. Sag. 1987. *Information-based Syntax and Semantics.* (CSLI Lecture Notes No. 13.) Stanford Calif.: Center for the Study of Language and Information.

Pollard, Carl and Ivan A. Sag. 1994. *Head-Driven Phrase Structure Grammar.* Stanford, Calif.: Center for the Study of Language and Information.

Pollock, Jean-Yves. 1989. Verb Movement, Universal Grammar, and the Structure of IP. *Linguistic Inquiry* 20.3, 365–424.

Postal, Paul M. and Geoffrey K. Pullum. 1988. Expletive Noun Phrases in Subcategorized Positions. *Linguistic Inquiry* 19.4, 635–670.

Przepiórkowski, Adam. 1997. On Case Assignment and "Adjuncts as Complements". Unpublished manuscript, University of Tübingen.

Pullum, Geoffrey K. and Arnold M. Zwicky. 1988. The Syntax-Phonology Interface. In Frederick J. Newmeyer, ed., *Linguistics: The Cambridge Survey, Volume 1, Linguistic Theory: Foundations.* Cambridge: Cambridge University Press, 255–280.

Reape, Mike. 1992. *A Theory of Word Order in Germanic Languages.* Doctoral dissertation, University of Edinburgh.

Reis, Marga. 1976. Reflexivierung in Deutschen A.c.I.-Konstruktionen. Ein transformationsgrammatisches Dilemma. *Papiere zur Linguistik* 9, 5–82.

Riehemann, Susanne. 1993. *Word Formation in Lexical Type Hierarchies: A Case Study of Bar-Adjectives in German.* Master's thesis, University of Tübingen.

Riehemann, Susanne. To appear. Type-Based Derivational Morphology. *Journal of Comparative Germanic Linguistics.*

Ritter, Elizabeth. 1991. Two Functional Categories in Noun Phrases: Evidence from Modern Hebrew. In Susan D. Rothstein, ed., *Perspectives on Phrase Structure: Heads and Licensing.* (Syntax and Semantics, Vol. 25). San Diego: Academic Press, 37–62.

Rombandeeva, E.I. 1973. *Mansiiskii (Vogul'skii) Iazyk.* Moscow: Akademii Nauk SSSR.

Rosen, Sara Thomas. 1990. *Argument Structure and Complex Predicates.* New York: Garland. [1989. Doctoral dissertation, Brandeis University.]

Rumelhart, David and Jay McClelland. 1986. On Learning the Past Tenses of English Verbs: Implicit Rules or Parallel Distributed Processing. In James L. McClelland, David E. Rumelhart, and the PDP Research Group, eds., *Parallel Distributed Processing: Explorations in the Microstructure of Cognition, Volume 2. Psychological and Biological Models.* Cambridge, Mass.: MIT Press, 216–271. [1994. In Paul Bloom, ed., *Language Acquisition: Core Readings.* Cambridge, Mass.: MIT Press, 423–471.]

Ruwet, Nicolas. 1991. *Syntax and Human Experience.* Chicago: The University of Chicago Press.

Sadler, Louisa. 1997. Clitics and the Structure-Function Mapping. In Miriam Butt and Tracy Holloway King, eds., *Proceedings of the LFG97 Conference.* <http://www-csli.stanford.edu/publications/ LFG2/lfg97.html>.

Sadock, Jerrold M. 1991. *Autolexical Syntax: A Theory of Parallel Grammatical Representations.* Chicago: University of Chicago Press.

Sag, Ivan. 1997. English Relative Clause Constructions. *Journal of Linguistics* 33.2, 431–483.

Sapir, Edward. 1924. The Grammarian and His Language. *American Mercury* 1, 149–155.

Saussure, Ferdinand de. 1986 [1922]. *Course in General Linguistics.* La Salle, Ill.: Open Court Press.

Sells, Peter. To appear a. Optimality and Economy of Expression in Japanese and Korean. In *Proceedings of the 7th Japanese/Korean Conference.* Stanford, Calif.: CSLI Publications.

Sells, Peter. To appear b. Positional Constraints and Faithfulness in Morphology. In S. Kuno et al., eds., *Harvard Studies in Korean Linguistics, Volume 7.* Cambridge, Mass.: Harvard University.

Shlonsky, Ur. 1989. The Hierarchical Representation of Subject-Verb Agreement. Unpublished manuscript, University of Haifa, Israel.

Simpson, Jane Helen. 1991. *Walpiri Morpho-syntax: A Lexicalist Approach.* Dordrecht: Kluwer Academic Publishers. [1983. *Aspects of Warlpiri Morphology and Syntax.* Doctoral dissertation, Massachusetts Institute of Technology.]

Slobin, Dan Isaac. 1997. The Origins of Grammaticizable Notions: Beyond the Individual Mind. In Dan Isaac Slobin, ed., *The Cross-Linguistic Study of Language Acquisition,* Volume 5. New York: Erlbaum, 265–322.

Sobin, Nicholas J. 1985. Case Assignment in Ukrainian Morphological Passive Constructions. *Linguistic Inquiry* 16.4, 649–662.

Soltész, Katalin J. 1959. *Az Ösi Magyar Igekötök: meg, el, ki, be, fel, le.* Budapest: Akadémiai Kiadó.

Spencer, Andrew. 1991. *Morphological Theory: an Introduction to Word Structure in Generative Grammar.* Oxford: Blackwell.

Spencer, Andrew. 1997. Inflectional Morphology and Functional Heads. In Wolfgang U. Dressler, Martin Prinzhorn, and John R. Rennison, eds., *Advances in Morphology.* Berlin: Mouton, 31–49.

Sportiche, Dominique. 1992. Clitic Constructions. Unpublished manuscript, University of California at Los Angeles.

Stechow, Arnim von. 1990. Status Government and Coherence in German. In Günther Grewendorf and Wolfgang Sternefeld, eds., *Scrambling and Barriers.* Amsterdam: John Benjamins, 143–198.

Steever, Sanford B. 1993. *Analysis to Synthesis. The Development of Complex Verb Morphology in the Dravidian Languages.* New York: Oxford University Press.

Stiebels, Barbara. 1996. *Lexikalische Argumente und Adjunkte: Zum semantischen Beitrag von verbalen Präfixen und Partikeln.* Berlin: Akademie Verlag.

Stiebels, Barbara and Dieter Wunderlich. 1992. A Lexical Account of Complex Verbs. *Arbeiten des Sonderforschungsbereichs* 282, Nr. 30. Düsseldorf: Seminar für Allgemeine Sprachwissenschaft.

Stowell, Tim. 1992. Talk Presented at the Department of Linguistics, University of Wisconsin-Madison.

Stump, Gregory T. 1991. A Paradigm-Based Theory of Morphosemantic Mismatches. *Language* 67.4, 675–725.

Subramanian, Uma. 1988. Subcategorization and Derivation: Evidence from Tamil. In *CLS 24: Papers from the 24th Annual Regional Meeting of the Chicago Linguistic Society*. Chicago: Chicago Linguistic Society, 353–361.

Tereschenko, N. M. 1973. *Sintaksis Samodiijskix Jazykov*. Moscow: Nauk.

Traugott, Elizabeth Closs and Bernd Heine, eds., 1991. *Approaches to Grammaticalization*. Amsterdam: John Benjamins.

Uriagereka, Juan. 1995. Aspects of the Syntax of Clitic Placement in Western Romance. *Linguistic Inquiry* 26.1, 79–123.

Vászolyi, E. 1976. Wunambal. In Robert M. W. Dixon, 1976, 629–646.

Vennemann, Theo. 1972. On the Theory of Syllabic Phonology. *Linguistische Berichte* 18, 1–18.

Watkins, Calvert. 1964. Preliminaries to the Reconstruction of Indo-European Sentence Structure. In Horace G. Lunt, ed., *Proceedings of the Ninth International Conference of Linguists*. The Hague: Mouton, 1035–1045.

Webelhuth, Gert. 1992. *Principles and Parameters of Syntactic Saturation*. New York: Oxford University Press.

Webelhuth, Gert, ed., 1995a. *Government and Binding Theory and the Minimalist Program: Principles and Parameters in Syntactic Theory* . Oxford: Blackwell.

Webelhuth, Gert. 1995b. X-bar Theory and Case Theory. In Webelhuth, 1995a, 15–95.

Webelhuth, Gert and Farrell Ackerman. 1998. Topicalization, Complex Predicates, and Functional Uncertainty in German. Unpublished manuscript, University of North Carolina at Chapel Hill and University of California at San Diego.

Williams, Edwin. 1980. Predication. *Linguistic Inquiry* 11, 203–38.

Zaenen, Annie, Joan Maling, and Höskuldur Thráinsson. 1985. Case and Grammatical Functions: The Icelandic Passive. *Natural Language and Linguistic Theory* 3.4, 441–483.

Zwicky, Arnold. 1990. Syntactic Words and Morphological Words, Simple and Composite. *Yearbook of Morphology* 3, 201–216.

Index of Type Names and Attribute Names

A Type Names

B Attribute Names

General Index

tense, 6–7, 10, 20–21, 30, 33,
39–40, 45, 50, 52, 54–55,
62–65, 74, 78–79, 89–90,
142, 144, 146, 171, 174,
194, 197, 211, 214, 217–
218, 314, 316, 327, 345.
See also aspect *and* tense-
aspect
aorist, 55–56
future, 10, 55–56, 62, 73, 78,
115, 118, 139, 174–218,
206, 212, 233
future perfect, 174, 206–218
head, 178
inflection, 63, 90
marker, 56
participle of the perfect, 146
participle of the present, 146
past, 50, 52, 54, 146–147,
149, 159, 162, 174–218,
316, 323, 327, 345
perfect, 27, 62, 146–147, 151,
153, 167, 170, 174, 183,
185–218, 233, 328
pluperfect 174, 206–218
present, 45, 50, 74, 118–119,
139, 144, 146, 155, 174–
218, 257, 316, 323, 327–
328, 345
progressive, 212
tense-aspect, 8, 112, 115, 122,
129, 141, 146–147, 149,
151, 170, 249, 268, 312,
320, 322, 326. *See also*
tense *and* aspect
archetype, 174, 186, 195, 205
meaning, 345
paradigm, 170, 174–176, 313,
320
pattern, 255, 257, 290
predicate, 148, 184–185, 279,
345
tensed predicate, 87, 148, 346
tenseless predicate, 191
Tereshchenko, N. M., 47, 51

term grammatical function, 250,
303, 310–311
thematic role, 222–229, 232
hierarchy, 309
thematic structure, 309
theme, 12, 221, 227
theoretical
construct, 37, 63
linguistics, 194
parsimony, 24, 78
theory
construction, 9, 36
of grammar, 96, 103, 126–
131, 154, 162, 182, 345
of language, 130, 229
of lexicalism, 342
of signs, 84
unity, 345
theta criterion, 30, 230
theta marking, 166, 232
Thráinsson, Höskuldur, 31, 215–
216
three-place verb, 276
Timberlake, Alan, 68, 249
time, 218
token identity, 79, 90, 182, 190
topic-focus, 97, 109
topicality, 130
topicalization, 279
traditional grammar, 81, 125
transformational grammar, 97,
166, 219–220, 228, 230,
232, 234, 348. *See also*
Principles and Parameters
theory *and* Minimalist
Program
transitive, 38, 66–67, 229, 275–
277, 285, 295–298, 307
predicate, 3, 54, 66–67, 130,
221, 225, 270, 274–275,
287, 292, 300
Traugott, Elizabeth Closs, 35, 39
Turkish, 68, 80, 131, 249, 269,
285–288, 310—312, 346